무지개보카

고등 초급편

목차

Chapter 1.

1	humid	[ˈhjuː.mɪd]	a. 습한, 습기가 있는
2	barn	[bɑːn]	n. 외양간, 헛간
3	gulf	[gʌlf]	n. 만, 격차
4	ruin	[ˈruː.ɪn]	v. 망치다, 파산시키다; 파산, 붕괴
5	torture	[ˈtɔː.tʃər]	n. 고문, 심한 고통 v. 고문하다
6	vegetation	[ˌvedʒ.ɪˈteɪ.ʃən]	n. 생장, 초목; 무위도식
7	surplus	[ˈsɜː.pləs]	a. 과잉, 과잉의
8	drown	[draʊn]	v. 익사하다, 익사시키다
9	paddle	[ˈpæd.əl]	n. (작은 보트의) 노, 주걱
10	pedestrian	[pəˈdes.tri.ən]	n. 보행자; 평범한, 진부한
11	rear	[rɪər]	a. 뒤쪽; 뒤쪽의; 기르다, 양육하다
12	swell	[swel]	n. 팽창 v. 부풀다, 부풀어 오르다
13	aspiration	[ˌæs.pɪˈreɪ.ʃən]	n. 열망, 포부, 대망, 동경
14	approximate	[əprάksəmət | -rɔ́k-]	v. 가까워지다, 근접하다 a. 근사치의, 대략적인
15	revenue	[ˈrev.ən.juː]	n. 수입, 세입, 세수
16	county	[ˈkaʊn.ti]	n. 자치주, 군(미국 대부분 주의 최소 행정 구역)
17	crater	[ˈkreɪ.tər]	n. 분화구
18	desolate	[ˈdes.əl.ət]	a. 황량한, 쓸쓸한
19	district	[ˈdɪs.trɪkt]	n. 선거구 지역, 구역
20	clone	[kləʊn]	n. 복제 생물, 클론; 복제하다
21	embassy	[ˈem.bə.si]	n. 대사관
22	equator	[ɪˈkweɪ.tər]	n. (지구를) 동일하게 나누는 것, 적도
23	exotic	[ɪgˈzɒt.ɪk]	a. 바깥의, 해외의, 이국적인
24	magnificent	[mægˈnɪf.ɪ.sənt]	a. 장엄한, 당당한
25	mast	[mɑːst]	n. 돛대, 마스트, 기둥
26	sheer	[ʃɪər]	a. 얇은, 순수한
27	summit	[ˈsʌm.ɪt]	n. 정상, 산꼭대기 a. 정상회담의
28	vine	[vaɪn]	n. 포도나무, 덩굴 식물
29	comet	[ˈkɒm.ɪt]	n. 혜성
30	dissolve	[dɪˈzɒlv]	v. 녹이다; 종료시키다, 없어지다, 소실되다
31	belong to N		p. ~에 속하다
32	appear to do		p. ~하는 것으로 보이다
33	A rather than B		p. A다 B라기 보다는
34	hand down		p. ~을 물려주다
35	at a low price		p. 낮은 가격으로
36	recover from		p. ~에서 회복하다
37	be divided into		p. 나누어지다, 분할되다
38	by turns		p. 차례로
39	consist in		p. ~에 근거하다
40	adapt to N		p. ~에 적응하다

1

humid
[ˈhjuːmɪd]

a. 습한, 습기가 있는

humidity n. 습도, 습함
humble a. 겸손한, 자기를 낮추는
humane a. 인도적인
dehumanize v. 비인간적으로 만들다

어원	-hum, -humili : earth 땅 → '땅에서 습기가 올라와 습한' - moist 수분이 있는 VS damp 눅눅한 습기
유의어	damp, moist, muggy
반의어	Dry, arid, parched
영영	Having a high level of moisture or water vapor in the air.
예문	The weather in the rainforest is often hot and humid. 우기림에서 날씨는 종종 더운과 습한 편입니다.

2

barn
[baːn]

n. 외양간, 헛간

barrier n. 장벽, 장애물
barricade n. 통행 차단물, 장애물
embargo n. 제재 v. 출입항을 금지하다
barbarian n. 이방인, 야만인

어원	-bar, -bat 말뚝, 막대 때리며 싸우다(E) → '막대로 막아 소, 말 등이 머물게 만든 외양간, 헛간'
유의어	shed, stable, warehouse
반의어	Shed, stable, outbuilding
영영	A building used to store or shelter animals, hay, or farm equipment.
예문	The farmer stored his hay in the barn. 농부는 건초를 헛간에 저장했습니다.

3

gulf
[gʌlf]

n. 만, 격차

gull n. 갈매기
garb n. 복장
garment n. 의류, 옷가지
gust n. 돌풍 v. 몰아치다

어원	-gulf 바다가 육지쪽으로 들어와 있는 상태 *이라크가 쿠웨이트를 침공했던 페르시아만 전쟁
유의어	bay, inlet, cove
반의어	Connection, linkage, unity
영영	A large body of water that is partly enclosed by land, often larger than a bay but smaller than an ocean.
예문	The Gulf of Mexico is known for its warm waters. 멕시코 만은 따뜻한 물로 유명합니다.

4

ruin
[ˈruːɪn]

v. 망치다, 파산시키다; 파산, 붕괴

ruined a. 멸망한, 파멸된, 파멸한
ruinous a. 파괴적인, 재해를 가져오는
ruination n. 파괴, 파멸의 원인, 화근
bruin n. 갈색곰

어원	-gru, -ruin : fall → '함께 떨어지니 망치니 파산, 붕괴'
유의어	wreckage, destruction, decay
반의어	Restore, rebuild, renovate
영영	The state of being in a severely damaged or destroyed condition.
예문	The ancient ruins were a popular tourist attraction. 고대 유적지는 인기 있는 관광 명소였습니다.

5

torture
[ˈtɔːtʃər]

n. 고문, 심한 고통 v. 고문하다

torturer n. 고문자
torment n. 고통, 고뇌
torturing a. 극심한 고통을 주는
torrent n. 급류, 격류

어원	-tort, -tor : twist 비틀다 → '비틀어서 고문하니 생기는 고통'
유의어	deluge, flood, downpour
반의어	Drought, dry spell, aridity
영영	A strong and fast-moving stream of water or other liquid.
예문	The heavy rain caused a torrent of water to flow down the street. 폭우로 인해 길 아래로 거대한 물의 토렌트가 흘렀습니다.

6

vegetation
[ˌvedʒɪˈteɪʃən]

n. 생장, 초목; 무위도식

vegetate v. 생장하다; 하는 일 없이 지내다
vegetated a. 초목이 있는
vegetrian n. 채식주의자
vegan n. (엄격한) 채식주의자

어원	-vid, -viv, -vit, -vig, -veget : live 살다, life : 생명(L) → '활기 있게 쑥쑥 자라는 식물
유의어	plants, flora, greenery
반의어	Barrenness, desolation, aridness
영영	Plants in general, especially the plants that grow in a specific area or habitat.
예문	The lush vegetation in the jungle is home to many animals. 밀림 속의 푸른 식물은 많은 동물들의 서식지입니다.

7

surplus

[ˈsɜː.pləs]

a. 과잉, 과잉의

surplusage n. 잉여, 과잉
nonplus n. 어찌할 바를 모름
plural a. 여러 개의
plumber n. 배관공

어원	-sur : super + -plus 더하기 (L) → '넘치게 더하니 과잉의' * plus '더해서 남게 되는 것' VS sum '더해서 목표에 도달한다'
유의어	excess, extra, surplusage
반의어	Deficiency, shortage, insufficiency
영영	An excess or abundance of something beyond what is required or needed.
예문	After the harvest, there was a surplus of crops that we couldn't store. 수확 후에는 저장할 수 없을 정도로 농작물이 초과되었습니다.

8

drown

[draʊn]

v. 익사하다, 익사시키다

drowning a. 익사하는; 혼란한, 이해할 수 없는
drowned a. 익사한; ~에 몰입한
drown in p. ~에 압도당하다, ~에 싸이다
drill n. 드릴, 송곳; 반복 연습, 훈련

어원	-dro : drink + -down 아래로 → '물을 먹여 익사시키다'
유의어	suffocate, submerge, immerse
반의어	Save, rescue, survive
영영	To die from suffocation in water, typically by inhaling water into the lungs.
예문	She nearly drowned while swimming in the deep pool. 그녀는 깊은 수영장에서 거의 익사했습니다.

9

paddle

[ˈpæd.əl]

n. (작은 보트의) 노, 주걱

pad n. 패드, 묶음
pave v. 포장하다
be paired with p. ~와 병행되다
paleolith n. 구석기

어원	-paddle 노
유의어	row, oar, boat
반의어	Stillness, immobility, inaction
영영	A short, flat-bladed instrument used for rowing a boat.
예문	They decided to paddle a canoe down the calm river. 그들은 고요한 강을 카누로 패들링하기로 결정했습니다.

10

pedestrian

[pəˈdes.tri.ən]

n. 보행자; 평범한, 진부한

pedal n. 발의 발판
pedestal n. 주춧돌; 기초
bipedal a. 두 발로 걷는 n. 두발 동물
expedition n. 원정, 탐험

어원	-ped : foot 발(L) + -str : street → '발로 길을 걷는 보행자'
유의어	walker, foot-traveler, walker
반의어	Driver, motorist, commuter
영영	A person who is walking on foot, especially in an area designed for walking.
예문	There's a pedestrian crossing ahead, so be careful. 앞에 횡단보도가 있으니 조심하세요.

11

rear

[rɪər]

a. 뒤쪽; 뒤쪽의; 기르다, 양육하다

rearing n. 양육
rearmost a. 최후의
rear seat p. 뒷자석

어원	-re : back * 리어카는 자전거 뒤에 놓고 끄는 마차 → '뒤에 업어 키우니 양육하다'
유의어	back, posterior, behind
반의어	Front, anterior, fore
영영	The back part of something, typically a vehicle.
예문	The car's rear window was shattered in the accident. 차의 후면 창이 사고로 깨졌습니다.

12

swell

[swel]

n. 팽창 v. 부풀다, 부풀어 오르다

swellfish n. 복어
swollen a. 부풀어 오른, 부은
swelling a. 증가하는, 팽창하는
swell up p. 부어오르다, 솟아오르다

어원	-swell 팽창; 부풀다 I swell really easily. 나 정말 잘 부어요.
유의어	expand, inflate, enlarge
반의어	Shrink, contract, decrease
영영	To become larger or rounder in size, often due to inflation or expansion.
예문	The ocean swell made the surfing conditions perfect. 바다의 물결이 서핑 조건을 완벽하게 만들었습니다.

13		어원	-a : to + -spire : breath → '~를 향해 영혼을 불어 넣으니 열망'
		유의어	ambition, goal, desire
aspiration		반의어	Resignation, acceptance, contentment
[ˌæs.pɪˈreɪ.ʃən]		영영	A strong desire, ambition, or goal; the act of breathing in.
n. 열망, 포부, 대망, 동경			
aspire v. 열망하다, 야망을 품다 aspirational a. 동경의 대상인 inspire v. 고무하다 expire v. 만기가 되다, 끝나다		예문	His aspiration was to become a successful entrepreneur and create innovative products. 그의 포부는 성공한 기업가가 되어 혁신적인 제품을 만드는 것이었습니다.
14		어원	-ap : to + -proach, -prov, -prob, -proxim 가까이 → '목표로 한 방향 가까워지니 근사치'
		유의어	estimated, rough, close
approximate		반의어	Precise, exact, accurate
[əpráksəmət ǀ -rɔ́k-]		영영	Close to the actual, but not completely accurate or exact.
v. 가까워지다, 근접하다 a. 근사치의, 대략적인			
approximation n. 비슷한 것, 근사치 approximately adv. 대략, 대체로, 거의 proximate a. 가장 가까운, 직전의 proximal a. 기부에 가까운, 기부의		예문	Can you give me an approximate estimate of the cost? 비용의 대략적인 견적을 알려줄 수 있나요?
15		어원	-re : again + -ven : come → '정부, 기관 등이 상품이나 서비스를 주고 얻는 세입'
		유의어	income, earnings, profits
revenue		반의어	Loss, deficit, expenditure
[ˈrev.ən.juː]		영영	Income generated by a business, organization, or government through its operations.
n. 수입, 세입, 세수			
adventure n. 모험 souvenir n. 기념품, 기념 선물 prevent v. 막다, 예방하다 revenue tax p. 수입세		예문	The company's revenue increased significantly this year. 회사의 수익이 올해에 크게 증가했습니다.
16		어원	-county 자치주, 군 * country 국가 안에 있는 자치주
		유의어	region, district, administrative division
county		반의어	City, municipality, metropolis
[ˈkaʊn.ti]		영영	A political and administrative division of a state or country.
n. 자치주, 군(미국 대부분 주의 최소 행정 구역)			
country n. 국가, 나라 countless a. 무수한 encounter v. 우연히 만나다 counteract v. 대항하다, 거스르다		예문	He was elected as the sheriff of the county. 그는 그 군의 보안관으로 선출되었습니다.
17		어원	-crater 손님 접대를 위해 와인과 물을 섞어 냈던 커다란 그릇을 의미. 빨간 와인과 색깔이 닮아 분화구
		유의어	hollow, pit, cavity
crater		반의어	Hill, mound, elevation
[ˈkreɪ.tər]		영영	A bowl-shaped depression or cavity, often found on the surface of a planet or moon.
n. 분화구			
crate n. 큰 나무 상자, 운송용 상자 create v. 창조하다; 야기하다 crease n. 주름 v. 주름이 생기게 하다 increase n. 늘리다, 증가시키다		예문	The volcano's crater was smoking and dangerous. 화산의 분화구는 연기를 내며 위험했습니다.
18		어원	-de : away + -sol : alone → '떨어져 혼자 있으니 황량한, 쓸쓸한
		유의어	barren, bleak, deserted
desolate		반의어	Inhabited, populated, thriving
[ˈdes.əl.ət]		영영	Empty, barren, and devoid of life or inhabitants.
a. 황량한, 쓸쓸한			
sole a. 유일한, 단 하나의 solely adv. 오로지, 전적으로 solar a. 태양의 solemn a. 엄숙한, 침통한		예문	The desert was desolate, with no signs of life. 사막은 어떤 생명의 흔적도 없는 황량한 곳이었습니다.

19

district

[ˈdɪs.trɪkt]

n. 선거구 지역, 구역

restrict v. ~을 제한하다, 금지하다
stricture n. 혹평, 비난
stringent a. 엄중한, 긴박한
distress n. 고통, 괴로움, 고뇌

어원 -di : away + -strict, -strai, -strain, -frain, -stress, -stig : bind
→ '떨어뜨려 묶어 놓은 구역'

유의어 area, region, locality

반의어 Central, main, city center

영영 An area or region, often with specific boundaries or characteristics.

예문 The school district covers a large area of the city.
학군은 도시의 큰 지역을 포함하고 있습니다.

20

clone

[kloʊn]

n. 복제 생물, 클론; 복제하다

anticyclone n. 고기압, 역선풍
cliff n. 절벽, 낭떠러지
close to one's heart p. ~에게 소중한
draw to a close p. 끝나가다

어원 -clon : klon 나뭇가지(G) → '나뭇가지에 똑같이 복제된 열매들' * 춤을 똑같이 복제해서 추는 가수 클론 그룹

유의어 duplicate, replica, copy

반의어 Original, unique, individual

영영 An organism or cell produced asexually that is genetically identical to its parent.

예문 Scientists are working on cloning endangered species.
과학자들은 멸종 위기에 처한 종을 복제하는 연구를 하고 있습니다.

21

embassy

[ˈem.bə.si]

n. 대사관

ambassador n. 대사, 사절
ambiguous a. 모호한
unambiguously adv. 명백하게
invalid a. 병약한

어원 -amb, -ambi, -ambit, -emb : two + -assad : work
→ '양 국가의 문제를 해결하는 대사' * 앰배서더 호텔

유의어 consulate, diplomatic mission, foreign office

반의어 Host country, local authorities, consulate

영영 A diplomatic mission or official residence of an ambassador in a foreign country.

예문 He had to visit the embassy to renew his passport.
그는 여권을 갱신하기 위해 대사관을 방문해야 했습니다.

22

equator

[ɪˈkweɪ.tər]

n. (지구를) 동일하게 나누는 것, 적도

equals v. ~와 같다 n. 등호
equivalent to p. 동등한, 대등한; ~에 상당하는
equipped with p. ~을 갖춘
adequate a. 적절한

어원 -equ, -equi, -ident : same 같은(L)
→ '남반구와 북반구를 똑같이 나눈 적도'

유의어 line of latitude, halfway point, equatorial circle

반의어 Poles, north pole, south pole

영영 An imaginary line that divides the Earth into northern and southern hemispheres, situated equidistant from the North and South Poles.

예문 The equator divides the Earth into the Northern and Southern Hemispheres.
적도는 지구를 북반구와 남반구로 나눕니다.

23

exotic

[ɪɡˈzɒt.ɪk]

a. 바깥의, 해외의, 이국적인

exorbitant a. 터무니 없는, 과도한
exile n. 추방, 유배
expand v. 확장하다, 확대하다
suborbital a. 궤도에 오르지 않은

어원 -ex, -exo : outside 밖, 더 밖 (G) + -tic 형용사
→ '경계를 벗어난 바깥이니 해외의 이국적인'

유의어 foreign, unusual, unfamiliar

반의어 Familiar, common, ordinary

영영 Unusual, foreign, or strikingly different from what is familiar.

예문 The exotic fruits at the market were intriguing.
시장에서 파는 이국적인 과일들이 흥미로웠습니다.

24

magnificent

[mæɡˈnɪf.ɪ.sənt]

a. 장엄한, 당당한

magnify v. 과장하다, 확대하다
magnifiable a. 확대할 수 있는
magnification n. 확대, 칭찬
magnitude n. (엄청난) 규모, 거대함, 중요성

어원 -mag : great + -fi : make
→ '위대하게 만드니 장엄한'

유의어 splendid, grand, impressive

반의어 Ordinary, unimpressive, mediocre

영영 Extremely impressive, grand, or beautiful.

예문 The palace was a magnificent example of architecture.
궁전은 건축의 웅장한 예였습니다.

25

mast

[mɑːst]

n. 돛대, 마스트, 기둥

masterly a. 훌륭한, 명인다운
masterpiece n. 걸작, 명작
too much for p. ~을 감당하기에 너무한
mastermind n. 지도자, 주모자, 조종자

어원	-mast 긴 장대
유의어	pole, spar, sail support
반의어	Bow, front, prow
영영	A tall vertical pole on a ship that supports sails or other equipment.
예문	The ship's mast was damaged during the storm. 배의 돛대가 폭풍 중에 손상되었습니다

26

sheer

[ʃɪər]

a. 얇은, 순수한

shave v. 깎다, 면도하다
scatter v. 흩뜨리다, 흩어지게 하다
shatter v. 산산이 부수다 n. 파편
shed n. 헛간 v. 깎다 v. 비추다

어원	-sha, -shi, -she, -sho : cut → '잘라져서 순수한 부분만 남은'
유의어	steep, abrupt, vertical
반의어	Gradual, gentle, sloping
영영	Completely vertical or steep, often used to describe cliffs or drops.
예문	The sheer cliff was a challenging climb. 순백한 절벽은 도전적인 등반이었습니다.

27

summit

[ˈsʌm.ɪt]

n. 정상, 산꼭대기 a. 정상회담의

superior a. 우월한, 우수한, 상급의
summarize v. 요약하다
summation n. 덧셈
superb a. 장엄한, 화려한, 훌륭한

어원	-sum : 더하다 (L) 최고, 정점; 개요 + -it : go → '최고로 높은 곳까지 가니 정상' * plus '더해서 남게 되는 것' VS sum '더해서 목표에 도달하는 것'
유의어	peak, pinnacle, zenith
반의어	Bottom, base, nadir
영영	The highest point of a mountain or hill; also used metaphorically to refer to the highest point of achievement or success.
예문	Reaching the summit of the mountain was their goal. 산 정상에 도달하는 것이 그들의 목표였습니다.

28

vine

[vaɪn]

n. 포도나무, 덩굴 식물

vintage n. 포도주; 년식, 오래됨
vineyard n. 포도밭
vinegar n. 식초
acetic a. 신랄한, 산뜻한

어원	-vine 포도나무, 덩굴 식물 * v 하나를 더 붙이면 wine, 포도주는 포도 * vintage → 포도를 수확하고 오래 숙성을 해야 포도주
유의어	creepers, climbing plant, grapevine
반의어	Dry, wither, wilt
영영	A climbing or trailing plant that produces grapes or other fruits.
예문	The grapevine produced sweet, juicy grapes. 포도 덩굴은 달콤하고 즙이 많은 포도를 생산했습니다.

29

comet

[ˈkɒm.ɪt]

n. 혜성

come up with p. ~을 떠올리다
come up p. 발생하다, 생기다
commence v. 시작하다, 시작되다, 개시하다
commodious a. 널찍한

어원	-comet : kome, kometes 머리털(G) → '떨어질 때 모습이 마치 머리털 같음'
유의어	celestial body, space object, astral body
반의어	Planet, asteroid, celestial body
영영	A celestial object composed of ice, dust, and gas that orbits the Sun and often develops a bright tail as it approaches.
예문	The comet could be seen in the night sky with a telescope. 혜성은 망원경으로 밤하늘에서 볼 수 있었습니다.

30

dissolve

[dɪˈzɒlv]

v. 녹이다; 종료시키다, 없어지다, 소실되다

solution n. 해결, 녹임; 용액
soluble a. 해결 가능한; 녹는
solvent a. 지급 능력이 있는; 용해력이 있는
insoluble a. 용해하지 않는; 해결할 수 없는

어원	-dis : apart + -sol, -solu, -solut : loosen → '나누어 풀어지니 녹이다' * solu(t) '물에 녹아 없어 지는 것' VS lo(t) '물로 씻어내는 것'
유의어	melt, liquefy, disintegrate
반의어	Solidify, congeal, coagulate
영영	To mix a substance in a liquid until it becomes a part of the liquid.
예문	You need to dissolve the powder in water to make the solution. 용매를 만들려면 분말을 물에 녹여야 합니다.

31

belong to N

p. ~에 속하다

belong to p. ~에 속하다
long for p. ~을 간절히 원하다, 갈망하다
as long as p. ~하는 한
at length p. 오랫동안, 상세히

어원	-be + -long, -leng,-ling : want 갈망하다, long 긴 → '~에 있기를 갈망하다'
갈의어	pertain to N, be affiliated with N
반의어	exclude from N, disown
영영	be owned by N
예문	The car belongs to John. 그 차는 존의 소유물이다.

32

appear to do

p. ~하는 것으로 보이다

appear v. 나타나다, 출현하다
appearance n. 모습, 외모, 나타남, 출현
disappear v. 사라지다
appease v. 달래다, 진정시키다

어원	-ap : to + -par, -pear : visible 보이는(L) → '~에 보여지는'
유의어	seem to do, look like
반의어	disappear from doing, vanish from view
영영	seem to do
예문	She appears to be tired. 그녀는 피곤해 보인다.

33

A rather than B

p. A다 B라기 보다는

rather adv. 꽤, 약간, 상당히; 오히려, 차라리
rather than p. ~보다 오히려
rather than to do p. ~하는 것보다 ...를 선호
rebel n. 반역자, 반항아 v. 반란을 일으키다

어원	-rath : ready + -than → '준비됐으니 B라기 보다는 A
유의어	A instead of B, A in preference to B
반의어	B rather than A, B over A
영영	A instead of B
예문	I prefer tea rather than coffee. 나는 커피 대신에 차를 선호한다.

34

hand down

p. ~을 물려주다

on one hand p. 한편으로는
second-hand p. 간접적으로
at hand p. 당면한
near at hand p. 가까이에

어원	-hand 손 + -down → '손으로 일군 모든 것을 아래 대에 물려주다'
갈의어	pass down, transmit
반의어	receive up, take up
영영	pass down
예문	My grandmother handed down her wedding ring to me. 내 할머니는 결혼 반지를 내게 유산으로 내려줬다.

35

at a low price

p. 낮은 가격으로

at all cost p. 기어코, 무슨 수를 써서라도
at an angle p. 비스듬히
at first glance p. 처음에는, 언뜻 보기에는
at a distance p. 멀리서

어원	-at 점 + low 낮은 + -price 가격 → '생각한 지점까지 낮은 가격으로'
갈의어	inexpensively, affordably
반의어	at a high price, expensive
영영	at an inexpensive cost
예문	I bought this book at a low price. 나는 이 책을 저렴한 가격에 샀다.

36

recover from

p. ~에서 회복하다

recover v. 회복하다, 되찾다
recovery n. 회복, 되찾음
uncover v. 발견하다, 폭로하다
discover v. 발견하다

어원	-re : again + -cover 덮다 + -from → '다시 상처가 덮이는 것이니 회복'
갈의어 paire	recuperate from, bounce back from
반의어	succumb to, worsen
영영	regain health after illness or injury
예문	He is recovering from a severe illness. 그는 심한 병으로부터 회복 중이다.

37	어원	-di : apart + -vid, -vis, -wid : separate 분리하다(L) → '떨어지게 나누는 경계선으로 분할되다'
	유의어	be segmented into, be separated into
be divided into	반의어	be united into, merge together
	영영	be separated into parts
p. 나누어지다, 분할되다		
divide v. 나누다, 분할하다; 경계선, 분수령 division n. 분할, 분배; 나눗셈 division of labor p. 분업 dividened n. 배당금	예문	The cake can be divided into six equal pieces. 케이크는 여섯 개의 동일한 조각으로 나눌 수 있다.

38	어원	-tour, turn 뒤집다, 회전하다 (L) → '돌아가며 차례로' * role '같은 자리를 회전' VS tour, turn '방향을 바꿈'
	유의어	alternately, in succession
by turns	반의어	consistently, continuously
	영영	alternately or in succession
p. 차례로		
in return p. ~에 대한 보상으로 trun A into B p. A를 B로 전환하다 turn down p. 거절하다 trun in p. ~을 제출하다; 되돌려 주다	예문	The friends took turns driving on the road trip. 친구들은 로드 트립에서 운전을 번갈아 했다.

39	어원	-con : together + -sist : stand → '함께 서 있는 구성에 근거'
	유의어	be comprised of, be characterized by
consist in	반의어	consist of, exclude from
	영영	have as its essential feature
p. ~에 근거하다		
consist of p. ~으로 구성되다 consistency n. 일관성 consistently adv. 일관되게, 지속적으로 consistent with p. ~와 일치하는	예문	Success consists in hard work and perseverance. 성공은 노력과 인내에 있다.

40	어원	-ad : to + -apt : fit, adjust → '같은 방향으로 조정하니 적응'
	유의어	adjust to N, acclimate to N
adapt to N	반의어	resist N, oppose N
	영영	adjust to N or change to fit N
p. ~에 적응하다		
adaption n. 조정, 적응 adaptive a. 적응할 수 있는, 적응하는 maladaptive a. 적응하지 못하는, 부적응의 maladapt p. 악용하다	예문	He had to adapt to the new environment. 그는 새로운 환경에 적응해야 했다.

Chapter 2.

41	enclosure	[ɪnˈkləʊ.ʒər]	n. (울타리로 쳐 놓은) 구역
42	extinct	[ɪkˈstɪŋkt]	a. 전멸한, 멸종한
43	infer	[ɪnˈfɜːr]	v. 추론하다; 암시하다
44	linear	[ˈlɪn.i.ər]	a. 선형의, 선적인
45	lunar	[ˈluː.nər]	a. 달의, 음력의
46	metabolic	[met.əˈbɒl.ɪk]	a. 신진대사의, 물질대사의
47	orbit	[ˈɔː.bɪt]	n. 궤도, 영향권; 범위; 궤도를 돌다
48	precise	[prɪˈsaɪs]	a. 정확한
49	reservoir	[ˈrez.ə.vwɑːr]	n. 저장소, 저수지
50	thermal	[ˈθɜː.məl]	a. 열의, 보온성이 좋은
51	underpin	[ˌʌn.dəˈpɪn]	v. (주장 등을) 뒷받침하다; 토대를 제공하다
52	velocity	[vəˈlɒs.ə.ti]	n. 속도, 빠른 속도
53	cluster	[ˈklʌs.tər]	n. 무리; 송이; 성단; v. 밀집시키다
54	compost	[ˈkɒm.pɒst]	n. 퇴비, 두엄 v. 퇴비를 만들다
55	dehydrate	[ˌdiː.haɪˈdreɪt]	v. 수분을 제거하다, 건조시키다
56	flock	[flɒk]	n. 떼, 무리; 떼 지어가다
57	fur	[fɜːr]	n. 모피, 털
58	impure	[ɪmˈpjʊər]	a. 더러운, 불결한, 불순한
59	magnetism	[ˈmæg.nə.tɪ.zəm]	n. 자성, 자력; 매력
60	mutation	[mjuːˈteɪ.ʃən]	n. 돌연변이, 변화, 변천
61	reed	[riːd]	n. 갈대, 갈대밭
62	specimen	[ˈspes.ə.mɪn]	n. 견본, 표본
63	substance	[ˈsʌb.stəns]	n. 본질, 실체; 물질
64	wither	[ˈwɪð.ər]	v. 시들다, 말라 죽다
65	capacity	[kəˈpæs.ə.ti]	n. 용량, 능력, 수용력
66	cavity	[ˈkæv.ə.ti]	n. 구멍; 충치
67	extract	[ɪkˈstrækt]	n. 발췌, 추출물
68	icing	[ˈaɪ.sɪŋ]	a. 당의(설탕을 입힌 과자)
69	proportion	[prəˈpɔː.ʃən]	n. 비율; 조화, 균형
70	radius	[ˈreɪ.di.əs]	n. 반지름, 반경
71	work out		p. 운동하다; 알아내다, 해결하다; 계산하다
72	what is more		p. 게다가, 더욱이
73	occur to N		p. ~에게 생각이 떠오르다
74	get past		p. ~을 넘어서다, ~을 지나가다
75	take after		p. ~을 닮다
76	under consideration		p. 고려 중인
77	be attached to		p. ~에 붙어 있다
78	break in		p. 침입하다
79	capitalize on		p. ~을 이용[활용]하다
80	come across		p. ~을 우연히 발견하다

41	어원	-en : in + -clo, -clos, -clu, -clud 닫다 → '울타리 안에 닫아 놓은 구역' * clo(s), -lu(d) 문을 닫는 것 VS velop envelope(봉투)와 같이 에워싸는 것
	유의어	enclosure, confinement, closure
enclosure	반의어	Opening, aperture, entrance
[ɪnˈkloʊ.ʒər]	영영	An area that is closed off or surrounded by a barrier, such as a fence or wall.
n. (울타리로 쳐 놓은) 구역		
closure n. 폐쇄, 종결 conclude v. 결론을 내리다; 종결하다 jump to a conclusion p. 성급하게 결론을 내리다 conclusive a. 결정적인	예문	The zoo has a special enclosure for the lions. 그 동물원에는 사자를 위한 특별한 울타리가 있습니다.
42	어원	-ex : out + -tinc, -tinct, -stinct 튕기다 → '손을 튕겨서 불을 끄는 것처럼 멸종한'
	유의어	vanished, eradicated, no longer existing
extinct	반의어	Alive, living, existing
[ɪkˈstɪŋkt]	영영	No longer in existence or living; typically used to describe species that have died out.
a. 전멸한, 멸종한		
extinguisher n. 소화기 extinction n. 멸종 extinctive a. 소멸적인, 소멸성의 insult v. 모욕하다, 창피를 주다	예문	The dodo bird is an example of an extinct species. 달갈새는 멸종된 종의 예입니다.
43	어원	-in + -fer : carry → '마음 속으로만 생각을 나르니 추론하고 암시'
	유의어	deduce, conclude, gather
infer	반의어	Ascertain, determine, conclude
[ɪnˈfɜːr]	영영	To deduce or conclude information based on evidence or reasoning.
v. 추론하다; 암시하다		
inference n. 추론 differentiate v. 구별하다 different from p. ~와 다른 indifferent a. 무관심한, 사심이 없는	예문	Based on the evidence, we can infer that he was at the scene. 증거를 바탕으로 우리는 그가 현장에 있었다고 추론할 수 있습니다.
44	어원	-lin 선 + -ar 형접
	유의어	straight, direct, in a line
linear	반의어	Nonlinear, curved, twisted
[ˈlɪn.i.ər]	영영	Arranged in or extending along a straight line.
a. 선형의, 선적인		
line up p. 줄 서다 down the line p. 미래에, 나중에; 완전히 underline v. 강조하다; 주장을 밝히다 align v. 일렬로 하다, 정렬시키다, 조정하다	예문	The linear arrangement of the books made them easy to find. 책들의 선형 배치로 인해 그들을 찾기 쉬웠습니다.
45	어원	-lun, -lus, -lustr, -lumin : shine 빛 → '밤하늘에 빛나는 달' * '루나'는 로마 신화에서 달의 신의 이름
	유의어	moon-related, moonlit, moonlike
lunar	반의어	Solar, earthly, terrestrial
[ˈluː.nər]	영영	Related to the Moon or its characteristics.
a. 달의, 음력의		
lustrate v. 깨끗하게 만들다, 정화시키다 luminous a. 빛을 내는; 총명한 lunatic a. 미친 n. 미치광이 irradiate v. (햇빛이) 비추다, 방사하다	예문	The lunar eclipse was a rare celestial event. 달의 일식은 드문 천체 사건이었습니다.
46	어원	-met, -meta 변화하는 (G) + -bol, phor, -fer, -port : carry → '음식을 에너지로 바꿔 몸 곳곳으로 나르니 신진대사'
	유의어	metabolic, bodily, physiological
metabolic	반의어	Nonmetabolic, inactive, dormant
[met.əˈbɒl.ɪk]	영영	Relating to the chemical processes that occur within living organisms to maintain life.
a. 신진대사의, 물질대사의		
metabolism n. 신진대사 metamorphosis n. (생물의) 변태, 변형 metaphysics n. 형이상학 metaphor n. 은유	예문	Exercise can boost your metabolic rate. 운동은 대사율을 증가시킬 수 있습니다.

47

orbit
[ˈɔːbɪt]

n. 궤도, 영향권; 범위; 궤도를 돌다

orb n. 구, 천체
orbital a. 궤도의
suborbital a. 궤도에 오르지 않은
exorbitant a. 터무니 없는, 과도한

어원	-orb 구, 천체 + -it :go → '구를 도는 궤도의 범위'
유의어	path, trajectory, course
반의어	Standstill, halt, stationary
영영	The path followed by a celestial object as it revolves around another object in space.
예문	The Earth orbits the Sun once a year. 지구는 일 년에 한 번 태양을 공전합니다.

48

precise
[prɪˈsaɪs]

a. 정확한

precisely adv. 정확히, 바로
decisive a. 결정적인
concise a. 거두절미한, 간결한
homicide n. 살인

어원	-pre : before + -cis 잘라 죽이다 → '불필요한 것을 미리 잘랐으니 정확한'
유의어	accurate, exact, meticulous
반의어	Inexact, imprecise, approximate
영영	Exact, accurate, and without error.
예문	The scientist made precise measurements to ensure accuracy. 과학자는 정확성을 보장하기 위해 정밀한 측정을 했습니다.

49

reservoir
[ˈrez.ə.vwɑːr]

n. 저장소, 저수지

preserve v. 보존하다
reserve 예약하다; 보류하다
reserved a. 보류된, 예약의
unreserve n. 스스럼 없음, 솔직

어원	-re : back + -serv, -serve : slave / keep 지키다, 보호하다 → '물을 지키니 저장소고 저수지다'
유의어	water source, storage, tank
반의어	Drainage, outflow, depletion
영영	A natural or artificial storage area for water or other substances.
예문	The reservoir provides water to the entire city. 저수지는 도시 전체에 물을 공급합니다.

50

thermal
[ˈθɜːməl]

a. 열의, 보온성이 좋은

thermometer n. 온도계
thermostat n. 온도조절장치
thermostable a. 내열성의, 열안정의
thermogenesis n. 열발생

어원	-thermos : heat * thermometer 온도계
유의어	heat-related, hot, warm
반의어	Cold, frigid, icy
영영	Related to heat or temperature.
예문	The thermal springs are known for their healing properties. 열수 온천은 치유 효과로 유명합니다.

51

underpin
[ˌʌn.dəˈpɪn]

v. (주장 등을) 뒷받침하다; 토대를 제공하다

underestimate v. 과소평가하다
understate v. 축소해서 말하다
misunderstanding n. 오해
underwater a. 물 속의, 수중의

어원	-under 아래 + -pin → '아래 핀을 꽂고 뒷받침해서 보강'
유의어	support, uphold, reinforce
반의어	Undermine, weaken, sabotage
영영	To provide a firm foundation or support for something.
예문	Strong foundations underpin the stability of the building. 견고한 기초가 건물의 안정성을 뒷받침합니다.

52

velocity
[vəˈlɒs.ə.ti]

n. 속도, 빠른 속도

velocimeter n. 속도계
velociraptor n. 벨로키랍토르(작은 공룡)
velocity of light p. 광속
vegetate v. 생장하다; 하는 일 없이 지내다

어원	-veloc → '속도' * velocimeter 속도계 * -velociraptor 벨로키랍토르(작은 공룡) '빠른 약탈자' 별명
유의어	speed, rate, swiftness
반의어	Standstill, immobility, inertia
영영	The speed of an object in a specific direction.
예문	The velocity of the car increased as it went downhill. 차의 속도가 내리막길을 내려감에 따라 증가했습니다.

53	어원	-cluster 무리 * -club에 -ste : star 별 무리가 모였다
cluster [ˈklʌs.tər]	유의어	group, bunch, collection
	반의어	Disperse, scatter, separate
n. 무리; 송이; 성단; v. 밀집시키다	영영	A group of similar things or objects gathered closely together.
clustery a. 무리를 이룬 clutch v. 잡다, 붙들다 coalesce v. 연합하다, 합병하다 coalition n. 연합, 제휴	예문	A cluster of stars formed a beautiful constellation in the night sky. 별들의 집합체가 밤하늘에 아름다운 별자리를 형성했습니다.

54	어원	-com : together + -pos, -pon, -pound : put 놓다 (L) → '함께 놓아 만드는 퇴비'
compost [ˈkɒm.pɒst]	유의어	organic matter, decayed material, fertilizer
	반의어	Decompose, decay, rot
n. 퇴비, 두엄 v. 퇴비를 만들다	영영	Decayed organic matter used as fertilizer for plants.
composion n. 구성; 작곡 be composed of p. ~로 구성되어 있다 component n. 성분, 구성요소 compound n.합성물, 합성어 v. 혼합하다, 합성하다	예문	We use compost to enrich our garden soil. 우리는 정퇴토를 풍부하게 하기 위해 퇴비를 사용합니다.

55	어원	-de :off + -hydr, -aqua : water → '물질에서 물이 떨어져 나가니 건조'
dehydrate [ˌdiːhaɪˈdreɪt]	유의어	dry out, remove moisture, desiccate
	반의어	Hydrate, moisten, soak
v. 수분을 제거하다, 건조시키다	영영	To remove water or moisture from something.
hydration n. 수화작용, 수분 유지 hydrant n. 소화전, 급수장치 hydrated a. 수화의; 함수의 aquaculture n. (어류 등의) 양식, 수경 재배	예문	Dehydration can lead to serious health problems. 탈수는 심각한 건강 문제로 이어질 수 있습니다.

56	어원	* -fl, -fli, -fly 날다 → 날개가 있는 새들의 무리 떼
flock [flɒk]	유의어	herd, group, crowd
	반의어	Individual, lone, solitary
n. 떼, 무리; 떼 지어가다	영영	A group of birds or animals that gather together.
flap v. 날개를 치다, 펄럭거리다 flapper n. 파리채 fleet a. 신속한, 잽싼; 함대, 선단 flat a. 평평한 n. 아파트(영국); 손바닥	예문	A flock of birds flew across the sky in formation. 여러 마리의 새들이 형성된 형태로 하늘을 날았습니다.

57	어원	* 털을 다 퍼(fur)트린다
fur [fɜːr]	유의어	pelage, hair, coat
	반의어	Skin, hide, pelage
n. 모피, 털	영영	The thick hair covering the skin of some animals, often used for clothing.
furious a. 격노하는, 몹시 화를 내는 fungus n. 균류, 곰팡이류; 균상종 fuzzy a. 보풀로 덮인; 흐릿한 funeral n. 장례식	예문	The fur of the bear kept it warm in the cold winter. 곰의 털은 추운 겨울에 따뜻하게 유지시켰습니다.

58	어원	-in : not + -pure 순수한 → '순수하지 않은'
impure [ɪmˈpjʊər]	유의어	contaminated, tainted, impurities
	반의어	Pure, uncontaminated, untainted
a. 더러운, 불결한, 불순한	영영	Not pure or free from contamination.
purity n. 순수성, 순도 impurity n. 불순, 불순물 purify v. 정화시키다, 깨끗하게 만들다 purified a. 정화된, 정제된	예문	The impure water needed to be filtered before drinking. 불순한 물은 마시기 전에 여과되어야 했습니다.

59

magnetism

[ˈmæg.nə.tɪ.zəm]

n. 자성, 자력; 매력

magnet n. 자석
magnetic field p. 자기장
magnesium n. 마그네슘(Mg)

어원	-magnet 자석 * 그리스의 매그네시아에 살던 한 목동이 크고 검은 바위에 못이 달라붙는 걸 발견
유의어	magnetic force, attraction, magnetization
반의어	Non-magnetic, non-attractive, non-repulsive
영영	The force exerted by magnets and the property of attracting or repelling objects.
예문	Magnetism is the force that attracts or repels objects with magnetic properties. 자석력은 자성을 가진 물체를 끌거나 밀어내는 힘입니다.

60

mutation

[mjuːˈteɪ.ʃən]

n. 돌연변이, 변화, 변천

mutant a. 돌연변이의
mutual a. 상호간의, 서로의
commute v. 교환하다, 대체하다; 통근하다
immutable a. 불변의

어원	-mut : change 바꾸다 → '형태나 성질이 바뀐 돌연변이'
유의어	genetic change, alteration, variation
반의어	Stasis, stability, uniformity
영영	A change in the genetic material of an organism.
예문	The genetic mutation resulted in a new trait in the organism. 유전적 돌연변이로 인해 생물체의 새로운 특징이 나타났습니다.

61

reed

[riːd]

n. 갈대, 갈대밭

reef n. 암초
reel n. 릴, 얼레; 비틀거리다
redress v. 고치다, 교정하다
redundant a. 과잉의

어원	-reed 갈대 * reel 비틀거리다 → '비틀거리는 갈대'
유의어	tall grass, marsh plant, cane
반의어	Hard, firm, rigid
영영	A tall, slender plant with hollow stems, often found near water.
예문	The musician played a melody on his flute made of reed. 음악가는 미풍으로 만든 플루트에서 음악을 연주했습니다.

62

specimen

[ˈspes.ə.mɪn]

n. 견본, 표본

species n. 종, 종류
specified a. 명시된
specification n. 열거, 명세사항
speculate v. 추측하다

어원	-spec 보다 → '보이는 특성대로 나누어 놓은 견본'
유의어	sample, example, representative
반의어	Entirety, whole, complete entity
영영	An individual example or sample of something.
예문	The scientist collected a rare insect specimen for research. 과학자는 연구용으로 희귀한 곤충 견본을 수집했습니다.

63

substance

[ˈsʌb.stəns]

n. 본질, 실체; 물질

substantial a. 실질적인, 상당한
substantially adv. 상당히, 많이, 주로, 대체로
substitute v. 대체하다, 바꾸다; 대신하다
substantiate v. 구체화 하다, 증명하다

어원	-sub 아래 + -stance 서다 → '아래 서 있는 것이 본질'
유의어	material, matter, stuff
반의어	Nothingness, nonentity, void
영영	A particular kind of matter with uniform properties.
예문	Water is a vital substance for all living organisms. 물은 모든 생물에게 필수적인 물질입니다.

64

wither

[ˈwɪð.ər]

v. 시들다, 말라 죽다

withdraw n. 철회
withdrawal n. (예금의) 인출
withhold v. 주지 않다, 박지 않다; 억제하다
withstand v. 반항하다, 저항하다

어원	-with 밖으로, 반대쪽으로 → '생명이 반대로 가니 시들다'(E)
유의어	shrivel, wilt, fade
반의어	Thrive, flourish, bloom
영영	To shrivel, dry up, or lose vitality.
예문	The plant began to wither due to lack of water. 물 부족으로 식물이 시들기 시작했습니다.

65

capacity

[kəˈpæs.ə.ti]

n. 용량, 능력, 수용력

be capable of p. ~을 할 수 있는
capability n. 능력
inescapable a. 피할 수 없는, 달아날 수 없는
captive n. 포로 a. 사로잡힌, 억류된

어원	-cap, -chief, -chiev, -cupy, -cip, -cept, -ceive, -ceit : head 머리, 우두머리 → '우두머리의 능력이 곧 조직의 크기'
유의어	capability, ability, potential
반의어	Incapacity, inability, disability
영영	The maximum amount that something can hold or contain.
예문	The stadium has a seating capacity of 50,000 spectators. 경기장은 5만 명의 관중 수용 능력이 있습니다.

66

cavity

[ˈkæv.ə.ti]

n. 구멍; 충치

cave n. 동굴
concave a. 오목한
cage n. 우리; 새장
cavitate v. 공동을 만들다

어원	-cav : hollow → '움푹 패인'
유의어	hollow, hole, void
반의어	Solidity, density, compactness
영영	A hollow space or hole within a solid object.
예문	The dentist found a cavity in one of my teeth. 치과 의사가 내 이빨 중 하나에 충치를 발견했습니다.

67

extract

[ɪkˈstrækt]

n. 발췌, 추출물

contract n. 계약 v. 수축하다
abstract a. 추상적인, 관념적인
attract v. 끌어들이다
retract v. 철회하다, 거부하다

어원	-ex : out + -tract : draw → 밖으로 끌어내니 추출'
유의어	derive, obtain, draw out
반의어	Insert, replace, put in
영영	To remove or obtain something, often through a process of separation or concentration.
예문	To make tea, you need to extract flavor from the tea leaves. 차를 만들려면 차잎에서 맛을 추출해야 합니다.

68

icing

[ˈaɪ.sɪŋ]

a. 당의(설탕을 입힌 과자)

iceberg n. 빙산
icily adv. 싸늘한 태도로, 냉담하게
icicle n. 고드름
icing sugar p. 가루 설탕

어원	-ice 얼음 * 얼음처럼 과자의 변질을 막기 위해 약의 표면을 입힌 것
유의어	frosting, glaze, icing sugar
반의어	Dry, unfrosted, unglazed
영영	A sweet glaze or coating, often used on cakes and pastries.
예문	The cake was covered with sweet icing. 케이크는 달콤한 아이싱으로 덮여 있었습니다.

69

proportion

[prəˈpɔː.ʃən]

n. 비율; 조화, 균형

portion n. 부분, 몫, 할당
inverse proportion p. 반비례
in direct proportion to p. ~에 정비례해서
in proportion to as p. ~에 비례하여

어원	-pro : for + -port, -part : divide → 비율을 계산을 위해 나누니 조화롭고 균형이 맞는다'
유의어	ratio, percentage, fraction
반의어	Disproportion, imbalance, inequality
영영	The relationship between the parts of a whole in terms of size, quantity, or degree.
예문	The proportion of men to women in the class was almost equal. 수업에 참여한 남성과 여성의 비율은 거의 동일했습니다.

70

radius

[ˈreɪ.di.əs]

n. 반지름, 반경

radioactive a. 방사선의
radio n. 라디오
radiant a. 빛나는, 눈부신
diameter n. 지름

어원	-rad 광선; 방사 → '원점에서 방사된 원의 반경'
유의어	distance, range, extent from center
반의어	Diameter, width, breadth
영영	The distance from the center of a circle to its outer edge.
예문	The radius of the circle is half of its diameter. 이 원의 반지름은 지름의 절반입니다.

71

work out

p. 운동하다; 알아내다, 해결하다; 계산하다

work on p. 애쓰다
work at p. ~을 하려고 애쓰다
worked up p. 흥분한, 화난
workmanship n. 솜씨, 기술, 기량

어원	-work, -erg, -urg, -ag 일, 일하다 + -out → '아웃될 때까지 하는 운동' , '아웃될 때까지 일해서 알아내니 해결', ' 정답 해결이 곧 계산'
유의어	figure out, solve
반의어	fail, give up
영영	be successful or result in success
예문	Let's work out a solution to this problem. 이 문제에 대한 해결책을 찾아보자.

72

what is more

p. 게다가, 더욱이

what A like p. A는 어떠한가?
what is knows as p. 소위
what with A and B p. A그리고 B 때문에
the so-called p. 소위

어원	-what 무엇 + -more 더욱 → '무언가를 더해서 더욱'
유의어	furthermore, moreover
반의어	what is less, what is equally
영영	moreover; in addition to what has been said
예문	She is talented, and what is more, she is hardworking. 그녀는 재능 있고 더욱이 열심히 일한다.

73

occur to N

p. ~에게 생각이 떠오르다

occur v. 발생하다
concur v. 일치하다
recur v. 재발하다
cursory a. 대충의

어원	-oc : to + -cur : run → '~에게 달리다 충돌이 발생'
유의어	come to mind for N, dawn on N
반의어	escape from N, evade N
영영	come to N's mind; to happen or take place
예문	It suddenly occurred to me that I had forgotten my keys. 나는 갑자기 내 열쇠를 잊었다는 생각이 떠올랐다.

74

get past

p. ~을 넘어서다, ~을 지나가다

get A out of the way p. A를 치우다
get something out p. ~을 생산하다
get to the point p. 핵심에 이르다
get the hang of p. ~에 익숙해지다

어원	-get 얻다 + -past 과거 → '과거를 넘어서 지나가다'
유의어	overcome, surpass
반의어	get stuck, be hindered
영영	move beyond or overcome an obstacle
예문	We need to find a way to get past this obstacle. 우리는 이 장애물을 극복할 방법을 찾아야 한다.

75

take after

p. ~을 닮다

after all p. 결국
one after another p. 차례로, 잇따라서
after the fact p. 사건 후에
thereafter adv. 그 후

어원	after(태어난 이후) 누군가의 특징을 take(취해서) 닮다
유의어	resemble, inherit traits from
반의어	differ from, deviate from
영영	resemble in appearance or behavior
예문	She takes after her mother in terms of appearance. 그녀는 외모적으로 어머니를 닮았다.

76

under consideration

p. 고려 중인

considerate a. 사려 깊은, 배려하는
considerable a. 상당한
reconsider v. 재고하다
sidereal a. 별자리의, 항성의

어원	-con : together + -sider 별 → '함께 별을 셀 정도로 상당히 많이'
유의어	being considered, on the table
반의어	disregarded, ignored
영영	being thought about or discussed
예문	Your proposal is still under consideration by the board. 당신의 제안은 아직 이사회에서 검토 중이다.

77	어원	-at : to + -tach, -tak 말뚝, 막대; 들러붙게 하다 → '말뚝 가까이 부착시키다'
be attached to	유의어	be connected to, be affixed to
	반의어	detach from, separate from
p. ~에 붙어 있다	영영	be connected or joined to
attach A to B p. A를 B에 붙이다 attachment n. 부착 detachment n. 분리, 탈착 be detached from p. ~에서 분리되다	예문	The photo is attached to the email. 그 사진은 이메일에 첨부되어 있다.
78	어원	-break 깨지다(E) + -in → '깨고 안으로 침입'
break in	유의어	interrupt, interject
	반의어	break out, escape from
p. 침입하다	영영	forcibly enter a building or interrupt
break down p. 분해되다 break the new to p. ~에 나쁜 소식을 전하다 breakthrough n. 획기적 발전; 돌파구 break into p. 침입하다, 난입하다	예문	Someone tried to break in while we were away. 우리가 없는 동안 누군가가 침입을 시도했다.
79	어원	-cap, -chief : head 머리, 우두머리 / take, hold 잡다, 취하다 (L) → '최고가 될 수 있는 자본을 이용하다'
capitalize on	유의어	take advantage of, exploit
	반의어	miss out on, squander
p. ~을 이용[활용]하다	영영	take advantage of an opportunity
capital n. 수도; 대문자; 자본 capability n. 능력 capable of p. ~을 할 수 있는 capacity n. 용량, 능력, 수용력	예문	They capitalized on their competitor's mistake. 그들은 경쟁사의 실수를 이용했다.
80	어원	-come 오다 + -across → '건너 오는 길에 우연히 발견하다'
come across	유의어	encounter, stumble upon
	반의어	avoid, bypass
p. ~을 우연히 발견하다	영영	encounter or find by chance
come about p. 일어나다, 생기다 come in handy p. 쓸모가 있다 come on p. 시작하다; ~이 닥쳐오다 come out ahead p. 결국 이득을 보다	예문	I came across an interesting article while browsing the internet. 나는 인터넷을 뒤져서 흥미로운 기사를 우연히 발견했다.

Chapter 3.

81	rag	[ræg]	n. 넝마 조각, 누더기 옷
82	rub	[rʌb]	v. 문지르다
83	courteous	[ˈkɜ:.ti.əs]	a. 공손한, 정중한
84	compound	[ˈkɒm.paʊnd]	n. 합성물, 합성어 v. 혼합하다, 합성하다
85	rejoice	[rɪˈdʒɔɪs]	v. 크게 기뻐하다
86	alternative	[ɒlˈtɜ:.nə.tɪv]	a. 양자택일의 n. 양자택일, (보통 복수형)
87	inhibit	[ɪnˈhɪb.ɪt]	v. 저해하다, 못하게 하다, 억제하다
88	adore	[əˈdɔ:r]	v. 존경하다
89	pendulum	[ˈpen.dʒəl.əm]	n. (시계의) 추, 진자
90	assassinate	[əˈsæs.ɪ.neɪt]	v. 암살하다
91	outright	[aʊˈtraɪˈt]	a. 분명한, 솔직한; 철저한; 모두, 완전히
92	obvious	[ˈɒb.vi.əs]	a. 명백한, 분명한
93	outcast	[ˈaʊt.kɑ:st]	a. 버림받은, 쫓겨난, 버림받은 사람
94	segregation	[ˌseg.rɪˈgeɪ.ʃən]	n. 분리; 인종 차별
95	stubborn	[ˈstʌb.ən]	a. 완고한; 다루기 힘든; 지우기 힘든
96	deliberate	[dɪˈlɪb.ər.ət]	a. 고의적인, 계획적인; 신중한, 심사숙고하는
97	retail	[ˈri:.teɪl]	n. 소매, 소매상 a. 소매의, 소매상의
98	grasp	[grɑ:sp]	v. 잡다; 파악하다, 이해하다
99	complement	[kάmpləmənt]	n. 보충, 보충물; 보어
100	scent	[sent]	n. 향기, 냄새
101	murmur	[ˈmɜ:.mər]	v. 속삭이다, 중얼거리다, 소곤거리다
102	convince	[kənˈvɪns]	v. 확신시키다, 납득시키다, 수긍하게 하다
103	deduction	[dɪˈdʌk.ʃən]	n. 추론, 연역; 공제, 공제액
104	dose	[dəʊs]	n. (약의 1회분) 복용량, 투여량
105	preside	[prɪˈzaɪd]	v. 주관하다, 주재하다
106	arise	[əˈraɪz]	vi. (문제 상황이) 일어나다, 발생하다
107	misery	[mízəri]	n. 불행, 고통, 비참(함)
108	convert	[kənˈvɜ:t]	v. 변환하다, 전환하다, 개종시키다
109	exaggerate	[ɪgˈzædʒ.ə.reɪt]	v. 과장하다
110	gratitude	[ˈgræt.ɪ.tʃu:d]	n. 감사
111	be capable of		p. ~을 할 수 있는
112	cut down on		p. ~를 줄이다
113	come about		p. 일어나다, 생기다
114	integrate A with B		p. A와 B를 통합시키다
115	on the contrary		p. 오히려(도리어)
116	depending on		p. ~에 따라서
117	merge into		p. ~로 합병하다, ~에 융합하다
118	except for		p. ~을 제외하고
119	be exposed to		p. ~을 접하다, ~에 노출되다
120	on the surface		p. 외견상으로는

81

rag

[ræg]

n. 넝마 조각, 누더기 옷

ragged a. 남루한
rug n. 양탄자, 깔개, 융단, 카펫
ragga n. 랩을 도입한 레게
rage n. 분노, 격렬, 대유행

어원	-rug, -rag : rough
유의어	cloth scrap, tatter, shred
반의어	Valuable cloth, new fabric, fine material
정의	A torn or tattered piece of cloth or fabric.
예문	He used an old rag to clean the dirty window. 그는 더러운 창문을 청소하기 위해 오래된 헝겊을 사용했습니다.

82

rub

[rʌb]

v. 문지르다

rubber n. 고무; 지우개
rubber band p. 고무줄
rubbish n. 쓰레기, 헛소리
rude a. 무례한

어원	-rub 문지르다
유의어	friction, massage, stroke
반의어	Smooth, polish, clean
정의	To move one's hand or a surface back and forth against something with pressure.
예문	He used a soft cloth to rub the surface of the antique furniture gently. 그는 고미술품 가구의 표면을 부드럽게 문지르기 위해 부드러운 천을 사용했습니다.

83

courteous

[ˈkɜːtiəs]

a. 공손한, 정중한

courtesy n. 공손함, 정중함
court n. 궁정, 법원, 코트
escort n. 호위, 안내
cohort n. 집단; 지지자

어원	-court, -cohort : garden 정원, 울타리 → '집단 안에서는 공손한 자세 유지'
유의어	polite, respectful, considerate
반의어	rude, impolite
정의	polite, respectful, and considerate in one's behavior and manners
예문	He was always courteous and polite to everyone he met. 그는 항상 만난 모든 사람에게 예의 바르고 공손했다.

84

compound

[ˈkɒm.paʊnd]

n. 합성물, 합성어 v. 혼합하다, 합성하다

composition n. 구성; 작곡
be composed of p. ~로 구성되어 있다
impose v. 부과하다, 강요하다
depose v. 물러나게 하다, 퇴위시키다

어원	-com : together + -pos, -pon, -pound : put 놓다 (L) → '함께 놓으니 합성물을 파운드 씩이나'
유의어	mixture, combination, complex
반의어	Simplify, reduce, break down
정의	A substance formed by the chemical combination of two or more elements.
예문	Water is a compound made up of hydrogen and oxygen. 물은 수소와 산소로 이루어진 화합물입니다.

85

rejoice

[rɪˈdʒɔɪs]

v. 크게 기뻐하다

ravel v. 복잡하게 만들다, 꼬이게 만들다
revel v. 주연을 베풀다
reveal v. 드러내다, 나타내다
retaliate v. 복수하다, 보복하다

어원	-re : back + -join : enjoy → '일이 끝난 뒤에 모여 크게 기뻐하다'
유의어	celebrate, be happy, delight
반의어	mourn, grieve, lament
정의	to feel or express great joy and happiness.
예문	The team and their fans had reason to rejoice after winning the championship. 팀과 그들의 팬들은 챔피언십 우승 후 기쁨을 나타낼 이유가 있었다.

86

alternative

[ɒlˈtɜːnətɪv]

a. 양자택일의 n. 양자택일, (보통 복수형)

alternatively adv. 그렇지 않으면, 대신에
alter v. 바꾸다, 변경하다
alternation n. 변화, 개조
alternating a. 번갈아 하는, 교대의

어원	-al, -alien, -alter, altru : other 다른(L) → '다른 대안' * alter 특성·성질·모양 등이 변함 VS shift 위치·방향을 이동
유의어	choice, option, substitute
반의어	Standard, common, regular
정의	An option or choice that is different from the usual or conventional one.
예문	There are alternative methods for solving this problem. 이 문제를 해결하기 위한 대안적인 방법들이 있습니다.

87

inhibit
[ɪnˈhɪb.ɪt]

v. 저해하다, 못하게 하다, 억제하다

inhibition n. 억제, 금지
inhibitor n. 억제제
inhibitory a. 억제하는
rehabilitate v. 원상태로 돌리다

어원	-in + -hib : hold → 안에 있는 걸 나오지 못하도록 억제시키다
유의어	restrain, suppress, hinder
반의어	encourage, stimulate
영영	prevent or restrain someone from doing something
예문	Fear can sometimes inhibit one's ability to make rational decisions. 두려움은 때로 합리적인 결정을 내리는 능력을 억제할 수 있다.

88

adore
[əˈdɔːr]

v. 존경하다

adorable a. 사랑스러운
adoration n. 숭배, 동경
adorn v. 꾸미다, 장식하다
orchard n. 과수원

어원	-ad : to + -or : speak → '~쪽으로만 말하니 존경하고 동경'
유의어	worship, love, venerate
반의어	despise, detest
영영	feel deep love or admiration for someone or something
예문	She adores her new puppy and spends hours playing with it. 그녀는 새로운 강아지를 아주 아끼며 시간을 보내면서 놀아준다.

89

pendulum
[ˈpen.dʒəl.əm]

n. (시계의) 추, 진자

expensive a. 비싼
pendant v. 펜던트, 목걸이
pendent a. 매달린, 미결의, 드리워진
pend v. 미결인 채로 두다, 결정을 미루다

어원	-pend, -pens, -pond : hang 매달다, weigh 무게를 달다 → '매달린 추' * pend(d,s)은 '매달리다', grav는 '고통'의 의미
유의어	swing, oscillator, timekeeper
반의어	Static, immobile, motionless
영영	A weight suspended from a fixed point that swings back and forth under the influence of gravity.
예문	The grandfather clock's pendulum swung back and forth. 할아버지 시계의 진자가 왔다갔다 흔들렸습니다.

90

assassinate
[əˈsæs.ɪ.neɪt]

v. 암살하다

assassinator n. 암살자
resilience n. 탄성력, 회복력
salient a. 두드러진, 현저한
assail v. 공격하다, 습격하다

어원	-as : to + -sail, -sali, -sali, -saul,- sul, -xul : leap → '~를 향해 뛰어들어 암살'
유의어	murder, kill, eliminate
반의어	protect, guard, defend
영영	To murder someone, especially a prominent or political figure, often for political reasons.
예문	The plot to assassinate the political leader was uncovered by the authorities. 정치 지도자를 암살하려는 계획이 당국에 의해 밝혀졌다.

91

outright
[auˈtraɪt]

a. 분명한, 솔직한; 철저한; 모두, 완전히

outlaw n. 무법자, 범법자
outlay n. 지출, 지출액
outrageous a. 모욕적인, 잔인무도한
outcome n. 결과

어원	-out : outside + -right → '옳은 상황을 밖으로 나타내는'
유의어	absolute, complete, total
반의어	ambiguous, unclear, uncertain
영영	completely or utterly; without reservation.
예문	Her comments were downright offensive. 그녀의 의견은 명백한 모욕이었다.

92

obvious
[ˈɒb.vi.əs]

a. 명백한, 분명한

obviously adv. 명백하게, 명확하게
convey v. 전하다; 나르다
vehicle n. 차량, 탈 것
obviate v. 없애다, 제거하다

어원	-ob : on + -via, -vi, -vey, -voy, -via : way → '길 위에서 명백히 보이는'
유의어	clear, apparent, evident
반의어	hidden, concealed
영영	easily perceived or understood; clear, apparent, or self-evident
예문	The solution to the problem was so obvious that everyone could see it. 문제의 해결책은 너무 명백해서 누구나 볼 수 있었다.

93

outcast

[ˈaʊt.kɑːst]

a. 버림받은, 쫓겨난, 버림받은 사람

forecast v. 예측하다, 예보하다
cast A aside p. A를 버리다
cast a shadow p. 그림자를 드리우다
broadcast v. 방송하다; 알리다

어원	-out + -cast : throw → '밖으로 던져지니 버림받은'
유의어	pariah, exile, social outcast
반의어	Insider, accepted, included
영영	A person who has been rejected or excluded from a group or society; an outsider.
예문	He felt like an outcast in the new school until he made some friends. 그는 새로운 학교에서 친구들을 사귀기 전까지는 배척당한 듯한 기분이었습니다.

94

segregation

[ˌseg.rɪˈgeɪ.ʃən]

n. 분리; 인종 차별

segregate v. 분리하다; 인종차별하다
segregative a. 분리시키는
seize v. 붙잡다, 장악하다
segregate A from B p. A를 B로부터 분리하다

어원	-se : apart + -greg : flock → '모임에서 분리해 떨어뜨리는'
유의어	separation, division, isolation
반의어	integration, inclusion
영영	the act or practice of separating or isolating certain groups or individuals based on characteristics like race, ethnicity, or religion
예문	Segregation based on race is considered unjust and discriminatory. 인종에 따른 격리는 부당하고 차별적으로 여겨진다.

95

stubborn

[ˈstʌb.ən]

a. 완고한; 다루기 힘든; 지우기 힘든

sturdy a. 튼튼한, 건장한, 확고한
stout a. 통통한, 튼튼한; 흑맥주
stalwart a. 충실한, 튼튼한
sgrengthen v. 강화하다

어원	* -st : stand + -born 태어난 → '고집만 세우도록 태어난', '고집을 지우기 힘들어 다루기도 힘든'
유의어	obstinate, inflexible, unyielding
반의어	flexible, pliable
영영	having a firm or determined attitude that is difficult to change; unyielding
예문	Despite everyone's advice, he remained stubborn and refused to change his mind. 모두의 충고에도 불구하고, 그는 완고하게 자신의 생각을 바꾸지 않았다.

96

deliberate

[dɪˈlɪb.ər.ət]

a. 고의적인, 계획적인; 신중한, 심사숙고하는

deliberately adv. 고의적으로
deliberation n. 토의, 심의; 숙고, 숙의
equlibrium n. 균형
delineate v. 윤곽을 그리다; 묘사하다

어원	-de : intensive + -liber, -libr : balance → '균형을 맞춰보며 신중히 숙고하다'
유의어	intentional, calculated, planned
반의어	accidental, unintentional, inadvertent
영영	Done consciously and with careful consideration or intent.
예문	The decision was made after careful and deliberate consideration. 그 결정은 신중하고 숙고한 고려 끝에 내려졌다.

97

retail

[ˈriː.teɪl]

n. 소매, 소매상 a. 소매의, 소매상의

retailer n. 소매업자
in detail p. 상세하게
trim v. (깎아) 다듬다, 없애다
tailor n. 재봉사 v. 맞추다, 조정하다

어원	-re : again + -tail 자르다 (L) → '다시 잘라 판매하니 소매
유의어	sell, market, peddle
반의어	Wholesale, bulk, large-scale
영영	The sale of goods or commodities to individual consumers or end-users.
예문	The company sells its products through both wholesale and retail channels. 그 회사는 도매 및 소매 채널을 통해 제품을 판매합니다.

98

grasp

[ɡrɑːsp]

v. 잡다; 파악하다, 이해하다

govern v. 다스리다, 통치하다
gorge n. 협곡 v. 게걸스레 먹다
gourd n. (식물) 박, 조롱박
get a grade p. 성적을 받다

어원	-grasp : grap → '개념을 잡으니 이해까지'
유의어	hold, grip, seize
반의어	release, let go, surrender
영영	Hold firmly or understand comprehensively.
예문	It took him a while to grasp the concept of advanced calculus. 그가 고급 미적분학의 개념을 이해하는 데에는 시간이 걸렸습니다.

99

complement

[kάmpləmənt]

n. 보충, 보충물; 보어

complete v. 완성하다
completely adv. 완전히
complementary a. 상호보완적인, 보충하는
compliment n. 칭찬

어원	-com : intensive + -ple, -pli : fill → '완전히 채우기 위한 보충'
유의어	supplementary, additional, matching
반의어	Non-complementary, non-matching, mismatched
영영	Completing or enhancing each other by combining qualities or elements.
예문	Their skills were complementary, making them a strong team. 그들의 기술은 상호 보완적이었으며 그들을 강력한 팀으로 만들었습니다.

100

scent

[sent]

n. 향기, 냄새

sensation n. 감각, 느낌, 기분
sensational a. 선풍적인
sentiment n. 감정, 정서
assent v. 동의하다

어원	-scent : feel → '냄새를 느끼다'
유의어	aroma, fragrance, smell
반의어	stench, odor
영영	pleasant or distinctive smell
예문	The scent of fresh flowers filled the room. 신선한 꽃의 향기가 방안에 가득했다.

101

murmur

[ˈmɜː.mər]

v. 속삭이다, 중얼거리다, 소곤거리다

mure v. ~에 가두다 n. 벽
mural a. 벽의, 벽화, 벽면의
murky a. 탁한, 매우 어두운, 흐린
murk n. 암흑, 어둠 a. 어두운

어원	-mut 소리 없는 + -utter 말하다 → '조용히 중얼거리며 투덜거리다'
유의어	mumble, whisper, mutter
반의어	shout, yell
영영	speak or make a low, indistinct sound
예문	The sound of the river's murmur was soothing and calming. 강물의 속삭임 소리는 달래고 진정시키는 효과가 있었다.

102

convince

[kənˈvɪns]

v. 확신시키다, 납득시키다, 수긍하게 하다

conviction n. 유죄 판결; 설득, 납득; 확신
convict v. 유죄를 선고하다
victory n. 승리
convincing a. 설득력 있는

어원	-con : together + -vict : conquer → '모두를 이기고 납득시키다'
유의어	persuade, assure, assure
반의어	dissuade, deter
영영	to persuade or make someone believe or accept something by providing reasons or evidence
예문	He tried to convince me to join his new business venture. 그는 나에게 그의 새로운 사업 참여를 설득하려고 노력했다.

103

deduction

[dɪˈdʌk.ʃən]

n. 추론, 연역; 공제, 공제액

deduct v. 빼다, 공제하다
deduce v. 연역하다, 추론하다
ductile a. 유연한
conducive a. 도움이 되는

어원	-de : down + -duc : lead → '숫자로 아래로 끌어내리는'
유의어	inference, conclusion, reasoning
반의어	Induction, addition, inclusion
영영	The process of reaching a conclusion based on evidence or reasoning.
예문	He made a deduction based on the evidence presented. 그는 제시된 증거를 기반으로 추론을 했습니다.

104

dose

[dəʊs]

n. (약의 1회분) 복용량, 투여량

dosage n. (약의) 정량, 투약
endow v. 기부하다, 재능을 부여하다
doze v. 깜빡 잠이 들다, 졸다
anecdote n. 일화

어원	-don, -dot, -dos 주다(L) → '환자에게 주기로 한 약물의 양'
유의어	amount, quantity, portion
반의어	overdose, excessive, surplus
영영	A specific amount or quantity of a substance, typically a medication or drug.
예문	The doctor prescribed a specific dose of medication for the patient. 의사는 환자에게 특정 용량의 약을 처방했다.

105

preside

[prɪˈzaɪd]

v. 주관하다, 주재하다

president n. 대통령, 회장
presidency n. 대통령직, 의장직
residue n. 나머지, 찌꺼기
reside on p. ~에 머물다

어원	-pre : before + -sid : sit → '앞에 앉아 주관하는'
유의어	chair, lead, conduct
반의어	Attend, participate, be present
영영	To serve as the chairperson or leader of a meeting, event, or organization.
예문	The judge will preside over the court proceedings. 판사는 법정 절차를 주관할 것입니다.

106

arise

[əˈraɪz]

vi. (문제 상황이) 일어나다, 발생하다

rise v. 오르다
arouse vt. (감정·생각 등을) 일으키다, 자극하다
arousal n. 자극, 각성
awaken v. 깨우치다

어원	-a : intensive + -rise 일어나다 → '일이 일어나니 발생'
유의어	emerge, occur, develop
반의어	subside, abate
영영	to originate, come into existence, or occur as a result of a situation or event
예문	Unexpected problems can arise during any project. 예상치 못한 문제는 어떤 프로젝트에서든 발생할 수 있다.

107

misery

[mízəri]

n. 불행, 고통, 비참(함)

miserable a. 비참한
miserably adv. 비참하게, 불쌍하게
miser n. 구두쇠, 수전노

어원	-mis : wrong + -sert 삽입 → '잘못된 일이 들어오니 불행'
유의어	suffering, distress, wretchedness
반의어	happiness, joy
영영	extreme suffering or unhappiness
예문	The war brought misery and suffering to countless families. 전쟁은 무수한 가정에 고통과 괴로움을 가져왔다.

108

convert

[kənˈvɜːt]

v. 변환하다, 전환하다, 개종시키다

converse v. 대화하다
conversation n. 대화
conversely adv. 반대로, 거꾸로
conversant a. ~에 정통한, 잘 알고 있는

어원	-con : together + -vert, -vers, -vorc : turn 돌리다(L) → '모든 것을 돌려 바꾸다'
유의어	change, transform, switch
반의어	Remain, stay, hold onto
영영	To change or transform from one state, belief, or condition to another.
예문	He decided to convert his garage into a home office. 그는 차고를 집 사무실로 변환하기로 결정했습니다.

109

exaggerate

[ɪgˈzædʒ.ə.reɪt]

v. 과장하다

exaggeration n. 과장
exaggerated a. 과장된
exceed v. 넘다, 초과하다
excess n. 초과, 잉여

어원	-ex : out + -ger : carry → 바깥으로 끝없이 말을 나르니 과장이다
유의어	overstate, inflate, embellish
반의어	minimize, downplay
영영	to represent something as being larger, greater, better, or worse than it really is; to overstate or magnify
예문	He tends to exaggerate the size of the fish he catches. 그는 자주 그가 잡는 물고기의 크기를 과장하는 경향이 있다.

110

gratitude

[ˈgræt.ɪ.tʃuːd]

n. 감사

grateful a. 감사하는, 고마워하는
be grateful for p. ~을 고맙게 여기다
gratify v. 기쁘게 하다, 만족시키다
gratification n. 만족감

어원	-grat, -gree, -grac : thankful 감사하는 * gratification 일시적인 만족감 VS gratitude 지속적인 만족감
유의어	thankfulness, appreciation, recognition
반의어	ingratitude, unthankfulness
영영	the quality of being thankful or appreciative
예문	She expressed her gratitude to her parents for their support. 그녀는 부모님에게 지원에 대한 감사의 뜻을 표현했다.

111

be capable of

p. ~을 할 수 있는

capacity n. 용량, 능력, 수용력
capability n. 능력
inescapable a. 피할 수 없는, 달아날 수 없는
captive n. 포로 a. 사로잡힌, 억류된

어원	-cap, -chief : head 머리, 우두머리 / take, hold 잡다, 취하다 (L) + -able → '우두머리의 능력이 유능한'
유의어	have the ability to, be able to
반의어	be incapable of, unable to
영영	have the ability or capacity to do something
예문	Despite his age, he is still capable of doing heavy physical work. 그의 나이에도 불구하고, 그는 여전히 무거운 육체적인 일을 할 수 있다.

112

cut down on

p. ~를 줄이다

cut out p. 멈추다; 급히 떠나다
cut A with B p. A를 B로 자르다
cut from the same cloth p. 같은 부류인
cut off p. 잘라버리다; 서둘러 떠나다

어원	-cut 자르다
유의어	reduce, decrease
반의어	increase, amplify
영영	reduce the amount of something
예문	I need to cut down on my sugar intake. 나는 설탕 섭취를 줄여야 한다.

113

come about

p. 일어나다, 생기다

come in handy p. 쓸모가 있다
come on p. 시작하다; ~이 닥쳐오다
come across p. ~을 우연히 발견하다
come across as p. ~이라는 인상을 주다

어원	-come 오다 + -about 여기저기 → '사건이 여기저기서 오니 일이 생기다'
유의어	happen, occur
반의어	cease, stop
영영	happen or occur
예문	The change came about because of new regulations. 그 변화는 새로운 규정 때문에 일어났다.

114

integrate A with B

p. A와 B를 통합시키다

integration n. 통합, 완성; 적분법
intergrative a. 통합적인
disintegrate v. 분해하다
intangible a. 무형의; 모호한

어원	-in 안 + -ti, -tig, -ting, - tag, -tac, -tan, -ten : touch → '~안에 접촉이 가능하니 통합'
유의어	merge A and B, combine A and B
반의어	separate A from B, disconnect A and B
영영	combine A and B into a unified whole
예문	The goal is to integrate technology with education. 목표는 기술을 교육과 통합하는 것이다.

115

on the contrary

p. 오히려(도리어)

to the contrary p. 그 반대로
contrary to p. ~와는 달리
controvert v. 논쟁하다, ~에 반박하다
contravene v. 반대하다, 위반하다

어원	-contr, -counter, -contra, -contro 반대쪽으로, 밖으로(L) → 의미상 연결되어 있으면서 반대의 말
유의어	conversely, however
반의어	on the same side, likewise
영영	in contrast; expressing the opposite idea
예문	I thought she would be upset, but on the contrary, she was quite pleased. 나는 그녀가 화가 날 것이라고 생각했는데, 그러나 그와는 반대로 그녀는 꽤 기뻤다.

116

depending on

p. ~에 따라서

dependent on p. ~에게 의존하고 있는
independent a. 독립적인, 자주적인
interdependent a. 상호 의존적인
impend v. 절박하다, 임박하다

어원	-de : down + -pend, -pens, -pond : hang 매달다 → '매달려 의존하니 ~에 따라서' (L) * pend(d,s) '매달리다' VS grav '고통'
유의어	contingent on, subject to
반의어	regardless of, irrespective of
영영	contingent on; influenced or determined by
예문	The price varies depending on the size. 가격은 크기에 따라 다릅니다.

117

merge into

p. ~로 합병하다, ~에 융합하다

merge with p. ~와 하나가 되다
empathize v. 공감하다
immersive n. 몰입; 본능
immersion n. 몰입, 몰두

어원	-merg, -mers : dip 잠기다 → '큰 기업에 작은 기업이 잠기니 합병'
유의어	blend into, combine into
반의어	separate from, disconnect from
영영	combine or blend together
예문	The two companies decided to merge into one. 두 회사는 하나로 합병하기로 결정했다.

118

except for

p. ~을 제외하고

except to do p. ~하는 것을 제외하고
exceptional a. 예외적인
excavate v. ~에 구멍을 파다
excerpt n. 발췌, 인용

어원	-ex : out + -cept : take → 'take out 밖으로 빼서 제외하고'
유의어	apart from, aside from
반의어	including, encompassing
영영	apart from; with the exclusion of
예문	Everyone was present except for Tom. 톰을 제외하고 모두가 참석했다.

119

be exposed to

p. ~을 접하다, ~에 노출되다

expose v. 드러내다, 폭로하다, 노출하다
exposure n. 노출, 폭로, 접함
exposed a. 비바람을 맞는
exposition n. 전시회, 박람회

어원	-ex : out + -pos, -posit : put → '바깥에 드러나니 비바람을 맞는'
유의어	be subjected to, be vulnerable to
반의어	be protected from, shielded from
영영	come into contact with; be subjected to
예문	Children should not be exposed to violent content. 어린이들은 폭력적인 콘텐츠에 노출되어서는 안 된다.

120

on the surface

p. 외견상으로는

interface n. 사이의 면, 경계면 v. 조정하다
forefront n. 맨 앞, 가장 중요한 위치
supeficial a. 표면상의
facile a. 손쉬운 , 수월한

어원	-sur 위 + -fac 겉면, 앞면(L)
유의어	superficially, outwardly
반의어	beneath the surface, deep within
영영	superficially; appearing to be true but not necessarily so
예문	On the surface, everything seemed fine, but underneath there were many problems. 표면상으로는 모든 것이 괜찮아 보였지만, 실제로는 많은 문제가 있었다.

Chapter 4.

121	liable	[ˈlaɪ.ə.bəl]	a. 책임을 져야 할, ~ 경향이 있는, ~하기 쉬운
122	accomplish	[əˈkʌm.plɪʃ]	v. 달성하다, 이루어 내다
123	bald	[bɔːld]	a. 대머리의, 머리가 벗겨진
124	constrict	[kənˈstrɪkt]	v. 압축하다, 죄다
125	limp	[lɪmp]	a. 기운이 없는, 다리를 절다, 절뚝거림
126	cognitive	[ˈkɒg.nə.tɪv]	a. 인식의, 인지의
127	quotation	[kwəʊˈteɪ.ʃən]	n. 인용구, 인용; 견적
128	potential	[pəˈten.ʃəl]	n. 잠재력 a. 잠재력이 있는, 가능성이 있는
129	reverse	[rɪˈvɜːs]	v. 거꾸로 하다
130	duplicate	[ˈdʒuː.plɪ.keɪt]	v. 복제하다, 되풀이하다 a. 복제의 n. 복제
131	detective	[dɪˈtek.tɪv]	n. 탐정 a. 탐정의
132	insomnia	[ɪnˈsɒm.ni.ə]	n. 불면증
133	outweigh	[ˌaʊtˈweɪ]	v. ~보다 뛰어나다
134	impolite	[ìmpəláit]	a. 무례한, 버릇없는
135	punctuate	[ˈpʌŋk.tʃuː.eɪt]	v. 구두점을 찍다, (말을) 중단시키다
136	accurate	[ˈæk.jə.rət]	a. 정확한, 정밀한
137	coordinate	[kəʊˈɔː.dɪ.neɪt]	v. 조직화하다, 조정하다
138	abundant	[əˈbʌn.dənt]	a. 풍부한
139	console	[kənsóul]	v. 달래다, 위로하다
140	consonant	[ˈkɒn.sə.nənt]	n. 자음
141	comply	[kəmˈplaɪ]	v. (명령, 요구 등에) 따르다, 준수하다
142	ripe	[raɪp]	a. 익은, 숙성한
143	elementary	[ˌel.ɪˈmen.tər.i]	a. 초보의, 초급의, 기본적인
144	observe	[əbzɜ́ːrv]	v. 지키다, 준수하다; 관찰하다
145	conceive	[kənˈsiːv]	v. 마음에 품다, 고안하다, 상상하다; 이해하다
146	shiver	[ˈʃɪv.ər]	n. 떨림, 전율; v. (몸을) 떨다
147	smear	[smɪər]	n. 얼룩; v. 마구 바르다, 더럽히다
148	monarchy	[ˈmɒn.ə.ki]	n. 군주제, 군주국, 군주 일가, 왕가
149	diffuse	[dɪˈfjuːz]	v. 확산시키다, 분산되다
150	eligible	[ˈel.ɪ.dʒə.bəl]	a. 적격의, 자격이 있는
151	come out		p. 나오다, 등장하다
152	with A in mind		p. A를 염두에 두고
153	prefer A to B		p. B보다 A를 더 선호하다
154	in the absence of		p. ~이 없을 때에, ~이 없어서
155	be absorbed in		p. ~에 열중하다, 몰두하다
156	with access to		p. 직접 만날 수 있는
157	account for		p. 설명하다; (부분·비율을) 차지하다
158	one after another		p. 차례로, 잇따라서, 하나하나
159	act against one's will		p. ~의 의지에 반하여 행동하다
160	adjust to N		p. ~에 적응하다, ~에 조정하다

121

liable

[ˈlaɪ.ə.bəl]

a. 책임을 져야 할, ~ 경향이 있는, ~하기 쉬운

reliant a. 의존하는, 의지하는
rely on p. 의지하다, 신뢰하다
be liable to do p. ~할 것 같다, ~책임이 있다
liability n. 책임, 의무

어원	-li : bind + -able 형접 → '~에 얽매어 책임져야 할'
유의어	responsible, accountable, susceptible
반의어	immune, resistant
영영	legally responsible or accountable for something; likely or prone to experience something
예문	The police suspected that the burglary was an inside job. 경찰은 절도 사건이 내부에서 계획된 일이라고 의심했다.

122

accomplish

[əˈkʌm.plɪʃ]

v. 달성하다, 이루어 내다

accomplished a. 기량이 뛰어난, 재주가 많은
accomplishment n. 달성, 성취
accompany v. 동반하다, 동행하다
accomplice n. 공범자

어원	-ac : to + -com : completely + -ply 채우다 → '한 방향으로 완전히 채우니 달성하다'
유의어	achieve, complete, fulfill
반의어	fail, fall short, miss
영영	To successfully complete a task or achieve a goal.
예문	They set out to accomplish their goals and succeeded in the end. 그들은 목표를 달성하려고 노력하고 마침내 성공했다.

123

bald

[bɔːld]

a. 대머리의, 머리가 벗겨진

bold a. 대담한; 선이 굵은
blame A on B p. A를 B의 책임으로 보다
blaze n. 화재 v. 불길이 타오르다
blend in with p. ~와 잘 섞이다

어원	* -bal : blaze → '빛나는 머리가 대머리'
유의어	hairless, barren, bald-headed
반의어	hairy, furry, well-covered
영영	Lacking hair on the head; having a smooth, hairless scalp.
예문	He started to go bald in his early thirties. 그는 30대 초반에 대머리가 되기 시작했습니다.

124

constrict

[kənˈstrɪkt]

v. 압축하다, 죄다

strict a. 엄격한, 정확한
restrict v. ~을 제한하다, 금지하다
stringent a. 엄중한, 긴박한
district n. 선거구 지역, 구역

어원	-con : together + -strict, -strai, -strain, -frain, -stress, -stig 팽팽히 누르다 → '모든 것을 팽팽하게 눌러 압축하다' (L)
유의어	tighten, squeeze, compress
반의어	expand, dilate, widen
영영	To tighten or squeeze something, usually causing it to become smaller or narrower.
예문	The snake can constrict its prey to immobilize it before eating. 뱀은 먹기 전에 먹잇감을 꼼짝 못하게 조여 죽이는 능력을 가지고 있다.

125

limp

[lɪmp]

a. 기운이 없는, 다리를 절다, 절뚝거림

limbo n. 불확실한 상태
eliminate v. 제거하다
delimit v. 범위를 정하다
along the way p. 그 과정에서

어원	-limp 절뚝거림 * limbo 절뚝거리며 통과하는 게임
유의어	hobble, stagger, walk lamely
반의어	walk confidently, strut
영영	walk with difficulty, typically due to injury or weakness
예문	After spraining his ankle, he walked with a limp for a few days. 발목을 삐고 나서 그는 몇 일 동안 절뚝거리며 걸었다.

126

cognitive

[ˈkɒɡ.nə.tɪv]

a. 인식의, 인지의

congnitively adv. 인지적으로, 지각력 있게
cognition n. 인식, 인지
diagnose v. 진단하다; 원인을 규명하다
recognize v. 알아보다, 식별하다; 인정하다

어원	-cogn, -gno, -kno, -no, -quaint : know → '알고 있으니 인지의'
유의어	mental, intellectual, psychological
반의어	noncognitive, nonmental
영영	related to mental processes and activities, such as thinking, learning, and memory
예문	Cognitive development is an important aspect of early childhood education. 인지 발달은 유아 교육의 중요한 측면이다.

127

quotation
[kwoʊˈteɪ.ʃən]

n. 인용구, 인용; 견적

quote v. 인용하다; 견적을 내다
quotation mark p. 인용 부호
double quotation marks p. 큰 따옴표
quarter n. 1/4

어원	-quote : how many, how much → '많은 이들이 인용하는', '얼마나 많은 금액인지 견적을 내다'
유의어	citation, quote, excerpt
반의어	Original text, source material, primary text
영영	The act of repeating or citing someone else's words or the words themselves.
예문	The wedding ceremony included traditional rituals from both cultures. 결혼식은 양쪽 문화의 전통 의식을 포함했습니다.

128

potential
[pəˈten.ʃəl]

n. 잠재력 a. 잠재력이 있는, 가능성이 있는

potent a. 유력한, 강력한
potential energy p. 위치 에너지
potentially adv. 가능성 있게, 잠재적으로
impotent a. 무력한, 무기력한

어원	-po, -pos, -pot : 힘 (L) + -tend, -tent : 끌어 오다 → '힘을 끌어 모으니 잠재력이 있는'
유의어	possibility, capability, potentiality
반의어	Non-potential, incapable, incapable of development
영영	The possibility or capacity for future development or success; latent ability.
예문	The young athlete has great potential for success. 젊은 선수는 성공을 위한 큰 잠재력을 가지고 있습니다.

129

reverse
[rɪˈvɜːs]

v. 거꾸로 하다

invert v. 뒤집다, 거꾸로하다
divorce v. 이혼하다; 분리하다
introvert n. 내향적인 사람
verse n. 운문, (시의) 연

어원	re : back + -vert, -vers, -vorc : turn 돌리다(L) → '거꾸로 뒤집다'
유의어	overturn, turn around, flip
반의어	Forward, progress, advancement
영영	To change the direction, order, or course of something to its opposite.
예문	To reverse the car, turn the steering wheel to the left. 차를 후진시키려면 조향 휠을 왼쪽으로 돌리세요.

130

duplicate
[ˈdʒuː.plɪ.keɪt]

v. 복제하다, 되풀이하다 a. 복제의 n. 복제

duel n. 결투, 다툼
dual a. 둘의, 이중의
duet n. 이중창, 이중주
doubly adv. 이중으로

어원	-du : two + -plic 접다 → '접어서 똑같은 둘을 만드니 복제하다'
유의어	copy, replicate, reproduce
반의어	Original, prototype, one-of-a-kind
영영	An identical copy or replica of something; to make a copy of.
예문	Please make a duplicate copy of this important document. 이 중요한 문서의 복제본을 만들어 주세요.

131

detective
[dɪˈtek.tɪv]

n. 탐정 a. 탐정의

detect v. 발견하다, 감지하다
detection n. 감지, 발견
detector n. 발견자, 탐지 장치
undetected a. 간파되지 않은

어원	-de : down + -tect : cover → '덮고 있던 것을 떨어뜨리니 발견하는 탐정'
유의어	investigator, sleuth, private eye
반의어	Criminal, wrongdoer, perpetrator
영영	A person who investigates crimes and gathers evidence to solve cases.
예문	The detective was assigned to solve the mysterious case. 탐정은 미스터리한 사건을 해결하기 위해 배정되었습니다.

132

insomnia
[ɪnˈsɒm.ni.ə]

n. 불면증

somnambulist n. 몽유병자
somnambulistic a. 몽유병의
ambulance n. 구급차
hypnology n. 최면학

어원	-in : not + -somn : sleep → '잠을 자지 못하니 불면증' * 솜누스Somnus : 잠의 신으로 밤의 여신 닉스가 혼자서 낳은 자식
유의어	sleeplessness, wakefulness, restlessness
반의어	sleep, rest
영영	a condition characterized by difficulty falling asleep or staying asleep, often resulting in inadequate rest
예문	He suffered from chronic insomnia and had trouble sleeping at night. 그는 만성 불면증으로 고민하며 밤에 잠을 이루기 어려웠다.

133

outweigh

[ˌaʊtˈweɪ]

v. ~보다 뛰어나다

outcompete v. 경쟁에서 이기다
outset n. 착수, 시작
outlive v. ~보다 오래 살다
outdo v. ~을 능가하다

어원	-out : more than + -weigh → '무게감이 더 있으니 뛰어나다'
유의어	surpass, eclipse, exceed
반의어	underweight, be lighter than
영영	be greater in value or importance than something else
예문	The benefits of regular exercise far outweigh the risks. 규칙적인 운동의 혜택은 위험을 훨씬 능가한다.

134

impolite

[impəláit]

a. 무례한, 버릇없는

politely adv. 공손히
politic a. 현명한, 정치상의
acropolis n. 언덕 위 도시
metropolis n. 모체가 되는 도시

어원	-im : not + -polit, -polic, -polis 많은, 시민, 도시 (G) → '많은 사람 사람 앞에서 예의바르지 못하니 무례한'
유의어	rude, discourteous, disrespectful
반의어	Polite, courteous, well-mannered
영영	Lacking manners or courtesy; rude or disrespectful in behavior.
예문	It's impolite to interrupt someone while they are speaking. 누군가가 말하는 동안 중단하는 것은 예의가 없습니

135

punctuate

[ˈpʌŋk.tʃuː.eɪt]

v. 구두점을 찍다, (말을) 중단시키다

puntual a. 시간을 엄수하는
punctually adv. 제시간에, 늦지 않게
puncture n. 펑크
pupil n. 학생; 눈동자(동공)

어원	-punct, -point 점 → '점을 찍어 끝나게 중단시키다'
유의어	emphasize, accentuate, highlight
반의어	Uninterrupted, continuous, constant
영영	To interrupt or emphasize something with punctuation marks or actions; to break up or divide with intervals.
예문	The fireworks punctuated the night sky with bursts of color. 폭죽이 밤하늘에 색깔의 폭발로 마침표를 찍었습니다.

136

accurate

[ˈæk.jə.rət]

a. 정확한, 정밀한

accurately adv. 정확하게, 정밀하게
accuracy n. 정확함, 정밀함, 정확성
inaccurately adv. 부정확하게, 정밀하지 않게
ache v. 아프다

어원	-ac : to + -cure : care → '그 방향으로만 신경을 쓰니 정확한'
유의어	precision, correctness, exactness
반의어	inaccuracy, imprecision, error
영영	The degree of correctness, precision, or exactness in something.
예문	The accuracy of the measurements was crucial for the experiment. 측정값의 정확성은 실험에 매우 중요했습니다.

137

coordinate

[koʊˈɔː.dɪ.neɪt]

v. 조직화하다, 조정하다

coordination n. 조정력, 공동 작용
incordinate a. 과도한
subordinate a. 종속적인, 하위의
extraordinary a. 특별한, 비상한

어원	-cor : together + -ordin : arrange → '모두의 순서를 함께 조정하여 조직화'
유의어	organize, arrange, synchronize
반의어	Disarrange, disrupt, disorganize
영영	To organize, harmonize, or arrange elements or activities to work together effectively.
예문	The team needs to coordinate their efforts to complete the project on time. 팀은 프로젝트를 제 시간에 완료하기 위해 노력을 협조해야 합니다.

138

abundant

[əˈbʌn.dənt]

a. 풍부한

redendant a. 과잉의
redound v. ~에 크게 도움이 되다
reed n. 갈대, 갈대밭
reef n. 암초

어원	-ab : from + -und : wave → '~로부터 물결쳐 흘러나올 정도로 풍부한'
유의어	plenty, wealth, profusion
반의어	Scarcity, shortage, dearth
영영	A large quantity or plentiful supply of something.
예문	The garden was filled with an abundance of colorful flowers. 그 정원은 다양한 색상의 꽃으로 가득 차 있었습니다.

139

console

[kənsóul]

v. 달래다, 위로하다

solitary a. 고독한, 혼자의
solace v. 위로하다
disconsolate a. 불행한
consolidate v. 합병하다; 강화하다

어원	-con : together + -sol : solo → '솔로들끼리 함께 모여 달래고 위로하다'
유의어	comfort, soothe, reassure
반의어	distress, upset, trouble
영영	To comfort or provide solace to someone who is experiencing grief, sadness, or distress.
예문	She tried to console her friend who was feeling sad. 그녀는 슬픈 친구를 위로하려고 노력했습니다.

140

consonant

[ˈkɒn.sə.nənt]

n. 자음

dissonant a. 조화되지 않는, 불협화의
dissonantly adv. 불협화음을 내어
resonant a. 울리는, 울려 퍼지는
sonata n. 소나타(이탈리아어)

어원	-con : together + -son 소리 (L) → '모음과 함께 해야 소리가 나는 자음'
유의어	harmonious, agreeable, compatible
반의어	Vowel, non-consonant, non-vocalic
영영	A speech sound characterized by the closure or partial closure of certain articulatory organs, such as lips, tongue, or teeth.
예문	The English alphabet consists of both vowels and consonants. 영어 알파벳은 모음과 자음으로 구성됩니다.

141

comply

[kəmˈplaɪ]

v. (명령, 요구 등에) 따르다, 준수하다

compliant a. 순응하는, 잘 따르는
supply v. 공급하다 n. 공급
in support of p. ~을 지지하여
supple a. 유연한

어원	-com : together + -ple, -ply 엮다 / fill 채우다 → '요구 받은 것을 모두 채우니 준수'
유의어	conform, obey, adhere
반의어	Defy, resist, oppose
영영	To obey or adhere to rules, instructions, or requests.
예문	It is important to comply with safety regulations in the workplace. 직장에서 안전 규정을 준수하는 것이 중요합니다.

142

ripe

[raɪp]

a. 익은, 숙성한

ripen v. 익다, 숙성시키다
ripeness n. 무르익음, 성숙
on the rise p. 증가 추세인, 상승세인
strife n. 분쟁, 불화, 반목

어요	-ripe : ready for reap(수확) → '수확할 준비가 되니 익은'
유의어	mature, ready, developed
반의어	unripe, immature, green
영영	Fully matured and ready for harvesting or consumption.
예문	The fruit is ripe and ready to be picked from the tree. 과일은 익어서 나무에서 따먹을 준비가 되어 있다.

143

elementary

[ˌel.ɪˈmen.tər.i]

a. 초보의, 초급의, 기본적인

element n. 요소, 원소, 성분
the elements n. [날씨] 악천후
elect v. 선출하다, 선택하다
eligible a. 적격의, 자격이 있는

어원	-e: out + -lec, -lect, -leg, -lig : gather 모으다 → '모아서 분류해 놓은 요소로 가르치는 초보'
유의어	basic, fundamental, primary
반의어	Advanced, complex, sophisticated
영영	Relating to the basic or fundamental principles or elements of a subject or field.
예문	Elementary education is the foundation of a child's learning journey. 초등 교육은 아이의 학습 여정의 기반입니다.

144

observe

[əbzɜ́ːrv]

v. 지키다, 준수하다; 관찰하다

observance n. 준수, 습관
observant n. 엄수자
observation n. 관찰, 주시
disservice n. 학대, 구박

어원	-ob : on + -serv : keep → '가까이에서 서로 지키고 살피며 법 준수 ' * 스타크래프트 '옵저버'
관의어	watch, view, witness
반의어	ignore, disregard, neglect
영영	To watch, perceive, or notice something through careful attention; to follow or adhere to a practice, rule, or custom.
예문	Scientists observe the behavior of animals in the wild. 과학자들은 야생동물의 행동을 관찰합니다.

145

conceive

[kənˈsiːv]

v. 마음에 품다, 고안하다, 상상하다; 이해하다

concept n. 개념, 생각, 구상
conceivable a. 생각할 수 있는
conceivably adv. 상상컨데
preconseive v. 미리 생각하다, 예상하다

어원	-con : together + -cept, -ceit, -ceive : take 취하다, 잡다 → '모았던 생각으로 상상하다'
유의어	imagine, envision, think up
반의어	forget, ignore, disbelieve
영영	to form or develop an idea or concept in one's mind.
예문	She was able to conceive a brilliant idea for their marketing campaign. 그녀는 그들의 마케팅 캠페인을 위한 뛰어난 아이디어를 고안할 수 있었다.

146

shiver

[ˈʃɪv.ər]

n. 떨림, 전율; v. (몸을) 떨다

shudder v. 몸을 떨다, 전율하다
shrug v. (어깨를) 으쓱하다
shake v. 흔들다; 충격을 주다
shuffle v. 발을 끌며 걷다; 카드를 섞다

어원	-sh, -shi : shake → '몸이 떨리는 전율'
유의어	tremble, quiver, shake
반의어	steady, remain still, stay calm
영영	to tremble or shake involuntarily due to fear, cold, or disgust.
예문	The cold wind made her shudder. 차가운 바람이 그녀로 하여금 떨게 만들었다.

147

smear

[smɪər]

n. 얼룩; v. 마구 바르다, 더럽히다

smeary a. 더럽혀진, 끈적거리는
smeared a. 오염된, 스며든
stain n. 얼룩
smudge n. 자국, 얼룩 v. 더럽히다

어원	* -sme : smell → 냄새 나는 것을 마구 발라 더럽힌 것이 얼룩' * 얼룩이 스미어 더럽혀지다
유의어	smudge, daub, spread
반의어	clean, wipe
영영	to spread a substance or material over a surface, often in a messy or careless manner; a stain or mark created by smearing
예문	She accidentally smeared the paint on the canvas. 그녀는 실수로 캔버스에 페인트를 묻혔다.

148

monarchy

[ˈmɒn.ə.ki]

n. 군주제, 군주국, 군주 일가, 왕가

monarch n. 군주
anarchy n. 무정부 상태; 난장판
patriarchy n. 가부장제
archon n. 집정관, 지배자, 장

어원	-mon, -mono : solo + -arch : rule → '혼자 지배하니 군주'
유의어	chaos, lawlessness, disorder
반의어	Order, governance, lawfulness
영영	A state of lawlessness or absence of government or authority.
예문	The absence of government led to a state of anarchy in the region. 정부의 부재로 인해 그 지역은 무질서 상태에 빠졌습니다.

149

diffuse

[dɪˈfjuːz]

v. 확산시키다, 분산되다

fusion n. 융합, 결합
diffusion n. 발산, 확산; 전파
fission n. (핵·세포 등의) 분열
perfume n. 향수

어원	-dif : away + -fus, -fut, -fund : pour 붓다 → '여러 떨어져 있는 곳에 부으며 확산시키다'
유의어	spread, disperse, scatter
반의어	concentrate, condense, focus
영영	to spread or disperse widely.
예문	The scent of flowers began to diffuse throughout the room. 꽃 향기가 방 안에 퍼져 나가기 시작했다.

150

eligible

[ˈel.ɪ.dʒə.bəl]

a. 적격의, 자격이 있는

element n. 요소, 원소, 성분
the elements n. [날씨] 악천후
elect v. 선출하다, 선택하다
edeligence n. 근면, 부지런함

어원	-e, -ex : out + -lig, -leg, -lec, -lic : select → '선택해서 밖으로 꺼내 놓은 후보니 적격의'
유의어	qualified, suitable, entitled
반의어	Ineligible, disqualified, unqualified
영영	Meeting the necessary requirements or qualifications to be considered or chosen for something.
예문	Only those who meet the criteria are eligible to apply for the scholarship. 기준을 충족하는 사람만이 장학금 신청 자격이 있습니다.

151

come out

p. 나오다, 등장하다

come across p. 우연히 발견하다
come in handy p. 쓸모가 있다
come true p. 실현되다
come out ahead p. 결국 이득을 보다

어원	-come 오다 + -out → '밖으로 나오니 등장하다'
유의어	emerge, surface
반의어	go in, retract
영영	be published or become known
예문	The sun came out after the rain stopped. 비가 그치고 나서 해가 나왔다.

152

with A in mind

p. A를 염두에 두고

out of one's mind p. 미친, 정신 이상의
take one's mind off p. ~을 잠시 잊게 하다
open-minded p. 개방적인
mindful a. 염두에 두는

어원	-with + -in mind → '마음에 함께 두고'
유의어	considering A, bearing A in consideration
반의어	without A in mind, absent A
영영	considering A; with the intention or purpose of A
예문	I made this plan with your preferences in mind. 나는 너의 선호도를 생각해서 이 계획을 세웠다.

153

prefer A to B

p. B보다 A를 더 선호하다

prefer to do p. ~하는 것을 더 선호하다
preference n. 선호도
preferable a. 더 좋은, 선호되는
proper a. 적절한, 적당한

어원	-pre, -pri : before (L) + -fer : carry → '먼저 나를 정도로 선호하는'
유의어	favor A over B, choose A over B
반의어	prefer B to A, favor B over A
영영	like or desire A more than B
예문	I prefer tea to coffee. 나는 차를 커피보다 선호한다.

154

in the absence of

p. ~이 없을 때에, ~이 없어서

absence n. 결석, 부재, 결여
absentee n. 결석자, 부재자
absent a. 결석한, 부재 중인
presently adv. 이내, 곧; 현재, 지금

어원	-ab, -a, -abs : away, from (L) + -se, -es : 손재하다 → '존재하지 않으니 부재고 결석' cf. absent 결석한, 결근한, absently 멍하니
유의어	without, lacking
반의어	in the presence of, with
영영	without; lacking
예문	In the absence of evidence, the case was dismissed. 증거가 없는 상황에서, 그 사건은 기각되었다.

155

be absorbed in

p. ~에 열중하다, 몰두하다

absorbed a. 몰두한
absorption n. 흡수; 열중, 전념
absorbing a. 마음을 사로잡는, 재미있는
absolve v. 면제하다, 용서하다

어원	-ab: from + -sorb, -sorp : soak 흡수하다 + -in → '~안에 완전히 흡수된 것이니 열중하고, 몰두하다'
유의어	be engrossed in, be immersed in
반의어	be disinterested in, uninterested in
영영	deeply engrossed or involved in
예문	She was absorbed in her book and didn't notice the time passing. 그녀는 책에 몰두해서 시간이 흐르는 것을 눈치채지 못했다.

156

with access to

p. 직접 만날 수 있는

access n. 접근, 접속
accessible a. 접근하기 쉬운
accessibility n. 접근성
excess n. 초과, 잉여

어원	-ac : to + -ce, -ced, -cess, -cede, -cesler : go → '그쪽으로 가니 접근, 접속'(L)
유의어	with the opportunity to, with entry to
반의어	without access to, deprived of access to
영영	having the opportunity or permission to use or obtain
예문	Students have access to the library resources. 학생들은 도서관 자료에 접근할 수 있다.

157

account for

p. 설명하다; (부분·비율을) 차지하다

take A into account p. A를 고려하다
account n. 계산, 회계; 책임
accountability n. 책임(성)
accounting n. 경리, 회계, 회계학

어원	-ac, -ad : add + -count 세다 → '셈을 더하며 차지한 비율을 설명하다'
동의어	explain, justify
반의어	defy explanation, remain unexplained
영영	explain or justify
예문	Can you account for your absence yesterday? 어제의 결석에 대한 이유를 설명할 수 있나요?

158

one after another

p. 차례로, 잇따라서, 하나하나

one after the other p. 차례로
after all p. 결국
after the fact p. 사건 후에
take after p. ~을 닮다

어원	-one + -after 이후(E) → '하나 이후 차례로'
동의어	consecutively, sequentially
반의어	all at once, simultaneously
영영	sequentially; in succession
예문	The guests arrived one after another. 손님들이 차례로 도착했다.

159

act against one's will

p. ~의 의지에 반하여 행동하다

against the laws p. 불법인, 법에 저촉하는
against the wall p. 벽에 기대다
act up p. 버릇없이 굴다; 상태가 나쁘다
agape adv. 입을 딱 벌리고

어원	-a : anti + -ga : gone * 그리스 신화에서 영원한 생명을 얻은 영웅 고네(Gone) → '영원한 생명에 반하여'
동의어	act involuntarily, act reluctantly
반의어	act willingly, voluntarily
영영	act involuntarily or against one's desires
예문	He was forced to sign the contract against his will. 그는 자신의 의지에 반하여 계약서에 서명하도록 강요당했다.

160

adjust to N

p. ~에 적응하다, ~에 조정하다

adjust A around B p. A를 B중심으로 맞추다
adjusted a. 조정된, 조절된
maladjusted a. 적응이 안 되는
adjustment n. 조절 적응

어원	-ad : to + -just : right → '올바른 방향으로 맞추니 적응하다'
동의어	adapt to N, acclimatize to N
반의어	resist N, oppose N
영영	adapt or modify oneself to fit N
예문	It took her some time to adjust to her new job. 새로운 직장에 적응하는 데에 시간이 걸렸다.

Chapter 5.

161	exquisite	[ɪkˈskwɪz.ɪt]	a. 정교한, 매우 아름다운
162	synthetic	[sɪnˈθet.ɪk]	a. 합성한, 인조의, 종합적인
163	faint	[feɪnt]	a. 희미한, 어렴풋한; 힘 없는, 겁 많은; n. 기절
164	nourish	[ˈnʌr.ɪʃ]	v. 영양분을 주다, 육성하다
165	keen	[kiːn]	a. 예민한, 신중한, 매우 관심이 많은; 깊은, 강한
166	infection	[ɪnˈfek.ʃən]	n. 감염, 전염병
167	mourn	[mɔːn]	v. 애도하다, 슬퍼하다
168	invert	[ɪnˈvɜːt]	v. 뒤집다, 거꾸로 하다
169	deluxe	[dɪˈlʌks]	a. 고급의, 사양이 높은
170	standpoint	[ˈstænd.pɔɪnt]	n. 입장, 견지, 관점
171	yield	[jiːld]	v. (결과·이익 등을) 내다, 생산하다; 항복하다
172	congress	[ˈkɒŋ.gres]	n. 국회 v. 모이다
173	privilege	[ˈprɪv.əl.ɪdʒ]	n. 특권, 특전
174	terrific	[təˈrɪf.ɪk]	a. 대단한, 지독한; 훌륭한
175	deficit	[ˈdef.ɪ.sɪt]	n. 적자, 부족액, 결손
176	commend	[kəˈmend]	v. 칭찬하다; 맡기다, 위탁하다
177	predator	[ˈpred.ə.tər]	n. 포식자, 약탈자, 육식동물
178	bygone	[ˈbaɪ.gɒn]	a. 지나간, 과거의
179	sow	[səʊ]	v. (씨를) 뿌리다
180	thread	[θred]	v. 실을 꿰다 n. 실
181	compact	[kəmˈpækt]	a. 빽빽한; 간결한 n. 협정, 계약
182	permit	[pəˈmɪt]	v. 허락하다, 인가하다
183	assert	[əsɜ́ːrt]	v. (말을) 끼워 넣어 억지 주장하다
184	phenomenon	[fəˈnɒm.ɪ.nən]	n. 현상, 사건
185	statistics	[stəˈtɪs·tɪks]	n. 통계; 통계학, 통계 자료
186	outlandish	[ˌaʊtˈlæn.dɪʃ]	a. 이국풍의, 색다른, 이상한, 기이한
187	carpenter	[ˈkɑː.pɪn.tər]	n. 목수
188	unearth	[ʌnˈɜːθ]	v. 파내다, 발굴하다; 밝혀 내다
189	resemble	[rɪˈzem.bəl]	v. 닮다, 비슷하다
190	emerge	[ɪˈmɜːdʒ]	v. 나오다, 나타나다; 벗어나다
191	be accustomed to N		p. ~에 익숙해지다
192	strive for		p. ~을 얻으려고 노력하다
193	be to blame for		p. ~ 비난을 받아야 한다, ~의 책임이 있다
194	from above		p. 위에서, 위로부터
195	come of age		p. 발달한 상태가 되다, 성년이 되다
196	be aimed at		p. ~을 목표로 하다
197	all the more		p. 그만큼 더
198	allow for		p. ~을 허용하다, ~을 가능하게 하다
199	connect with		p. ~과 친해지다, ~을 이해하다, ~와 교류하다
200	answer for		p. ~을 책임지다

161	어원	-ex : out + -quir, -quer, -quest, -quisit : seek 구하다, ask 묻다 → '구한 것을 밖으로 내어 자랑할 만큼 정교한'(L)
exquisite [ɪkˈskwɪz.ɪt] a. 정교한, 매우 아름다운 requisite a. 필요한; 필수품 exquisitely adv. 아주 아름답게, 절묘하게 inquisition n. 조사, 탐구 rescind v. 폐지하다, 무효로 하다	유의어	beautiful, elegant, lovely
	반의어	ordinary, plain, unexceptional
	영영	Extremely beautiful or delicate; of exceptional quality or craftsmanship.
	예문	The craftsmanship on the antique vase was exquisite. 고미술이 된 그 고미술은 정교했습니다.

162	어원	-syn : together + thes : put → '함께 모아 두니 합성'
synthetic [sɪnˈθet.ɪk] a. 합성한, 인조의, 종합적인 synergy n. 공동 작용, 시너지 효과 synthesis n. 종합, 통합; 합성 snydrome n. 증후군 aerodrome n. 비행장	유의어	artificial, man-made, fabricated
	반의어	Natural, organic, non-man-made
	영영	Made or produced by chemical synthesis, often referring to man-made materials or substances.
	예문	Synthetic fabrics are often used in the fashion industry. 합성 섬유는 패션 산업에서 자주 사용됩니다.

163	어원	-fein, -feign, -fain, -fake 가짜의; 게으른, 나약한 → '빛이 나약하여 희미한'
faint [feɪnt] a. 희미한, 어렴풋한; 힘 없는, 겁 많은; n. 기절 faintly adv. 희미하게 faintheart n. 겁쟁이 fainthearted a. 소심한, 용기 없는 fad n. (일시적인) 유행	유의어	weak, feeble, faint-hearted
	반의어	strong, bold
	영영	lacking strength or brightness
	예문	She felt faint after standing in the hot sun for hours. 그녀는 오랜 시간 동안 뜨거운 햇빛 아래 서 있어서 어지러움을 느꼈다.

164	어원	-nutri, -nur, -nour : nourish 영양분을 주다, feed 기르다 * nurse 간호사, 유모
nourish [ˈnʌr.ɪʃ] v. 영양분을 주다, 육성하다 nurse n. 간호사, 유모 nursery n. 탁아소, 양성소 nutrition n. 영양분 nurture v. 기르다, 양육하다	유의어	feed, sustain, nurture
	반의어	starve, deprive, neglect
	영영	To provide sustenance and support for growth or development.
	예문	A healthy diet is essential to nourish the body and mind. 건강한 식사는 몸과 마음을 양분하는 데 필수적이다.

165	어원	-keen : sharp (E) → '날카롭게 살피니 빈틈없이', '날카롭고 예민한 의지가 강한'
keen [kiːn] a. 예민한, 신중한, 매우 관심이 많은; 깊은, 강한 keenly adv. 매우, 단단히; 예리하게, 빈틈없이 be keen to p. ~하기를 간절히 바라다 keep A from -ing p. A가 ~하지 못하게 막다 keep up p. 유지하다	유의어	sharp, perceptive, observant
	반의어	indifferent, apathetic, disinterested
	영영	Eager, enthusiastic, or sharp in perception or understanding.
	예문	She was keen to learn new skills. 그녀는 새로운 기술을 배우려는 열망이 있었습니다.

166	어원	-in + -fac, -fec, -fic, -fy, -fair : make → '세균이 몸 안에서 병을 만들어 감염시키다'
infection [ɪnˈfek.ʃən] n. 감염, 전염병 perfect a. 완전한, 완벽한 defect n. 결점, 결함, 결핍 affect v. 영향을 주다 infect v. 감염시키다	유의어	disease, contagion, illness
	반의어	health, wellness
	영영	the invasion and multiplication of harmful microorganisms, such as bacteria or viruses, in the body
	예문	The doctor prescribed antibiotics to treat the bacterial infection. 의사는 세균 감염을 치료하기 위해 항생제를 처방했다.

167

mourn

[mɔːn]

v. 애도하다, 슬퍼하다

amount n. 총액, 총계, 양
surmount v. 극복하다
paramount a. 최고의
mournful a. 애절한

어원	-mo : move + -orn, urn : rise → '떠오른 생명이 멀어지니 애도하다'
유의어	grieve, lament, weep for
반의어	celebrate, rejoice, be happy
영영	to express sorrow or grief over a loss.
예문	The community came together to mourn the loss of a beloved member. 지역사회는 사랑받는 회원의 손실을 애도하기 위해 모였다.

168

invert

[ɪnˈvɜːt]

v. 뒤집다, 거꾸로 하다

diverse a. 다양한, 가지각색의
divorce v. 이혼하다; 분리하다
divert v. (방향을) 전환하다
inverted a. 거꾸로 된

어원	-in + -vert, -vers, -vorc : turn 돌리다(L) → '안에 있던 걸 밖으로 뒤집다'
유의어	reverse, flip, turn upside down
반의어	Retain, keep, maintain
영영	To turn something upside down or reverse its position.
예문	To invert the colors, press the button on the remote control. 색상을 반전하려면 리모컨의 버튼을 누르세요.

169

deluxe

[dɪˈlʌks]

a. 고급의, 사양이 높은

luxury n. 사치(품); 쾌락
deluxe room p. 고급 객실
luster n. 광택
elucidate v. 밝히다, 명료하게 설명하다

어원	-de : intense + -luxury : 초과 → '초과된 가격이니 고급의'
유의어	luxurious, lavish, opulent
반의어	basic, standard, ordinary
영영	Extremely luxurious, often referring to high-quality or extravagant products or services.
예문	The deluxe hotel room had a stunning view of the ocean. 고급 호텔 객실은 바다의 멋진 전망을 가지고 있었다.

170

standpoint

[ˈstænd.pɔɪnt]

n. 입장, 견지, 관점

standby n. 예비물, 대기신호
standee n. 입석
stance n. 입장, 태도, 자세
standstill n. 막힘, 정돈

어원	-sta,-sist, -ste, -st, -stitu, -stin, -sti : stand 서다, 세우다 → '내가 서 있는 입장'
유의어	viewpoint, perspective, position
반의어	Non-standpoint, disregard, neglect
영영	A person's perspective or point of view on a particular matter or situation.
예문	From a historical standpoint, this event had a profound impact on the region. 역사적인 관점에서 이 사건은 그 지역에 깊은 영향을 미쳤습니다.

171

yield

[jiːld]

v. (결과·이익 등을) 내다, 생산하다; 항복하다

yearn v. 열망하다, 갈망하다
yield to p. ~로 대체되다
yawn n. 하품 v. 하품하다
yarn n. 직물을 짜는 실, 뜨개실; 방적사

어원	-yield * 중세 이익집단인 guild(상인협회)에서 yield가 파생. → '생산한 작물을 넘겨준다, 그래서 항복'
유의어	produce, generate, supply
반의어	resist, withhold, keep
영영	To produce or provide a result, product, or outcome; to give in or surrender under pressure.
예문	The farm yielded a plentiful harvest this year. 올해 농장은 풍작을 내놓았습니다.

172

congress

[ˈkɒŋ.ɡres]

n. 국회 v. 모이다

progress n. 전진, 진보 v. 전진하다, 발전하다
aggress v. 공격하다, 시비를 걸다
regress v. 후퇴하다
congress hearing p. 의회 청문회

어원	-con : together + -gress : go * congress : 상원과 하원이 함께 일하는 미국
유의어	legislature, parliament, assembly
반의어	Dissolution, disbandment, breakup
영영	A formal assembly of representatives or delegates, often for legislative purposes.
예문	The congress passed a new law to address environmental concerns. 의회는 환경 문제에 대응하기 위한 새로운 법률을 통과시켰습니다.

173

privilege

[ˈprɪv.əl.ɪdʒ]

n. 특권, 특전

privileged a. 특권을 가진
underprivileged a. 혜택받지 못한
delegate n. 대표자, 대리인
legacy n. 유산, 유물

어원	-privi : individual + -leg, -leag, -loy : law 법률, 위임하다 → '개인에게만 적용되는 법이니 특권'
유의어	advantage, benefit, special right
반의어	Disadvantage, disadvantageousness, lack of advantage
영영	A special advantage, right, or benefit granted to a specific individual or group.
예문	It's a privilege to have access to quality healthcare. 고품질 의료 서비스에 접근할 수 있는 것은 특권입니다.

174

terrific

[təˈrɪf.ɪk]

a. 대단한, 지독한; 훌륭한

terrible a. 무서운
terror n. 공포, 두려움, 폭력 행사
terrify v. 겁나게 하다, 무섭게 하다
deter v. 그만두게 하다, 단념시키다, 저지하다

어원	-terr : frighten 두려워하게 하다 → '두려울 정도로 대단한'
유의어	fantastic, excellent, wonderful
반의어	awful, terrible
영영	extremely good or excellent
예문	The movie received terrific reviews from both critics and audiences. 이 영화는 평론가와 관객 모두로부터 훌륭한 평가를 받았다.

175

deficit

[ˈdef.ɪ.sɪt]

n. 적자, 부족액, 결손

profit n. 수익, 혜택
proficient a. 능숙한
sufficient a. 충분한
deficient a. 부족한, 결핍한

어원	-de : down + -fac, -fec, -fic, -fy, -fair : make → '떨어지게 만드니 적자'
유의어	shortfall, shortage, deficiency
반의어	Surplus, excess, surplus
영영	A deficiency or shortage, often referring to a financial deficit where expenses exceed income.
예문	The country is facing a budget deficit this year. 이 나라는 올해 예산 적자에 직면하고 있습니다.

176

commend

[kəˈmend]

v. 칭찬하다; 맡기다, 위탁하다

command v. 명령하다
commendable a. 칭찬할 만한, 훌륭한
countermand v. 취소하다, 철회하다
in high demand p. 수요가 많은

어원	-com : together + -mend : 규칙 → '규칙을 잘 지키는 곳에 다 맡기고 칭찬하다'
유의어	praise, applaud, compliment
반의어	criticize, condemn, denounce
영영	Praise or express approval for someone's actions or qualities.
예문	He received a commendation for his outstanding work. 그는 훌륭한 업적에 대한 칭찬을 받았습니다.

177

predator

[ˈpred.ə.tər]

n. 포식자, 약탈자, 육식동물

prey n. 먹이
predatory a. 약탈하는, 욕심 많은, 육식의
predatism n. 동물의 포식(습성)
depredate v. 강탈하다

어원	-predat : prey → '먹이를 쫓는 거이니 포식자'
유의어	carnivore, hunter, killer
반의어	Prey, victim, target
영영	An animal or organism that hunts and preys on other organisms for food.
예문	The lion is a top predator in the African savannah. 사자는 아프리카 사바나의 최상위 포식자입니다.

178

bygone

[ˈbaɪ.ɡɒn]

a. 지나간, 과거의

bygones n. 지나간 일
bypass v. 우회하다; 무시하다
bystander n. 방관자
byproduct n. 부산물

어원	-by 옆에, 나란히(E) + -gone → '옆으로 지나가버린 과거'
유의어	past, former, previous
반의어	Current, present, modern
영영	Belonging to a past era or time; no longer in existence or use.
예문	The bygone era is remembered through historical records. 과거의 시대는 역사적 기록을 통해 기억됩니다.

179

sow

[soʊ]

v. (씨를) 뿌리다

season n. 계절 v. 양념하다, 양념을 넣다
seasoning n. 양념, 조미료
seasoned a. 노련한, 경험이 많은
in the space of p. ~의 기간 내내

어원	-s : seed + -ow : plow → '쟁기로 갈고 씨를 뿌리다'
유의어	plant, seed, scatter
반의어	reap, harvest, gather
영영	To plant seeds in the ground for the purpose of growing crops.
예문	Farmers sow seeds in the spring to grow crops. 농부들은 봄에 작물을 키우기 위해 씨앗을 뿌린다.

180

thread

[θred]

v. 실을 꿰다 n. 실

twist v. 꼬(이)다, 비틀다 n. 꼬임, 엉킴
threat n. 위협, 협박
thrust v. 세게 밀다; 찌르다
thrill v. 흥분시키다; 흥분, 전율

어원	-thread : twisted → '꼬여질 때 특히 가는 끈이 실'
유의어	filament, string, strand
반의어	tangle, knot
영영	a long, thin strand of material, such as cotton or nylon; to pass a thread through a needle for sewing
예문	She carefully threaded the needle to start sewing. 그녀는 손끝에 실을 실어 바늘에 끼웠다.

181

compact

[kəmˈpækt]

a. 빽빽한; 간결한 n. 협정, 계약

pact n. 계약, 협정
impact n. 영향; 충돌
pave v. 포장하다
pad n. 패드; 묶음

어원	-com : together + -pact : fasten → '모든 조항을 간결하게 묶어 놓은 계약'
유의어	dense, compressed, closely packed
반의어	Large, spacious, roomy
영영	Closely packed together; small and efficiently organized.
예문	The compact car is easy to park in tight spaces. 소형 자동차는 협소한 공간에 주차하기 쉽습니다.

182

permit

[pəˈmɪt]

v. 허락하다, 인가하다

permission n. 허가, 면허
have permission to do p. ~할 허가를 받다
permissible a. 허용할 수 있는
permise n. 전제

어원	-per 완전히 통해서 (L) + -miss, -mitt, -mise, -mess : send → '완전히 보내준다고 허락'
유의어	allow, authorize, consent to
반의어	forbid, prohibit, ban
영영	to allow or grant permission for something.
예문	You need a permit to build a new structure in this area. 이 지역에서 새 건물을 지으려면 허가가 필요합니다.

183

assert

[əsɔ́ːrt]

v. (말을) 끼워 넣어 억지 주장하다

desert n. 사막; 버리다
assertive a. 자기 주장이 강한, 단정적인
assertion n. 단정, 확고한 주장
exert v. 행사하다, 애쓰다, 노력하다

어원	-as : to + -ser, -sert 밀어 넣어 합치다 (L)→ '~방향으로 강하게 끼워 넣는 의견이니 억지 주장' * join, junc(t) '서로 다른 것이 만나 합침' VS ser(t) '밀어 넣어 합침'
유의어	declare, claim, state
반의어	deny, disclaim, negate
영영	To state or declare something confidently and forcefully; to insist or affirm.
예문	He had to assert his authority as the team leader. 그는 팀 리더로서 권한을 주장해야 했습니다.

184

phenomenon

[fəˈnɒmˌɪˌnən]

n. 현상, 사건

phenomena n. (복수) 현상, 사건
phenomenal a. 현상의, 놀랄 만한
phantom n. 유령, 허깨비, 환상
pant v. 숨을 헐떡이다

어원	-pha,-phan, -phas, -pan, -fan : show 보이다, 보여주다(G) → '밖으로 보이는 현상이나 사건'
유의어	occurrence, event, happening
반의어	Normality, regular occurrence, common event
영영	An observable event or occurrence, often with scientific or cultural significance.
예문	The Northern Lights are a natural phenomenon that is awe-inspiring. 북극광은 경외감을 일으키는 자연 현상입니다.

185

statistics

[stəˈtɪs·tɪks]

n. 통계; 통계학, 통계 자료

static a. 정적인
statistic n. 통계치, 통계량
statistical a. 통계상의, 통계학의
statute n. 법령, 법규

어원	-stat : 국가 → '국가가 인구 조사를 하니 통계'
유의어	data, numbers, figures
반의어	Anecdotes, individual cases, singular data
영영	The collection, analysis, interpretation, and presentation of numerical data.
예문	The statistics show a decline in unemployment rates. 통계는 실업률의 감소를 보여줍니다.

186

outlandish

[ˌaʊtˈlæn.dɪʃ]

a. 이국풍의, 색다른, 이상한, 기이한

outlet n. 배출구, 표출; 콘센트; 상점, 아울렛
outdated a. 시대에 뒤진, 진부한
outdistance v. ~을 훨씬 앞서다
outlast v. ~보다 더 오래 살다

어원	-out + -land → '우리 땅을 벗어나니 이국풍이라 색다른'
유의어	strange, bizarre, peculiar
반의어	familiar, ordinary
영영	strange or bizarre in appearance or behavior
예문	His outlandish clothing choices always attracted attention. 그의 이상한 의상 선택은 항상 주목을 끌었다.

187

carpenter

[ˈkɑː.pɪn.tər]

n. 목수

carriage n. 마차
cargo n. 화물
caretaker n. 관리인
excursion n. 짧은 여행, 소풍

어원	-carpent : carriage 마차 → '마차를 만들던 목수'
유의어	woodworker, joiner, craftsman
반의어	Non-carpenter, non-builder, non-artisan
영영	A skilled craftsman who works with wood to build or repair structures and furniture.
예문	The carpenter built custom furniture for the client. 목수는 고객을 위해 맞춤 가구를 제작했습니다.

188

unearth

[ʌnˈɜːθ]

v. 파내다, 발굴하다; 밝혀 내다

unbiased a. 편견이 없는, 공정한
unceasing a. 끊임 없는, 부단한
unbind v. 해방하다, 석방하다
unconvincing a. 설득력 없는

어원	-un : under + -earth 땅 → '땅 밑을 파내다'
유의어	discover, dig up, excavate
반의어	bury, conceal
영영	dig up or uncover something buried or hidden
예문	Archaeologists unearthed ancient artifacts at the dig site. 고고학자들은 발굴 현장에서 고대 유물을 발굴했다.

189

resemble

[rɪˈzem.bəl]

v. 닮다, 비슷하다

assemble v. 모으다 n. 조립
ensemble n. 합창, 합주; 앙상블
dissemble v. 숨기다, 가장하다
resent v. ~에 분개하다, 원망하다

어원	-re : back + -sem 비슷한 → '대를 거슬러도 비슷한'(L) * resemble '시간을 거슬러 닮은 것' VS similar '시간에 관련 없이 닮은 것'
유의어	look like, mirror, simulate
반의어	differ, contrast, deviate
영영	To have a similar appearance or likeness to something or someone else.
예문	The twins closely resemble each other in appearance. 쌍둥이들은 외모에서 서로 무척 닮았다.

190

emerge

[ɪˈmɜːdʒ]

v. 나오다, 나타나다; 벗어나다

emergency n. 비상사태, 위급
emerging a. 떠오르는
emergence n. 출현
immerse v. 잠기게 하다, 담그다; 몰두시키다

어원	-e, -ex : out + -merg, -mers : dip → '물 속에 잠겨 있다가 밖으로 나오는'
유의어	appear, surface, come forth
반의어	disappear, vanish
영영	come out or become visible after being hidden
예문	The talented young musician started to emerge as a rising star in the music industry. 재능 있는 젊은 음악가가 음악 산업에서 떠오르기 시작했다.

191

be accustomed to N

p. ~에 익숙해지다

customize v. 주문 제작하다
costume n. 의상, 복장
accustom v. 익히다, 익숙케 하다
accustomedly adv. 평소대로, 습관대로

어원	-ac : to + -custom 습관 → '습관처럼 한 방향으로 익히다'
유의어	be familiar with N, be used to N
반의어	be unaccustomed to N, unfamiliar with N
영영	be familiar with N due to frequent exposure
예문	She is accustomed to waking up early. 그녀는 일찍 일어나는 것에 익숙하다.

192

strive for

p. ~을 얻으려고 노력하다

strive to do p. ~하려고 노력하다, 애쓰다
strife n. 분쟁, 불화, 반목
struggle v. 고군분투하다 n. 투쟁, 싸움
stride v. 성큼성큼 걷다, 활보하다

어원	-str : strength 싸우다 + -riv : rival → '라이벌과 싸우며 투쟁하고 노력하다'
유의어	aim for, endeavor for
반의어	settle for, give up on
영영	make great efforts to achieve or attain
예문	He strives for excellence in everything he does. 그는 자신이 하는 모든 일에 뛰어남을 추구한다.

193

be to blame for

p. ~ 비난을 받아야 한다, ~의 책임이 있다

blame A on B p. A를 B의 책임으로 보다
blameworthy a. 탓할 만한, 책임이 있는
blaze n. 화재 v. 불길이 활활 타다, 타오르다
blend in with p. ~와 잘 섞이다

어원	-black 불에 탄 + -name → '검게 물들은 이름이라 비난'
유의어	be responsible for, be at fault for
반의어	be blameless for, exonerate from
영영	be responsible or accountable for
예문	He is to blame for the mistake. 그는 그 실수의 책임이 있다.

194

from above

p. 위에서, 위로부터

from a distance p. 멀리서
from time to time p. 가끔[이따금]
from square one p. 처음부터
abode n. 거주지, 집

어원	-ab : up + -over → 'over보다 위에'
유의어	from a higher position, from the top
반의어	from below, from beneath
영영	from a higher position or authority
예문	The decision came from above, so we have to follow it. 결정은 상위에서 내려왔으므로 우리는 그것을 따라야 한다.

195

come of age

p. 발달한 상태가 되다, 성년이 되다

in this day and age p. 요즘 같은 시대에
come off p. 성공하다; 떨어지다
come about p. 일어나다, 생기다
adage n. 격언

어원	-come 되다 + -age → '적절한 나이에 이르니 성년이 되다'
유의어	reach adulthood, mature
반의어	remain immature, stay youthful
영영	reach the age at which one is legally recognized as an adult
예문	When she turned 18, she came of age. 그녀가 18세가 되었을 때 성인이 되었다.

196

be aimed at

p. ~을 목표로 하다

aim to do p. ~하는 것을 목표로 하다
aimlessly adv. 목적 없이
aisle n. 통로, 복도
akin a. 친척의; 유사한

어원	-aim 조준 → '조준하려는 목표'
유의어	be targeted at, be directed towards
반의어	be deterred from, be discouraged from
영영	be intended or directed towards a particular goal or target
예문	This campaign is aimed at raising awareness about climate change. 이 캠페인은 기후 변화에 대한 인식을 높이는 데 목표를 두고 있다.

197

all the more

p. 그만큼 더

all-around p. 다재다능한
all but p. 사실상, 거의
all the same p. 그럼에도 불구하고
all too p. 완전 너무, 너무나, 정말

어원	-all 전부 + -more 더 → '전부만큼 더'
유의어	even more, especially
반의어	all the less, even less
영영	to an even greater extent
예문	His failure made him all the more determined to succeed. 그의 실패는 그를 더욱 성공하려는 결의를 갖게 했다.

198

allow for

p. ~을 허용하다, ~을 가능하게 하다

allocate v. 할당하다, 배분하다
allowance n. 용돈, 비용; 허용량
amenity n. 편의시설; 예의
arouse v. 자극하다, 깨우다

어원	-al : to + -low : laud 칭찬하다 → '~방향으로 칭찬하며 장려하니 허락'
유의어	accommodate, make room for
반의어	prohibit, disallow
영영	make provisions or considerations for
예문	The schedule allows for breaks every two hours. 일정은 두 시간마다 휴식을 허용한다.

199

connect with

p. ~과 친해지다, ~을 이해하다, ~와 교류하다

connected a. 관련이 있는
connection n. 연결
disconnect p. ~와 연락을 끊다
annexure n. 합병 v. 합병하다

어원	-con : together + -nect : bind → '같이 하나로 묶으니 연결' * Vt. connect 연결하다
유의어	link with, associate with
반의어	disconnect from, detach from
영영	establish a relationship or link with
예문	I find it easy to connect with people who share my interests. 나는 나와 같은 관심사를 가진 사람들과 연결하기 쉽다.

200

answer for

p. ~을 책임지다

answer to p. ~에 대한 대답
answer up p. 재빠르게 대답하다
answer with p. ~으로 반응하다
answer back p. 말대꾸하다, 자기 변명하다

어원	for(누군가를 위해) answer(대답하니) 책임지다
유의어	be accountable for, be responsible for
반의어	question, challenge
영영	be responsible or accountable for one's actions or decisions
예문	He had to answer for his actions. 그는 그의 행동에 대해 책임져야 했다.

Chapter 6.

201	compassion	[kəmˈpæʃ.ən]	n. 연민, 동정
202	decade	[ˈdek.eɪd]	n. 10년
203	persevere	[pɜ̀ːrsəvíər]	v. 고집하다, 노력하다, 견디다
204	stitch	[stɪtʃ]	v. 바느질하다; 바늘땀, 코, 바느질
205	cradle	[ˈkreɪ.dəl]	n. 요람, 아기 침대; 발상지
206	symmetry	[ˈsɪm.ə.tri]	n. 대칭, 균형
207	spontaneous	[spɒnˈteɪ.ni.əs]	a. 자발적인, 자연스러운
208	inquire	[ɪnˈkwaɪər]	v. 묻다, 조사하다
209	impair	[ɪmˈpeər]	v. 손상시키다
210	deflect	[dɪˈflekt]	v. 빗나가다, 빗나가게 하다
211	coverage	[ˈkʌv.ər.ɪdʒ]	n. 보도, 방송, 보급
212	mandatory	[ˈmæn.də.tər.i]	a. 규칙으로 명령하는, 의무적인, 필수의
213	prolong	[prəˈlɒŋ]	v. 연장하다
214	exile	[ˈek.saɪl]	n. 추방, 유배
215	pioneer	[ˌpaɪəˈnɪər]	n. 선구자, 선도자
216	sufficient	[səˈfɪʃ.ənt]	a. 충분한
217	flourish	[ˈflʌr.ɪʃ]	v. 번창하다, 잘 자라다
218	hypothesis	[haɪˈpɒθ.ə.sɪs]	n. 가설
219	epidemic	[ˌep.ɪˈdem.ɪk]	a. 널리 퍼져 있는 n. 유행(병)
220	fatigue	[fəˈtiːg]	n. 피로(* 밭일로 피곤한)
221	innate	[ɪˈneɪt]	a. 타고난, 선천적인
222	exhaust	[ɪgˈzɔːst]	v. 다 써버리다, 기진맥진하게 만들다 n. 배출
223	attain	[əˈteɪn]	v. 얻다; 달성하다, 도달하다
224	manipulate	[məˈnɪp.jə.leɪt]	v. 조종하다, 조작하다; 잘 다루다
225	fling	[flɪŋ]	v. 내던지다, 퍼붓다
226	stun	[stʌn]	v. 기절시키다, 망연자실하게 만들다
227	ethics	[ˈeθ·ɪks]	n. 윤리학
228	vanish	[ˈvæn.ɪʃ]	v. 사라지다, 소멸하다
229	straightforward	[ˌstreɪtˈfɔː.wəd]	a. 간단한, 솔직한
230	speculate	[ˈspek.jə.leɪt]	v. 추측하다
231	be frightened of		p. ~을 무서워하다
232	be conscious of		p. ~을 의식하다, ~을 알고 있다
233	confuse A with B		p. A를 B와 혼동하다
234	in the long run		p. 결국, 결국에는; 긴 악목으로
235	near at hand		p. 가까이에
236	in harmony with		p. ~와 조화를 이루다, 일치하다
237	hand over		p. 인도하다, 넘기다
238	get into shape		p. 몸매를 가꾸다
239	blame A on B		p. A를 B의 책임[때문]으로 보다
240	at the least		p. 적어도

201

compassion

[kəmˈpæʃ.ən]

n. 연민, 동정

passion n. 열정
pity n. 연민, 동정, 유감
passionate a. 열정적인
passive a. 수동의, 수동적인

어원	-com : together + -path, -pati, -pass : suffer → '고통을 함께 겪는'
유의어	empathy, sympathy, kindness
반의어	indifference, cruelty
영영	a feeling of deep sympathy and sorrow for another who is stricken by misfortune, accompanied by a strong desire to alleviate the suffering
예문	Her compassion for animals led her to become a vegetarian. 그녀의 동물에 대한 동정심은 그녀를 채식주의자로 만들었다.

202

decade

[ˈdek.eɪd]

n. 10년

decimal a. 십진법의
Decalogue n. 십계명
december n. 12월
dean n. 십부장, 학과장

어원	-deca, -dece 10(G)
유의어	ten years, decennium, decagon
반의어	century, millennium
영영	a period of ten years
예문	They've been friends for over a decade. 그들은 10년 이상의 친구이다.

203

persevere

[pɜːrsəˈvɪər]

v. 고집하다, 노력하다, 견디다

perseverance n. 인내
perseverant a. 불굴의
persecution n. 박해, 박대
asseverate v. 단언하다

어원	-per 완전히 통해서 (L) + -sever : strict → '원칙을 엄격하게 지키니 고집'
유의어	persist, endure, continue
반의어	Quit, give up, surrender
영영	To persist or continue in a course of action despite challenges or difficulties.
예문	Despite the challenges, he continued to persevere in his goals. 어려움에도 불구하고, 그는 자신의 목표를 계속해서 끈질기게 추구했습니다.

204

stitch

[stɪtʃ]

v. 바느질하다; 바늘땀, 코, 바느질

sewer n. 하수관, 수채통
sewage n. 하수, 오물, 오수
sew v. 바느질하다, 깁다
shiver n. 떨림, 전율

어원	-stinct, -sting : prick 찌르다 → '옷감에 찔러 바느질하다'
유의어	sew, needlework, suture
반의어	unstitch, rip
영영	a loop of thread used to join fabric
예문	She needed a few stitches to close the wound. 상처를 닫기 위해 몇 바퀴를 봤어요.

205

cradle

[ˈkreɪ.dəl]

n. 요람, 아기 침대; 발상지

in the cradle p. 초기에
rock a cradle p. 요람을 흔든다
cradling n. 육성
cradle of civilization p. 문명의 요람

어원	-cradle : cot 작은 아기 침대 * 클 애들이 쓰는 침대
유의어	infancy, beginnings, starting point
반의어	Tomb, grave, resting place
영영	A small bed for an infant; the place of origin or beginning of something.
예문	The baby slept soundly in the cradle. 아기는 요람에서 편안하게 잤습니다.

206

symmetry

[ˈsɪm.ə.tri]

n. 대칭, 균형

symmetric a. 균형이 잡힌, 대칭적인
asymmetric a. 불균형의, 비대칭의
symbolic a. 상징적인, 상징하는
synchronize v. 동시에 일어나다

어원	-sym : same + -metr : measure → '같은 수치를 잰 거니 좌우가 대칭'
유의어	balance, harmony, proportion
반의어	Asymmetry, imbalance, irregularity
영영	A balanced and harmonious arrangement of parts or elements on either side of a central axis.
예문	The butterfly's wings had perfect symmetry. 나비의 날개는 완벽한 대칭을 갖고 있었습니다.

207

spontaneous

[spɒnˈteɪ.ni.əs]

a. 자발적인, 자연스러운

respond v. 응답하다
correspond to p. ~과 일치하다, ~에 상응하다
despond vi. 낙심하다, 실망하다
spontaneously adv. 자발적으로, 자연스럽게

어원	-spond : promise + -tane : take → '약속했던 것처럼 자연스럽게 취하는'
유의어	impulsive, unplanned, natural
반의어	planned, deliberate, intentional
영영	Occurring naturally or without prior planning; impulsive.
예문	Their spontaneous decision to go on a road trip turned out to be a great adventure. 길을 나서기로 한 그들의 자발적인 결정은 큰 모험으로 이어졌다.

208

inquire

[ɪnˈkwaɪər]

v. 묻다, 조사하다

inquiry n. 문의, 질문
inquisitive a. 꼬치꼬치 캐묻는
inquirer n. 조사자, 탐구자
inquiring a. 묻는, 조회하는

어원	-in + -quir, -quer, -quest, -quisit : seek 구하다, ask 묻다 → '안에 무엇이 있는지 묻다'(L)
유의어	ask, query, question
반의어	Ignore, neglect, disregard
영영	To seek information or investigate by asking questions or making inquiries.
예문	Customers can inquire about product availability at the store. 고객은 상점에서 제품의 입고 여부를 문의할 수 있습니다

209

impair

[ɪmˈpeər]

v. 손상시키다

repair v. 수리하다; 회복하다
despair n. 절망 v. 절망하다
impaired a. 손상된, 약화된
impairment n. 손상

어원	-im : not + -re : again + -peer, -par : equal 동등한 (L) → '다시 원래와 같게 만들지 못하니 손상'
유의어	damage, weaken, diminish
반의어	enhance, improve, strengthen
영영	to weaken or damage the quality or function of something.
예문	Lack of sleep can impair cognitive functions and decision-making. 수면 부족은 인지 능력과 결정력을 손상시킬 수 있다.

210

deflect

[dɪˈflekt]

v. 빗나가다, 빗나가게 하다

flex v. 구부리다, 구부러지다
reflect v. 반사하다, 반영하다; 숙고하다
deflected a. 아래로 굽은
deflection n. 편향, 비뚤어짐; 굴절

어원	-de : away , + -flect : bend → '다른 방향으로 휘게 하다'
유의어	divert, avert, turn aside
반의어	attract, draw, allure
영영	To cause something to change direction, often by turning it aside.
예문	The shield was designed to deflect arrows and protect the knight. 방패는 화살을 튕겨내고 기사를 보호하기 위해 디자인되었다.

211

coverage

[ˈkʌv.ər.ɪdʒ]

n. 보도, 방송, 보급

cover v. 덮다, 포함하다; 지불하다
discover v. 발견하다
recover from p. ~에서 회복하다
covert a. 비밀의, 은밀한

어원	-cover 덮다 → '모든 정보를 다루는 보도로 방송'
유의어	reporting, news, media coverage
반의어	Omission, exclusion, lack of inclusion
영영	The extent or scope of protection, insurance, or news reporting.
예문	The news coverage of the event was extensive. 그 이벤트에 대한 뉴스 보도는 광범위했습니다.

212

mandatory

[ˈmæn.də.tər.i]

a. 규칙으로 명령하는, 의무적인, 필수의

mandate n. 명령 v. 위임하다
chain of command p. 지휘 계통
command v. 명령하다
commander n. 지휘관, 사령관; 중령

어원	-man, -mand, mend 명령, 법(L) / 손을 주다 → '명령하니 의무적인'
유의어	compulsory, required, obligatory
반의어	Optional, voluntary, discretionary
영영	Required by law, rule, or authority; obligatory.
예문	Wearing a seatbelt is mandatory for all passengers in the car. 자동차 안의 모든 승객은 시트벨트를 착용하는 것이 의무입니다.

213

prolong

[prəˈlɒŋ]

v. 연장하다

prolonged a. 오랫동안의, 장기간의
prolongment n. 연장, 연기
prolongedly adv. 질질 끌면서, 장기간에 걸쳐
proliferate v. 증식하다

어원	-pro : forth + -long : long → '앞쪽으로 길게 늘리다'
유의어	extend, lengthen, protract
반의어	shorten, abbreviate
영영	to extend the duration or length of something; to lengthen or protract
예문	Regular exercise can prolong your life and improve your health. 규칙적인 운동은 당신의 수명을 연장시키고 건강을 개선시킬 수 있다.

214

exile

[ˈek.saɪl]

n. 추방, 유배

exile from p. ~로부터의 망명
exorbitant a. 터무니 없는, 과도한
expand v. 확장하다, 확대하다
suborbital a. 궤도에 오르지 않은

어원	-ex : out + -il, -sed : sit → '밖으로 보내 눌러앉게 하는'
유의어	banish, deport, expel
반의어	inclusion, acceptance
영영	the state of being forcibly removed from one's home country or place of residence; to banish or expel someone from their homeland
예문	The political dissident was forced into exile for speaking out against the government. 정부에 반대하여 말한 정치적 반대자는 추방당하게 되었다.

215

pioneer

[ˌpaɪəˈnɪər]

n. 선구자, 선도자

frontier n. 국경, 변경
pioneering a. 선구적인
on the surface p. 외견상으로는
interface n. 사이의 면, 경계면 v. 조정하다

어원	-pioneer : frontier → '앞서나가는 선구자'
유의어	trailblazer, innovator, groundbreaker
반의어	Follower, imitator, copycat
영영	A person who is among the first to explore or settle in a new area or undertake a new endeavor.
예문	She was a pioneer in the field of scientific research. 그녀는 과학 연구 분야의 선구자였습니다.

216

sufficient

[səˈfɪʃ.ənt]

a. 충분한

proficient a. 숙달된, 능숙한
insufficiently adv. 불충분하게
self-sufficient p. 자급자족
sufficiently adv. 충분히

어원	-suf, -sur : over + -fac, -fec, -fic, -fy, -fair : make → '흘러넘치게 만들 정도로 충분한'
유의어	enough, adequate, ample
반의어	Insufficient, inadequate, lacking
영영	Adequate or enough to meet a particular need or requirement.
예문	The food provided was sufficient to feed all the guests at the event. 제공된 음식은 행사의 모든 손님들을 먹여 채우기에 충분했습니다.

217

flourish

[ˈflʌr.ɪʃ]

v. 번창하다, 잘 자라다

flower n. 꽃
flour n. (고운) 가루, 밀가루
flora n. 식물군
florist n. 꽃집 주인, 꽃집 직원; 화초 재배자

어원	-flour, -flori : flower → '꽃이 활짝 핀 것처럼 번성하는'
유의어	thrive, prosper, blossom
반의어	decline, wither, wilt
영영	to grow or develop in a healthy or vigorous way.
예문	The local economy began to flourish after the opening of the new factory. 새로운 공장이 개장한 후 지역 경제가 번창하기 시작했다.

218

hypothesis

[haɪˈpɒθ.ə.sɪs]

n. 가설

parody n. 패러디
parasite n. 기생충
hypothetical a. 가상의
hypocrisy n. 우유부단; 위선

어원	-hyp, -hypo 더 아래 + -the, -thes, -thet : place 놓다 → 더 아래 놓여 있는 가설
유의어	theory, supposition, conjecture
반의어	Fact, truth, reality
영영	A proposed explanation or educated guess that can be tested through research and experimentation.
예문	The scientist proposed a hypothesis to explain the phenomenon. 과학자는 현상을 설명하기 위한 가설을 제안했습니다.

219

epidemic

[ˌep.ɪˈdem.ɪk]

a. 널리 퍼져 있는 n. 유행(병)

democracy n. 민주주의
pandemic a. 보편적인; n. 유행병
aristocracy n. 귀족 정치
epidemiological a. 역학의

어원	-epi : on, upon 주위, 위 + -dem 많은 사람들 → '주위 많은 사람들에게도 퍼져 있는'
유의어	outbreak, pandemic, widespread disease
반의어	containment, prevention, control
영영	A widespread occurrence of a disease or condition in a specific population or area.
예문	The influenza epidemic spread rapidly across the country. 인플루엔자 유행병이 빠르게 전국으로 퍼졌습니다.

220

fatigue

[fəˈtiːɡ]

n. 피로(* 발일로 피곤한)

fate n. 운명, 천명
fatigued a. 피로해진, 지친
indefatigable a. 지칠 줄 모르는

어원	-fatis : fate 운명 + -ue 불어에서 차용 → '주어진 운명을 다 행한 후 피곤한'
유의어	exhaustion, weariness, tiredness
반의어	energy, vigor
영영	extreme tiredness or physical and mental exhaustion
예문	After a long day of hiking, fatigue set in, and they set up camp. 긴 하이킹 후에 피로가 느껴지며, 그들은 캠프를 설치했다.

221

innate

[ɪˈneɪt]

a. 타고난, 선천적인

native a. 출생지의, 원주민의; 타고난
innately adv. 선천적으로
natural a. 자연스러운, 본연의
denature v. 변성시키다, 성질을 바꾸다

어원	-in : in + -na, -nat, -gna : born → '태어난 그대로의 선천적인'
contour	inborn, inherent, natural
반의어	Acquired, learned, acquired through experience
영영	Existing naturally or inherently; inborn or present from birth.
예문	Some people believe that kindness is an innate human quality. 어떤 사람들은 친절함이 선천적인 인간의 품질이라고 믿습니다.

222

exhaust

[ɪɡˈzɔːst]

v. 다 써버리다, 기진맥진하게 만들다 n. 배출

haul v. 끌다, 운반하다
exhausted a. 기진맥진한, 진이 빠진
exhausting a. 소모적인, 심신을 지치게 하는
exhaustion n. 기진맥진, 고갈, 소진

어원	-ex : out + -haust : 물을 긷다[L] → '물을 길어오느라 피곤한'
유의어	deplete, drain, wear out
반의어	refresh, rejuvenate, energize
영영	to use up completely; to drain of energy or resources.
예문	After the long hike, they were completely exhausted. 긴 하이킹 후에, 그들은 완전히 지친 상태였다.

223

attain

[əˈteɪn]

v. 얻다; 달성하다, 도달하다

obtain v. 얻다, 획득하다
contain v. 포함하다, 담고 있다
retain v. 계속 유지하다; 보유하다
sustain v. 유지하다, 지지하다

어원	-at : to + -ten, -tent, -tin, -tain : hold, grasp, have → '그곳으로 가서 얻다 그래서 목표를 달성'
유의어	achieve, reach, accomplish
반의어	Lose, fail, surrender
영영	To achieve or reach a particular goal or objective; to gain or acquire something.
예문	With hard work and dedication, she was able to attain her goals. 노력과 헌신으로 그녀는 목표를 달성할 수 있었습니다.

224

manipulate

[məˈnɪp.jə.leɪt]

v. 조종하다, 조작하다; 잘 다루다

manage v. 관리하다, 경영하다
maintain v. 유지하다, 가지다; 주장하다
manipulation n. 조작
maneuver n. 작전, 조작 연습

어원	-mani : hand + -pul : fill → '손에 가득 쥐고 조종하다'
antipha	control, influence, maneuver
반의어	leave untouched, keep intact, preserve
영영	Control or influence something or someone in a skillful or dishonest way.
예문	Some people try to manipulate others for their own gain. 어떤 사람들은 자신의 이익을 위해 다른 사람들을 조작하려고 합니다.

225

fling

[flɪŋ]

v. 내던지다, 퍼붓다

flight n. 비행
flip v. 홱 뒤집다 n. 공중제비
flit v. 훨훨 날다
flutter v. 펄럭이다

어원	-fl, -fli, -fly 날다 → '날리듯이 내던지다'
유의어	toss, throw, hurl
반의어	catch, hold
영영	throw or hurl something forcefully
예문	He had a fling with his coworker, but it didn't last long. 그는 동료 직원과 짧은 열애를 가졌지만 오래 가지 않았다.

226

stun

[stʌn]

v. 기절시키다, 망연자실하게 만들다

stunning a. 깜짝 놀랄, 굉장히 아름다운
stun gun p. 전기총
stunt n. 스턴트, 곡예
astounded a. 아연실색한

어원	-ton, -toun, -stun : thunder 놀라게 하다 → '놀라게 하여 기절시키다'
유의어	amaze, astonish, shock
반의어	bore, disinterest, underwhelm
영영	To shock or astonish someone to the point of temporary loss of consciousness or mental clarity; to amaze or overwhelm.
예문	The surprising news stunned everyone in the room. 놀라운 소식으로 방 안의 모든 사람들이 깜짝 놀라게 되었습니다.

227

ethics

[ˈeθ·ɪks]

n. 윤리학

ethnicity n. 민족(집단)
ethnocentric a. 자기 민족 중심적인
ethic n. 도덕, 윤리
ethical a. 도덕적인, 윤리적인

어원	-eth 도덕, 윤리 + -ics 학문 → '도덕을 연구하는 학문이니 윤리학'
유의어	moral principles, morals, values
반의어	Unethical behavior, immorality, wrongdoing
영영	The moral principles or values that guide behavior and decision-making.
예문	The company's code of ethics promotes honesty and integrity. 회사의 윤리규범은 정직과 덕실을 촉진합니다.

228

vanish

[ˈvæn.ɪʃ]

v. 사라지다, 소멸하다

vacation n. 방학
avoid v. 피하다, 회피하다
devoid a. ~이 빠진, 전혀 없는
vacant a. 빈 자리의

어원	-van, -vain, -void, -vac : empty 빈 → '비게 만드니 사라지다'
유의어	disappear, fade, evaporate
반의어	Appear, materialize, emerge
영영	To disappear suddenly or completely from sight or existence.
예문	The magician made the rabbit vanish into thin air. 마술사가 토끼를 공중으로 사라지게 만들었습니다.

229

straightforward

[ˌstreɪtˈfɔːwəd]

a. 간단한, 솔직한

straight adv. 똑바로, 곧장, 곧바로
straightforwardly adv. 있는 그대로, 솔직하게
strighten v. 자세를 바로 하다
strain v. 긴장시키다 n. 힘을 주어 팽팽함

어원	-straight 곧바로 + -forward 앞으로 → '곧바로 필요한 얘기만 간단히 말하니 솔직한'
유의어	direct, simple, uncomplicated
반의어	complicated, complex
영영	clear, direct, and honest in communication or action; simple and easy to understand
예문	His straightforward answer left no room for confusion. 그의 직접적인 대답은 혼란의 여지가 없게 했다.

230

speculate

[ˈspek.jə.leɪt]

v. 추측하다

spectator n. 관중, 구경꾼
spectrum n. 범위, 영역, 빛의 띠
specimen n. 견본, 표본
speculation n. 추측

어원	-spec 보다 → '보이는 사실로 추측'
유의어	hypothesize, conjecture, guess
반의어	Confirm, ascertain, verify
영영	To form conjectures or theories about something without sufficient evidence; to make educated guesses.
예문	Investors often speculate on the future performance of stocks. 투자자들은 종종 주식의 미래 성과에 대해 추측합니다.

231

be frightened of

p. ~을 무서워하다

frighten v. 겁먹게 만들다, 깜짝 놀라게 하다
in awe of p. ~을 두려워하다
fright n. 공포, 경악
frigid a. 몹시 추운, 냉담한

어원	-fre, -fri : freeze 얼음으로 변하다(E) → '얼음처럼 몸이 굳도록 겁먹게 만들다'
be skilled	be afraid of, be scared of
반의어	be unafraid of, fearlessly face
영영	be afraid or scared of
예문	The child is frightened of the dark. 그 아이는 어둠을 무서워한다.

232

be conscious of

p. ~을 의식하다, ~을 알고 있다

consciously adv. 의식적으로
consciousness n. 의식, 자각
conscience n. 양심, 도덕심
unconscious a. 의식을 잃은, 의식이 없는

어원	-con : completely + -sci : know 알다 → '완전히 안다는 건 의식이 있는 것'
유의어	be aware of, be mindful of
반의어	be unaware of, oblivious to
영영	be aware or mindful of
예문	She was conscious of the fact that she was being watched. 그녀는 자신이 지켜보고 있다는 사실을 의식했다.

233

confuse A with B

p. A를 B와 혼동하다

confused with p. ~과 혼동되는
confusing a. 혼란스러운
confusion n. 혼란
refuse v. 거절하다, 사절하다

어원	-con : together + -fus : pour → '함께 부어 뒤섞다'
유의어	mix up A and B, mistake A for B
반의어	differentiate A from B, distinguish A and B
영영	mistake A for B; mix up A and B
예문	Don't confuse salt with sugar. 소금을 설탕과 혼동하지 마세요.

234

in the long run

p. 결국, 결국에는; 긴 안목으로

in the light of p. ~의 관점에서
in the face of p. ~에 직면하여
in the mood to do p. ~하고 싶은
in the same way p. 이와 마찬가지로

어원	-long 긴 + -run 달리다 → '오래 달려야 하니 긴 안목으로'
act as	eventually, ultimately
반의어	in the short term, immediately
영영	over an extended period of time; eventually
예문	Exercising regularly is beneficial for your health in the long run. 규칙적인 운동은 장기적으로 건강에 도움이 됩니다.

235

near at hand

p. 가까이에

on one hand p. 한편으로는
second-hand p. 간접적으로
hand down p. ~을 물려주다
hand out p. 나눠주다

어원	-at ~에 + -hand 손 → '손에 닿을 정도로 가까이에'
at home	close by, nearby
반의어	far away, distant
영영	close by; within reach or close proximity
예문	Help is near at hand if you need it. 필요하다면 도움이 손에 가까이 있습니다.

236

in harmony with

p. ~와 조화를 이루다, 일치하다

disharmony n. 불화, 부조화
harmful a. 해로운
harsh a. 혹독한, 가혹한
harry v. 약탈하다, 침략하다

어원	-in 안 + -harmony 조화 → '조화 안에서'
control over	in accordance with, in sync with
반의어	in conflict with, discordant with
영영	in agreement or accordance with; compatible with
예문	The colors in the painting are in harmony with each other. 그 그림 속 색상들이 서로 조화를 이루고 있다.

237

hand over

p. 인도하다, 넘기다

on one hand p. 한편으로는
second-hand p. 간접적으로
hand down p. ~을 물려주다
hand out p. 나눠주다

어원	-hand 손 → '손으로 나눠주다'
유의어	relinquish, transfer
반의어	withhold, keep
영영	relinquish or transfer control or possession of something to someone else
예문	He handed over the keys to the new owner. 그는 새 주인에게 열쇠를 건넸다.

238

get into shape

p. 몸매를 가꾸다

get by p. 그럭저럭 살아나가다
get into trouble p. ~을 어려움에 빠뜨리다
get off p. 떠나다, 출발하다
get out p. 생산하다

어원	-get into 들어가다 + -shape 이상적 몸매 → '이상적 몸매 가꾸기에 들어가다'
유의어	get fit, get in good condition
반의어	fall out of shape, become unfit
영영	become physically fit or improve one's physical condition
예문	He started going to the gym to get into shape. 그는 몸을 좀더 탄탄하게 하기 위해 체육관에 가기 시작했다.

239

blame A on B

p. A를 B의 책임[때문]으로 보다

to be blame for p. ~에 대해 비난 받아야 한다
blameworthy a. 탓할 만한, 책임이 있는
blaze n. 화재 v. 불길이 활활 타다, 타오르다
blend in with p. ~와 잘 섞이다

어원	-black 불에 탄 + -name → '검게 물들은 이름이라 비난'
aggressive to	attribute A to B, hold B responsible for A
반의어	absolve A from B, exonerate A for
영영	attribute responsibility for A to B
예문	Don't blame your mistakes on others. 당신의 실수를 다른 사람에게 돌리지 마세요.

240

at the least

p. 적어도

at the latest p. 늦어도 ~까지는
at the height of p. ~가 한창일 때
at the cost of p. ~의 비용을 지불하고
at the most p. 기껏해야

어원	* little의 최상급 → '최고로 적게 잡아도'
유의어	at the very least, at minimum
반의어	at the most, at most
영영	at the minimum; at the very least or smallest amount
예문	It will take a week at the least to finish this project. 이 프로젝트를 마치는 데 최소 일주일이 걸릴 것입니다.

Chapter 7.

241	committee	[kəˈmɪt.i]	v. 의뢰하다; 주문하다 n. 위원회; 후견인
242	expend	[ɪkˈspend]	v. (돈 , 시간, 노력 등을) 쏟다, 들이다
243	reflect	[rɪˈflekt]	v. 반사하다, 반영하다; 생각하다, 숙고하다
244	tribe	[traɪb]	n. 종족(로마제국의 3종족에서 유래)
245	moderate	[ˈmɒd.ər.ət]	v. 절제하다, 조절하다 a. 보통의, 중간의, 적당한
246	linger	[ˈlɪŋ.gər]	v. 오래 머무르다; 지속되다
247	demote	[dimóut]	v. 강등시키다
248	significant	[sɪgˈnɪf.ɪ.kənt]	a. 의미 심장한, 중요한, 상당한
249	ambiguous	[æmˈbɪg.ju.əs]	a. 모호한, 여러 가지로 해석할 수 있는
250	multitude	[ˈmʌl.tɪ.tʃuːd]	n. 다수, 수많음, 많은 사람
251	contaminate	[kənˈtæm.ɪ.neɪt]	v. 더럽히다, 오염시키다
252	subtract	[səbˈtrækt]	v. 빼다, 감하다
253	delegate	[ˈdel.ɪ.gət]	n. 대표자, 대리인 v. 권한을 위임하다
254	degenerate	[dɪˈdʒen.ə.reɪt]	v. 퇴화하다, 퇴보하다, 타락하다
255	outset	[ˈaʊt.set]	n. 착수, 시작
256	component	[kəmˈpoʊ.nənt]	n. 성분, 구성요소
257	banquet	[ˈbæŋ.kwɪt]	n. 연회, 만찬
258	withhold	[wɪðˈhoʊld]	v. 주지 않다, 받지 않다, 억제하다
259	wholesome	[ˈhoʊl.səm]	a. 전체의, 건강에 좋은, 건전한
260	untapped	[əntæˈpt]	a. 이용되지 않은, 미개발의
261	stationary	[ˈsteɪ.ʃən.ər.i]	a. 움직이지 않는, 고정된
262	harsh	[hɑːʃ]	a. 혹독한, 가혹한
263	intimate	[ˈɪn.tɪ.mət]	a. 가장 깊은, 친밀한
264	dense	[dens]	a. 빽빽한, 밀집한, 짙은
265	perceive	[pəˈsiːv]	v. 인지하다, 인식하다, 지각하다, 알아차리다
266	dynamic	[daɪˈnæm.ɪk]	a. 힘의, 역동적인, 활발한
267	sake	[seɪk]	n. 이익, 목적, 위험
268	hardwire	[hɑːrdwàɪər]	v. 고정화하다, 굳어버리게 하다
269	confine	[kənˈfaɪn]	v. 한정하다, 제한하다; 가두다, 감금하다
270	burglar	[bə́ːrglər]	n. 강도, 빈집털이, 밤도둑
271	immune to N		p. ~의 영향을 받지 않는
272	around the clock		p. 24시간 내내
273	far from		p. 전혀 ~이 아닌, ~와는 거리가 먼
274	catch up on		p. (소식·정보를) 알아내다
275	coincide with		p. ~와 부합하다, 일치하다
276	in favor with		p. ~에 호의적이다
277	break the news to		p. ~에게 (나쁜) 소식을 전하다
278	in passing		p. 지나가는 말로
279	back down		p. (주장 등을) 굽히다, 양보하다
280	act upon		p. ~에 따라 행동하다; 조치를 취하다

241

committee

[kəˈmɪt.i]

v. 의뢰하다; 주문하다 n. 위원회; 후견인

commission n. 위원회(정부에 의해 지정)
conucil n. 위원회(선출에 의해 지정); 회의
commit v. 전념하다, 헌신하다; 약속하다
commission n. 수수료

어원	-com : together + -miss, -mitt, -mist, -mess : course, send → '같은 과정을 밟으며 헌신하자고 모인 하위 위원회'
유의어	board, panel, council
반의어	Individual, separate, non-committee
영영	A group of people appointed or elected to perform a specific task, often in an organization or government.
예문	The committee is responsible for reviewing the proposed changes. 위원회는 제안된 변경 사항을 검토하는 책임이 있습니다.

242

expend

[ɪkˈspend]

v. (돈 , 시간, 노력 등을) 쏟다, 들이다

expand v. 확장하다, 확대하다
expendable a. 소모용의
at one's expense p. ~의 부담으로
at the expense of p. ~을 희생하면서

어원	-ex : out + -pense : money → '밖으로 돈을 쏟다'
유의어	spend, use up, consume
반의어	Save, hoard, conserve
영영	To spend or use up resources, energy, or effort.
예문	It's important to carefully plan how you expend your resources. 자원을 어떻게 소비할지 신중하게 계획하는 것이 중요합니다.

243

reflect

[rɪˈflekt]

v. 반사하다, 반영하다; 생각하다, 숙고하다

inflexible a. 구부러지지 않는; 불변의
reflect on p. ~에 관해 곰곰이 생각하다
reflect upon p. ~을 숙고하다
deflect v. 빗나가다, 빗나가게 하다

어원	-re : against + -flect 구부리다 → '역으로 구부러져 반사하는', '역으로 생각하며 숙고하며 상대의 의견을 반영'
Incidence	ponder, contemplate, consider
반의어	conceal, hide
영영	to think deeply or carefully about something; to give back an image or sound, such as a mirror does
예문	She took a moment to reflect on her past mistakes. 그녀는 자신의 과거 실수를 돌아보는 시간을 가졌다.

244

tribe

[traɪb]

n. 종족(로마제국의 3종족에서 유래)

tribal a. 부족의
tribute n. 헌사, 공물
attribute v. ~탓으로 돌리다 n. 속성, 성질
contribute v. 기부하다

어원	-tri : three + -be → 고대 로마는 3부족으로 구성
유의어	clan, ethnic group, community
반의어	Individual, person, single person
영영	A social group or community of people sharing common customs, traditions, and often a common ancestry.
예문	The indigenous tribe has lived in this area for generations. 원주민 부족은 세대를 거쳐 이 지역에서 살아왔습니다.

245

moderate

[ˈmɒd.ər.ət]

v. 절제하다, 조절하다 a. 보통의, 중간의, 적당한

mould v. 틀에 넣어 만들다
mole n. 두더지; 스파이
modern a. 현대의, 근대의
modest a. 적합한, 겸손한

어원	-mod : fit → '~에 맞추려면 조절을 해서 적당한 선에 맞춰야지'
유의어	temperate, reasonable, middle-of-the-road
반의어	extreme, excessive, immoderate
영영	not extreme; reasonable or mild.
예문	She prefers a moderate level of spice in her food. 그녀는 음식에 중간 정도의 향신료를 선호한다.

246

linger

[ˈlɪŋ.ɡər]

v. 오래 머무르다; 지속되다

at length p. 오랫동안, 상세히
lengthen v. 길어지다
longevities n. 오래 사는 기간, 수명
longitude n. 경도

어원	-long, -leng,-ling : want 갈망하다, long 긴 → '길게 남아 있으니 지속되다'
brace	remain, loiter, stay
반의어	rush, hurry
영영	stay in a place longer than necessary
예문	The aroma of freshly baked bread lingered in the kitchen. 막 구운 빵의 향기가 부엌에 남아 있었다.

247

demote

[dimóut]

v. 강등시키다

emotion n. 감정, 정서, 감동
locomote v. (제 힘으로) 움직이다
mob n. 군중, 폭도, 떼
remove v. 제거하다, 치우다; 벗다

어원	-de : down + -mot : move → '밑으로 움직이니 강등'
유의어	downgrade, reduce, lower
반의어	promote, advance, elevate
영영	To lower someone's rank or position, often in a workplace.
예문	He was demoted to a lower position due to poor performance. 그는 성적이 좋지 않아 하위 직책으로 강등되었다.

248

significant

[sɪɡˈnɪf.ɪ.kənt]

a. 의미 심장한, 중요한, 상당한

signature n. 서명
sign up for p. 가입하다, 신청하다, 참가하다
signify v. 나타내다, 표시하다
insignificance n. 의미 없음, 사소함, 하찮음

어원	-sign, -sea : mark 표시 + -fic : make → '특별한 표시를 할만큼 중요한'
유의어	important, meaningful, substantial
반의어	Insignificant, unimportant, trivial
영영	Important, noteworthy, or having a meaningful impact.
예문	The discovery of a new species was a significant event in the scientific community. 새로운 종의 발견은 과학 커뮤니티에서 중요한 사건이었습니다.

249

ambiguous

[æmˈbɪɡ.ju.əs]

a. 모호한, 여러 가지로 해석할 수 있는

ambivalent a. 양면적인, 모순된 감정을 가진
ambiguity n. 애매모호함
unambiguously adv. 명백하게
ambassadoe n. 대사, 사절

어원	-ambit : two + -gu : lead → 두 가지 이상으로 가니 모호한
유의어	unclear, vague, uncertain
반의어	Clear, definite, unambiguous
영영	Having more than one possible interpretation or meaning; unclear or vague.
예문	His ambiguous response left us confused about his intentions. 그의 애매한 답변으로 우리는 그의 의도를 혼란스러워 했습니다.

250

multitude

[ˈmʌl.tɪ.tʃuːd]

n. 다수, 수많음, 많은 사람

multiply v. 곱하다
multiplex a. 복합적인
multipurpose a. 다목적의
a multitude of p. 다수의, 아주 많은

어원	-multi : many, much
유의어	crowd, mass, throng
반의어	Few, handful, limited number
영영	A large number or multitude of people or things; a crowd.
예문	A multitude of people gathered for the music festival. 음악 축제를 위해 많은 사람들이 모였습니다.

251

contaminate

[kənˈtæm.ɪ.neɪt]

v. 더럽히다, 오염시키다

untained a. 때 묻지 않은, 흠 없는
sustain v. 유지하다
decontamination n. 오염 제거, 정화
contemn v. ~를 경멸하다

어원	-con : together + -tam, -tan, -tag : touch → '함께 만져 세균이 달라붙다' * contamination 다른 물질과 섞임 VS pollution '환경 오염
유의어	pollute, taint, infect
반의어	purify, clean
영영	to make something impure or polluted by introducing harmful or undesirable substances; to taint or pollute
예문	The chemical spill contaminated the soil and water in the area. 화학 누출로 지역의 토양과 물이 오염되었다.

252

subtract

[səbˈtrækt]

v. 빼다, 감하다

attract v. 매혹하다
attract A to B p. A를 B로 끌어들이다
subtraction n. 빼기, 공제
subtractive a. 빼는, 차감하는

어원	-sub : under + -tract : draw → '밑으로 당기니 빼다'
유의어	deduct, take away, minus
반의어	Add, increase, augment
영영	To take away or deduct one quantity from another.
예문	To find the difference, you need to subtract one number from another. 차이를 찾으려면 한 숫자에서 다른 숫자를 빼야 합니다.

253

delegate

[ˈdel.ɪ.gət]

n. 대표자, 대리인 v. 권한을 위임하다

legitimate a. 합법의, 적법의
illicit a. 불법의
delegate A to B p. A를 B에게 위임하다
legacy n. 유산, 유물

어원	-de : down + -leg, -leag, -loy : law 법률, 위임하다 → '법적 권한을 받은 대표나 대리인'
유의어	representative, envoy, proxy
반의어	Retain, keep, hold onto
영영	A person who is authorized to represent or act on behalf of another person, organization, or group.
예문	The manager will delegate the project to a capable team. 관리자는 프로젝트를 능력 있는 팀에 위임할 것입니다.

254

degenerate

[dɪˈdʒen.ə.reɪt]

v. 퇴화하다, 퇴보하다, 타락하다

genome n. 유전자 총체, 게놈
generosity n. 관용
homogeneous a. 동종의, 동질적인
in general p. 일반적으로

어원	-de : down + -gen, -gn : birth 태어나다, 낳다 (G) → '능력이 떨어지게 출생하니 퇴화하다'
유의어	decline, deteriorate, worsen
반의어	improve, advance, progress
영영	to decline or deteriorate in quality or moral character.
예문	The once thriving neighborhood has degenerated into a high-crime area. 한때 번창한 지역은 범죄가 많은 지역으로 퇴보되었다.

255

outset

[ˈaʊt.set]

n. 착수, 시작

onset n. 착수; 공격
beset v. 에워싸다, 포위하다; 괴롭히다
set A apart from B p. A와 B를 구별하다
set A aside p. A를 제쳐 두다

어원	-out : outside + -set → '밖에 최초로 내놓아 착수'
유의어	beginning, start, commencement
반의어	Conclusion, end, termination
영영	The beginning or start of something; the initial stage.
예문	From the outset, he was determined to succeed. 처음부터 그는 성공하기로 결심했습니다.

256

component

[kəmˈpoʊ.nənt]

n. 성분, 구성요소

compose v. 구성하다, 작곡하다
be composed of p. ~로 구성되어 있다
compost n. 퇴비, 두엄
compound v. 혼합하다, 합성하다

어원	-com : together + -pos, -pon, -pound : put 놓다 (L) → '함께 놓아 구성된 성분'
유의어	element, part, ingredient
반의어	Whole, entirety, complete entity
영영	A part or element that makes up a larger whole or system.
예문	The computer has several key components, including a CPU and memory. 컴퓨터에는 CPU와 메모리와 같은 주요 구성 요소가 여러 개 있습니다.

257

banquet

[ˈbæŋ.kwɪt]

n. 연회, 만찬

bench n. 벤치; 판사(석/직)
belly n. 배, 복부
for the benefit of p. ~을 위하여
benefit from p. ~로부터 혜택을 받다

어원	-banquet : bench → '긴 의자와 긴 테이블에서 열렸던 연회'
유의어	feast, gala, celebration
반의어	fast, hunger strike, starvation
영영	a large and lavish meal or feast.
예문	The royal banquet was a grand and extravagant affair. 왕실 연회는 화려하고 호화로운 행사였다.

258

withhold

[wɪðˈhoʊld]

v. 주지 않다, 받지 않다, 억제하다

withdraw n. 철회
withdrawal n. (예금의) 인출
wither v. 시들다, 말라 죽다
withstand v. 반항하다, 저항하다

어원	-with 밖으로, 반대쪽으로 + -hold → '뒤로 가지 못하도록 잡고 억제하다'
유의어	retain, reserve, keep back
반의어	reveal, disclose, divulge
영영	To refuse to give or share something, often information or resources.
예문	He decided to withhold the information until the right moment. 그는 정보를 적절한 순간까지 숨겨두기로 결정했다.

259

wholesome

[ˈhəʊl.səm]

a. 전체의, 건강에 좋은, 건전한

wholesale a. 도매의
retail n. 소매
wholehearted a. 성심 성의의
wholly adv. 완전히, 전적으로

어원	-whole 전체 (E) + -some 명접 → '전반적으로 완전하니 건강에 좋은'
유의어	healthy, nutritious, beneficial
반의어	unhealthy, harmful, detrimental
영영	conducive to or promoting good health and well-being.
예문	Fresh fruits and vegetables are part of a wholesome diet. 신선한 과일과 채소는 건강한 식단의 일부이다.

260

untapped

[əntæˈpt]

a. 이용되지 않은, 미개발의

tap v. 톡톡 두드리다 n. 수도꼭지
take over p. 넘겨 받다; 장악하다
take possession of p. ~을 점유하다
take sides p. 편을 들다

어원	-un : not + -tap 톡톡 두드리다 → '두드리는 손길이 닿지 않았으니 미개발의'
affix	unused, undeveloped, unexplored
반의어	Utilized, exploited, harnessed
영영	Not fully utilized or developed; having unused potential or resources.
예문	The region has vast untapped natural resources. 그 지역은 방대한 미개척 자연 자원을 보유하고 있습니다.

261

stationary

[ˈsteɪ.ʃən.er.i]

a. 움직이지 않는, 고정된

stationery n. 문방구, 문구류
stationer n. 문구상
stain n. 얼룩 v. 얼룩지다, 더럽히다
stainless a. 때 끼지 않은, 얼룩지지 않은

어원	-sta,-sist, -ste, -st, -stitu, -stin, -sti : stand 서다, 세우다 → '가만 서 있으니 정지되고 고정된'
humanitarian	immobile, fixed, motionless
반의어	moving, mobile
영영	not moving or changing position; fixed or immobile
예문	The car was stationary at the traffic light. 차는 신호등에서 정지해 있었다.

262

harsh

[hɑːʃ]

a. 혹독한, 가혹한

harmful a. 해로운
harrowed a. 불안한, 고통스러운
harass v. 괴롭히다
harry v. 약탈하다, 침략하다

어원	-harm, -har 해를 끼치다 → '해를 끼칠 정도로 혹독한'
유의어	severe, rigorous, stern
반의어	gentle, mild, soft
영영	Severe, rigorous, or unpleasant in quality, tone, or effect.
예문	The harsh winter weather made it difficult to travel. 가혹한 겨울 날씨로 여행하기 어려웠습니다.

263

intimate

[ˈɪn.tɪ.mət]

a. 가장 깊은, 친밀한

interval n. 간격, 틈
intimately adv. 밀접하게
intimacy n. 친밀함
internal a. 내부의, 내면의

어원	-intimus : in의 라틴어 최상급 + * -mat : mate 친구 → '가장 속에 있는 것까지 나누는 친구 사이의 친밀함'
유의어	close, personal, familiar
반의어	Distant, remote, detached
정의	Relating to close personal relationships or private and personal aspects of life.
예문	They shared an intimate moment by the fireplace. 그들은 벽난로 앞에서의 아주 가까운 순간을 공유했습니다.

264

dense

[dens]

a. 빽빽한, 밀집한, 짙은

densely adv. 빽빽이, 밀집하여
condense v. 압축하다; 액화되다, 고체화되다
density n. 밀도
densify v. 밀도를 높이다

어원	-dens : -densus(L) 두꺼운, 복잡한(thick); 흐린(cloudy) * 댄스는 클럽처럼 밀집한 곳에서?
유의어	thick, compact, crowded
반의어	Sparse, scattered, scattered
정의	Closely compacted in substance; having a high mass per unit volume.
예문	The forest was so dense that it was hard to see through the trees. 숲은 나무 사이로 보기가 어려울 정도로 빽빽했습니다.

265

perceive

[pəˈsiːv]

v. 인지하다, 인식하다, 지각하다, 알아차리다

perceive A to be B p. A를 B라고 인식하다
perceive A as B p. A를 B라고 인식하다
perceptive a. 통찰력 있는, 지각할 수 있는
precept n. 교훈, 격언

어원	-per : throughly 완전히 + -ceive : take → '완전히 받아들이니 인지한 것이다'
유의어	notice, discern, detect
반의어	overlook, miss
영영	to become aware of, notice, or understand something through the senses or mental processes
예문	Different people may perceive the same situation differently. 다른 사람들은 같은 상황을 다르게 인식할 수 있다.

266

dynamic

[daɪˈnæm.ɪk]

a. 힘의, 역동적인, 활발한

dynamics n. 역학 관계, 역학
dynast n. 군주, 왕
dynastic a. 왕조의
dynamite n. 다이너마이트

어원	-dynam 힘 (G) → '힘이 있으니 역동적인'
유의어	energetic, lively, vigorous
반의어	Static, motionless, unchanging
영영	Energetic, forceful, or characterized by constant change and activity.
예문	The dynamic performance of the athlete impressed the audience. 그 스포츠 선수의 역동적인 경기는 관객들을 감동시켰습니다.

267

sake

[seɪk]

n. 이익, 목적, 위험

forsake v. 저버리다, 미련없이 떠나다
for the sake of p. ~때문에, ~을 위해서
salvage v. 구조하다, 인양하다
safely adv. 별로 틀리지 않게, 무난하게

어원	-sake : seek → '당장의 목적인 이익만 찾으면 위험' * sake 사케로 술 취할 목적이면 위험
유의어	reason, cause, purpose
반의어	Detriment, harm, disadvantage
영영	A reason or purpose; often used in the phrase "for the sake of."
예문	She worked hard for the sake of her family's well-being. 그녀는 가족의 복지를 위해 열심히 일했습니다.

268

hardwire

[hɑːrdwàiər]

v. 고정화하다, 굳어버리게 하다

hardwired a. 하드웨어에 내장된; 타고나는
harden v. 고정화하다
hale v. 잡아끌다
hare n. 산토끼

어원	-hard 단단한, 어려운 + -wire 연결하다 → '단단하게 연결하여 고정화'
유의어	wire, connect, establish a connection
반의어	Wireless, cordless, untethered
영영	To connect something directly with wires, typically in an electrical or electronic context.
예문	The security system is hardwired into the building's electrical system. 보안 시스템은 건물의 전기 시스템에 하드웨어로 연결되어 있습니다.

269

confine

[kənˈfaɪn]

v. 한정하다, 제한하다; 가두다, 감금하다

by definition p. 당연히, 정의상
indefinite a. 무기한의, 규정되지 않은
find out p. 알아내다
firmly adv. 단호히, 확고히

어원	-con : together + -fin : end → '모두 경계를 두고 한정, 제한하다'
유의어	restrict, limit, enclose
반의어	release, free
영영	to restrict or limit someone or something within certain boundaries or limits; to enclose or imprison
예문	They had to confine the dog to a kennel while they were away. 그들은 나가 있을 동안 개를 개구리장에 가둬야 했다.

270

burglar

[bə́ːrglər]

n. 강도, 빈집털이, 밤도둑

burglary n. 주거 침입, 강도질
budget n. 예산, 경비
bulge n. 부푼 것
bulk n. 대부분, 규모(양)

어원	-burg : break into + * -urg : work → '부수고 들어가는 게 일인 강도'
유의어	thief, intruder, robber
반의어	homeowner, resident
영영	a person who illegally enters buildings to commit theft
예문	A burglar broke into their house while they were away on vacation. 휴가 중일 때 침입범이 그들의 집에 들어갔다.

271

immune to N

p. ~의 영향을 받지 않는

company n. 회사, 단체
immune a. 면제된, 면역된
commotion n. 소요, 소동
communize v. 공유화하다, 공산화하다

어원	-im, -in : not + -mun : duty / -munic, -mon 모으다 → '일 등의 의무에서 벗어난 상태'
유의어	resistant to N, unaffected by N
반의어	susceptible to N, vulnerable to N
영영	not affected or influenced by N; resistant to N
예문	Vaccinated individuals are immune to certain diseases. 백신 접종을 받은 사람들은 특정 질병에 면역이 있다.

272

around the clock

p. 24시간 내내

clone n. 복제 생물, 클론
cliff n. 절벽, 낭떠러지
close to one's heart p. ~에게 소중한
draw to a close p. 끝나가다

어원	-around 원, 주변 + -clock 시계 → '시계가 계속 원을 그리며 도니 24시간 내내
유의어	24/7, continuously
반의어	intermittently, occasionally
영영	continuously or constantly; without interruption
예문	Doctors work around the clock in hospitals. 의사들은 병원에서 주야간으로 일한다.

273

far from

p. 전혀 ~이 아닌, ~와는 거리가 먼

as far as it goes p. 그 정도까지
way too far p. 너무 멀리 온, 지나친
take A further p. A추가적인 조치를 취하다
fare n. 요금; 승객

어원	-far 멀리 + -from → '원천으로부터 거리가 머니 전혀 ~이 아닌'
유의어	distant from, nowhere near
반의어	close to, near
영영	distant from; significantly different from
예문	His behavior is far from acceptable. 그의 행동은 받아들일 만한 것에서 거리가 멀다.

274

catch up on

p. (소식·정보를) 알아내다

get caught in p. ~에 사로 잡히다
catch oneself p. 하던 말(일)을 갑자기 멈추다
catch wind of p. ~의 낌새를 알아채다
get a handle on p. 이해하다, 알아듣다

어원	-catch 잡다 + -on → '사건에 딱 붙어 정보를 알아내다'
유의어	make up for lost time, get up to date on
반의어	fall behind on, lag behind in
영영	bring up to date or make progress with something that has been neglected
예문	I need to catch up on my reading during the weekend. 주말에 독서를 하며 미처 따라잡아야겠다.

275

coincide with

p. ~와 부합하다, 일치하다

hesitate v. 망설이다
coincidence n. 우연의 일치
coincident a. 일치하는, 동시에 일어나는
adhere v. 부착하다, 고수하다

어원	-co, -com : together + -in : upon + cid : fall → '같이 위로 동시에 떨어지는 일'
유의어	coincide, correspond with
반의어	differ from, be unrelated to
영영	occur at the same time or correspond with
예문	Her birthday coincides with Thanksgiving this year. 올해 그녀의 생일이 추수감사절과 겹친다.

276

in favor with

p. ~에 호의적이다

in contrast to p. ~와는 대조적으로
in mind p. ~을 염두에 두다
in one's interest p. 가장 이익이 되는
in one's place p. ~의 의견으로는

어원	-fav, -fev : burn → '마음이 탈 정도로 따뜻한 호의'
유의어	favored by, popular with
반의어	out of favor with, unpopular with
영영	enjoying approval or support from someone or a group
예문	The new policy is not in favor with the employees. 새로운 정책은 직원들에게 호의적이지 않다.

277

break the news to

p. ~에게 (나쁜) 소식을 전하다

break into p. 침입하다, 난입하다
breakthrough n. 획기적 발전; 돌파구
breakage n. 파손, 손상
brew v. 끓이다, 양조하다

어원	-break 깨지다(E) → '분위기 깨는 소식을 전하다'
유의어	inform, tell
반의어	keep the news from, conceal the news from
영영	inform someone about something important or surprising
예문	It's never easy to break the news to someone about a loss. 누군가에게 손실에 대해 알리는 것은 언제나 쉽지 않다.

278

in passing

p. 지나가는 말로

pass up p. ~의 기회를 놓치다, 포기하다
pass down p. 전해주다
in retrospect p. 돌이켜 생각해보면
insofar as p. ~하는 한은

어원	-pass, -pace 통과하다, step 발걸음 (L) → '귀를 통과하는 말이니 지나가는 말로'
유의어	incidentally, casually
반의어	deliberately, purposefully
영영	briefly or casually; without much attention or detail
예문	He mentioned it in passing during our conversation. 그는 우리 대화 중에 흘려듣듯이 언급했다.

279

back down

p. (주장 등을) 굽히다, 양보하다

back and forth p. 왔다 갔다 하는
back out p. 물러나다, ~에서 빠지다
backdrop n. 배경
bacteria n. 박테리아, 세균

어원	-back 뒤, 거꾸로, 다시(E) + -down 아래로 → '거꾸로 숙이고 굽히니 양보하다'
유의어	retreat, concede
반의어	stand firm, persist
영영	retreat or withdraw from a position or stance
예문	Despite pressure, he refused to back down from his position. 압력에도 불구하고, 그는 자신의 입장에서 물러서지 않았다.

280

act upon

p. ~에 따라 행동하다; 조치를 취하다

act as p. ~의 역할을 하다; ~로 작용하다
inactive a. 활동하지 않는, 소극적인
activate v. 작동시키다, 활동시키다
take action p. 활동을 취하다

어원	-ac, -act, -ag, -ig : do 행하다, act 작용하다, drive 몰다(L) → 'as 이하로서 행동하다' * action 활동, 움직임
유의어	follow, adhere to
반의어	ignore, neglect
영영	take action based on or in response to something
예문	The committee will act upon your recommendation. 위원회는 당신의 권고에 따라 행동할 것입니다.

Chapter 8.

281	hygiene	[ˈhaɪ.dʒiːn]	n. 위생
282	coffin	[ˈkɒf.ɪn]	n. 관; 시체를 담는 상자
283	retrospect	[ˈret.rə.spekt]	v. 돌이켜보다, 추억하다; 추억, 회상
284	impersonal	[impə́ːrsənl]	a. 냉담한
285	fierce	[fɪəs]	a. 사나운, 맹렬한
286	fraud	[frɔːd]	n. 사기, 사기꾼
287	indulge	[ɪnˈdʌldʒ]	v. 탐닉하다, ~에 빠지다; 내버려 두다
288	nod	[nɒd]	v. 끄덕이다, (고개를) 까딱하다
289	empathic	[empǽθik, im-]	a. 공감할 수 있는, 감정 이입의
290	primitive	[ˈprɪm.ɪ.tɪv]	a. 원시의, 원시적인
291	yearn	[jɜːn]	v. 갈망하다, 그리워하다
292	stride	[straɪd]	v. 성큼성큼 걷다, 활보하다; 큰 걸음, 보폭
293	frank	[fræŋk]	a. 솔직한, 숨김없는, 명백한, 공정한
294	carefree	[ˈkeə.friː]	a. 근심 걱정 없는, 무관심한
295	consecutive	[kənˈsek.jə.tɪv]	a. 연속적인, 계속적인, 일관된
296	commentary	[ˈkɒm.ən.tər.i]	n. 논평, 해설
297	entrust	[ɪnˈtrʌst]	v. 믿음을 주다(믿고 맡기다)
298	reveal	[rɪˈviːl]	v. 드러내다, 나타내다, 보여주다
299	catastrophe	[kəˈtæs.trə.fi]	n. 재앙
300	medieval	[ˌmed.ˈiː.vəl]	a. 중세의 [ev 시대(age)]
301	colony	[ˈkɒl.ə.ni]	n. 식민지; 집단, 부락, 군집, 군체
302	downplay	[ˌdaʊnˈpleɪ]	v. 경시하다
303	definite	[ˈdef.ɪ.nət]	a. 확실한, 확고한, 분명한
304	favoritism	[ˈfeɪ.vər.ɪ.tɪ.zəm]	n. 치우친 사랑, 편애
305	elaborate	[iˈlæb.ər.ət]	a. 정성들인, 정교한 v. 상세히 설명하다
306	linguistic	[liŋgwístik]	a. 언어의, 언어학의
307	utmost	[ʌtmòust]	a. 최대의, 극도의
308	infrastructure	[ˈɪn.frəˌstrʌk.tʃər]	n. 하부조직(구조), 기초, 토대; 사회 기반 시설
309	legacy	[ˈleg.ə.si]	n. 유산, 유물, 물려받은 것
310	vital	[ˈvaɪ.təl]	a. 생명의, 치명적인
311	appeal to N		p. ~에 호소하다
312	at a discount		p. 할인하여
313	cast A aside		p. A를 버리다
314	be terrified of		p. ~을 두려워하다, ~을 경외하다
315	deal with		p. ~을 상대하다, 다루다
316	qualified to do		p. ~할 자격이 있는
317	have an impact on		p. 효과를 미치다
318	be fond of		p. ~을 좋아하다
319	caught in		p. ~에 사로잡힌
320	damaging to N		p. ~에 피해를 주는

281	어원	-hyge, -hygi, -hyde : water * Hygea 히게이아 : 그리스 愼火에 나오는 건강의 여신, 죽은 자가 레테의 강물(망각의 물)을 마시면 몸과 마음이 깨끗해 짐
	유의어	cleanliness, sanitation, healthiness
hygiene	반의어	filth, dirt
[ˈhaɪ.dʒiːn]	영영	conditions or practices that promote cleanliness and health
n. 위생		
hygienic a. 위생적인 hygienist n. 치과 위생사 hygienically adv. 위생적으로, 철저하게 hydrate v. 수화시키다, 수분을 유지시키다	예문	Good hygiene practices are essential for maintaining health. 건강을 유지하기 위해 좋은 위생 습관이 필수적이다.
282	어원	-coffin : casket : basket → 소중한 것을 담는 상자'
	유의어	casket, burial box, sarcophagus
coffin	반의어	cradle, crib, bassinet
[ˈkɒf.ɪn]	영영	A box or container for a deceased person's body before burial or cremation.
n. 관; 시체를 담는 상자		
casket n. 장식함, 손궤 cafeteria n. 구내식당 keg n. (맥주 저장용의) 작은 통 basin n. 대야, (큰 강의) 유역	예문	The pallbearers carried the coffin to the burial site. 시신 보살펴주는 사람들이 관을 묻는 곳까지 나르고 갔습니다.
283	어원	-retro : back + -spect : see → '뒤로 돌이켜 보다'
	유의어	hindsight, review, reflection
retrospect	반의어	Prospect, outlook, future
[ˈret.rə.spekt]	영영	The act of looking back on or reviewing past events or situations.
v. 돌이켜보다, 추억하다; 추억, 회상		
retrogress v. 쇠퇴하다, 퇴보하다 resort to p. ~에 의지하다 redeem v. ~을 되찾다; 메우다, 보상하다 redemption n. 상환, 회수; 구원	예문	In retrospect, I realize I should have made a different decision. 회고를 통해 나는 다른 결정을 내릴 필요가 있었다는 것을 깨달았습니다.
284	어원	-im : not + -personal 인간적인 → '인간적이지 못하니 냉담한' * 프랑스어로 '페르소나' → '입이 뚫린 가면을 쓴 존재'
	유의어	unemotional, detached, objective
impersonal	반의어	Personal, individual, subjective
[impə́ːrsənl]	영영	Lacking personal involvement or emotional connection; formal and objective in nature.
a. 냉담한		
in person p. 직접 personnel n. 인원, 직원; 인사과 to a person p. 만장일치로 personality n. 개성, 성격	예문	The email response was polite but impersonal. 이메일 응답은 공손하지만 감정이 없었습니다.
285	어원	-fier : fire 불 → '불처럼 사납고 맹렬한'
	유의어	ferocious, aggressive, intense
fierce	반의어	gentle, mild, tame
[fɪəs]	영영	marked by intense or aggressive behavior.
a. 사나운, 맹렬한		
misfire v. 불발이 되다 infirm a. 허약한 fiery a. 불의, 불같은, 화염의 affirm v. 확언하다, 단언하다	예문	The fierce competition made it challenging to secure a job. 치열한 경쟁 때문에 일자리를 확보하기 어려웠다.
286	어원	-fraud : fake(L) 사기, 속임수
	유의어	deception, scam, swindle
fraud	반의어	Honesty, truthfulness, integrity
[frɔːd]	영영	Deceptive or dishonest behavior intended to gain an unfair or unlawful advantage, often involving deception for financial gain.
n. 사기, 사기꾼		
defraud v. 사기치다 fradulent a. 사기적인 fradulently adv. 사기를 쳐서 fraudster n. 사기꾼	예문	The company uncovered a case of financial fraud within its ranks. 그 회사는 내부에서의 금융 사기 사례를 발견했습니다.

287

indulge

[ɪnˈdʌldʒ]

v. 탐닉하다, ~에 빠지다; 내버려 두다

overindulge v. 지나치게 내버려두다
indulgent a. 관대한
indulgence n. 하고 싶은 대로 함; 사치; 관용
indulger n. 빠지는 사람, 탐닉자

어원	-in 안 + -dulg, -dulc 달콤한, 감미로운 ; 양보하다, 친절하다 → '달콤함 안에 빠져 탐닉하다'
유의어	pamper, spoil, treat
반의어	restrain, control, withhold
영영	To allow oneself to enjoy or partake in something pleasurable, often in excess.
예문	She liked to indulge in chocolate on special occasions. 그녀는 특별한 날에 초콜릿을 즐기는 것을 좋아했다.

288

nod

[nɒd]

v. 끄덕이다, (고개를) 까딱하다

give a nod to p. ~을 인정하다, 승인하다
nod off p. 잠들다, 졸다
nomad n. 유목민, 방랑자
nominate v. 임명하다, 공천하다

어원	-nod 고개를 끄덕이다 * no doubt 아마, 틀림없는 → '틀림없으니 고개를 끄덕이다'
유의어	gesture, agree, acknowledge
반의어	shake, decline
영영	move one's head up and down to signal agreement or understanding
예문	She gave a nod of approval when she liked the idea. 그녀는 아이디어가 마음에 들 때 찬성의 뜻을 표현했다.

289

empathic

[empǽθik, im-]

a. 공감할 수 있는, 감정 이입의

empathy n. 감정이입
empathize v. 공감하다
emphatic a. 단호한, 강조된, 강경한
empirical a. 경험의, 경험적인

어원	-em, -en : into + -pat : feeling → '느낌을 넣으니 공감'
유의어	empathetic, compassionate, understanding
반의어	apathetic, indifferent
영영	showing empathy or understanding of others' feelings
예문	She had an empathic response to her friend's pain. 그녀는 친구의 고통에 공감했다.

290

primitive

[ˈprɪm.ɪ.tɪv]

a. 원시의, 원시적인

prime a. 가장 중요한, 최상의 n. 전성기
primacy n. 제일
primarily adv. 주로, 본래
optimus prime p. 옵티머스 프라임

어원	-prim, -prin, -pri : first (L) → '최초니 원시의'
유의어	ancient, prehistoric, primitive
반의어	advanced, modern
영영	relating to an early stage of development or existence; basic, simple, or rudimentary
예문	In the early days of human civilization, people lived in primitive shelters. 인류 문명의 초기 시기에는 사람들이 원시적인 보호소에서 살았다.

291

yearn

[jɜːn]

v. 갈망하다, 그리워하다

yield v. 산출하다, 생산하다; 항복하다
yield to p. ~로 대체되다
yawn n. 하품 v. 하품하다
yarn n. 직물을 짜는 실, 뜨개실; 방적사

어원	-year 연 → '1년이 넘게 그리워하다'
유의어	crave, desire, long
반의어	despise, loathe, detest
영영	To have a strong and persistent desire or longing for something.
예문	He yearned to travel the world and explore new cultures. 그는 세계를 여행하고 새로운 문화를 탐험하고 싶었다.

292

stride

[straɪd]

v. 성큼성큼 걷다, 활보하다; 큰 걸음, 보폭

strive to do p. ~하려고 노력하다, 애쓰다
strenuous a. 몹시 힘든, 격렬한
strife n. 분쟁, 불화, 반목
struggle v. 고군분투하다 n. 투쟁, 싸움

어원	-str : strength 싸우다 → '싸움을 앞에 두고 성큼성큼 나아가다'
유의어	step, walk, pace
반의어	Stagnation, standstill, immobility
영영	A long step or the manner of walking with long steps; also, progress or advancement.
예문	He walked with confident strides towards the finish line. 그는 확신에 찬 보폭으로 결승선 쪽으로 걸어갔습니다.

293

frank

[fræŋk]

a. 솔직한, 숨김없는, 명백한, 공정한

infringe v. 위반하다, 어기다
infuriate v. 격노하다, 격분하다
influx n. 유입, 쇄도
frankly adv. 솔직히

어원	-fra, -frag, -frac, -fring : break → '다 부서져 모두가 보이는'
유의어	candid, open, honest
반의어	dishonest, deceptive, insincere
영영	Open, honest, and straightforward in speech or behavior; candid and sincere.
예문	He appreciated her frank and honest feedback. 그는 그녀의 솔직하고 정직한 피드백을 감사했습니다.

294

carefree

[ˈkeə.friː]

a. 근심 걱정 없는, 무관심한

caring a. 배려하는
daycare a. 탁아소의, 보육의
be careful of p. ~을 주의하다
reck v. 개의하다, 마음을 쓰다

어원	-car, -cur, -cour : care 돌봄, 관심, 주의 + -free 無 → '관심이 없으니 무관심한'
유의어	worry-free, lighthearted, relaxed
반의어	worried, anxious, concerned
영영	free from worry or responsibility; lighthearted.
예문	They spent a carefree summer vacation by the beach. 그들은 해변에서 즐겁게 보낸 여름 휴가를 보냈다.

295

consecutive

[kənˈsek.jə.tɪv]

a. 연속적인, 계속적인, 일관된

consecrate v. 신성하게 하다, 봉헌하다
execrate v. 저주하다, 비난하다
consent v. 동의하다, 찬성하다
dissent vi. 의견을 달리하다; n. 불찬성, 이의

어원	-con : intensive + -secu, -sequ : follow → '계속 뒤따르니 연속적인'
유의어	successive, sequential, in a row
반의어	Non-consecutive, sporadic, intermittent
영영	Following in uninterrupted order, one after another.
예문	The team won three consecutive championships. 그 팀은 연속으로 세 번의 챔피언십을 차지했습니다.

296

commentary

[ˈkɒm.ən.tər.i]

n. 논평, 해설

comment on p. ~에 관해 논평하다
commentate v. 논평하다, 해설하다
commentator n. 논평가, 해설가
monument n. 기념품, 기념관

어원	-com : together + -ment : announcement → '모두가 멘트로 의견을 말하며 논평'
유의어	analysis, explanation, narration
반의어	silence, quiet, hush
영영	A written or spoken explanation or analysis of an event, situation, or piece of work.
예문	The sports commentator provided live commentary during the game. 스포츠 해설가는 경기 중에 실시간 해설을 제공했다.

297

entrust

[ɪnˈtrʌst]

v. 믿음을 주다(믿고 맡기다)

truly adv. 진짜로
mistrust n. 불운, 재난 v. 의심하다
truce n. 진실, 휴전
truthful a. 정직한

어원	-en : make + -trust 믿음 → '신뢰하여 중요한 일을 맡기다'
유의어	assign, delegate, hand over
반의어	withhold, retain, keep
영영	Assign the responsibility or care of something to someone.
예문	She decided to entrust her pets to a reliable pet sitter. 그녀는 자신의 애완 동물들을 신뢰할 수 있는 펫 시터에게 맡기기로 결정했습니다.

298

reveal

[rɪˈviːl]

v. 드러내다, 나타내다, 보여주다

revealation n. 폭로, 누설, 반각
unveil v. 베일을 벗기다; 밝혀내다
revel v. 주연을 베풀다, 마시고 흥청거리다
ravel v. 복잡하게 만들다, 꼬이게 만들다

어원	-re : against + -veal, -veil : cover → '덮는 것의 반대니 드러내다'
유의어	disclose, unveil, make known
반의어	conceal, hide, cover
영영	to make something known or visible; to disclose.
예문	The detective will reveal the identity of the murderer in the final scene. 형사는 마지막 장면에서 살인범의 정체를 드러낼 것이다.

299

catastrophe

[kəˈtæs.trə.fi]

n. 재앙

category n. 범주
catalog n. 목록, 카탈로그; 일람표
calamitous a. 재앙을 초래하는
cascade n. 작은 폭포

어원	-cata 아래 + -strophe 돌다 → '아래로 돌아 떨어지니 재앙'
유의어	disaster, calamity, tragedy
반의어	Success, achievement, triumph
영영	A sudden and widespread disaster or calamity, often resulting in significant damage or loss.
예문	The earthquake was a catastrophic event, causing widespread destruction. 지진은 대규모 파괴를 일으켜 참사적 사건이었습니다.

300

medieval

[ˌmed.ˈiː.vəl]

a. 중세의 [ev 시대(age)]

medium a. 중간의 n. 매개, 매개체; 재료
meditation n. 명상
meditate v. 명상하다
median a. 중간의

어원	-me, -med, -men, -medi : middle 중간 (L) / think 생각하다 / macula 흠
유의어	Middle Ages, ancient, historical
반의어	Modern, contemporary, current
영영	Relating to the Middle Ages, a historical period between the fall of the Roman Empire and the Renaissance.
예문	The castle was built during the medieval period. 이 성은 중세 시대에 건축되었습니다.

301

colony

[ˈkɒl.ə.ni]

n. 식민지; 집단, 부락, 군집, 군체

culture n. 문화
colon n. 대장, 대장암; 콜론
colors n. 기, 깃발
colonel n. 대령

어원	-cult, -colon 재배하다, 경작하다 (L) → '경작을 시작하며 집단 부락이 생기고 식민지가 생겼다'
유의어	settlement, outpost, territory
반의어	Homeland, native land, motherland
영영	A group of people or organisms living together in a specific area; a settlement in a distant land.
예문	The British established a colony in North America in the 17th century. 17세기에 영국이 북아메리카에 식민지를 설립했습니다.

302

downplay

[ˌdaʊnˈpleɪ]

v. 경시하다

play a trick p. (눈을) 속이다
play tricks p. 농간을 부리다
play on p. (감정 등을) 이용하다
playful a. 장난스러운

어원	-down + -play 놀다 → '수준 낮은 놀이라며 경시하다'
유의어	minimize, de-emphasize, understress
반의어	emphasize, highlight, stress
영영	Minimize the significance or importance of something.
예문	He tends to downplay his achievements to stay humble. 그는 겸손하게 남기기 위해 자신의 성취를 경시하는 경향이 있습니다.

303

definite

[ˈdef.ɪ.nət]

a. 확실한, 확고한, 분명한

definitely adv. 확실히, 분명히, 절대
definition n. 정의, 선명도
by definition p. 당연히, 정의상
indefinitely adv. 무한하게

어원	-de : from + -fin : limit → '~로부터 한계를 정하니 확실'
유의어	certain, specific, clear
반의어	Indefinite, vague, uncertain
영영	Clearly defined, certain, or fixed; without ambiguity or doubt.
예문	Please provide a definite answer by the end of the week. 이번 주 끝까지 명확한 답변을 제공해 주세요.

304

favoritism

[ˈfeɪ.vər.ɪ.tɪ.zəm]

n. 치우친 사랑, 편애

favorite a. 가장 좋아하는
favorably adv. 호의적이게
in favor of p. ~에 찬성하는, 지지하는
fever n. 열, 흥분

어원	-fav, -fev : burn → '마음이 탈 정도로 치우친 사랑이 편애'
유의어	bias, discrimination, partiality
반의어	fairness, impartiality
영영	unfair preference for one person or group
예문	Favoritism in the workplace can lead to a toxic environment. 직장에서의 편견은 유해한 환경을 초래할 수 있다.

305

elaborate

[iˈlæb.ər.ət]

a. 정성들인, 정교한 v. 상세히 설명하다

laboratory n. 실험실, 연구소
collaboration n. 협업, 협력
be laced with p. ~이 짜넣어져 있다
lag v. 뒤쳐지다, 뒤떨어지다

어원	-e, -ex : out + labor 노동 → '바깥으로 힘쓴게 드러나니 공들인, 정성들인'
유의어	detailed, intricate, complex
반의어	simplify, condense
영영	detailed, complex, or intricate
예문	He gave an elaborate explanation of the complex scientific theory. 그는 복잡한 과학 이론을 상세하게 설명했다.

306

linguistic

[liŋgwístik]

a. 언어의, 언어학의

lingua n. 혀, 언어
linguist n. 언어학자
monolingual a. 단일 언어를 사용하는
lexicon n. 어휘 (목록)

어원	-lingu : tongue 혀 / language 언어 → '언어를 연구하는 학문'
유의어	verbal, language-related, lexical
반의어	non-linguistic, non-verbal, a-linguistic
영영	Related to the study of language or the ability to use language effectively.
예문	The study of linguistic diversity explores different languages and their structures. 언어 다양성의 연구는 다양한 언어와 그 구조를 탐구한다.

307

utmost

[ʌtmòust]

a. 최대의, 극도의

do one's utmost p. 전력을 다하다
utter a. 극단적인 v. 밖으로 소리를 내다
utterly adv. 완전히, 철저히
utterance n. 말, 발화

어원	-ut : out + -most → '가장 최고의'
유의어	greatest, maximum, extreme
반의어	minimum, least, smallest
영영	The highest degree or most extreme point.
예문	He put forth his utmost effort to complete the project on time. 그는 프로젝트를 시간 내에 완료하기 위해 최선의 노력을 기울였다.

308

infrastructure

[ˈɪn.frəˌstrʌk.tʃər]

n. 하부조직(구조), 기초, 토대; 사회 기반 시설

inflate v. 부풀리다, 팽창시키다
flatter v. 아첨하다, 추켜세우다
infatuate v. 얼빠지게 하다, 홀딱 반하게 하다
infiltrate v. 스며들게 하다, 침투하다

어원	-infra 아래에 + -structure 기반 → '아래 기반이 기초로 사회 기반 시설'
유의어	facilities, network, structure
반의어	Non-infrastructure, absence of development
영영	The fundamental physical and organizational structures and facilities needed for the operation of a society, such as roads, bridges, utilities, and communication systems.
예문	The government plans to invest in improving the country's infrastructure. 정부는 국가의 인프라를 개선하기 위한 투자 계획을 세우고 있습니다.

309

legacy

[ˈleg.ə.si]

n. 유산, 유물, 물려받은 것

legitimate a. 합법의, 적법의
illicit a. 불법의
delegate A to B p. A를 B에게 위임하다
loyalty n. 충성, 충실, 충성심

어원	-leg, -leag, -loy : law 법률, 위임하다 → '법으로 인정 받은 유산'
유의어	inheritance, bequest, heritage
반의어	Non-legacy, absence of inheritance, lack of heritage
영영	Something passed down from a previous generation; a bequest or inheritance.
예문	She was a notable figure in the field of science, known for her groundbreaking discoveries. 그녀는 과학 분야에서 주목받는 인물로, 혁신적인 발견으로 유명합니다.

310

vital

[ˈvaɪ.təl]

a. 생명의, 치명적인

revival n. 회복, 부흥, 부활
vivid a. 생생한, 선명한
survive v. 살아남다, 생존하다
revive v. 소생시키다, 회복시키다

어원	-vid, -viv, -vit, -vig, -veget : live 살다, life : 생명(L) * 의학 드라마 "바이탈 체크하세요"
유의어	essential, crucial, important
반의어	nonessential, insignificant, trivial
영영	Essential, crucial, or necessary for life, existence, or success.
예문	Proper nutrition is vital for good health. 적절한 영양은 건강에 중요합니다.

311

appeal to N

p. ~에 호소하다

appealing a. 매력적인
propel v. 나아가게 하다, 추진하다
propeller n. 프로펠러, 추진기
compel v. 강요하다, ~하게 하다

어원	-ap : to + -peal : drive → '마음을 몰고가며 호소하니 관심을 끌다'
유의어	appeal to, attract, entice
반의어	repel, deter
영영	attract interest or support
예문	The new policy is designed to appeal to younger voters. 새로운 정책은 젊은 유권자들에게 호소하도록 설계되었습니다.

312

at a discount

p. 할인하여

encounter v. 우연히 만나다
counteract v. 대항하다, 거스르다
counterfeit a. 가짜의, 위조의 v. 위조하다
counterpart n. 상대물, 복사물; 상대, 대응

어원	-at 점 + -discount 할인 → '생각한 지점까지 할인하여'
유의어	discounted, at a reduced price
반의어	at full price, at the regular price
영영	offered at a reduced price
예문	I bought this shirt at a discount because it was on sale. 이 셔츠를 할인 가격에 샀는데, 세일 중이었기 때문입니다.

313

cast A aside

p. A를 버리다

cast a shadow p. 그림자를 드리우다
broadcast v. 방송하다, 알리다
forecast v. 예측하다, 예보하다
outcast a. 버림받은, 쫓겨난

어원	-cast : throw 던지다 + -aside 옆 → '옆으로 제껴두는 것이니 버리다'
유의어	discard A, disregard A, dismiss A
반의어	retain A, keep A, embrace A
영영	dismiss or reject A
예문	She felt cast aside when her friends excluded her from their plans. 친구들이 계획에서 그녀를 배제하자, 그녀는 외면당한 느낌이었습니다.

314

be terrified of

p. ~을 두려워하다, ~을 경외하다

terrible a. 무서운
terror n. 공포, 두려움, 폭력 행사
terrify v. 겁나게 하다, 무섭게 하다
deter v. 그만두게 하다, 단념시키다, 저지하다

어원	-terr : frighten 두려워하게 하다 + -fy : make → '두렵게 만들다'
유의어	be afraid of, be scared of, fear
반의어	be unafraid of, be fearless of, be brave in the face of
영영	be extremely frightened of
예문	John is terrified of spiders. 존은 거미를 무서워합니다.

315

deal with

p. ~을 상대하다, 다루다

strike a deal p. 계약을 맺다
new deal p. 뉴딜 정책
deal in p. 장사하다
a great deal of p. 많은

어원	-deal 거래 + -with 함께 → '함께 거래하니 다루는 상대'
유의어	handle, manage, address
반의어	avoid, ignore, neglect
영영	handle, manage, or cope with
예문	We need to deal with this issue before it gets worse. 더 악화되기 전에 이 문제를 처리해야 합니다.

316

qualified to do

p. ~할 자격이 있는

qualify v. 자격을 주다, 적임이다
qualify A for B p. A자격을 주다 B에게
qualify for p. ~할 자격이 있다
quality n. 특성

어원	-quality 품질 + -fy : make → '품질을 만드는 사람에게 자격을 주다'
유의어	capable of, competent to do, eligible to do
반의어	unqualified to do, ineligible to do, incompetent to do
영영	having the necessary skills, knowledge, or experience to do
예문	She is highly qualified to lead the research team. 그녀는 연구 팀을 이끌 자격이 충분히 있습니다.

317

have an impact on

p. 효과를 미치다

have nothing to do with p. ~와 전혀 관계가 없다
have game p. 수준 높은 경기력을 가지다
have trouble -ing p. ~하는 데 어려움을 겪다

어원	-have 갖다 + -impact 영향 → '영향을 갖는 것이니 효과를 미치다'
유의어	influence, affect, make a difference to
반의어	have no effect on, be inconsequential to, be insignificant to
영영	affect or influence
예문	Social media has a significant impact on modern communication. 소셜 미디어는 현대 커뮤니케이션에 상당한 영향을 미칩니다.

318

be fond of

p. ~을 좋아하다

fond a. 좋아하는, 애정을 느끼는
fondly adv. 상냥하게
face up to p. ~을 받아들이다, 직시하다
frontal a. 정면의 n. 기상 전선

어원	-fond : found 기초 → '감정의 기초가 되는 사랑'
유의어	like, enjoy, be attached to
반의어	dislike, detest, loathe
영영	have a liking or affection for
예문	Sarah is fond of playing the piano in her free time. 사라는 여가 시간에 피아노 연주를 좋아합니다.

319

caught in

p. ~에 사로잡힌

catch on p. 이해하다, 알아듣다
catch oneself p. 하던 말(일)을 갑자기 멈추다
catch wind of p. ~의 낌새를 알아채다
get a handle on p. 이해하다, 알아듣다

어원	-caught : catch의 과거 → '사로잡히다'
유의어	trapped in, ensnared in, entangled in
반의어	free from, liberated from, released from
영영	trapped or ensnared in
예문	He was caught in a dilemma between choosing his career and spending time with his family. 그는 직업을 선택하고 가족과 시간을 보내는 사이에 딜레마에 빠졌습니다.

320

damaging to N

p. ~에 피해를 주는

damn v. 비난하다, 저주하다
indemnify v. ~에게 변상하다, 보상하다
do damage p. 피해를 주다
damages n. 손해액

어원	-dam, -demn : loss 손실 / blame 비난 → '손실을 주니 피해'
유의어	harmful to N, detrimental to N, injurious to N
반의어	beneficial to N, advantageous to N, helpful to N
영영	causing harm or injury to N
예문	Smoking is damaging to your health. 흡연은 당신의 건강에 해로울 수 있습니다.

Chapter 9.

321	**prompt**	[prɒmpt]	a. 즉석의, 신속한
322	**ferry**	[féri]	n. 나루터, 나룻배, 연락선 v. 수송하다
323	**array**	[əˈreɪ]	v. 정렬시키다; 잘 차려 입히다 n. 대형, 배치
324	**drawback**	[ˈdrɔː.bæk]	n. 결점, 문제점
325	**scarcity**	[ˈskeə.sə.ti]	n. 부족, 결핍
326	**concise**	[kənˈsaɪs]	a. 거두절미한, 간결한
327	**janitor**	[ˈdʒæn.ɪ.tər]	n. 문지기, 수위, 관리인
328	**vertical**	[ˈvɜː.tɪ.kəl]	a. 수직의, 세로의
329	**divine**	[dɪˈvaɪn]	a. 신성한, 신의
330	**parallel**	[ˈpær.ə.lel]	v. 평행하다, 유사하다
331	**consent**	[kənˈsent]	v. 동의하다, 승인하다 n. 동의, 허가
332	**charity**	[ˈtʃær.ə.ti]	n. 사랑, 박애, 관용; 자선(행위), 자선(단체)
333	**reprove**	[rɪˈpruːv]	v. ~을 야단치다, 비난하다
334	**minister**	[ˈmɪn.ɪ.stər]	n. 장관, 성직자, 목사
335	**shred**	[ʃred]	v. 갈기갈기 찢다, 째다
336	**sarcastic**	[sɑːˈkæs.tɪk]	a. 풍자적인, 빈정대는, 비꼬는
337	**soothe**	[suːð]	v. 달래다, 누그러뜨리다
338	**ware**	[weər]	n. 제품, 상품
339	**distinguish**	[dɪˈstɪŋ.gwɪʃ]	v. 구별하다, 구분하다
340	**scorn**	[skɔːn]	v. 조롱하다, 경멸하다; n. 조롱, 경멸
341	**render**	[ˈren.dər]	v. ~한 상태로 만들다; 주다, 제공하다; 표현하다
342	**frustrate**	[frʌstreit]	v. 좌절감을 주다; 방해하다
343	**compass**	[ˈkʌm.pəs]	n. 나침반, 컴퍼스; v. 둘러싸다, 에워싸다
344	**indifferent**	[ɪnˈdɪf.ər.ənt]	a. 무관심한, 사심이 없는
345	**sway**	[sweɪ]	n. 흔들림; v. 흔들리다
346	**nurture**	[ˈnɜː.tʃər]	v. 기르다, 양육하다
347	**irrational**	[ɪˈræʃ.ən.əl]	a. 비이성적인, 무분별한
348	**ignoble**	[ɪgˈnəʊ.bəl]	a. 비열한, 비천한
349	**profit**	[ˈprɒf.ɪt]	n. 이익, 수익 v. 이익을 얻다
350	**marvel**	[ˈmɑː.vəl]	n. 놀라운 일 v. 놀라다
351	**in awe of**		p. ~을 두려워[경외]하다
352	**at the height of**		p. ~가 한창일 때
353	**live beyond one's income**		p. 수입을 초과하여 살다
354	**have no choice but to do**		p. ~할 수 밖에 없다
355	**have a discussion with**		p. ~와 토론을 벌이다
356	**hold on**		p. 붙잡고 있다, 기다리다, 고정시키다
357	**for a change**		p. 여느 때와 달리, 기분 전환으로
358	**by way of**		p. ~ 의 방법으로, ~에 의해서, ~을 거쳐서
359	**enter into**		p. 시작하다, [계약 따위를] 맺다
360	**in a timely fashion**		p. 시기 적절하게

321

prompt
[prɒmpt]

a. 즉석의, 신속한

promptly adv. 즉각적으로, 신속히
prompter n. 프롬프터
promptitude n. 신속
preempt v. 선매하다, 선취하다

어원	-pro : prepare + -mpt : take → '미리 준비해서 상황을 준비하니 신속한'
유의어	encourage, motivate, stimulate
반의어	Delay, hesitation, procrastination
영영	To incite or inspire action or response; to cause something to happen quickly.
예문	She received a prompt response to her inquiry from the customer service team. 그녀는 고객 서비스 팀에서 그녀의 문의에 신속한 답변을 받았습니다.

322

ferry
[féri]

n. 나루터, 나룻배, 연락선 v. 수송하다

reference n. 추천서, 참고; 언급, 논급
with reference to p. ~에 관하여
referee n. 중재인, 심판원
freight n. 화물 운송 v. 운송하다

어원	-fer, fur, far : carry → '물건이나 사람을 나르는 연락선'
유의어	transport, shuttle, boat
반의어	Stay, remain, abide
영영	A boat or ship used to transport people, vehicles, or goods across a body of water.
예문	The ferry transported passengers across the river. 페리는 강을 건너는 승객을 운송했습니다.

323

array
[əˈreɪ]

v. 정렬시키다; 잘 차려 입히다 n. 대형, 배치

an array of p. 많은
arraign v. 기소하다, 고발하다
arrogant a. 거만한, 오만한
arrogate v. 침해하다, 가로채다

어원	-ar : to + -ray, -rei : order → '정돈시키다'
유의어	range, assortment, collection
반의어	disorder, disarray, confusion
영영	A large and orderly arrangement or display of things.
예문	The store had a wide array of products to choose from. 그 가게에는 선택할 수 있는 다양한 제품이 있었다.

324

drawback
[ˈdrɔːbæk]

n. 결점, 문제점

draw on p. ~에 의존하다
draw A out p. A를 끌어내다
drawer n. 서랍; 수표 발행인
drain v. 배수하다, 물을 빼내다

어원	-draw 당기다 + -back → '뒤로 당겨 놓아야 할 문제점'
유의어	disadvantage, limitation, downside
반의어	Advantage, benefit, positive aspect
영영	A disadvantage or negative aspect of a situation or decision.
예문	The drawback of the new technology is its high cost. 새로운 기술의 단점은 높은 비용입니다.

325

scarcity
[ˈskeə.sə.ti]

n. 부족, 결핍

scarce a. 부족한
scarcely adv. 간신히, 겨우, 거의 ~않다
scare a. 희귀한, 드문 v. 위협하다
scarecrow n. 허수아비

어원	-scare : rare 드문 → '드물게 있으니 부족한' (* 중세 영어로 '겁, 두려움' 뜻)
유의어	shortage, lack, insufficiency
반의어	Abundance, plentifulness, profusion
영영	A limited supply or insufficient amount of something relative to demand.
예문	The scarcity of clean drinking water is a global concern. 깨끗한 마실 물의 부족은 전 세계적인 문제입니다.

326

concise
[kənˈsaɪs]

a. 거두절미한, 간결한

precisely adv. 정확히, 바로
decisive a. 결정적인
genocide n. 인종말살, 대량학살
homicide n. 살인

어원	-con : together + -cis 죽이다 → '머리와 꼬리를 잘라내고 본론만'
유의어	brief, succinct, terse
반의어	Wordy, verbose, long-winded
영영	Giving a lot of information clearly and in a few words; brief and to the point.
예문	She gave a concise presentation that lasted only ten minutes. 그녀는 단 10분 동안 지속되는 간결한 프레젠테이션을 했습니다.

327

janitor

[ˈdʒæn.ɪ.tər]

n. 문지기, 수위, 관리인

jam vt. 밀어넣다 vi. 가득 채워지다
jammed up p. 꽉 막힌
jail n. 교도소, 감옥
jargon n. 전문 용어

어원	-Janus 야누스 → '두 얼굴을 가진 문·출입구의 수호신'
유의어	custodian, caretaker, cleaner
반의어	CEO, executive, manager
영영	A person employed to clean and maintain a building, especially in a school, office, or public facility.
예문	The school janitor keeps the campus clean and tidy. 학교 관리인은 캠퍼스를 청결하고 정돈되게 유지합니다.

328

vertical

[ˈvɜː.tɪ.kəl]

a. 수직의, 세로의

vertically adv. 수직으로, 세로로
vertebrate n. 척추동물
adverse a. 반대의, 역의; 불리한
adversity n. 역경, 고난

어원	-vert, -vers, vorc : turn 돌리다(L) → '수평선을 돌려서 수직선의'
유의어	upright, perpendicular, straight up
반의어	Horizontal, parallel, level
영영	Positioned or oriented in an upright direction, perpendicular to the horizontal.
예문	The flagpole stood tall and vertical in the center of the plaza. 깃발대는 광장 중앙에 키가 크고 수직으로 섰습니다.

329

divine

[dɪˈvaɪn]

a. 신성한, 신의

divinity n. 신성, 신성함
divinize v. 신격화하다, 신성화하다
divinization n. 신격화, 신성화
devil n. 악마

어원	-div : deva 신 * devil 악마
유의어	heavenly, godly, sacred
반의어	Human, earthly, mortal
영영	Of or related to a god or deity; often used to describe something as heavenly or perfect.
예문	The view from the mountaintop was truly divine. 산 정상에서의 경치는 정말로 신성한 것이었습니다.

330

parallel

[ˈpær.ə.lel]

v. 평행하다, 유사하다

parade n. 퍼레이드, 행진
paradigm n. 패러다임, 모범, 질서, 양식
paradise n. 낙원, 천국, 파라다이스
parasite n. 기생충

어원	-para 옆에, 나란히 (G) → '서로 다른 것이 옆에 나란히 있으니 유사한'
유의어	similar, comparable, analogous
반의어	Perpendicular, intersecting, crossing
영영	Extending in the same direction and always equidistant from each other, never meeting.
예문	The train tracks run in parallel to each other. 기차 선로는 서로 평행하게 놓여 있습니다.

331

consent

[kənˈsent]

v. 동의하다, 승인하다 n. 동의, 허가

consecrate v. 신성하게 하다, 봉헌하다
execrate v. 저주하다, 비난하다
consecutive a. 연속적인, 계속적인, 일관된
dissent vi. 의견을 달리하다; n. 불찬성, 이의

어원	-con : together + -sens, -sent : feel → '함께 느끼니 동의하다'
유의어	agree, permit, allow
반의어	refuse, deny, decline
영영	To give permission or approval for something to happen.
예문	They obtained informed consent from the participants before the study. 연구 전에 참가자로부터 알림 동의를 얻었다.

332

charity

[ˈtʃær.ə.ti]

n. 사랑, 박애, 관용; 자선(행위), 자선(단체)

charitable a. 자비로운
charitably adv. 자비롭게, 관대하게
cherish v. 소중히 여기다, 아끼다
charm n. 매력, 마력; 주문

어원	-charis, -charit 은혜, 감사 → '은혜로운 사랑을 베푸는 단체'
유의어	benevolence, philanthropy, generosity
반의어	cruelty, selfishness
영영	providing help or support to those in need
예문	He regularly donates to charity to help those in need. 그는 정기적으로 자선에 기부하여 필요한 사람들을 돕는다.

333

reprove

[rɪˈpruːv]

v. ~을 야단치다, 비난하다

approve v. 승인하다
disapprove of p. ~을 못마땅하게 여기다
proberb n. 속담, 격언
reproval n. 책망, 비난

어원	-re : back + -prove 증명하다 → '이전 잘못을 증명하며 야단치다'
유의어	admonish, rebuke, scold
반의어	praise, commend, applaud
영영	To express disapproval or criticism; to scold or rebuke someone for their actions.
예문	The teacher had to reprove the student for misbehaving. 선생님은 학생을 잘못 행동한 것으로 꾸짖어야 했습니다.

334

minister

[ˈmɪn.ɪ.stər]

n. 장관, 성직자, 목사

minority n. 소수
minimum n. 최소한도, 최저치
ministry n. 내각, 성직자
eminent a. 저명한, 탁월한

어원	-min, -mini, -minim 작은 (L) → '몸을 작게하여 봉사하는 장관'
유의어	clergyman, pastor, preacher
반의어	Layperson, non-clergy, commoner
영영	A person who is authorized to perform religious duties and lead worship in a church or religious organization, or a government official responsible for a specific department or area.
예문	The prime minister addressed the nation in a televised speech. 총리는 텔레비전 연설에서 국민에게 말했습니다.

335

shred

[ʃred]

v. 갈기갈기 찢다, 째다

scrap with p. ~와 다투다
scrutinize v. 세밀히 조사하다
scratch v. 긁다, 할퀴다
crack v. 깨다, 갈라지다; 풀다

어원	-scru : shred + -tin : tiny → '조각처럼 작은 부분까지 갈기갈기 찢다'
유의어	tear, rip, slice
반의어	assemble, unite, join
영영	To tear or cut into small pieces or fragments.
예문	She carefully shredded the documents to protect sensitive information. 그녀는 민감한 정보를 보호하기 위해 문서를 조심스럽게 파쇄했다.

336

sarcastic

[sɑːˈkæs.tɪk]

a. 풍자적인, 빈정대는, 비꼬는

satirical a. 풍자적인, 해학적인
satisfy v. 만족시키다, 충족시키다
to one's satisfaction p. ~가 만족스럽게도
dissatisfy v. 불만을 갖게 하다, 실망시키다

어원	-sarc : flesh 고기 + -tic 형접 → '고기를 씹어대는 것처럼 비꼬는'
유의어	sardonic, ironic, cutting
반의어	sincere, genuine, heartfelt
영영	Using irony or sarcasm to mock or convey contempt.
예문	She often used sarcastic humor to make her friends laugh. 그녀는 자주 비꼬는 유머를 사용하여 친구들을 웃기려고 했다.

337

soothe

[suːð]

v. 달래다, 누그러뜨리다

soft a. 부드러운, 연한, 매끄러운
soil n. 흙, 토양
solar a. 태양의
desolate a. 황량한, 쓸쓸한

어원	* -so : soft → '부드럽게 달래다'
유의어	calm, comfort, pacify
반의어	agitate, disturb
영영	calm or comfort someone or alleviate their distress
예문	The soothing music helped him relax after a long day at work. 직장에서 긴 하루를 보낸 후 진정시키는 음악이 그를 도와주었다.

338

ware

[weər]

n. 제품, 상품

warehouse n. 창고
wallet n. 지갑
warrior n. 전사, 용사
warm up to p. ~에 관심을 더 가지게 되다

어원	-ware : warn → '주의하며 꼼꼼히 따져봐야 할 제품''
유의어	merchandise, goods, products
반의어	Empty, vacant, bare
영영	An item of merchandise or goods, often used in the context of pottery or ceramics.
예문	The store displayed a wide variety of kitchen wares. 그 가게는 다양한 주방 용품을 전시했습니다.

339

distinguish
[dɪˈstɪŋ.gwɪʃ]

v. 구별하다, 구분하다

distinct a. 뚜렷한, 구별되는, 별개의
in distinction to p. ~과 구별하여
distinguish A from B p. A를 B와 구별하다
instinct n. 본능, 직관, 육감, 천성

어원	-dis : away + -stinct, -sting : prick 찌르다 → '떨어지도록 사이에 막대기를 찔러 넣으니 구별되는'
유의어	differentiate, discern, separate
반의어	confuse, mix up, blur
영영	To recognize and highlight the differences between two or more things.
예문	She could distinguish between the two identical-looking keys. 그녀는 두 개의 똑같이 보이는 열쇠를 구별할 수 있었다.

340

scorn
[skɔːn]

v. 조롱하다, 경멸하다; n. 조롱, 경멸

corn n. 곡물, 옥수수
cone n. 원뿔, 원뿔형 물체
scronful a. 조롱하는, 경멸하는
scronfully adv. 조롱하면서, 경멸적으로

어원	-s, -se : cut + -corn, -con, -cop, -crop,-gon, -hor, -bull 모서리, 뿔(L) → '뿔이 잘린 상대를 조롱하고 경멸하다'
유의어	contempt, disdain, derision
반의어	admiration, respect
영영	a feeling of contempt or disdain; to show disdain or contempt for someone or something
예문	He looked at her with scorn when she suggested a silly idea. 그녀가 어리석은 아이디어를 제안하자 그는 경멸의 눈총을 보냈다.

341

render
[ˈren.dər]

v. ~한 상태로 만들다; 주다, 제공하다; 표현하다

rendering n. 연주, 연기; 번역; 시멘트 칠
surrender v. 항복하다, 넘겨주다
rental n. 임대료, 임대, 대여
rent out p. ~을 임대하다

어원	-re : back + -der, -t, -d : give → '다시 돌려주며 ~한 상태로 만들다'
유의어	depict, represent, portray
반의어	obscure, hide
영영	make or cause to be in a particular state or condition
예문	The artist tried to render the beauty of the landscape in his painting. 예술가는 풍경의 아름다움을 그림에 담으려 노력했다.

342

frustrate
[frʌstreit]

v. 좌절감을 주다; 방해하다

fragile a. 부서지기 쉬운; 허약한
fraction n. 단편, 일부, 소량; 분수
fragrant a. 향기로운, 향긋한
frantic a. 미친듯이 서두르는, 제정신이 아닌

어원	-frust, -fra, -frag, -frac : break → '희망을 부수며 좌절감을 주다'
유의어	thwart, hinder, impede
반의어	assist, aid
영영	to cause feelings of disappointment, discouragement, or annoyance; to hinder or prevent the achievement of a goal
예문	The constant setbacks began to frustrate their progress. 계속된 좌절이 그들의 진전을 좌절시키기 시작했다.

343

compass
[ˈkʌm.pəs]

n. 나침반, 컴퍼스; v. 둘러싸다, 에워싸다

encompass v. 둘러싸다, 망라하다, 포함하다
surpass v. ~을 능가하다, ~보다 낫다
passerby n. 통행인
pass up p. ~의 기회를 놓치다

어원	-com : together + -pass, -pace 통과하다, step 발걸음 (L) → '모든 여정을 통과할 때 필요한 나침반'
유의어	navigator, guide, director
반의어	disorient, confuse, mislead
영영	A navigational instrument used to determine direction, often with magnetic properties.
예문	A compass can help you find your way when you're lost. 나침반은 길을 잃었을 때 도움이 될 수 있다.

344

indifferent
[ɪnˈdɪf.ər.ənt]

a. 무관심한, 사심이 없는

different from p. ~와 다른
infer v. 추론하다, 암시하다
proffer v. 증정하다 n. 제출, 제안
offering n. 봉납물

어원	-in : not + -different 다른 → '다름을 보지 않으니 무관심한'
유의어	apathetic, uninterested, uncaring
반의어	concerned, interested, caring
영영	Having no strong feelings or interest, showing apathy or neutrality.
예문	She seemed indifferent to the outcome of the game. 그녀는 경기 결과에 무관심한 것처럼 보였다.

345

sway

[sweɪ]

n. 흔들림; v. 흔들리다

swing v. 흔들다, 빙 돌다 n. 그네
switch n. 스위치; 회초리 v. 전환하다
switch over p. 전환하다, 바꾸다
swift a. 신속한, 빠른

어원	-sway : swing 흔들리다, 그네 → '그네처럼 흔들리다'
유의어	swing, influence, control
반의어	stabilize, balance, steady
영영	To move or swing back and forth or influence or control something.
예문	The gentle breeze made the trees sway in the wind. 부드러운 바람으로 나무들이 바람에 흔들렸다.

346

nurture

[ˈnɜː.tʃər]

v. 기르다, 양육하다

nurse n. 간호사, 유모
nurshing home p. 양로원
nourish v. 영양분을 주다, 육성하다
nursery n. 탁아소, 양성소

어원	-nutri, -nur, -nour : nourish 영양분을 주다, feed 기르다 → '영양분을 주며 양육하다'
유의어	nourish, foster, raise
반의어	neglect, abandon
영영	to care for and encourage the growth and development of someone or something; to foster or support
예문	Parents should nurture their children's talents and interests. 부모는 자녀의 재능과 관심을 양성해야 한다.

347

irrational

[ɪˈræʃ.ən.əl]

a. 비이성적인, 무분별한

rationalize v. 합리화하다
irrationality n. 불합리, 부조리
irrationalism n. 비합리주의; 무분별, 불합리
irrationally adv. 이성을 잃어, 분별 없이

어원	-ir : not + -rat, -reas 생각하여 평가하다[E] → '생각하여 평가하지 못하니 비이성적인'
유의어	illogical, unreasonable, nonsensical
반의어	Rational, logical, reasonable
영영	Not based on reason or logic; lacking sound judgment.
예문	His fear of spiders is irrational because they pose no real danger. 그의 거미에 대한 공포는 실제로 위험이 없기 때문에 비합리적입니다.

348

ignoble

[ɪɡˈnoʊ.bəl]

a. 비열한, 비천한

morality n. 도덕성
amoral a. 도덕을 모르는
anonym n. 가명, 익명
ignominious a. 수치스러운, 치욕적인

어원	-ig, -in : not + -noble 귀족의 → '귀족이 아니니 천한'
유의어	dishonorable, disgraceful, shameful
반의어	noble, honorable, virtuous
영영	Not honorable or noble in character; lacking moral or ethical principles.
예문	His ignoble actions tarnished his reputation. 그의 천하무시한 행동이 그의 평판을 손상시켰습니다.

349

profit

[ˈprɒf.ɪt]

n. 이익, 수익 v. 이익을 얻다

fiction n. 소설, 허구
profitable a. 수익이 되는, 이익이 되는
profitability n. 수익성, 유익성, 수익률
proficient a. 숙달된, 능숙한

어원	-pro : forth + -fac, -fec, -fic, -fy, -fair : make → '먼저 만들어야 이익이 난다'
유의어	earnings, income, gain
반의어	Loss, deficit, financial loss
영영	The financial gain or positive difference between revenue and expenses in a business or endeavor.
예문	The company's profit margin increased significantly this year. 그 회사의 이윤 마진은 올해 크게 증가했습니다.

350

marvel

[ˈmɑː.vəl]

n. 놀라운 일 v. 놀라다

marvelousness n. 경이로움, 놀라운 정도
miracle n. 기적
admirable a. 존경할 만한, 놀랄 만한

어원	-mir, -mar : wonder 놀라다 * 마블 영화를 보며 어벤저스에 놀라는
유의어	wonder, amazement, astonishment
반의어	ordinary, mundane, commonplace
영영	a wonderful or astonishing thing; to be filled with wonder.
예문	The breathtaking view from the mountain made us marvel at the beauty of nature. 산에서의 숨막히는 경치는 우리로 하여금 자연의 아름다움에 감탄하게 만들었다.

351	어원	* 의성어 / * -awe : away → 멀리 떨어져 경외심을 느끼는'
in awe of	유의어	in admiration of, amazed by, reverent towards
	반의어	unimpressed by, indifferent to, blasé about
p. ~을 두려워[경외]하다	영영	filled with admiration, reverence, or fear
awe n. 경외심 v. 경외심을 느끼다 awe-inspiring a. 경외심을 자아내는 awful a. 끔찍한 지독한 awesome a. 아주 멋진, 굉장한	예문	The audience was in awe of the magician's incredible tricks. 관객들은 마술사의 놀라운 마술에 감탄했습니다.
352	어원	-height 키 → '가장 높은 높이로 한창일 때'
at the height of	유의어	at the peak of, at the zenith of, at the summit of
	반의어	at the nadir of, at the lowest point of, at the bottom of
p. ~가 한창일 때	영영	at the highest point or level of
at no cost p. 공짜로 at no time p. 결코 ~하지 않다 at one's option p. ~의 마음대로 highten v. 고조시키다	예문	The fashion trend was at the height of its popularity last year. 패션 트렌드는 작년에 인기의 정점에 있었습니다.
353	어원	-in + -come 오다(E) → '안으로 들어온 소득'
live beyond one's income	유의어	overspend, live beyond one's means, be extravagant
	반의어	live within one's means, budget, economize
p. 수입을 초과하여 살다	영영	spend more money than one earns
income n. 소득 low-income p. 저소득의 per capita income p. 1인당 소득 overcome v. 극복하다, 이기다	예문	If you continue to live beyond your income, you will accumulate debt. 소득을 초과하여 살면, 빚을 더욱 쌓게 될 것입니다.
354	어원	no choice(선택 없이) to do(해야만) 하는
have no choice but to do	유의어	be compelled to do, be forced to do, have to do
	반의어	have a choice not to do, be voluntary to do
p. ~할 수 밖에 없다	영영	be compelled or forced to do
choose v. 선택하다 choice n. 선택물, 선택 사항 chore n. 잡일, 허드렛일 chord n. 코드, 화음	예문	She had no choice but to resign from her job after the company downsized. 회사가 축소되자 그녀는 직장을 사임할 수밖에 없었습니다.
355	어원	-have 갖다 + -discussion 토론 → '토론 시간을 갖는 것이니 토론을 벌이다'
have a discussion with	유의어	converse with, talk to, engage in a discussion with
	반의어	avoid a discussion with, evade a conversation with
p. ~와 토론을 벌이다	영영	engage in conversation with
discuss v. 토론하다, 논의하다 have a fit p. 화내다 have a taste for p. ~에 취미가 있다 have a breakdown p. 고장이 나다	예문	I need to have a discussion with my boss about my workload. 내 업무 부담에 대해 상사와 논의해야 합니다.
356	어원	-hold 잡다 + -on 붙어 → '딱 붙어 잡으니 ~에 매달리다'
hold on	유의어	wait, pause, hang on
	반의어	let go, release, relinquish
p. 붙잡고 있다, 기다리다, 고정시키다	영영	grasp or cling to something
get hold of p. ~을 구하다, 손에 넣다 hold A in check p. A를 억제하다 hold good p. 유효하다 hold one's tongue p. 입을 다물다	예문	Please hold on for a moment while I transfer your call. 전화를 연결하는 동안 잠시 기다려 주세요.

357

for a change

p. 여느 때와 달리, 기분 전환으로

change into p. ~으로 바뀌다
exchange v. 교환하다, 환전하다
interchange v. 교환하다
unchanged a. 불변의

어원	change(변화)를 for(위한) 것이니 기분 전환으로
유의어	for variety, as a variation, for something different
반의어	consistently, habitually, regularly
영영	as a variation or departure from the usual
예문	Let's eat out for a change instead of cooking at home. 집에서 요리하는 대신에 한 번 밖에서 식사를 해봐요.

358

by way of

p. ~ 의 방법으로, ~에 의해서, ~을 거쳐서

all the way p. 줄곧, 내내
make one's way p. 나아가다
in a big way p. 대규모로
in no way p. 결코 ~하지 않다

어원	-by는 수단, 방법 앞에 주로 쓰인다.
유의어	via, through, by means of
반의어	bypassing, avoiding, circumventing
영영	via, through, or by means of
예문	She traveled to Europe by way of London. 그녀는 런던을 경유하여 유럽으로 여행했습니다.

359

enter into

p. 시작하다, [계약 따위를] 맺다

enter v. 들어가다
entrance fee p. 입장료
entry n. 진입, 출입; 기입, 기재사항
entrant n. 신참, 참가자

어원	(사무실) enter into (안으로 들어가) 계약 맺기를 시작하다
유의어	engage in, participate in, embark on
반의어	withdraw from, retreat from, exit from
영영	become involved in or start participating in
예문	They entered into a partnership to launch the new product. 그들은 새 제품 출시를 위해 파트너십을 맺었습니다.

360

in a timely fashion

p. 시기 적절하게

fashion n. 유행, 인기, 풍조
in a timely manner p. 시기 적절한 방법으로
in a series p. 잇달아, 연이어
in accordance with p. ~에 준하여

어원	-time 시간 + fashion 유행 → '적시에 맞춘 유해으로'
유의어	promptly, punctually, on time
반의어	belatedly, tardily, behind schedule
영영	promptly or punctually
예문	Please submit your report in a timely fashion to meet the deadline. 마감일을 준수하기 위해 제때에 보고서를 제출해 주세요.

Chapter 10.

361	contradict	[ˌkɒn.trəˈdɪkt]	v. 반박하다
362	unease	[ʌnˈiːz]	n. 불안, 우려, 불안감
363	inspire	[inspáiər]	v. 고무하다, 격려하다, 영감을 주다
364	recollect	[ˌrek.əˈlekt]	v. 생각해내다, 회상하다
365	shrug	[ʃrʌg]	v. (어깨를) 으쓱하다
366	boredom	[ˈbɔː.dəm]	n. 지루함
367	prohibit	[prəˈhɪb.ɪt]	v. 금지하다, 제지하다
368	halve	[hɑːv]	v. 반으로 줄다, 이등분하다
369	nerve	[nɜːv]	n. 신경, 긴장, 불안
370	causal	[ˈkɔː.zəl]	a. 원인이 되는
371	accord	[əˈkɔːd]	v. 일치하다, 조화되다 n. 합의
372	unanimous	[juːˈnæn.ɪ.məs]	n. 만장일치
373	provision	[prəˈvɪʒ.ən]	n. 규정, 조항, 공급, 대비
374	shatter	[ˈʃæt.ər]	v. 산산이 부수다; n. 파편
375	pessimist	[ˈpes.ɪ.mɪst]	n. 비관론자, 염세주의자
376	severe	[sɪˈvɪər]	a. 엄격한, 가차없는, 혹독한
377	ballot	[ˈbæl.ət]	n. 투표
378	hoop	[huːp]	n. 테, 쇠테, 링, 굴렁쇠
379	resolute	[ˈrez.ə.luːt]	a. 결심이 굳은, 단호한
380	affect	[əˈfekt]	v. 영향을 주다, 작용하다; ~인 체하다
381	doctrine	[ˈdɒk.trɪn]	n. 가르침, 원리, 주의, 학설
382	renown	[rináun]	n. 명성, 유명
383	sob	[sɒb]	v. 흐느껴 울다
384	erect	[ɪˈrekt]	a. 똑바로 선 v. 세우다, 직립시키다
385	compel	[kəmˈpel]	v. 강요하다, ~하게 하다
386	sew	[səʊ]	v. 바느질하다, 깁다; 만들다; 달다, 꿰매다
387	stain	[steɪn]	n. 얼룩; 얼룩지다, 더럽히다
388	superstition	[ˌsuː.pəˈstɪʃ.ən]	n. 미신, 미신적 행위
389	depress	[dɪˈpres]	v. 낙담시키다; 불경기로 만들다
390	adhere	[ədˈhɪər]	v. 부착하다, 고수하다, 지지하다
391	can afford to do		p. ~할 여유가 있다, ~할 수 있다
392	have a point		p. 일리가 있다; 장점이 있다
393	take hold		p. 자리를 잡다, 확립하다, 정착하다
394	at a charge of		p. ~의 비용 부담으로
395	fall away		p. 서서히 사라지다
396	chances are		p. 아마 ~일 것이다
397	ahead of		p. ~앞에, ~보다 앞서는
398	at all costs		p. 무슨 수를 써서라도, 기어코
399	have a problem with		p. ~에 문제가 있다; ~에 반대하다
400	in the same way		p. 이와 마찬가지로

361

contradict
[ˌkɒn.trəˈdɪkt]

v. 반박하다

predict v. 예측하다, 예견하다
unpredictable a. 예측불가능한
dedicate v. 헌신하다, 전념하다, 바치다
valediction n. 고별

어원	-contra : opposite + -dict : say → '반대로 말하니 반박하다'
유의어	oppose, dispute, deny
반의어	agree, concur, correspond
영영	to deny or disagree with a statement or assertion.
예문	Her statements seem to contradict each other. 그녀의 진술은 서로 모순된 것처럼 보인다.

362

unease
[ʌnˈiːz]

n. 불안, 우려, 불안감

ill at ease p. 불편한
easygoin a. 느긋한, 태평스러운
easily adv. 쉽게
eat into p. ~을 잠식하다

어원	-un : not + -ease 완화하다 → '완화될 않으니 불안'
유의어	discomfort, anxiety, apprehension
반의어	comfort, ease, tranquility
영영	A feeling of discomfort, anxiety, or tension; a sense of being unsettled or uneasy.
예문	The constant noise from the construction site unased the residents. 건설 현장에서 계속되는 소음이 주민들을 불안하게 했습니다.

363

inspire
[inspáiər]

v. 고무하다, 격려하다, 영감을 주다

inspiration n. 영감, 고취, 고무
expiring a. 만료의, 숨을 거두려 하는
aspire v. 열망하다
respire v. 호흡하다, 숨쉬다

어원	-in : in + -spir, -spar : breathe → '안에 영혼을 불어 넣어 고무하다'
유의어	motivate, encourage, influence
반의어	Discourage, demotivate, dishearten
영영	To stimulate, encourage, or motivate someone to do something creative or extraordinary.
예문	Her determination and hard work inspired others to pursue their dreams. 그녀의 결심과 노력은 다른 사람들에게 꿈을 추구하도록 영감을 주었습니다.

364

recollect
[ˌrek.əˈlekt]

v. 생각해내다, 회상하다

collect on p. 회수하다
dialect n. 사투리, 방언
elect v. 선출하다, 선택하다
recollection n. 기억(력), 기억나게 하는 것

어원	-re : again + -col : together + -lec, -lect, -leg, -lig : gather 모으다 → '다시 함께 모은 생각이 회상'
유의어	remember, recall, reminisce
반의어	forget, erase, abandon
영영	To remember or recall something from the past.
예문	She tried to recollect the details of the conversation from memory. 그녀는 대화의 세부 내용을 기억에서 되새기려고 노력했다.

365

shrug
[ʃrʌg]

v. (어깨를) 으쓱하다

shudder v. 몸을 떨다, 전율하다
shiver n. 떨림, 전율 v. 몸을 떨다
shake v. 흔들다; 충격을 주다
shuffle v. 발을 끌며 걷다; 카드를 섞다

어원	* -sh, -shi : shake / shoulder 어깨 → '어깨를 흔들며 으쓱'
유의어	raise shoulders, dismiss, disregard
반의어	emphasize, accentuate
영영	raise and lower one's shoulders to express indifference or uncertainty
예문	When asked about his mistake, he just shrugged and walked away. 자신의 실수에 대해 물어보면 그는 어깨를 으쓱하고 걸어갔다.

366

boredom
[ˈbɔː.dəm]

n. 지루함

bore v. 지루하게 만들다
bored a. 지루한
boring a. 지루하게 만드는
botany n. 식물학

어원	-bore 지루하게 만들다 + -dom 명접
유의어	tedium, ennui, monotony
반의어	Interest, excitement, enthusiasm
영영	The state of being uninterested or disengaged due to lack of excitement or stimulation.
예문	The long wait at the airport led to a sense of boredom among passengers. 공항에서의 긴 대기는 승객들 사이에서 지루함을 느끼게 했습니다.

367

prohibit

[prəˈhɪb.ɪt]

v. 금지하다, 제지하다

on exhibit p. 전시되어, 출품되어
inhibit v. 저해하다, 억제하다
habitat n. 서식지, 거주지
inhabit v. 살다, 거주하다

어원	-pro : in front + -hib : hold → '앞에서 잡고 하지 못하게 하다'
유의어	forbid, ban, disallow
반의어	permit, allow
영영	to formally forbid or prevent something by law or regulation; to ban or disallow
예문	The prohibition of alcohol during the event helped maintain order. 행사 중의 주류 금지가 질서를 유지하는 데 도움이 되었다.

368

halve

[hɑːv]

v. 반으로 줄다, 이등분하다

halfway a. 중간의, 불완전한
half off p. 반값 할인
halfhearted a. 열의가 없는
hallway n. 복도

어원	-halve : half 절반 → '절반으로 이등분하다'
유의어	cut in half, divide by two, split
반의어	double, increase, multiply
영영	to divide into two equal parts; to cut in half.
예문	She decided to halve the recipe to make a smaller portion. 그녀는 작은 양을 만들기 위해 레시피를 반으로 나누기로 결정했다.

369

nerve

[nɜːv]

n. 신경, 긴장, 불안

nervous a. 긴장되는
nervously adv. 초조하게
neurological a. 신경학의
neurology n. 신경학

어원	-nerv, -neur, -neuro 신경
유의어	courage, bravery, audacity
반의어	cowardice, fearfulness, timidity
영영	Courage, boldness, or fortitude in the face of challenges or danger.
예문	It takes a lot of nerve to speak in front of a large audience. 대규모 관객 앞에서 말하는 데에는 많은 용기가 필요합니다.

370

causal

[ˈkɔː.zəl]

a. 원인이 되는

cause v. 초래하다; n. 원인, 이유
causality n. 인과 관계
causative a. 원인이 되는
caution n. 주의, 조심

어원	-cause, -cuse : reason → '이유가 원인이 되는'
유의어	causative, resulting, connected
반의어	resultant, secondary
영영	relating to a cause and effect relationship
예문	The causal relationship between smoking and lung cancer is well-established. 흡연과 폐암 사이의 인과관계는 잘 알려져 있다.

371

accord

[əˈkɔːd]

v. 일치하다, 조화되다 n. 합의

hard core p. 핵심적인
to the core p. 깊숙이, 핵심까지
in accord with p. ~와 부합하여, 일치하여
encore n. 앙코르

어원	-ac : to + -cord, -cour, -cor : heart 마음, 심장 → '한 방향으로 마음이 일치하니 합의'
유의어	agreement, pact, treaty
반의어	discord, disagreement, conflict
영영	An agreement or harmony between people or groups.
예문	They reached an accord after lengthy negotiations. 그들은 긴 협상 끝에 합의에 도달했다.

372

unanimous

[juːˈnæn.ɪ.məs]

n. 만장일치

animal n. 동물(영혼을 가진 것)
mammal n. 포유류, 포유동물
unanimously adv. 만장일치로
animosity n. 적의, 증오, 악의, 원한

어원	-uni : one + -anim 정신 → '하나의 정신으로 만장일치'
유의어	agreed, united, in accord
반의어	divided, split
영영	characterized by complete agreement or consensus among all parties or individuals involved
예문	The board of directors was unanimous in their decision to expand the company. 이사회는 회사를 확장하기로 결정한 데 동의했다.

373

provision

[prəˈvɪʒ.ən]

n. 규정, 조항, 공급, 대비

provide A to B p. A를 B에게 공급하다
provide A with B p. A를 B에게 공급하다
provisional a. 일시적인 잠정적인
provident a. 신중한 조심스러운

어원	-pro : forward + -vis : look → '미래에 문제가 생길 것을 대비해 규정과 조항을 준비'
유의어	supply, equipment, resources
반의어	deprivation, shortage
영영	the act of supplying or providing something; a clause or condition in a legal document or agreement
예문	The contract includes a provision for early termination if certain conditions are met. 계약에는 특정 조건이 충족되면 조기 해지를 위한 조항이 포함되어 있다.

374

shatter

[ˈʃæt.ər]

v. 산산이 부수다; n. 파편

shave v. 깎다, 면도하다
scatter v. 흩뜨리다, 흩어지게 하다
sprinkle v. 뿌리다
shed n. 헛간 v. 깎다 v. 비추다

어원	-sha, -shi, -she, -sho : cut → '날카롭게 부서진 조각'
유의어	break, fracture, smash
반의어	mend, repair
영영	to break into many pieces with a violent force; to destroy or damage severely
예문	The glass shattered into pieces when it fell on the floor. 유리가 바닥에 떨어져 조각으로 깨졌다.

375

pessimist

[ˈpes.ɪ.mɪst]

n. 비관론자, 염세주의자

opt v. 택하다
optimistic a. 낙관적인, 낙천적인
pessimism n. 비관론, 염세주의
suboptimal a. 차선의

어원	-pessim 최악 + -ist 사람 → '최악이 될 거라 말하는 사람'
유의어	cynic, downbeat, defeatist
반의어	optimist, positive thinker
영영	a person who tends to see or expect the worst outcome in situations; a negative thinker
예문	She tends to be a pessimist and always expects the worst outcome. 그녀는 비관주의자적 경향이 있고 항상 최악의 결과를 예상한다.

376

severe

[sɪˈvɪər]

a. 엄격한, 가차없는, 혹독한

sever v. 끊다, 절단하다
several a. 몇 개의
select v. 선택하다
severely adv. 심하게, 심각하게

어원	-se : cut + -ver, -par, -per : divide → '의견을 가차없이 자르니 엄격한'
유의어	harsh, intense, extreme
반의어	Mild, gentle, lenient
영영	Extremely serious or harsh in nature; causing great discomfort or damage.
예문	The severe weather conditions forced the event to be canceled. 엄격한 기상 조건으로 인해 행사가 취소되었습니다.

377

ballot

[ˈbæl.ət]

n. 투표

ball n. 볼; 무도회, 댄스 파티
ballet n. 발레
bullet n. 총알
bulla n. 인장, 수포

어원	-ball, -bull 둥근; 던지다 → '작은 공으로 투표' - 이태리에서는 검은 공으로 투표를 하기도 했다
유의어	vote, election, polling
반의어	Dictatorship, autocracy, one-person rule
영영	A method of voting or casting votes by secret written or printed ballot.
예문	Citizens cast their votes using a secret ballot in the election. 시민들은 선거에서 비밀 투표를 통해 투표를 했습니다.

378

hoop

[huːp]

n. 테, 쇠테, 링, 굴렁쇠

hula hoop p. 훌라후프 '훌라춤 모양의 링'
loop n. 고리
hop v. 깡충 뛰다
grasshopper n. 메뚜기

어원	-hoop 원형 밴드 → '둥글게 생긴 링으로 굴렁쇠 놀이'
유의어	ring, circle, band
반의어	gap, opening
영영	a circular or ring-shaped object; a flexible band often used for games or holding things
예문	The basketball player made a perfect shot through the hoop. 농구 선수가 훌륭한 숏을 바구니를 통해 넣었다.

379

resolute

[ˈrez.ə.luːt]

a. 결심이 굳은, 단호한

resolution n. 결심, 결의; 해결, 해답
resolve v. 결심하다, 해결하다
dissolute a. 방탕한, 타락한
with respect to p. ~에 관해서

어원	-re : against + -solu : loosen → '느슨하게 푸는 것의 반대니 단호한'
유의어	determined, steadfast, unwavering
반의어	indecisive, wavering
영영	determined and unwavering in purpose or opinion; characterized by firmness and determination
예문	She was resolute in her decision to pursue her dreams, no matter the obstacles. 그녀는 장애물이 무엇이든 간에 꿈을 추구하기로 결심했다.

380

affect

[əˈfekt]

v. 영향을 주다, 작용하다; ~인 체하다

perfect a. 완전한, 완벽한
defect n. 결점, 결함, 결핍
infect v. 감염시키다
affective a. 감정적인, 정서적인

어원	-af : to + -fac, -fec, -fic, -fy, -fair : do 하다 (L) → '~방향으로 행해서 영향을 미치다'
유의어	influence, impact, sway
반의어	effect, influence, impact
영영	Influence or have an impact on something.
예문	The economic downturn will affect many businesses. 경기 침체는 많은 기업에 영향을 미칠 것입니다.

381

doctrine

[ˈdɒk.trɪn]

n. 가르침, 원리, 주의, 학설

doctor n. 의사, 박사
document n. 문서
dodge v. 잽싸게 피하다
dodgy a. 교활한, 요리조리 피하는

어원	-doc 아이를 가르치다(L) → '가르치는 원리나 학설'
유의어	belief, teaching, ideology
반의어	Heresy, blasphemy, non-belief
영영	A set of beliefs or principles that form the basis of a religion, philosophy, or political system.
예문	The government plans to enact new legislation to address environmental issues. 정부는 환경 문제를 다루기 위해 새로운 법률을 시행하기로 계획하고 있습니다.

382

renown

[rináun]

n. 명성, 유명

anonymous a. 익명의
antonym a. 반의어
synonym n. 동의어, 유의어
renowned a. 유명한, 명성 있는

어원	-re : again + -no, -nomen : name → '자꾸 이름이 알려지니 유명한'
유의어	fame, reputation, celebrity
반의어	obscurity, anonymity, unknown status
영영	Being widely recognized and celebrated; fame or reputation.
예문	The author gained renown for her bestselling novels. 그 작가는 베스트셀러 소설로 명성을 얻었습니다.

383

sob

[sɒb]

v. 흐느껴 울다

sore a. 아픈 따가운
sorrow n. 슬픔, 비애
sour a. 신, 시큼한
a sort of p. 일종의

어원	-so : sorrow 슬픔 → '슬픔으로 흐느껴 울다' * ache 갑자기 생기는 통증 VS pain ache보다 아픈 고통 VS sore 신체의 일부에 생기는 고통
유의어	cry, weep, wail
반의어	laugh, chuckle
영영	cry loudly expressing deep sorrow or distress
예문	She couldn't help but sob when she heard the sad news. 그녀는 슬픈 소식을 듣자마자 흐느끼지 않을 수 없었다.

384

erect

[ɪˈrekt]

a. 똑바로 선 v. 세우다, 직립시키다

in the direction of p. ~의 방향으로
indirect a. 간접적인, 우회하는
rectify v. 개정하다
recuperate v. 회복하다, 만회하다

어원	-e : out + -rec, -rect, -reg, -reig, -roy 올바른(L) → '바깥 세상에 올바르게 선'
유의어	upright, standing, vertical
반의어	dismantle, disassemble, take apart
영영	upright or standing in position.
예문	The construction workers will erect the new building. 공사 근로자들이 새로운 건물을 세울 것입니다.

385

compel

[kəm|pel]

v. 강요하다, ~하게 하다

repel v. 물리치다, 쫓아버리다
propel v. 추진하다, 밀어내다
dispel v. 떨쳐 버리다, 없애다
impel v. 재촉하다

어원	-com : together + -pel, -peal, pul : drive 몰다 → '같이 몰아 붙이다' syn. propel, impel
유의어	force, oblige, require
반의어	discourage, dissuade, deter
영영	to force or drive someone to do something.
예문	His compelling story moved the audience to tears. 그의 강력한 이야기는 청중을 눈물짓게 만들었다.

386

sew

[səʊ]

v. 바느질하다, 깁다; 만들다; 달다, 꿰매다

sewer n. 하수관, 수채통
sewage n. 하수, 오물, 오수
stitch v. 바느질하다; n. 바늘땀, 코, 바느질
shiver n. 떨림, 전율

어원	-sew : stitch 바느질하다
유의어	stitch, stitch up, mend
반의어	rip, tear
영영	join or mend fabric using a needle and thread
예문	She learned how to sew and made her own clothes. 그녀는 바느질을 배우고 자신의 옷을 만들었다.

387

stain

[steɪn]

n. 얼룩; 얼룩지다, 더럽히다

smear n. 얼룩
stainless a. 때 끼지 않은, 녹슬지 않은
stationery n. 문방구, 문구류
stationer n. 문구상

어원	-stain 얼룩, 녹 → '얼룩으로 더럽히다
유의어	spot, blemish, discolor
반의어	clean, purify
영영	a mark or discoloration on a surface caused by a substance or material; to discolor or mar the appearance of something
예문	The red wine left a stubborn stain on the white tablecloth. 빨간 와인이 흰 식탁보에 난덕지게 얼룩을 남겼다.

388

superstition

[ˌsuːpə|stɪʃən]

n. 미신, 미신적 행위

superstitious a. 미신적인, 미신에 사로잡힌
supernatural a. 초자연적인, 불가사의한
subsist v. 살아가다; 존재하다
such A as B p. B와 같은 A

어원	-super : over + sti : stand → '위에 서 있는 존재니 미신적인'
유의어	belief in magic, irrational belief, folklore
반의어	Rationality, reason, logic
영영	A belief or practice resulting from ignorance or fear of the unknown, often with no scientific or logical basis.
예문	Some people believe in superstitions like avoiding black cats. 어떤 사람들은 흑고양이를 피하는 등의 미신을 믿습니다.

389

depress

[dɪ|pres]

v. 낙담시키다; 불경기로 만들다

depression n. 의기소침; 불경기
oppress v. 억압하다
suppress v. 진압하다, 억제하다; 참다
appress v. 억압하다, 우울하게 하다

어원	-de : down + -press 누르다 → '기분을 눌러 우울하게 만들다'
유의어	sadden, dishearten, demoralize
반의어	elevate, uplift, raise
영영	To make someone feel sad or discouraged; to lower or reduce something.
예문	Continuous rainy weather can sometimes depress one's mood. 계속되는 비날씨는 가끔 기분을 우울하게 할 수 있다.

390

adhere

[əd|hɪər]

v. 부착하다, 고수하다, 지지하다

coincide with p. ~와 부합하다, 일치하다
coincidence n. 우연의 일치
hesitate v. 주저하다, 망설이다
cohesion n. 응집력

어원	-ad : to + -her, -here, -hes : cling, stick → '~방향으로 딱 부착'
유의어	stick, cling, attach
반의어	detach, disconnect
영영	to stick or attach firmly to something; to remain loyal or committed to a particular belief or principle
예문	It's important to adhere to the safety guidelines when handling chemicals. 화학 물질을 다룰 때 안전 지침을 준수하는 것이 중요하다.

391

can afford to do

p. ~할 여유가 있다, ~할 수 있다

afford v. ~할 여유가 있다
affordable a. ~할 여유가 있는; 저렴한
affordability n. 구매 비용을 감당할 수 있음
affinity n. 유사성; 호감, 애정

어원	-af : to + -ord : order → '명령을 하는 입장이니 여유가 있다'
유의어	have the means to do, have the resources to do, be able to do
반의어	cannot afford to do, be unable to do
영영	have the financial means to do
예문	They can afford to go on vacation this year because they saved money. 그들은 돈을 저축했기 때문에 올해 휴가를 갈 수 있습니다.

392

have a point

p. 일리가 있다; 장점이 있다

make a point p. 강조하다; 주장을 밝히다
point of view n. 관점
point out p. 가리키다, 지적하다
at some point p. 어느 시점에서

어원	-have 갖다 + -point 요점 → '요점을 갖고 있으니 일리가 있다'
유의어	be right, be correct, have a valid argument
반의어	be mistaken, be incorrect, be wrong
영영	have a valid or reasonable argument
예문	Sarah has a point about the importance of time management. 사라는 시간 관리의 중요성에 대한 요점이 있습니다.

393

take hold

p. 자리를 잡다, 확립하다, 정착하다

get hold of p. ~을 구하다, 손에 넣다
hold A in check p. A를 억제하다
hold on p. 붙잡고 있다, 잠시만
hold out p. ~을 내밀다

어원	-take 취하다 + -hold 잡다 → '잡을 곳을 취해 자리 잡다'
유의어	grasp, seize, take control
반의어	release, let go, relinquish
영영	grasp or seize firmly
예문	The new policy began to take hold within the organization. 새로운 정책이 조직 내에서 정착하기 시작했습니다.

394

at a charge of

p. ~의 비용 부담으로

in charge of p. ~에 대한 책임이 있다
recharge v. 재충전하다
discharge v. 해임하다, 방출하다
at all cost p. 기어코, 무슨 수를 써서라도

어원	-at 점 + -charge 비용 → '지정한 비용으로'
유의어	for a fee of, for a price of, at a cost of
반의어	free of charge, without charge, at no cost
영영	for a specified price or fee
예문	The mechanic fixed the car at a charge of $200. 정비공은 자동차를 200달러에 고쳤습니다.

395

fall away

p. 서서히 사라지다

fall v. 떨어지다 n. 가을
fall down p. 넘어지다
fall apart p. 무너지다
fall on p. ~에게 부과되다, 맡겨지다

어원	-fall 떨어지다 + -away 멀리 → '멀리 떨어져 사라지다'
유의어	decline, diminish, decrease
반의어	rise, ascend, increase
영영	diminish or decline gradually
예문	As the project progressed, support for the initial proposal began to fall away. 프로젝트가 진행됨에 따라 초기 제안에 대한 지지가 사라지기 시작했습니다.

396

chances are

p. 아마 ~일 것이다

chance n. 기회, 우연 a. 우연한, 뜻밖의
above chance p. 우연의 확률을 넘는
by chance p. 어쩌다가
mischance n. 불운, 불행

어원	-chance 기회, 운 → '운으로 발생하는 것이니 아마 ~일 것이다' * chance '운에 의한 기회' VS opportunity '준비로 맞이한 기회'
유의어	likelihood is, it's probable that, it's likely that
반의어	chances aren't, it's improbable that
영영	it is likely or probable
예문	Chances are it will rain tomorrow based on the weather forecast. 기상 예보를 보면 내일 비가 올 가능성이 있습니다.

397

ahead of

p. ~앞에, ~보다 앞서는

ahead adv. 앞으로, 앞에; 미리
head on p. 정면으로
off the top of one's head p. 당장은
headlong adv. 거꾸로; 성급하게

어원	-a 하나 + -head 머리 → '머리보다 한 발 앞서'
유의어	in advance of, before, prior to
반의어	behind, after, following
영영	in advance of or before
예문	She finished the project ahead of schedule. 그녀는 일정보다 빠르게 프로젝트를 완료했습니다.

398

at all costs

p. 무슨 수를 써서라도, 기어코

at an angle p. 비스듬히
at all times p. 항상
at a loss p. 어쩔 줄을 모르는
at a distance p. 멀리서

어원	-all + -cost → '모든 비용을 들여서라도'
유의어	no matter what, regardless of the expense, by any means necessary
반의어	at no cost, at no expense, without any sacrifice
영영	regardless of the expense or sacrifice involved
예문	We must protect the environment at all costs. 우리는 환경을 위해 모든 비용을 들여 보호해야 합니다.

399

have a problem with

p. ~에 문제가 있다; ~에 반대하다

have no patience with p. 참을 수 없다
have trouble -ing p. ~하는데 어려움을 겪다
have a problem in -ing p. 어려움을 겪다
have A ready p. A를 준비시키다

어원	-have 갖다 + -problem 문제 → '문제를 갖고 있으니 문제가 있다'
유의어	disagree with, object to, take issue with
반의어	agree with, accept, support
영영	disagree with or object to
예문	He has a problem with authority figures. 그는 권위 있는 인물에 문제가 있습니다.

400

in the same way

p. 이와 마찬가지로

in the way p. ~의 방식대로
stand in the way p. 방해가 되다
be in the way p. 방해가 되다
in no way p. 결코 ~하지 않다

어원	-in 안 + -same 같은 + -way 방식 → '~의 같은 방식 안에서'
유의어	similarly, likewise, in a similar manner
반의어	differently, dissimilarly, disparately
영영	similarly or comparably
예문	Cats clean themselves in the same way as they groom each other. 고양이는 서로를 손질하는 것과 마찬가지로 스스로 청결을 유지합니다.

Chapter 11.

401	beloved	[bɪˈlʌv.ɪd]	a. (대단히) 사랑하는
402	obedient	[əˈbiː.di.ənt]	a. 순종하는
403	sneeze	[sniːz]	v. 재채기를 하다
404	transmit	[trænzˈmɪt]	v. 보내다, 전송하다; 전도하다; 전염시키다
405	optimal	[ˈɒp.tɪ.məl]	a. 최선의, 최적의
406	mindlessly	[ˈmaɪnd.ləs.li]	adv. 무심코, 분별없이, 어리석게
407	accuse	[əˈkjuːz]	v. 고발하다, 기소하다, 비난하다
408	parachute	[ˈpær.ə.ʃuːt]	n. 낙하산
409	derive	[dɪˈraɪv]	v. 비롯되다, 유래하다; 끌어내다, 유도하다
410	neutral	[ˈnjuː.trəl]	a. 중립의, 중간의; 감정이 드러나지 않는
411	intense	[ɪnˈtens]	a. 강렬한, 치열한, 심한
412	demand	[dɪˈmɑːnd]	v. 요구하다, 청구하다; 수요
413	statement	[ˈsteɪt.mənt]	n. 성명, 성명서; 명세서; 진술, 연설
414	solvent	[ˈsɒl.vənt]	a. 지급 능력이 있는; 용해력이 있는; 용매, 용제
415	neural	[njúərəl]	a. 신경의
416	cite	[saɪt]	v. 인용하다; 언급하다; 소환하다
417	esteem	[ɪˈstiːm]	n. 존경, 경의; 존경하다, 존중하다
418	perspective	[pəˈspek.tɪv]	n. 원근법; 경치; 관점, 시야
419	deter	[ditə́ːr]	v. 그만두게 하다, 단념시키다, 저지하다
420	lament	[ləˈment]	n. 애도; v. 애통하다
421	disorder	[dɪˈsɔː.dər]	n. 따라오지 않는(무질서)
422	evacuate	[ɪˈvæk.ju.eɪt]	v. 대피시키다, 철수시키다
423	pursue	[pəˈsjuː]	v. 해나가다, 추구하다
424	endanger	[ɪnˈdeɪn.dʒər]	v. 위태롭게 하다
425	obstruct	[əbˈstrʌkt]	v. 막다, 방해하다
426	alliance	[əˈlaɪ.əns]	n. 동맹, 동맹국, 협력, 협조, 친화
427	debate	[dɪˈbeɪt]	v. 논쟁하다, 토론하다 n. 논쟁
428	solemn	[ˈsɒl.əm]	a. 엄숙한, 침통한
429	pity	[ˈpɪt.i]	n. 연민, 동정, 유감
430	halt	[hɒlt]	n. 멈춤, 중단 v. 멈추다, 서다
431	at the beginning of		p. ~의 시작에
432	have a taste for		p. ~을 좋아하다, ~에 취미가 있다.
433	table of contents		p. (책 등의) 목차
434	get along with		p. ~와 잘 지내다
435	a quantity of		p. 많은, 다량의
436	after the fact		p. (이미 일이 벌어지고 난) 사후에
437	to that end		p. 이를 위해, 그 목적을 달성하기 위하여
438	fall on		p. ~에게 부과되다, ~ 맡겨지다; ~을 습격하다
439	draw A out		p. A를 끌어내다
440	in one's opinion		p. ~의 의견으로는, ~의 입장에서는

401

beloved

[bɪˈlʌv.ɪd]

a. (대단히) 사랑하는

lovely a. 사랑스러운, 아름다운
would love to p. ~하기를 정말 원하다
lead by example p. 솔선수범하다
lead up to p. ~까지 이르다

어원	-be loved 수동형
유의어	cherished, adored, dear
반의어	despised, detested, loathed
영영	Loved and cherished deeply, often referring to a person.
예문	The beloved family pet brought joy to everyone's lives. 사랑하는 가족 애완 동물은 모든 사람의 삶에 기쁨을 주었다.

402

obedient

[əˈbiː.di.ənt]

a. 순종하는

obey v. 순종하다
obedience n. 복종, 순종
disobey v. 반항하다
obesity n. 비만

어원	-ob : to + -eis, -ey, -aud : hear → '~쪽 방향으로 듣고 순종하는'
유의어	compliant, submissive, dutiful
반의어	Disobedient, rebellious, defiant
영영	Willing to comply or follow instructions or orders; submissive to authority.
예문	The obedient dog followed its owner's commands without hesitation. 순종적인 개는 소유자의 명령을 주저하지 않고 따랐습니다.

403

sneeze

[sni:z]

v. 재채기를 하다

snorty a. 공격적인, 경멸스러운
snortingly adv. 코를 불며
snore v. 코를 골다
sniff v. 코를 킁킁거리다, 훌쩍이다

어원	-sno, -sne : snort 코골이 + -no : noise → '코 안의 신경이 자극 받아 재채기'
유의어	snort, sniff, achoo
반의어	suppress, stifle
영영	to expel air suddenly and involuntarily from the nose and mouth, often in response to irritation or illness
예문	He couldn't help but sneeze when he inhaled the dusty air. 그는 먼지 낀 공기를 들이마실 때 재채기를 할 수밖에 없었다.

404

transmit

[trænzˈmɪt]

v. 보내다, 전송하다; 전도하다; 전염시키다

transmitter n. 송달자, 전달자, 송신기
transmittable a. 전할 수 있는, 전염성의
omit v. 생략하다, 빠뜨리다
remission n. 용서, 면제

어원	-trans : across + -mit : send → '건너서 보내니 전염까지'
유의어	send, transfer, broadcast
반의어	Receive, accept, take in
영영	To send or pass along something, such as information or signals, from one place to another.
예문	The radio tower can transmit signals over long distances. 라디오 타워는 멀리까지 신호를 전송할 수 있습니다.

405

optimal

[ˈɒp.tɪ.məl]

a. 최선의, 최적의

opt v. 택하다
optimistic a. 낙관적인, 낙천적인
pessimism n. 비관론, 염세주의
suboptimal a. 차선의

어원	-optim 최고 → '최고로 열심히 하니 최선의'
유의어	ideal, best, optimal
반의어	suboptimal, inferior
영영	best or most favorable under given circumstances
예문	The optimal time to plant tomatoes is in the spring. 토마토를 심는 최적의 시기는 봄이다.

406

mindlessly

[ˈmaɪnd.ləs.li]

adv. 무심코, 분별없이, 어리석게

mindfull of p. ~을 염두에 두는
keep in mind p. ~을 명심하다
keep A in mind p. A를 명심하다
mindless a. 아무 생각이 없는

어원	-mind 마음 + -less 無 → '마음이 없으니 분별없이 어리석게'
유의어	thoughtlessly, without thinking, automatically
반의어	consciously, purposefully, deliberately
영영	Acting or behaving without conscious thought or awareness; in a thoughtless or automatic manner.
예문	He mindlessly scrolled through his social media feed for hours. 그는 몇 시간 동안 무의식적으로 소셜 미디어 피드를 스크롤했습니다.

407

accuse

[əˈkjuːz]

v. 고발하다, 기소하다, 비난하다

cause v. 초래하다; n. 원인, 이유
causality n. 인과 관계
excuse oneself for p. ~에 대해 변명하다
accused n. 피고인, 피의자

어원	-ac : to + -cuse : reason → '~쪽으로 이유를 돌리는 것이 고발'
같은어	charge, indict, allege
반의어	exonerate, vindicate, absolve
영영	Charge someone with wrongdoing or make an allegation against them.
예문	She accused him of stealing her wallet. 그녀는 지갑을 훔쳤다고 그를 고발했습니다.

408

parachute

[ˈpær.əˌʃuːt]

n. 낙하산

chute n. 활강로, 비탈진 수로
paraglide v. 패러글라이딩하다
paragliding n. 패러글라이딩
appear to do p. ~하는 것으로 보이다

어원	-para 막다 + -chu 떨어지다 → 떨어지는 걸 막는 낙하산' * '슈~' 하고 떨어지는 것을 막아주는 낙하산
같은어	chute, descent device, skydiving equipment
반의어	Fall, drop, descend
영영	A device used for slowing the descent of a person or object through the air.
예문	The skydiver pulled the ripcord to release the parachute. 스카이다이버는 낙하산을 풀기 위해 리피드 코를 당겼습니다.

409

derive

[dɪˈraɪv]

v. 비롯되다, 유래하다; 끌어내다, 유도하다

derived a. 유래된
derivative a. ~에서 끌어낸, 모방적인
derive from p. ~에서 유래하다
riiverine a. 강변의

어원	-de : apart + -riv : river → 떨어져 흐르는 강을 보니 거기서 비롯되다, 유래하다'
같은어	obtain, extract, acquire
반의어	originate, begin
영영	to obtain or receive something from a source or origin; to deduce or infer something from information or evidence
예문	The scientist was able to derive valuable insights from the data. 과학자는 데이터에서 가치 있는 통찰력을 얻을 수 있었다.

410

neutral

[ˈnjuː.trəl]

a. 중립의, 중간의; 감정이 드러나지 않는

denial n. 부인, 부정
negatively adv. 부정적으로
neglect v. 소홀히 하다, 경시하다
neutrality n. 중립성, 중립

어원	-ne : deny + -utr : either → '이쪽도 저쪽도 부인하니 중립으로 감정이 드러나지 않는'
같은어	impartial, unbiased, uninvolved
반의어	Biased, prejudiced, partial
영영	Not taking sides or showing bias; having a pH level of 7 in chemistry.
예문	The car's transmission was in neutral, so it didn't move. 차의 변속기가 중립 상태였기 때문에 움직이지 않았습니다.

411

intense

[ɪnˈtens]

a. 강렬한, 치열한, 심한

intensely adv. 극심하게, 강렬하게
intensity n. 강렬함, 격렬함
intensive a. 집중적인
tension n. 긴장

어원	-in + -tend, -tens, -tent : stretch 뻗다, 넓게 펴다 → '안으로 신경이 뻗쳐 있으니 강렬하고 치열한'
같은어	fierce, extreme, concentrated
반의어	mild, gentle
영영	extreme in degree or strength
예문	The intense heat made it difficult to stay outside. 강렬한 더위로 밖에 머물기 어려웠다.

412

demand

[dɪˈmɑːnd]

v. 요구하다, 청구하다; 수요

commend v. 칭찬하다; 맡기다, 위탁하다
command v. 명령하다
demand for p. ~에 대한 요구
in high demand p. 수요가 많은

어원	-de : intensive + -mand, -mend : order / entrust → '명령하듯 요구하는 것이 요구'
같은어	request, call for, require
반의어	Supply, offer, provision
영영	The desire or need for a product, service, or resource, often in the marketplace.
예문	There is a high demand for the latest smartphones in the market. 시장에서 최신 스마트폰에 대한 높은 수요가 있습니다.

413

statement

[ˈsteɪt.mənt]

n. 성명, 성명서; 명세서; 진술, 연설

make a statement p. 성명하다, 진술하다
statesman n. 정치가
unstated a. 발표되지 않은
restate v. 새로 진술하다

어원	-stat,-sta, -sist, -ste, -st, -stitu, -stin, -sti : stand (E) → '똑바로 설 수 있는 상태', '똑바로 세운 국가에 서서 분명히 말하는 진술'
유의어	declaration, assertion, announcement
반의어	Silence, non-expression, lack of communication
영영	A written or spoken declaration, assertion, or remark that conveys information or an opinion.
예문	The CEO made a public statement regarding the company's future plans. CEO는 회사의 미래 계획에 관한 공개적인 성명을 내놓았습니다.

414

solvent

[ˈsɒl.vənt]

a. 지급 능력이 있는; 용해력이 있는; 용매, 용제

solution n. 해결, 녹임; 용액
soluble a. 해결 가능한; 녹는
insoluble a. 용해지지 않는; 해결할 수 없는
somber a. 어두운, 음침한; 우울한

어원	-sol, -solu : loosen → '물에서 느슨하게 녹이는', 느슨하게 문제를 풀어 해결' * solu(t) '물에 녹아 없어짐' VS lo(t) '물로 씻어냄'
유의어	liquid, solution, dissolvent
반의어	insolvent, bankrupt, indebted
영영	a substance capable of dissolving other substances.
예문	The company was not financially solvent and had to declare bankruptcy. 그 회사는 재정적으로 안정되지 않았으며 파산을 선언해야 했다.

415

neural

[njúərəl]

a. 신경의

nervous a. 긴장되는
neurological a. 신경학의
neurologist n. 신경학자
neurology n. 신경학

어원	-nerv, -neur, -neuro 신경
유의어	nerve-related, nerve-cell, neurological
반의어	Non-neural, non-nervous, non-neuronal
영영	Relating to the nerves or the nervous system.
예문	Neural networks are used in machine learning algorithms. 신경망은 기계 학습 알고리즘에서 사용됩니다.

416

cite

[saɪt]

v. 인용하다; 언급하다; 소환하다

recite v. 낭송하다
excite v. 흥분시키다
incite v. 자극하다, 선동하다
quotation n. 인용구, 인용

어원	-cit, -cite : summon, call 부르다 → '문장을 부르니 인용하다'
유의어	mention, quote, reference
반의어	omit, disregard, ignore
영영	To quote or mention as evidence or an example in support of an argument or statement.
예문	In his research paper, he will cite various sources to support his claims. 그의 연구 논문에서 그는 자신의 주장을 뒷받침하기 위해 다양한 출처를 인용할 것이다.

417

esteem

[ɪˈstiːm]

n. 존경, 경의; 존경하다, 존중하다

estimate v. 평가하다, 추정하다
self-esteem p. 자존감, 자부심
hold in low esteem p. ~을 낮게 평가하다
ethic n. 도덕, 윤리, 가치체계

어원	-esteem : value → '가치 있게 생각하는'
유의어	respect, admire, regard highly
반의어	disrespect, disdain, contempt
영영	respect and admiration for someone or something.
예문	She held her teacher in high esteem for the knowledge and guidance provided. 그녀는 선생님을 높이 존경했으며 지식과 지도력을 제공했다.

418

perspective

[pəˈspek.tɪv]

n. 원근법; 경치; 관점, 시야

prospective a. 미래의
proscribe v. 금지하다, 배척하다
prosecute v. 기소하다, 추진하다
prosper v. 번영하다, 성공하다

어원	-per : through + -spec : look → '두루 보는 경치는 원근법으로 보는 관점'
유의어	viewpoint, standpoint, outlook
반의어	Myopia, narrow view, limited outlook
영영	A particular point of view or way of looking at something; a mental outlook or frame of reference.
예문	Changing your perspective can lead to a deeper understanding of a situation. 시각을 바꾸면 상황에 대한 깊은 이해를 얻을 수 있을 수 있습니다.

419

deter
[dɪtə́ːr]

v. 그만두게 하다, 단념시키다, 저지하다

terrible a. 무서운
detergent n. 세제
deterrent a. 제지시키는, 방해하는
terrain n. 지형, 지역, 지세

어원	-de : off + -ter : frighted → '겁을 줘서 떨어뜨리는'
유의어	clean, clear, broom
반의어	scatter, disperse
영영	clean or clear an area by removing dirt or debris
예문	She used a broom to sweep the floor clean. 그녀는 바닥을 깨끗하게 쓸 때 빗자루를 사용했다.

420

lament
[ləˈment]

n. 애도; v. 애통하다

mourn v. 애도하다, 슬퍼하다
moan n. 신음 v. 신음하다
bemoan v. 슬퍼하다, 애도하다
lame a. 절름발이의

어원	-lament : mourn 슬픔 → '슬픔으로 애도하다'
유의어	mourn, grieve, bemoan
반의어	celebrate, rejoice, applaud
영영	To express deep sorrow, grief, or regret.
예문	The poet wrote a lament about the loss of a loved one. 그 시인은 사랑하는 사람을 잃음에 대한 애도 시를 썼다.

421

disorder
[dɪˈsɔːdər]

n. 따라오지 않는(무질서)

ordinary a. 보통의, 통상의, 평범한
adorable a. 사랑스러운
orchard n. 과수원
ordain v. 명령하다, 질서를 정하다

어원	-dis : not + -ord 쫓다, 따르다(E) → '따라오지 않으니 무질서'
유의어	chaos, confusion, disarray
반의어	order, organization, arrangement
영영	a state of confusion or lack of order.
예문	The doctor diagnosed him with a sleep disorder. 의사는 그에게 수면장애 진단을 내렸다.

422

evacuate
[ɪˈvæk.ju.eɪt]

v. 대피시키다, 철수시키다

vacation n. 방학
vain a. 허영심이 강한
in vain p. 허사가 되어, 헛되이
vacant a. 빈 자리의

어원	-e, ex : out + -vacu : empty → '밖으로 나가 비어있게 만드는'
유의어	empty, clear, vacate
반의어	Inhabit, occupy, reside
영영	To leave or remove people from a place of danger or disaster.
예문	The town had to evacuate due to the approaching hurricane. 도시는 다가오는 허리케인 때문에 대피해야 했습니다.

423

pursue
[pəˈsjuː]

v. 해나가다, 추구하다

pursuit n. 추구, 추적
pursuer n. 추격자
ensue v. 계속해서 일어나다
sequence n. 연속 사건

어원	-pur, -pro : forth + -sue, -su, -sequ : follow → '앞으로 계속해서 나아가는'
유의어	follow, chase, seek
반의어	retreat, abandon, surrender
영영	To follow or chase after something or someone in order to achieve a goal or catch them.
예문	She decided to pursue a career in medicine to help others. 그녀는 다른 사람들을 돕기 위해 의학 분야에서 경력을 쌓기로 결정했다.

424

endanger
[ɪnˈdeɪn.dʒər]

v. 위태롭게 하다

endangered a. 멸종 위기에 처한
in danger p. 위험에 빠진
endear v. 애정을 느끼게 하다
end up with p. 결국 ~을 가지게 되다

어원	-en : in + -danger 위험 → '위험에 빠져 위태로운'
유의어	imperil, jeopardize, threaten
반의어	protect, safeguard
영영	to put someone or something at risk or in a dangerous situation; to jeopardize or threaten
예문	The construction of the dam may endanger the habitat of several species. 댐의 건설은 여러 종의 서식지를 위협할 수 있습니다.

425

obstruct

[əbˈstrʌkt]

v. 막다, 방해하다

construction n. 건설, 공사
deconstruct v. 분해하다, 해체하다
reconstruct v. 재구성하다
obstacle n. 장애, 방해물

어원	-ob : against + -struct : build → '올리는 것을 막다'
유의어	block, hinder, impede
반의어	facilitate, assist, aid
영영	To block or hinder the progress of something, creating an obstacle.
예문	The fallen tree obstructed the path, making it impossible to pass. 넘어진 나무가 길을 막아서 통과할 수 없게 했다.

426

alliance

[əˈlaɪ.əns]

n. 동맹, 동맹국, 협력, 협조, 친화

ally v. 동맹하다, 결합시키다
allied a. 동맹한, 연합한
alligation n. 혼합, 혼합법
alloy n. 합금, 순도

어원	-al : to + + -lig, -ly, -li : bind 묶다 → '~와 묶었으니 동맹'
유의어	partnership, coalition, union
반의어	Enmity, rivalry, opposition
영영	A formal agreement or partnership between two or more parties for mutual benefit.
예문	The two countries formed a military alliance for mutual defense. 두 나라는 상호 방어를 위해 군사 동맹을 구축했습니다.

427

debate

[dɪˈbeɪt]

v. 논쟁하다, 토론하다 n. 논쟁

combat n. 전투, 싸움
upbeat a. 경쾌한, 매우 즐거운
downbeat a. 우울한, 침울한
be embattled in p. ~에 휘말리다

어원	-de : apart + bat 때리다 → '따로 말 때리는 논쟁'
유의어	discussion, argument, dispute
반의어	Agreement, consensus, harmony
영영	A formal discussion or argument between individuals or groups with differing opinions or viewpoints.
예문	The candidates engaged in a heated debate about healthcare reform. 후보들은 의료 개혁에 대한 고조된 토론에 참여했습니다.

428

solemn

[ˈsɒl.əm]

a. 엄숙한, 침통한

solely adv. 오로지, 전적으로
desolate a. 황량한, 쓸쓸한
solidify v. 응고하다; 단결하다
solidarity n. 연대, 결속

어원	-soli : alone 혼자(L) → '혼자만 남으니 침통하고 엄숙한'
유의어	serious, grave, earnest
반의어	Casual, informal, relaxed
영영	Serious, formal, and dignified in manner or tone; often associated with a significant event or ceremony.
예문	The ceremony had a solemn atmosphere with traditional music. 그 행사는 전통 음악과 함께 엄숙한 분위기를 가졌습니다.

429

pity

[ˈpɪt.i]

n. 연민, 동정, 유감

self-pity p. 자기 연민
pitful a. 측은한, 가엾은, 불쌍한
petal n. 꽃잎
compassion n. 연민, 동정

어원	-pity : -path, -pati, -pass : suffer / faith → '고통을 겪고 있으니 동정이 가는 연민'
유의어	compassion, sympathy, empathy
반의어	scorn, disdain, contempt
영영	Feeling sympathy or compassion for someone's suffering or misfortune.
예문	He felt pity for the stray dog and decided to adopt it. 그는 길고양이에 동정을 느끼고 입양하기로 결정했다.

430

halt

[hɒlt]

n. 멈춤, 중단 v. 멈추다, 서다

get hold of p. ~을 구하다, 손에 넣다
hold A in check p. A를 억제하다
hold on p. 붙잡고 있다, 잠시만
hold out p. ~을 내밀다

어원	-halt : hold 잡다 → '잡혀 멈춘 상태'
유의어	stop, cease, come to a standstill
반의어	continue, proceed, advance
영영	to come to a stop or pause; to cease.
예문	The train came to a sudden halt. 기차가 갑자기 정지했다.

431

at the beginning of

p. ~의 시작에

at no cost p. 공짜로
at no time p. 결코 ~하지 않다
begin with p. ~으로 시작하다
begin to talk p. 운을 떼다

어원	-be : to make + gin 기계 장치 → '만들기 시작하다'
유의어	at the start of, initially, in the early stages of
반의어	at the end of, in the middle of, midway through
영영	at the start or commencement of
예문	At the beginning of the movie, the main character faces a difficult decision. 영화의 시작부에서 주인공은 어려운 결정을 마주합니다.

432

have a taste for

p. ~을 좋아하다, ~에 취미가 있다.

tasty a. 맛있는
tasteless a. 무미건조한, 멋없는
distaste n. 불쾌감, 혐오감
have a fit p. 화내다

어원	-have 갖다 + -taste 취향 → '갖고 있는 취향이 있으니 ~을 좋아하다'
유의어	enjoy, appreciate, have a liking for
반의어	dislike, have an aversion to, be repelled by
영영	have a preference or liking for
예문	John has a taste for spicy food. 존은 매운 음식을 좋아합니다.

433

table of contents

p. (책 등의) 목차

content n. 내용(물); (책의) 목차
discontent n. 불만
contentedly adv. 만족스럽게, 기꺼이
be content to do p. 기꺼이 ~하다

어원	-table 테이블 + -content 목차 → '목차를 담은 리스트'
유의어	contents page, index, list of contents
반의어	body of text, main text, content
영영	a list of the chapters or sections of a book or document
예문	The table of contents helps readers navigate through the book. 목차는 독자들이 책을 쉽게 찾아보도록 도와줍니다.

434

get along with

p. ~와 잘 지내다

along prep. 함께; ~을 따라
get hold of p. ~을 구하다, 찾아내다
get a handle on p. 이해하다, 알아듣다
get rid of p. ~을 없애다

어원	-a : from + -long + -with → '~부터 먼 길을 따라 함께'
유의어	have a good relationship with, get on with, be compatible with
반의어	clash with, disagree with, conflict with
영영	have a harmonious or friendly relationship with
예문	Sarah gets along well with her coworkers. 사라는 동료들과 잘 지냅니다.

435

a quantity of

p. 많은, 다량의

quantity n. 양, 수량
quantify v. 분량을 정하다
quantification n. 정량화, 수량화
quantum n. 양자

어원	-quant 수량 → '수량이 많은' * quality 질, 품질
유의어	an amount of, a number of, a volume of
반의어	a lack of, an absence of, a scarcity of
영영	an amount or number of
예문	We need a large quantity of flour to bake all these cookies. 이 모든 쿠키를 굽기 위해 많은 양의 밀가루가 필요합니다.

436

after the fact

p. (이미 일이 벌어지고 난) 사후에

after all p. 결국
one after another p. 차례로, 잇따라서
take after p. ~을 닮다
thereafter adv. 그 후

어원	-after 이후 + -fact 사실 → '기정 사실 이후에'
유의어	post facto, retrospectively, after the event
반의어	before the fact, pre-emptively, beforehand
영영	occurring or done after an event has taken place
예문	We discovered the mistake only after the fact. 우리는 사실을 알아차리는 것이 너무 늦었습니다.

437

to that end

p. 이를 위해, 그 목적을 달성하기 위하여

end up in p. 결국 ~로 끝나다
end up ing p. 결국 ~하게 되다
end up with p. 결국 ~을 가지게 되다
end up alone p. 결국 혼자 있게 되다

어원	-to 까지 + -end 끝 → '끝까지 가려는 건 그 목적 달성을 위해'
유의어	for that purpose, with that aim, in order to achieve that
반의어	aimlessly, purposelessly, without intention
영영	for that purpose or with that aim
예문	We implemented new security measures to that end. 그 목적을 달성하기 위해 새로운 보안 조치를 시행했습니다.

438

fall on

p. ~에게 부과되다, ~ 맡겨지다; ~을 습격하다

fall v. 떨어지다 n. 가을
fall down p. 넘어지다
fall apart p. 무너지다
fall outside p. ~밖에 위치하다

어원	-fals, -fal, -fail, -faul : deceive 떨어지다 + -on 접촉 → '책임이 붙었으니 맡겨지고 부과되다'
유의어	descend on, land on, befall
반의어	avoid, evade, sidestep
영영	be experienced or encountered suddenly or unexpectedly
예문	The responsibility to organize the event fell on Sarah's shoulders. 행사를 조직하는 책임이 사라의 어깨에 떨어졌습니다.

439

draw A out

p. A를 끌어내다

draw on p. ~에 의존하다
draw A from B p. A를 B로부터 끌어내다
drawer n. 서랍; 수표 발행인
draw attention to p. ~에 관심을 끌다

어원	-draw 당기다, 뽑다 + -down 아래로 → '아래로 뽑아 내리다'
유의어	elicit A, extract A, bring out A
반의어	suppress A, inhibit A, restrain A
영영	elicit or bring forth A
예문	The interviewer tried to draw out more information from the hesitant candidate. 면접관은 주저하는 지원자로부터 더 많은 정보를 끌어내려고 노력했습니다.

440

in one's opinion

p. ~의 의견으로는, ~의 입장에서는

in mind p. ~을 염두에 두다
in one's interest p. 가장 이익이 되는
in order p. 순서대로
in particular p. 개별적으로, 특별하게

어원	-opt, opin : choose 선택 ((L) → '선택한 의견' * op(t) '둘 중 하나를 선택' VS lec(t) '보다 넓은 범위 선택'
유의어	according to one, from one's perspective, in one's view
반의어	objectively, factually, empirically
영영	according to one's viewpoint or belief
예문	In my opinion, the best solution is to compromise. 제 의견으로는, 최상의 해결책은 타협하는 것입니다.

Chapter 12.

441	**protest**	[ˈprəʊ.test]	v. 항의(하다)
442	**demerit**	[ˌdiːˈmer.ɪt]	n. 단점, 결점, 잘못
443	**suffix**	[ˈsʌf.ɪks]	n. 접미사
444	**imprint**	[ɪmˈprɪnt]	v. 찍다; ~에게 감명을 주다
445	**sewage**	[ˈsuː.ɪdʒ]	n. 하수, 오물, 오수
446	**curb**	[kɜːb]	v. 억제하다
447	**reduce**	[rɪˈdʒuːs]	v. 줄이다, 낮추다
448	**mob**	[mɒb]	n. 군중, 폭도, 떼
449	**fate**	[feɪt]	n. 운명, 숙명
450	**restrict**	[rɪˈstrɪkt]	v. ~을 제한하다, 금지하다, 한정하다
451	**conduct**	[kənˈdʌkt]	v. 행하다, 지휘하다, 안내하다; 지휘, 지도, 행위
452	**taboo**	[təˈbuː]	n. 금기, 금기시되는 것 a. 금제의
453	**relieve**	[rɪˈliːv]	v. 경감시키다, 완화시키다
454	**wield**	[wiːld]	v. 휘두르다, 쓰다
455	**coward**	[ˈkaʊ.əd]	n. 겁쟁이
456	**overlook**	[ˌəʊ.vəˈlʊk]	v. 묵살하다, 간과하다
457	**stall**	[stɔːl]	n. 마굿간; 매점; 가판대; 칸막이 벽, 칸
458	**decree**	[dɪˈkriː]	n. 법령, 포고
459	**initiate**	[ɪˈnɪʃ.i.eɪt]	v. 시작하다, 착수하다; 전수하다
460	**paradox**	[ˈpær.ə.dɒks]	n. 역설, 모순된 일
461	**extinguish**	[ɪkˈstɪŋ.gwɪʃ]	v. 끄다, 소멸시키다
462	**trace**	[treɪs]	v. 추적하다; 밝혀내다; n. 자취, 발자국
463	**inflame**	[ɪnˈfleɪm]	v. 자극하다, 불을 붙이다, 타오르다
464	**mobilize**	[ˈməʊ.bɪ.laɪz]	v. 동원하다
465	**absorb**	[əbˈzɔːb]	v. 흡수하다, 받아들이다
466	**attempt**	[əˈtempt]	n. 시도, 노력 v. 시도하다
467	**reside**	[rɪˈzaɪd]	v. 거주하다, 살다
468	**cemetery**	[ˈsem.ə.tri]	n. 공동묘지
469	**release**	[rɪˈliːs]	v. 석방하다, 놓아주다; 발표하다 n. 해방, 면제
470	**craft**	[krɑːft]	v. 공들여 만들다 n. 공예, 기술
471	**a bunch of**		p. 많은, 다수의
472	**invest A with B**		p. A에게 B를 주다, 투자하다
473	**more often than not**		p. 대개, 흔히
474	**at the moment**		p. 지금
475	**in common with**		p. ~와 공통으로 / ~와 같게
476	**feed on**		p. ~을 먹이로 하다
477	**at a 형 price**		p. ~한 가격으로
478	**cut out**		p. 멈추다; 급히 떠나다
479	**out of date**		p. 시대에 뒤떨어진, 구식의
480	**be subjected to N**		p. ~을 받다; ~을 겪다

441

protest

[ˈprɑʊ.test]

v. 항의(하다)

protester n. 항의자, 시위자
attest v. 증명하다
detest v. 몹시 싫어하다, 혐오하다
distend v. 팽창시키다

어원	-pro : forward + -test 증명하다, 증언하다(L) → '앞에 나가 증언으로 항의하다' * prove 코앞에 증거 VS test 객관적인 근거'
유의어	object, complain, demonstrate
반의어	support, agree
영영	express strong disapproval or objection
예문	Many people gathered to protest against the new government policies. 많은 사람들이 새로운 정부 정책에 반대하기 위해 모였다.

442

demerit

[ˌdiːˈmer.ɪt]

n. 단점, 결점, 잘못

deviant a. 벗어난, 일탈적인
deforestation n. 삼림 벌채, 삼림 개간
devitalize v. ~의 활력을 빼앗다
devise v. 궁리하다, 고안하다

어원	-de : not + merit 장점 → '장점이 아닌'
유의어	disadvantage, drawback, fault
반의어	Merit, advantage, benefit
영영	A fault or disadvantage; a mark or point against someone's record.
예문	The teacher noted a demerit on the student's behavior record. 선생님은 학생의 행동 기록에 불이익 사항을 남겼습니다.

443

suffix

[ˈsʌf.ɪks]

n. 접미사

interfix n. 삽입구
affix v. (우표 등을) 붙이다
fixate v. 정착시키다, 집착하다
fixed a. 고정된

어원	-suf, -sur : over + -fac, -fec, -fic, -fy, -fair : make → '더해서 품사를 다른 것으로 만드는 접미사'
유의어	ending, affix, postfix
반의어	Prefix, affix, preface
영영	A group of letters added to the end of a word to change its meaning or form.
예문	In English, "-ing" is a common suffix used to form gerunds. 영어에서 "-ing"은 분사를 형성하는 데 사용되는 일반적인 접미사입니다.

444

imprint

[ɪmˈprɪnt]

v. 찍다; ~에게 감명을 주다

out of print p. 절판된
blueprint n. 청사진, 계획
fine print p. 약관 등의 작은 글씨
exempt v. 면제하다 a. 면제의

어원	-im, -in : on + -print 찍다 → '마음 안에 찍으니 감명을 주다'
유의어	mark, impression, stamp
반의어	Erase, delete, remove
영영	A mark or indentation made by pressing or stamping.
예문	The shoe left an imprint in the mud. 그 신발은 진흙에 물림을 남겼습니다.

445

sewage

[ˈsuː.ɪdʒ]

n. 하수, 오물, 오수

sewer n. 하수관, 수채통
sewer system p. 하수 처리 시스템
sew v. 바느질하다, 깁다
shiver n. 떨림, 전율

어원	-sew : drain 물을 빼다 → '물을 빼는 하수관으로 오수와 오물이~'
유의어	wastewater, sewage system, effluent
반의어	Clean water, purified liquid, fresh fluid
영영	Waste and dirty water from households, industries, and commercial establishments that is carried away for treatment or disposal.
예문	nglish Sentence: The city upgraded its sewage treatment plant to improve water quality. 도시는 물 질질이 개선하기 위해 하수 처리 공장을 업그레이드했습니다.

446

curb

[kɑːb]

v. 억제하다

curl n. 곱슬머리; (몸을) 옹크리다
curl up p. 동그랗게 말리다
cosy a. 편안한
cope with p. 다루다, 대처하다

어원	-curb 재갈 → '재갈을 물려 움직임을 억제하다'
유의어	restrain, control, limit
반의어	encourage, promote, support
영영	to restrain or control something, typically an undesirable behavior.
예문	The city implemented measures to curb pollution. 도시는 오염을 억제하기 위한 조치를 시행했다.

447

reduce

[rɪˈdʒuːs]

v. 줄이다, 낮추다

produce v. 생산하다 n. 농산물
reproduce v. 재생하다, 번식하다; 복사하다
reduction n. 감소
profane a. 불경스런 v. 모독하다

어원	-re : back + -duce → '뒤로 끄니 줄인다'
같은의어	decrease, lessen, diminish
반의어	increase, enlarge, expand
영영	to make something smaller or decrease in size, quantity, or intensity.
예문	He decided to reduce his sugar intake for better health. 그는 건강을 위해 설탕 섭취량을 줄이기로 결정했다.

448

mob

[mɒb]

n. 군중, 폭도, 떼

mop n. 대걸레
mobility n. 기동력, 유동성
locomote v. (제 힘으로) 움직이다
remove v. 제거하다, 치우다; 벗다

어원	-mo, -mot, -mob, -mop, -mut 이동하다, 움직이다(L) → 이동하는 무리
같은의어	crowd, multitude, group
반의어	Individual, person, single person
영영	A large and disorderly crowd of people; often associated with unruly behavior.
예문	A mob of protestors gathered outside the government building. 시위대가 정부 건물 밖에서 모였습니다.

449

fate

[feɪt]

n. 운명, 숙명

fatal a. 치명적인, 결정적인, 중대한
fatally adv. 치명적으로
fable n. 우화
infatuate v. 열광시키다, 미쳐버리다

어원	-fa, -fe, -fess, -phe : talk 말하다 → '신의 말씀이니 운명'
같은의어	destiny, fortune, predestination
반의어	Free will, choice, agency
영영	The predetermined course of events in one's life; destiny or fortune.
예문	Folklore includes traditional stories, legends, and customs passed down through generations. 민속학은 세대를 거쳐 전해진 전통 이야기, 전설 및 관습을 포함합니다.

450

restrict

[rɪˈstrɪkt]

v. ~을 제한하다, 금지하다, 한정하다

strict a. 엄격한, 정확한
constrict v. 압축하다, 죄다
stringent a. 엄중한, 긴박한
district n. 선거구 지역, 구역

어원	-re : back + -stric : draw tight → '뒤로 단단히 묶어 한정하니 제한하다'
같은의어	limit, confine, restrain
반의어	Allow, permit, grant access
영영	To limit or confine within certain boundaries or rules; to impose limitations.
예문	The rules may restrict certain activities in the park. 규칙은 공원에서 특정 활동을 제한할 수 있습니다.

451

conduct

[kənˈdʌkt]

v. 행하다, 지휘하다, 안내하다; 지휘, 지도, 행위

conducive a. 도움이 되는, 공헌하는
induce v. 설득하여 ~하게 하다; 야기하다
seduce v. 부추기다; 매혹시키다
conduce v. 도움이 되다, 공헌하다

어원	-con : together + -duc, -duct : lead → '함께 좋은 방향으로 이끌어 행하다'
같은의어	behavior, demeanor, performance
반의어	misbehave, behave badly, transgress
영영	To manage or carry out a task, action, or behavior.
예문	The conductor will conduct the orchestra during the concert. 지휘자는 콘서트 중에 오케스트라를 지휘할 것이다.

452

taboo

[təˈbuː]

n. 금기, 금기시되는 것 a. 금제의

tabor n. 작은 북
tablet n. 알약, 현판
end table p. 소파 옆에 붙이는 작은 탁자
tail n. 꼬리 v. 미행하다

어원	-tabo : tabor 작은 북 * 18세기 말 영국의 탐험가 제임스 쿡이 폴리네시아의 섬에서 추장이 북을 치며 금기를 내리는 것을 보고 기록
같은의어	prohibition, restriction, ban
반의어	Acceptable, permissible, allowed
영영	A social or cultural prohibition or restriction, often based on moral or religious beliefs.
예문	In some cultures, discussing death is considered taboo. 어떤 문화에서는 죽음에 대한 토론이 금기로 여겨집니다.

453

relieve

[rɪˈliːv]

v. 경감시키다, 완화시키다

disbelief n. 불신
relief n. 안도, 안심
relish n. 맛, 즐거움 v. 즐기다
elicit v. 이끌어 내다, 유도하다

어원 -re : again + -lev, -liev, -lief : raise 올리다
→ '기분이 올라 마음이 가벼워지니 안심'

유의어 alleviate, ease, mitigate
반의어 intensify, exacerbate

영영 to alleviate or lessen the discomfort, pain, or stress of someone or something; to provide comfort or assistance

예문 Taking a break can relieve stress and improve your well-being.
휴식을 취하면 스트레스를 덜 수 있고 건강을 회복할 수 있다.

454

wield

[wiːld]

v. 휘두르다, 쓰다

weapon n. 무기, 병기
wear out p. 지치게 하다; 닳아서 헤지다
wear down p. 약화되다, 마모되다
worn out p. 진부한

어원 -wield : weapon
→ '무기를 휘두르다'

유의어 handle, use, exercise
반의어 relinquish, surrender, abandon

영영 To hold and use a weapon, tool, or power with skill and control.

예문 The knight could wield his sword with great skill in battle.
그 기사는 전투에서 그의 검을 능숙하게 다룰 수 있었다.

455

coward

[ˈkaʊəd]

n. 겁쟁이

cowardly a. 겁 많은, 소심한
cowardice n. 겁 먹음, 소심함
crane n. 기중기, 크레인; 학
copious a. 풍요로운

어원 -cow : 동물의 꼬리
→ '꼬리를 감추는 겁쟁이'

유의어 chicken, timid person, scaredy-cat
반의어 hero, brave, courageous

영영 a person who lacks courage or is easily frightened.

예문 He was labeled a coward for not standing up for his beliefs.
그는 자신의 신념을 지키지 않아 겁쟁이로 비난 받았다.

456

overlook

[ˌoʊvəˈlʊk]

v. 묵살하다, 간과하다

look to do p. ~하려고 애쓰다
look to A for B p. A사 B해주기를 기대하다
look over p. 전체를 훑어보다
look through p. ~을 훑어보다

어원 -over : above + -look 보다 (E)
→ '넘겨 보니 간과하다, 묵살하다'

유의어 ignore, neglect, miss
반의어 notice, observe

영영 to fail to notice or observe something; to neglect or disregard

예문 Don't overlook the small details; they can be important.
작은 세부 사항을 무시하지 마세요. 그것들은 중요할 수 있습니다.

457

stall

[stɔːl]

n. 마굿간; 매점; 가판대; 칸막이 벽, 칸

standby n. 예비물, 대기신호
standee n. 입석
stance n. 입장, 태도, 자세
standstill n. 막힘, 정돈

어원 -sta : stand + -tall 벽
→ '양 옆에 벽을 세우고 길에 새운 매점이 가판대'

유의어 delay, stop, hinder
반의어 Progress, advance, move forward

영영 A small enclosure or compartment for animals; to come to a halt or stop progressing.

예문 The car's engine suddenly stalled on the highway.
차의 엔진이 고속도로에서 갑자기 멈췄습니다.

458

decree

[dɪˈkriː]

n. 법령, 포고

discretion n. 분별, 분별력; 재량, 재량권
indict v. 기소하다, 고발하다
indiscreet a. 무분별한, 경솔한
by decree p. 명령에 따라

어원 -de : apart + -cre, -cret 걸러내다, 가려내다
→ '따로 엄선해서 가려낸 법령'

유의어 order, command, proclamation
반의어 repeal, annul

영영 an official order or decision issued by an authority

예문 The king issued a decree announcing a new law.
왕은 새로운 법률을 발표하는 법령을 공포했다.

459

initiate

[ɪˈnɪʃ.i.eɪt]

v. 시작하다, 착수하다; 전수하다

initial a. 처음의, 최초의 n. 머리글자
initially adv. 처음에는
initiative n. 진취성, 결단력, 주도권
initiation n. 착수, 시작

어원	-in : into + -it, -ish, -ir : go → '처음 들어가는 시작이니 착수'
유의어	begin, start, commence
반의어	conclude, finish, terminate
영영	Begin, start, or introduce someone to a new experience, organization, or group.
예문	She was the one who initiated the project. 그녀가 그 프로젝트를 시작한 사람이었습니다.

460

paradox

[ˈpær.ə.dɒks]

n. 역설, 모순된 일

paradoxical a. 역설적인, 불합리한
orthodox a. 정통의, 보수적인
irony n. 반어법
paralysis n. 마비, 불구

어원	-para : against + -dox : opinion → '정설에 반하는 의견'
유의어	contradiction, puzzle, enigma
반의어	Consistency, agreement, conformity
영영	A seemingly contradictory statement or situation that may reveal an underlying truth.
예문	Everyone has their own preference when it comes to food. 음식에 관한 입맛은 각자의 선호도가 있습니다.

461

extinguish

[ɪkˈstɪŋ.gwɪʃ]

v. 끄다, 소멸시키다

extinguisher n. 소화기
extinction n. 멸종
extinctive a. 소멸적인, 소멸성의
insult v. 모욕하다, 창피를 주다

어원	-ex : out + -tinc, -tinct, -stinct 튕기다 → '손을 튕겨서 불을 끄다'
유의어	put out, quench, douse
반의어	ignite, kindle, light
영영	to put out or quench, especially a fire or flame.
예문	Please extinguish all cigarettes before entering the building. 건물에 들어가기 전에 담배를 모두 끄세요.

462

trace

[treɪs]

v. 추적하다; 밝혀내다; n. 자취, 발자국

trace to p. ~을 ..까지 추적하여 찾아내다
trace back to p. ~가지 거슬러 올라가다
keep track of p. ~을 계속 파악하다
track down p. ~을 추적하다, 찾아내다

어원	-trac : track 자취 → '자취를 쫓아 추적하다
유의어	track, follow, find
반의어	erase, remove
영영	follow or mark the course or development of something
예문	They tried to trace the origin of the mysterious phone call. 그들은 신비로운 전화 통화의 출처를 추적하려고 노력했다.

463

inflame

[ɪnˈfleɪm]

v. 자극하다, 불을 붙이다, 타오르다

flame a. 격렬한, 불타는; 지독한 n. 화염, 불꽃
aflame adv. 불타서, 불꽃이 되어
inflammable a. 가연성의
flash n. 플래시; 불빛, 섬광

어원	-in : in + -flame 타오르다 → '마음 안이 타오르게 불을 붙여 자극하다'
유의어	provoke, irritate, agitate
반의어	soothe, calm
영영	to cause a part of the body to become swollen, hot, and painful due to infection or injury; to provoke strong emotions or reactions
예문	His inflammatory comments only served to escalate the argument. 그의 도발적인 발언은 다툼을 악화시키는 데 도움이 되지 않았다.

464

mobilize

[ˈmoʊ.bɪ.laɪz]

v. 동원하다

mobile a. 움직일 수 있는, 변덕스러운
mobility n. 기동력, 유동성
social mobility p. 사회 이동
motion n. 움직임, 동작, 운동

어원	-mo, -mot, -mob, -mop, -mut 이동하다, 움직이다(L) → '움직여서 집결시키다'
유의어	prepare, rally, assemble
반의어	Demobilize, deactivate, disband
영영	To prepare and organize resources, troops, or forces for a specific purpose or action.
예문	The government had to mobilize the army to respond to the crisis. 정부는 위기 대응을 위해 군대를 동원해야 했습니다.

465

absorb

[əbˈzɔːb]

v. 흡수하다, 받아들이다

absorbed a. 몰두한
be absorbed in p. ~에 열중하다, 몰두하다
absorbing a. 마음을 사로잡는, 재미있는
absolve v. 면제하다, 용서하다

어원	-ab: from + -sorb, -sorp : soak 흡수하다 → '~로부터 흡수하다'
유의어	soak up, take in, assimilate
반의어	Emit, release, expel
영영	To take in or soak up a substance or energy.
예문	Plants absorb nutrients from the soil through their roots. 식물은 뿌리를 통해 토양으로부터 영양분을 흡수합니다.

466

attempt

[əˈtempt]

n. 시도, 노력 v. 시도하다

attempt to do p. ~하려고 시도하다
temporary a. 시간적인, 일시의
contemporary a. 같은 시대의, 현대의
temptation n. 유혹

어원	-at 방향 + -tempt : taunt 시도하다, 시험하다, 유혹하다(L) → '그쪽으로 해보려고 시도하다'
유의어	try, endeavor, effort
반의어	Avoid, abstain, refrain
영영	To make an effort to do something, often with the intention of succeeding.
예문	He will attempt the challenging climb up the mountain. 그는 산을 오르는 도전적인 시도를 할 것입니다.

467

reside

[rɪˈzaɪd]

v. 거주하다, 살다

reside in p. ~에 거주하다
reside on p. ~에 머물다
resident n. 거주자, 주민
residue n. 나머지, 찌꺼기

어원	-re : again + -sid : sit → '계속해서 앉아 있는 곳이니 살며 거주하는 곳이다'
유의어	live, dwell, stay
반의어	depart, leave, vacate
영영	to live in a particular place.
예문	The Smiths reside in a beautiful house by the lake. 스미스 가족은 호수 옆 아름다운 집에 거주한다.

468

cemetery

[ˈsem.ə.tri]

n. 공동묘지

cement v. 굳게 하다, 강화하다 n. 시멘트
cemeterial a. 묘지의, 공동묘지의

어원	* -cemet : cement → '시멘트처럼 영혼과 땅을 단단히 묶은 무덤' * tomb 영혼이 출발하는 곳 VS grave 시체를 묻은 곳 VS cemetery 공동묘지
유의어	graveyard, burial ground, necropolis
반의어	birthplace, cradle, beginning
영영	a place where deceased people are buried; a graveyard.
예문	Many people visit the cemetery to pay respects to their loved ones. 많은 사람들이 그들의 사랑하는 사람들에게 경의를 표하기 위해 묘지를 방문합니다.

469

release

[rɪˈliːs]

v. 석방하다, 놓아주다; 발표하다 n. 해방, 면제

relax v. 휴식을 취하다, 안심하다
delay v. 연기하다, 늦추다
relay v. 전달하다; 중계하다
releaser n. 해발인; 자극

어원	-re : again + -lax, -ly, -leas, -lay : leave 내버려 두다 → '다시 풀어주니 석방이고 해방, 정보를 풀어주니 공개 발표'
유의어	set free, liberate, unleash
반의어	hold, retain
영영	set free or let go
예문	The company plans to release their new product next month. 회사는 다음 달에 새로운 제품을 출시할 계획이다.

470

craft

[krɑːft]

v. 공들여 만들다 n. 공예, 기술

minecraft n. 채굴하는 기술
crafty a. 술수가 뛰어난, 교활한
craftsman n. 공예가
craftsmanship n. 손재주, 솜씨

어원	-craft : force → '혼자 힘써 완성도를 높이는 기술'
유의어	skill, art, trade
반의어	Clumsiness, ineptitude, lack of skill
영영	A skill or activity that involves creating objects or performing tasks with manual dexterity.
예문	He has a talent for the craft of woodworking. 그는 목공예라는 기술에 재능이 있습니다.

471

a bunch of

p. 많은, 다수의

bunch n. 다발, 송이, 묶음
bunch of keys p. 열쇠 뭉치
bundle n. 다발, 꾸러미
bind v. 묶다, 결속시키다

어원	-band, bind, bund, bond → '묶인 다발이 많은'
유의어	a group of, a collection of, a cluster of
반의어	an individual, a single entity, a lone item
영영	a group or collection of things
예문	She bought a bunch of flowers for her mother's birthday. 그녀는 어머니 생일을 축하하기 위해 꽃 한 무리를 샀습니다.

472

invest A with B

p. A에게 B를 주다, 투자하다

vest n. 조끼, 셔츠
investment n. 투자, 투자금
return on investment p. 투자수익
divest v. 재산을 빼앗다, 박탈하다

어원	-in + -vest : clothes → '안에 조끼를 입혀 지위를 주고 투자하다'
유의어	endow A with B, imbue A with B, confer B upon A
반의어	divest A of B, strip A of B, dispossess A of B
영영	allocate or endow A with B
예문	The artist invested her paintings with deep emotional meaning. 그 예술가는 그녀의 그림에 깊은 감정적 의미를 부여했습니다.

473

more often than not

p. 대개, 흔히

no more than p. 꼭 ~만큼, ~일뿐인
no less than p. 꼭 ~만큼, ~못지 않게
not A any more than B p. A하지 않듯이 B하지 않다

어원	-more often + -than not → '아무것도 아닌 것보다는 좀 더 하니 대개, 흔히'
유의어	usually, frequently, commonly
반의어	less frequently than not, infrequently, rarely
영영	most of the time or frequently
예문	More often than not, he arrives late to meetings. 대부분의 경우 그는 회의에 늦게 도착합니다.

474

at the moment

p. 지금

at the cost of p. ~의 비용을 지불하고
at the latest p. 늦어도 ~까지는
at most p. 기껏해야
for a moment p. 잠시 동안

어원	-mom : move → '움직인 바로 이 순간, 지금'
유의어	currently, presently, right now
반의어	later, subsequently, afterwards
영영	currently or presently
예문	I'm busy at the moment, can I call you back later? 지금은 바쁩니다, 나중에 다시 전화드릴까요?

475

in common with

p. ~와 공통으로 / ~와 같게

in charge of p. ~을 담당하는
in commotion p. 동요하고 있는
in contact with p. ~와 연락하여
in contrast to p. ~와는 대조적으로

어원	-coun, -com : together → '불러서 함께 모이니 공통으로'
유의어	shared with, similar to, alike in
반의어	different from, dissimilar to, unlike
영영	shared with or similar to
예문	I have a lot in common with my best friend. 나와 나의 베스트 프렌드는 많은 공통점이 있습니다.

476

feed on

p. ~을 먹이로 하다

feedback n. 의견, 반응
feed into p. ~에 영향을 미치다
feed off p. ~을 먹이로 하다
feeble a. 허약한, 힘 없는; 희미한

어원	-food, -feed, -fost 음식
유의어	consume, devour, subsist on
반의어	starve, abstain from, refrain from
영영	consume as nourishment or sustenance
예문	Sharks feed on smaller fish and marine animals. 상어는 작은 물고기와 해양 동물을 먹습니다.

477

at a 형 price

p. ~한 가격으로

at a 형 speed p. ~한 속도로
at a 형 pace p. ~한 속도로
at a 형 charge of p. ~의 비용 부담으로
at a distance p. 멀리서, 거리를 두고

어원	-at 점 + -price 가격 → '지정한 가격으로'
유의어	at a specific price, at a certain price, at a particular price
반의어	at no cost, for free, without charge
영영	at a specific price or rate
예문	I bought this dress at a discounted price. 나는 이 드레스를 할인된 가격에 샀다.

478

cut out

p. 멈추다; 급히 떠나다

cut A with B p. A를 B로 자르다
cut from the same cloth p. 같은 부류인
cut off p. 잘라버리다; 서둘러 떠나다
chop up p. ~을 잘게 자르다

어원	-cut 자르다 + -out 밖 → '잘려서 나오니 일을 멈추고 급히 떠나다'
유의어	eliminate, remove, excise
반의어	add in, insert, include
영영	remove or eliminate
예문	She decided to cut out sweets from her diet to improve her health. 그녀는 건강을 회복하기 위해 다이어트에서 당을 배제하기로 결정했습니다.

479

out of date

p. 시대에 뒤떨어진, 구식의

keep up to date p. 최신 정보를 유지하다
date back to p. ~까지 거슬러 올라가다
daybreak n. 새벽, 동틀녘
heyday n. 전성기, 한창 때

어원	-out 벗어나다 + -date 날짜, 시기 → '시기에서 벗어나니 뒤떨어져 구식의'
유의어	outdated, obsolete, old-fashioned
반의어	up-to-date, current, modern
영영	no longer current or applicable
예문	This information is out of date; we need to find the latest version. 이 정보는 오래되었습니다. 최신 버전을 찾아야 합니다.

480

be subjected to N

p. ~을 받다; ~을 겪다

subject n. 주제, 학과, 주어; 피실험자
subjective a. 주관적인
subjectivity n. 주체성, 주관성
be subject to N p. ~의 영향을 받다

어원	-sub : under + -ject : throw → '아래에 던져져 ~을 당하는'
유의어	undergo N, experience N, endure N
반의어	be shielded from N, be protected from N, be defended from N
영영	be exposed to or experience N
예문	The suspect was subjected to intense questioning by the police. 용의자는 경찰에 의해 강한 심문을 받았습니다.

Chapter 13.

481	notable	[ˈnəʊ.tə.bəl]	a. 주목할 만한
482	eject	[iˈdʒekt]	v. 밖으로 던지다; 분출하다
483	complicate	kɑ́mpləkèit | kɔ́m-]	v. 복잡하게 하다
484	paralyze	[ˈpær.əl.aɪz]	v. 마비시키다, 활동 불능이 되게 하다
485	conscience	[ˈkɒn.ʃəns]	n. 양심, 도덕심
486	illiterate	[ɪˈlɪt.ər.ət]	a. 글을 모르는, 문맹의
487	comprise	[kəmˈpraɪz]	v. 구성하다
488	enrich	[ɪnˈrɪtʃ]	v. 부유하게 하다, 풍요롭게 하다
489	parliament	[ˈpɑː.lɪ.mənt]	n. 국회, 입법부
490	silhouette	[sìluét]	n. 검은 윤곽, 실루엣
491	anonymous	[əˈnɒn.ɪ.məs]	a. 이름이 없는 n. 익명
492	potable	[ˈpəʊ.tə.bəl]	a. 마실 수 있는
493	communism	[ˈkɒm.jə.nɪ.zəm]	n. 공산주의
494	distract	[dɪˈstrækt]	v. 딴 데로 돌리다, 산만하게 하다
495	geometry	[dʒiˈɒm.ə.tri]	n. 기하학, 기하학적 구조
496	stout	[staut]	a. 통통한, 튼튼한; n. 흑맥주
497	lyric	[ˈlɪr.ɪk]	n. 노래가사; a. 서정시의
498	profound	[prəˈfaʊnd]	a. 강한; 심오한; 깊은 n. 깊은 바다(심연)
499	adequate	[ˈæd.ə.kwət]	a. 적절한
500	interfere	[ˌɪn.təˈfɪər]	v. 방해하다, 간섭하다
501	anecdote	[ˈæn.ɪk.dəʊt]	n. 일화
502	archery	[ˈɑː.tʃər.i]	n. 양궁, 활쏘기
503	digest	[daɪˈdʒest]	v. 소화하다; 이해하다
504	watchful	[ˈwɒtʃ.fəl]	a. 지켜보는, 주의 깊은
505	cumulative	[ˈkjuː.mjə.lə.tɪv]	a. 누적되는, 가중의
506	listless	[ˈlɪst.ləs]	a. 힘이 없는, 무기력한
507	verbal	[ˈvɜː.bəl]	a. 말의, 문자 그대로의
508	composure	[kəmˈpəʊ.ʒər]	n. 침착함, 평정심
509	haste	[heɪst]	n. 급함, 서두름; v. 서두르다
510	terminate	[ˈtɜː.mɪ.neɪt]	v. 끝나다, 종료되다, 끝내다
511	in an effort to do		p. ~하려는 노력으로
512	in the face of		p. ~에도 불구하고, ~에 직면하여
513	in conclusion		p. 결론적으로, 끝으로
514	get A out		p. A를 생산하다
515	at latest		p. 늦어도 ~까지는
516	in good faith		p. 옳다고 믿으며, 선의로
517	at one another		p. 서로
518	by law		p. 법에 의해
519	in a series		p. 잇달아, 연이어
520	come to one's rescue		p. ~을 구조하러 오다

481 **notable** [ˈnəʊ.tə.bəl] a. 주목할 만한 notion n. 개념, 관념, 생각 connotation n. 함축, 내포 notation n. 표기법 annotate v. 주석을 달다	어원	-no, -not : mark 표시하다, know 알다(L) → '표시를 한 것이니 주목할 만한'
	유의어	noteworthy, remarkable, prominent
	반의어	Insignificant, unimportant, ordinary
	영영	Worthy of attention, recognition, or remark; distinguished or noteworthy.
	예문	The concept of time travel presents a paradox that challenges our understanding of physics. 시간 여행의 개념은 물리학에 대한 이해를 도전시키는 모순을 제시합니다.
482 **eject** [iˈdʒekt] v. 밖으로 던지다; 분출하다 project v. 계획하다, 투영하다, 발사하다 subject n. 주제; 학과; 주어; 피실험자 be subjected to p. ~의 영향을 받다 object n. 목표, 물체, 목적어; ~에 반대하다	어원	-e : out + -ject : throw (L) → '밖으로 던지니 쫓아내다'
	유의어	expel, oust, remove
	반의어	admit, allow, welcome
	영영	Expel or throw out forcibly.
	예문	The unruly passenger was ejected from the airplane. 안절부절 못하는 승객은 비행기에서 추방되었습니다.
483 **complicate** kámpləkèit | kɔ́m-] v. 복잡하게 하다 simplicity n. 단순함, 간단함, 평이함 complicated a. 복잡한 complicit a. 가담한, 공모한, 공범의 perplex v. 당황하게 하다	어원	-com : together + -pli, -ply, -ploy, -ploit, -plex : weave → '여러 가지를 함께 꼬니 복잡하다'
	유의어	complexify, entangle, confuse
	반의어	simplify, clarify
	영영	to make something more complex, difficult, or intricate; to add complications or difficulties to a situation
	예문	The instructions for assembling the furniture were quite complicated. 가구 조립을 위한 지시사항은 상당히 복잡했다.
484 **paralyze** [ˈpær.əl.aɪz] v. 마비시키다, 활동 불능이 되게 하다 paralyse v. 마비시키다, 쓸모없게 만들다 paradox n. 역설, 모순된 일 paralysis n. 마비, 불구 clumsy a. 서투른, 어색한	어원	-para : against + -ly : loosen → '몸에 풀리는 것에 반하는 것이 마비'
	유의어	immobilize, incapacitate, disable
	반의어	activate, energize
	영영	to cause someone or something to become unable to move or function, often temporarily
	예문	A sudden accident can paralyze a person's ability to walk. 갑작스러운 사고로 인해 사람의 걷기 능력이 마비될 수 있다.
485 **conscience** [ˈkɒn.ʃəns] n. 양심, 도덕심 consciously adv. 의식적으로 consciousness n. 의식, 자각 subconscious a. 잠재의식적인 n. 잠재의식 unconscious a. 의식을 잃은, 의식이 없는	어원	-con : together + -sci : know 알다 → '모두가 알고 있는 것은 양심'
	유의어	moral sense, ethics, inner voice
	반의어	Indifference, apathy, unconcern
	영영	A person's inner sense of what is morally right or wrong; a guide to ethical decision-making.
	예문	Her conscience told her to do the right thing. 그녀의 양심은 그녀에게 올바른 일을 하라고 말했습니다.
486 **illiterate** [ɪˈlɪt.ər.ət] a. 글을 모르는, 문맹의 literally adv. 그야말로, 문자 그대로 literary a. 문학의 문예의 illiterately adv. 문맹으로, 교양 없이 transliterate v. 다른 문자로 옮기다	어원	-il, -in : not + -liter : letter 글자 → '글을 모르니 문맹의'
	유의어	uneducated, unlettered, non-literate
	반의어	Literate, educated, knowledgeable
	영영	Lacking the ability to read or write; having limited or no literacy skills.
	예문	In some regions, a significant portion of the population is illiterate. 어떤 지역에서는 인구의 상당 부분이 글을 모르는 상태입니다.

487

comprise

[kəmˈpraɪz]

v. 구성하다

prison n. 감옥, 교도소
enterprise n. 기업, 회사; 경영
prey on p. ~을 먹고 살다
comprisal n. 포함 구성

어원	-com : together + -pri, -pris, -prehend 붙잡다 → '모든 요소를 묶어 구성' * pri(s)나 prehend는 sume보다 더 강한 의미
유의어	consist of, include, encompass
반의어	Exclude, omit, leave out
영영	To consist of or be made up of various parts or elements; to include.
예문	The committee comprises experts from various fields. 위원회는 다양한 분야의 전문가들로 구성되어 있습니다.

488

enrich

[ɪnˈrɪtʃ]

v. 부유하게 하다, 풍요롭게 하다

entitle v. 제목을 붙이다
enlarge v. 확대하다, 확장하다
empower v. 권한을 주다
entrap v. 함정에 빠뜨리다

어원	-en, -em ~하게 하다(E) + -rich 부유한 → '부유하게 만드니 풍요롭게 하다' * -en, -em은 명사 앞에 붙어 동사로 품사를 바꿔주는 역할
유의어	enhance, improve, make richer
반의어	Impoverish, deplete, impoverish
영영	To enhance or improve the quality or value of something; to make richer.
예문	Reading books can enrich your knowledge and vocabulary. 책을 읽는 것은 지식과 어휘를 풍부하게 할 수 있습니다.

489

parliament

[ˈpɑːlɪmənt]

n. 국회, 입법부

parlor n. 응접실, 거실
parley n. 회담, 협상, 대회
for the most part p. 대체로
have no part in p. ~에 관계가 없다

어원	-parlor, -parl 공식적으로 말하다 (E) → '공식적으로 말하는 국회'
유의어	legislature, congress, governing body
반의어	Non-parliament, non-legislative body, non-congress
영영	The highest legislative body in some countries, responsible for making laws and representing the people.
예문	The parliament passed a new law to address environmental issues. 국회는 환경 문제를 다루기 위해 새로운 법을 통과시켰습니다.

490

silhouette

[sìluét]

n. 검은 윤곽, 실루엣

silent a. 침묵을 지키는
seal n. 바다표범, 물개; 인장, 도장 v. 밀폐하다

어원	-silhouette 실루엣 * '18c 프랑스 재무장관 에띠앙 실루엣의 극단적인 긴축재정정책으로 하나의 색으로 초상화를 그리는 게 유행
유의어	outline, profile, contour
반의어	detail, elaboration, intricacy
영영	The dark shape or outline of an object or figure against a lighter background.
예문	The silhouette of the mountain against the sunset was breathtaking. 일몰에 맞춰진 산의 실루엣은 숨막히는 아름다움이었습니다.

491

anonymous

[əˈnɒn.ɪ.məs]

a. 이름이 없는 n. 익명

antonym a. 반의어
synonym n. 동의어, 유의어
economize v. 절약하다, 아끼다
antedate v. ~에 앞서다, 날짜를 앞당기다

어원	-an : not + -nomen, -onym 이름 → '이름이 없으니 익명' * anonymouse 이름을 찾을 수가 없음 VS nameless 이름을 알아도 달라질 게 없음
유의어	nameless, unidentified, unknown
반의어	Named, identified, known
영영	Without a known or revealed identity; nameless or unidentified.
예문	The donation was made by an anonymous benefactor. 기부는 익명의 후원자에 의해 이루어졌습니

492

potable

[ˈpəʊ.tə.bəl]

a. 마실 수 있는

poison n. 독약
pox n. 천연두
pot n. 냄비, 솥; 병, 항아리; 통
pottery n. 도자기, 도

어원	-pos, -pois, -pot 마시다 + -able * portable 휴대용의
유의어	drinkable, suitable for drinking, safe to consume
반의어	Non-potable, undrinkable, contaminated
영영	Suitable for drinking; safe to consume.
예문	The water from the well is potable and safe to drink. 우물에서 나오는 물은 마실 수 있고 안전합니다.

493

communism

[ˈkɒm.jə.nɪ.zəm]

n. 공산주의

in common p. 공통으로, 공동으로
community n. 사회, 공동체, 군집
excommunication n. 제명, 추방
communal a. 공동의, 자치 단체의

어원	-coun, -com : together + -sm 사상 → '불러서 함께 모이는 것이 공산주의'
유의어	socialism, collectivism, Marxist theory
반의어	Capitalism, free market, individualism
영영	A political and economic ideology advocating for common ownership of the means of production and the absence of social classes.
예문	Communism is a political ideology that advocates for collective ownership of resources. 공산주의는 자원의 집단 소유를 주장하는 정치 이념입니다.

494

distract

[dɪˈstrækt]

v. 딴 데로 돌리다, 산만하게 하다

retraction n. 철회
retract v. 취소하다, 철회하다
detract v. 떨어뜨리다, 손상시키다
distraction n. 주위를 산만하게 하는 것

어원	-dis : away + -tract : draw → '~에서 떨어지도록 주의를 끄니 산만한'
유의어	divert, sidetrack, disrupt
반의어	Focus, concentrate, pay attention
영영	To divert one's attention or focus away from something; to disturb or interrupt.
예문	Loud noises can distract students from their studies. 큰 소음은 학생들이 공부를 집중하지 못하게 할 수 있습니다.

495

geometry

[dʒiˈɒm.ə.tri]

n. 기하학, 기하학적 구조

diameter n. 직경, 지름
barometer n. 기압계
commensurate a. 같은 크기의, 적당한
geometric a. 기하학의, 기하학적인

어원	-geo : earth + -mens, -mod, -modus : measure → '땅을 측정하니 기하학'
유의어	mathematics, mathematical study, spatial relationships
반의어	Non-geometry, non-mathematics, non-mathematical
영영	A branch of mathematics that deals with the properties and relationships of points, lines, angles, surfaces, and solids.
예문	Geometry involves the study of shapes and their properties. 기하학은 도형과 그들의 특성을 연구하는 학문입니다.

496

stout

[staut]

a. 통통한, 튼튼한; n. 흑맥주

sturdy a. 튼튼한, 건장한, 확고한
stalwart a. 충실한, 튼튼한
sgrengthen v. 강화하다
substance n. 본질, 실체; 물질

어원	-stout : strong / stand → '서 있기만 하니 통통하면서도 튼튼한'
유의어	strong, robust, sturdy
반의어	thin, slender, slim
영영	Strong, robust, or physically sturdy.
예문	The stout oak tree had stood in the forest for centuries. 튼튼한 참나무는 수세기 동안 숲에 서 있었다.

497

lyric

[ˈlɪr.ɪk]

n. 노래가사; a. 서정시의

lyricist n. 작사가
lyre n. 수금(고대 현악기), 리라
lung n. 폐
lucrative a. 수익성 좋은, 수익성이 높은

어원	-lyr : lyra (G) -lyr : lyra (G) → '리라'라는 현악기를 연주하는 사람', '노래하는 사람의 가사 같은 서정시'
유의어	songlike, poetic, melodious
반의어	instrumental, non-lyrical, wordless
영영	Relating to the words of a song; expressing personal emotions or feelings in a poetic or musical way.
예문	The song's lyrics were filled with emotion. 그 노래 가사는 감정으로 가득 차 있었습니다.

498

profound

[prəˈfaʊnd]

a. 강한; 심오한; 깊은 n. 깊은 바다(심연)

foundation n. 토대, 기초
confound v. 당황케 하다, 혼동하다
fungus n. 균류, 곰팡이류
profoundly adv. 깊게, 대단히

어원	-pro : forth + -found 기초 → '바닥보다 앞에 있으니 깊은' * confound 설명이 섞여 혼동스러운 VS confuse 함께 있어 혼란스러운
유의어	deep, intense, significant
반의어	shallow, superficial, trivial
영영	Having deep meaning, significance, or knowledge.
예문	The philosopher's ideas had a profound impact on society. 그 철학자의 생각은 사회에 깊은 영향을 미쳤다.

499

adequate

[ˈæd.ə.kwət]

a. 적절한

equals v. ~와 같다 n. 등호
equivalent to p. 동등한, 대등한; ~에 상당하는
equipped with p. ~을 갖춘
adquately adv. 적절히

어원	-ad : to + -equ : equal → '동등한 것에 가까우니 적절한'
유의어	sufficient, enough, ample
반의어	insufficient, inadequate, lacking
영영	Sufficient or satisfactory in quality or quantity to meet a particular need or purpose.
예문	Make sure you have adequate supplies for the trip. 여행을 위한 충분한 물품을 준비해 두세요.

500

interfere

[ˌɪn.təˈfɪər]

v. 방해하다, 간섭하다

interfere with p. ~를 방해하다
interact with p. ~와 상호작용하다
interrelate v. 서로 연관시키다
intercede v. 중재하다, 조정하다

어원	-inter : between + -fere 치다 → '서로 상대방을 쳐서 방해하다'
유의어	intervene, intrude, meddle
반의어	assist, aid, facilitate
영영	To get involved in a situation or activity where one is not wanted or needed.
예문	It's important not to interfere with the natural habitat of wildlife. 야생동물의 자연 서식지에 개입하지 않는 것이 중요하다.

501

anecdote

[ˈæn.ɪk.doʊt]

n. 일화

donate v. 기부하다, 기증하다
dosage n. (약의) 정량, 투약
endow v. 기부하다, 재능을 부여하다
doze v. 깜빡 잠이 들다, 졸다

어원	-an : not + -ec, -ex : out + -do, -didon : give → '밖으로 드러나지 않은 이야기'
유의어	story, tale, narrative
반의어	Fact, reality, truth
영영	A short, amusing, or interesting story about a real incident or person.
예문	He shared an amusing anecdote from his recent vacation. 그는 최근 휴가에서의 재미있는 단편 이야기를 공유했습니다.

502

archery

[ˈɑː.tʃər.i]

n. 양궁, 활쏘기

arch n. 아치형 구조물 v. 동그랗게 구부리다
archibishop n. 대주교
anarchy n. 무정부 상태; 난장판
monarch n. 군주

어원	-arch 동그란 구조물 → '동그랗게 구부린 양궁으로 활쏘기'
유의어	bow and arrow, marksmanship, shooting
반의어	Non-archery, absence of bow and arrow use
영영	The sport or practice of using a bow to shoot arrows at a target.
예문	Archery is a precision sport that requires focus and skill. 양궁은 집중력과 기술이 필요한 정밀한 스포츠입니다.

503

digest

[daɪˈdʒest]

v. 소화하다; 이해하다

digestion n. 소화
indigestion n. 소화불량
digestive a. 소화의
ingest v. 섭취하다

어원	-di, -dis : apart + -gest : carry → '나누어 나르듯이 이해하고, 소화하다'
유의어	process, assimilate, metabolize
반의어	regurgitate, vomit
영영	break down food in the stomach and intestines
예문	It may take some time to digest all the information in this book. 이 책의 모든 정보를 소화하는 데 시간이 걸릴 수 있습니다.

504

watchful

[ˈwɒtʃ.fəl]

a. 지켜보는, 주의 깊은

watchdog n. 감시 단체
wachout n. 경계, 조심하기
watch for p. ~을 가만히 기다리다
watcher n. 경비원, 감시인

어원	-watch 지켜보다 + -full → '충분히 지켜보니 주의 깊은'
유의어	vigilant, alert, observant
반의어	careless, inattentive, negligent
영영	Being alert, attentive, or vigilant, often to guard against danger.
예문	The security guard remained watchful throughout the night. 경비원은 밤새 경계를 지켜보았다.

505

cumulative

[ˈkjuːmjələtɪv]

a. 누적되는, 가중의

accumulate v. 모으다, 축적하다, 누적시키다
cumulatively adv. 누적되어, 누계로
accuracy n. 정확함, 정밀함, 정확성
ache v. 아프다

어원	-cumul : heap up 쌓아 올리다 * accumulate 모으다, 축적하다
유의어	accumulative, collective, accrued
반의어	Isolated, separate, individual
영영	Increasing or growing by accumulation or addition.
예문	The cumulative effect of years of hard work finally paid off. 연간 노력의 누적 효과가 마침내 보람을 주었습니다.

506

listless

[ˈlɪstləs]

a. 힘이 없는, 무기력한

literally adv. 그야말로, 문자 그대로
literary a. 문학의 문예의
illiterately adv. 문맹으로, 교양 없이
transliterate v. 다른 문자로 옮기다

어원	-list 목록, 명단 → '명단에도 없으니 힘이 없는'
유의어	apathetic, indifferent, lethargic
반의어	energetic, lively
영영	lacking energy, enthusiasm, or interest; apathetic or lethargic
예문	After a long day of work, he felt listless and lacked energy. 긴 하루 일한 후 그는 기력을 잃고 활기가 없었다.

507

verbal

[ˈvɜːbəl]

a. 말의, 문자 그대로의

verb n. 동사
verbalize v. 말로 표현하다
verbally adv. 말로, 구두로
adverb n. 부사

어원	-verb : word 말, 언어 * verb 동사
유의어	spoken, oral, vocal
반의어	Non-verbal, non-linguistic, non-spoken
영영	Relating to words or spoken language; expressed in words or speech.
예문	He made a verbal agreement to complete the project by the end of the month. 그는 이달 말까지 프로젝트를 완료하기 위한 구두 합의를 했습니다.

508

composure

[kəmˈpoʊʒər]

n. 침착함, 평정심

composition n. 구성; 작곡
be composed of p. ~로 구성되어 있다
component n. 성분, 구성요소
compost n. 퇴비, 두엄

어원	-com : together + -pos : put → '모두 내려 놓으니 마음의 평정'
유의어	calmness, tranquility, poise
반의어	agitation, anxiety, restlessness
영영	Calmness and self-control, especially in stressful situations.
예문	Despite the stressful situation, she maintained her composure. 스트레스 받는 상황에도 불구하고 그녀는 침착함을 유지했다.

509

haste

[heɪst]

n. 급함, 서두름; v. 서두르다

hasten v. 서두르게 하다, 재촉하다
hastily adv. 급히, 허둥지둥
hasty a. 급한, 성급한
haunt v. 귀신이 나타나다, 출몰하다

어원	-hast : hurry → '급히 서두르다'
유의어	hurry, rush, speed
반의어	leisure, slowness
영영	excessive speed or urgency
예문	He completed the project in great haste, and it showed in the quality of his work. 그는 프로젝트를 매우 서두르게 완료했고, 그의 작업 품질에 나타났다.

510

terminate

[ˈtɜːmɪneɪt]

v. 끝나다, 종료되다, 끝내다

terminal n. 터미널
terminated a. 해고된
terminally adv. 종말에, 말단에
terminator n. 끝내는 사람, 명암 경계선

어원	-termin, -term, -tern 끝, 경계 (G) → '끝을 만드니 종료' * 고대 로마 신화, 테르미누스 Terminus 신은 '토지의 경계와 끝, 고정불변의 것'을 뜻함
유의어	end, conclude, finish
반의어	initiate, begin
영영	bring to an end or conclude
예문	The company decided to terminate the employee's contract due to poor performance. 회사는 성과가 나쁜 이직원의 계약을 종료하기로 결정했다.

511

in an effort to do

p. ~하려는 노력으로

in a degree p. 조금은, 어느 정도
in a hurry p. 서두르는
ina series p. 잇달아, 연이어
in a word p. 한 마디로

어원	-ex : out + -for, -forc, -fort : strength 강한(L) → '밖으로 힘을 보내는 것이 노력'
유의어	in an attempt to do, with the aim of doing, striving to do
반의어	without attempting to do, without trying to do
영영	with the aim or intention of doing
예문	He started jogging every morning in an effort to improve his health. 그는 건강을 회복하기 위해 아침마다 조깅을 시작했습니다.

512

in the face of

p. ~에도 불구하고, ~에 직면하여

at one's face value p. 액면 그대로
face up to p. ~을 받아들이다, 직시하다
straight face p. 무표정한 얼굴
in the air p. 헛된 근거 없는

어원	-fac 겉면, 앞면(L) * fac '얼굴이나 겉의 면' VS front '앞쪽의 면'
유의어	despite, notwithstanding, regardless of
반의어	unaffected by, unfazed by, undeterred by
영영	despite or in defiance of
예문	She remained calm in the face of adversity. 그녀는 역경에 직면해도 차분했습니다.

513

in conclusion

p. 결론적으로, 끝으로

jump to a conclusion p. 성급하게 결론내리다
conclusive a. 결정적인
in contrast to p. ~와는 대조적으로

어원	-con : intensive + -clud, -clude, -clos : close, shut → '논의를 완전히 끝내고 결론을 내리다'
유의어	finally, to sum up, in summary
반의어	in the introduction, in the beginning, initially
영영	finally or as a final point
예문	In conclusion, I believe we should invest more in renewable energy sources. 결론적으로, 저는 우리가 재생 가능한 에너지원에 더 많은 투자를 해야 한다고 생각합니다.

514

get A out

p. A를 생산하다

get A out of the way p. A를 치우다
get something out p. ~을 생산하다
get to the point p. 핵심에 이르다
get the hang of p. ~에 익숙해지다

어원	-get 얻다 + -out 꺼내다 → '꺼내서 얻어내는 것이 생산, 그 소식이 알려지다'
유의어	remove A, extract A, take A out
반의어	put A in, place A inside, insert A
영영	extract or remove A
예문	He managed to get the information out of the reluctant witness. 그는 마지못해 주인공으로부터 정보를 끌어냈습니다.

515

at latest

p. 늦어도 ~까지는

latest a. 최신의, 최근의
at the cost of p. ~의 비용을 지불하고
at the last minute p. 막판에, 마지막 순간에
at most p. 기껏해야

어원	-la : late 늦은 → '가장 늦어도 ~까지는'
유의어	at the latest, by the latest, no later than
반의어	at earliest, at the earliest possible time, at the soonest
영영	by the latest possible time or date
예문	Please submit your report by Friday at the latest. 최대한 늦어도 금요일까지 보고서를 제출해 주세요.

516

in good faith

p. 옳다고 믿으며, 선의로

family n. 가족
faithful a. 충실한, 충직한
fidelity n. 충실, 충성
fiance n. 약혼자

어원	-fid, -fy, -faith : trust 믿다
유의어	sincerely, genuinely, honestly
반의어	in bad faith, dishonestly, deceitfully
영영	with honesty or sincerity
예문	He acted in good faith, believing that his friend would pay him back. 그는 친구가 돈을 갚을 것이라고 믿어 선량한 신념으로 행동했습니다.

517

at one another

p. 서로

in other words p. 다시 말해서
on the other hand p. 반면에, 한편으로는
the other way around p. 반대로
otherwise adv. 그렇지 않으면, 다른 방법으로

어원	-one 하나 + -a 하나 + -other 다른 → '하나와 또 다른 하나가 서로'
규의어	towards each other, to one another, facing each other
반의어	apart from one another, separate from one another, isolated from one another
정영	toward each other or facing each other
예문	The two dogs growled at one another before becoming friends. 두 개의 개는 서로에게 으르렁거리다가 친구가 되었습니다.

518

by law

p. 법에 의해

outlaw n. 무법자, 범법자
lawful a. 합법적인
by cash p. 현금으로
by now p. 이제는, 이미

어원	-by 수단 + -law 법 → '법을 가지고'
규의어	legally, according to the law, pursuant to law
반의어	illegally, unlawfully, criminally
정영	according to the law or legally
예문	Wearing a seatbelt is required by law. 시트벨트 착용은 법적으로 의무화되어 있습니다.

519

in a series

p. 잇달아, 연이어

a series of p. 일련의
in a hurry p. 서두르는
in an effort to do p. ~하려는 노력으로
in a word p. 한 마디로

어원	-ser, -sert 밀어 넣어 합치다 → '개별 사건의 결합이니 연속' * join, junc(t) '서로 다른 것이 합침' VS ser(t) '밀어 넣어 합침'
규의어	sequentially, successively, one after the other
반의어	standalone, independent, separate
정영	occurring one after another or in succession
예문	The events unfolded in a series of unexpected twists. 사건들은 예상치 못한 연쇄적인 변화 속에 펼쳐졌습니다.

520

come to one's rescue

p. ~을 구조하러 오다

curative a. 치료의
incurable a. 치유할 수 없는, 불치의
come to do p. ~하게 되다
come to one's senses p. 정신이 들다

어원	-come 오다 + -rescue 구조하다 → '구조하러 오다'
규의어	aid, assist, help
반의어	abandon one, desert one, neglect one
정영	assist or aid someone in need
예문	The firefighters came to the family's rescue when their house caught fire. 집에 불이 났을 때 소방대가 가족을 구하기 위해 나섰습니다.

Chapter 14.

521	wreckage	[ˈrek.ɪdʒ]	n. 난파, 잔해물, 잔해
522	surpass	[səˈpɑːs]	v. ~을 능가하다, ~보다 낫다
523	celsius	[ˈsel.si.əs]	n. 섭씨
524	repute	[ripjúːt]	v. 평하다, 생각하다 n. 평판, 소문
525	council	[ˈkaʊn.səl]	n. 위원회, 심의회, 지방 의회
526	startle	[ˈstɑː.təl]	v. 깜짝 놀라게 하다
527	allocate	[ˈæl.ə.keɪt]	v. 할당하다, 배분하다
528	attribute	[ˈæt.rɪ.bjuːt]	v. ~탓으로 돌리다; n. 속성, 성질
529	outspoken	[ˌaʊtˈspəʊ.kən]	a. 거리낌 없는, 솔직한
530	align	[əˈlaɪn]	v. 일렬로 하다, 정렬시키다, 조정하다
531	curse	[kɜːs]	n. 저주; v. 저주하다
532	flavor	[ˈfleɪ.vər]	n. 풍미, 향미, 맛; 향미로, 조미료
533	kindle	[ˈkɪn.dəl]	v. (불을 붙이다), 태우다
534	resign	[rɪˈzaɪn]	v. 사임하다
535	atmosphere	[ˈæt.mə.sfɪər]	n. 공기의 영역(대기권), 분위기
536	devastate	[ˈdev.ə.steɪt]	v. 완전히 파괴하다, 유린하다, 황폐화하다
537	furnish	[ˈfɜː.nɪʃ]	v. (가구를) 비치하다, 제공하다
538	physiology	[fiziɑ́lədʒi]	n. 생리학, 생리 (기능)
539	beware	[bɪˈweər]	v. 조심하다, 주의하다
540	competent	[ˈkɒm.pɪ.tənt]	a. 유능한, 능숙한
541	lad	[læd]	n. 사내애, 청년
542	suppress	[səˈpres]	v. 진압하다, 억제하다; 참다
543	alienation	[ˌeɪ.li.əˈneɪ.ʃən]	n. 소외감
544	imperial	[ɪmˈpɪə.ri.əl]	a. 제국의, 황제의
545	affirm	[əˈfɜːm]	v. 확언하다, 단언하다, 주장하다
546	remark	[rɪˈmɑːk]	n. 논평, 말 v. 논평하다, 발언하다, 주목하다
547	frantic	[ˈfræn.tɪk]	a. 미친듯이 서두는, 제정신이 아닌
548	tempt	[tempt]	v. 유혹하다
549	hibernate	[háibərnèit]	v. 동면하다
550	irrespective	[irispéktiv]	a. 상관하지 않는, 고려하지 않고
551	impose A on B		p. A를 B에 부과하다, 선고하다
552	come to do		p. ~하게 되다
553	on one hand		p. 한편으로는
554	set an example of		p. ~의 본보기가 되다
555	excuse oneself for		p. ~에 대해 변명하다, 사과하다
556	in any case		p. 어떠한 경우에도
557	hold together		p. 단결시키다
558	catch hold of		p. ~을 (붙)잡다
559	get into trouble		p. ~을 어려움에 빠뜨리다
560	at all times		p. 항상

521

wreckage

[ˈrek.ɪdʒ]

n. 난파, 잔해물, 잔해

reck v. ~을 개의하다, 염려하다
wreck n. 난파선, 잔해
wrecker 파괴자; 레커차, 견인차
wretched a. 비참한 끔찍한

어원	-wreck 잔해 * wrecker = tow truck 견인차
유의어	debris, ruins, wreckage remains
반의어	Intact, undamaged, unharmed
영영	The remains or debris of something that has been destroyed or damaged.
예문	After the accident, the wreckage of the car was scattered on the road. 사고 후 자동차의 파편이 도로에 흩어져 있었습니다.

522

surpass

[səˈpɑːs]

v. ~을 능가하다, ~보다 낫다

encompass v. 둘러싸다, 망라하다, 포함하다
surpassing a. 뛰어난, 우수한
keep pace with p. ~과 보조를 맞추다
pass up p. ~의 기회를 놓치다

어원	-sur : super + -pass, -pace 통과하다 → '위를 통과하니 능가하다'
유의어	exceed, outperform, outdo
반의어	Lag behind, fall short, underperform
영영	To exceed or go beyond in quality, degree, or achievement.
예문	Her performance in the race surpassed everyone's expectations. 그녀의 경주에서의 성과는 모두의 기대를 뛰어넘었습니다.

523

celsius

[ˈsel.si.əs]

n. 섭씨

precent n. 백분율, 퍼센트
Fahrenheit n. 화씨
centennial a. 100년마다의 n. 100주년
centimeter n. 1/100미터

어원	* 스웨덴의 천문학자 안데르스 셀시우스의 이름을 땀 * centigrade 섭씨(-cent, -centi 100(L) + -grade 단계)
유의어	centigrade, temperature scale, degree Celsius
반의어	Fahrenheit, Kelvin, temperature scale
영영	A temperature scale used in most of the world, with 0°C as the freezing point of water and 100°C as the boiling point at sea level.
예문	The temperature in the room is set to 22 degrees Celsius. 방의 온도는 섭씨 22도로 설정되어 있습니다.

524

repute

[ripjúːt]

v. 평하다, 생각하다 n. 평판, 소문

reputation n. 명성, 평판
reputable a. 명성 높은, 평판이 좋은
reputed a. 평판이 좋은
imputation n. 전가, 비난

어원	-re : again + -put : think → '계속 생각하는 것이니 평하다'
유의어	reputation, status, renown
반의어	Disrepute, disgrace, dishonor
영영	The reputation or standing of someone or something in the eyes of others; regard or esteem.
예문	The restaurant has a good repute for its delicious cuisine. 그 레스토랑은 맛있는 음식으로 유명합니다.

525

council

[ˈkaʊn.səl]

n. 위원회, 심의회, 지방 의회

commision n. 수수료; 위원회
commissionary n. 대표자, 대리
commissary n. 매점, 간이 식당
in common p. 공통으로, 공동으로

어원	-coun, -com : together + -cil : call → '불러서 함께 모이는'
유의어	committee, assembly, board
반의어	individual, person
영영	a group of people convened for the purpose of discussion, decision-making, or advisory
예문	The city council met to discuss the proposed budget. 시의회가 제안된 예산을 논의하기 위해 모였다.

526

startle

[ˈstɑː.təl]

v. 깜짝 놀라게 하다

kick-start p. 시동을 걸다, 시작하다
startling a. 놀라울 정도의
starve to death p. 굶어 죽다
stick out of p ~에서 삐져나오다

어원	-start 시작 → '시작하기 전에 '땅'하고 총을 쏴서 놀라게 하다'
유의어	surprise, shock, alarm
반의어	calm, soothe, comfort
영영	To surprise or shock someone suddenly, often causing a quick reaction.
예문	The sudden loud noise made her startle and drop her book. 갑자기 큰 소음 때문에 그녀는 놀라서 책을 떨어뜨렸다.

527

allocate

[ˈæl.ə.keɪt]

v. 할당하다, 배분하다

allow for p. ~을 허용하다, ~을 가능케 하다
allowance n. 용돈, 비용; 허용량
amenity n. 편의시설; 예의
arouse v. 자극하다, 깨우다

어원	-al : to + -loc : place → '금액을 나눠 할당하니 배분' * allowance 일정 금액의 돈을 나눠주는 것, 영국은 pocket money
유의어	distribute, assign, allot
반의어	withhold, retain, keep
영영	To distribute or apportion resources, often money or time, for a specific purpose.
예문	The company decided to allocate more resources to the marketing department. 회사는 마케팅 부서에 더 많은 자원을 할당하기로 결정했다.

528

attribute

[ˈæt.rɪ.bjuːt]

v. ~탓으로 돌리다; n. 속성, 성질

atttribute A to B b. A를 B탓으로 돌리다
attorn v. 양도하다
attire v. 옷을 차려 입히다
tribe n. 종족

어원	-at : to + -tribu : assign → '~방향으로 책임을 할당하니 탓으로 돌리다', '~에게 할당된 성질' * tribute '존경의 표시로 값진 물건을 바친다'
유의어	ascribe, assign, credit
반의어	dissociate, disconnect
영영	a quality or characteristic of a person or thing
예문	She attributes her success to hard work and determination. 그녀는 자신의 성공을 노력과 결단력에 기인한다고 생각한다.

529

outspoken

[ˌaʊtˈspoʊ.kən]

a. 거리낌 없는, 솔직한

utter a. 극단적인 v. 밖으로 소리를 내다
utterly adv. 완전히, 철저히
bespeak v. 미리 부탁하다
stretch out p. ~을 내밀다, 뻗다

어원	-out : outside + -spoken → '밖으로 그냥 내뱉으니 거리낌 없는'
유의어	candid, frank, forthright
반의어	reserved, quiet, reticent
영영	Frank and candid in expressing opinions or feelings; not reserved or shy about expressing oneself.
예문	She is known for being outspoken and always speaking her mind. 그녀는 솔직하고 항상 생각을 표현하는 것으로 알려져 있습니다.

530

align

[əˈlaɪn]

v. 일렬로 하다, 정렬시키다, 조정하다

link A to B p. A를 B와 연관시키다
lineage n. 계통, 혈통
deadline n. 기한, 마감 시한
guideline n. 지침, 정책

어원	-a : to + -lign : line → '~방향, 일렬로 정렬'
유의어	arrange, adjust, coordinate
반의어	misalign, disarrange
영영	to arrange in a straight line or correct relative positions; to bring into cooperation or agreement
예문	The team needs to align their goals and work together towards a common objective. 팀은 목표를 일치시키고 공통의 목표를 향해 함께 일해야 한다.

531

curse

[kɜːs]

n. 저주; v. 저주하다

cursor n. 커서
course n. 진로 v. 뒤쫓다, 추적하다
run its course p. 경과를 거치다
cast A aside p. A를 버리다

어원	-curse 악을 부르는 기도 / -car, -cur, -cour 달리다, 탈 것(L) → '계속 달려서 도망가야 하는 저주'
유의어	swear, imprecate, maledict
반의어	blessing, boon
영영	a profane or offensive word or expression; to wish harm or misfortune upon someone or something
예문	Some people believe that curses can bring bad luck. 일부 사람들은 저주가 악운을 가져올 수 있다고 믿는다.

532

flavor

[ˈfleɪ.vər]

n. 풍미, 향미, 맛; 향미료, 조미료

flavorful a. 풍미가 가득한, 맛이 풍부한
flavoring n. 향신료, 맛성분
flame n. 화염, 불꽃
inflame v. 자극하다, 타오르다

어원	-fla : flame → '불맛으로 향미를 돋우는' * taste 혀로 느끼는 맛 VS flavor 냄새, 질감, 눈으로 예상
유의어	taste, seasoning, savor
반의어	Tastelessness, blandness, lack of flavor
영영	The taste or distinctive quality of a food or beverage.
예문	The chef added herbs to enhance the flavor of the dish. 요리사는 요리의 맛을 높이기 위해 허브를 추가했습니다.

533

kindle

[ˈkɪn.dəl]

v. (불을 붙이다), 태우다

candle n. 양초
carnage n. 살육, 대량 학살
incarnate v. 구체화하다; 양초를 갖게 하다
incense n. 향, 냄새 v. 격분시키다

어원	-kindle : candle 양초 → '양초에 불을 붙이다'
유의어	ignite, spark, arouse
반의어	extinguish, quench, douse
영영	To ignite or start a fire; metaphorically, to inspire or arouse emotions or interest.
예문	Reading a good book can kindle a love for literature. 좋은 책을 읽는 것은 문학에 대한 애정을 불러일으킬 수 있다.

534

resign

[rɪˈzaɪn]

v. 사임하다

design v. 고안하다
assign v. 할당하다
consign v. 맡기다, 넘겨주다
ensign n. 국기

어원	-re : back + -sign 표시 → '뒤로 물러나겠다고 표시하니 사임하다'
유의어	quit, step down, retire
반의어	Accept, embrace, take on
영영	To voluntarily leave a job, position, or responsibility; to formally quit.
예문	After many years of service, he decided to resign from his job. 오랜 업무를 한 후, 그는 직장에서 사임하기로 결정했습니다.

535

atmosphere

[ˈæt.mə.sfɪər]

n. 공기의 영역(대기권), 분위기

hemisphere n. 반구
biosphere n. 생물권
hemicycle n. 반원, 반원형 극장
sphere n. 구; 영역; 분야

어원	-atmo : air 공기, 수증기 + -sphere 구, 지구 → '지구의 공기 중 분위기'
유의어	air, environment, ambiance
반의어	Vacuum, emptiness, void
영영	The layer of gases surrounding a planet, including Earth, that is held in place by gravity.
예문	The atmosphere of the party was festive and lively. 파티 분위기는 축제적이고 활기찼습니다.

536

devastate

[ˈdev.ə.steɪt]

v. 완전히 파괴하다, 유린하다, 황폐화하다

vest n. 조끼, 속옷
vessel n. 선박; 혈관; 용기
devastating a. 엄청나게 충격적인
detonate v. 폭발시키다, 폭발하다

어원	-de : completely + -vat, -vas, -was : empty → '철저히 비어있게 만드니 파괴'
유의어	destroy, ruin, devastate
반의어	Rebuild, restore, reconstruct
영영	To cause extensive and severe damage or destruction; to overwhelm with grief or shock.
예문	The natural disaster devastated the coastal town. 자연 재해로 인해 해안 도시가 완전히 파괴되었습니다.

537

furnish

[ˈfɜː.nɪʃ]

v. (가구를) 비치하다, 제공하다

furniture n. 가구
furnished a. 가구가 비치된
furnishing n. 가구, 비품, 건구, 복식품
provident a. 신중한, 조심스러운

어원	-furn, furnit, form : provide 공급하다 → '가구를 공급하니 가구 비치'
유의어	provide, supply, equip
반의어	strip, empty, vacate
영영	To provide or supply something, often referring to furniture or equipment.
예문	The newlywed couple is excited to furnish their first home together. 신혼 부부는 함께 처음으로 집을 꾸밀 것을 기대하고 있다.

538

physiology

[fiziάlədʒi]

n. 생리학, 생리 (기능)

physiological a. 생리학의, 생리적인
physics n. 물리학
physician n. 내과 의사
meta-physical p. 형이상학의

어원	-physio 물체의, 육체의 / 자연 + -logy 학문 → '육체의 모든 것을 연구하는 학문'
유의어	biology, study of the body, bodily functions
반의어	Anatomy, morphology, bodily structure
영영	The branch of biology that deals with the functions and processes of living organisms.
예문	The study of human physiology examines the functions of the body's organs. 인체 생리학 연구는 몸의 기관 기능을 조사합니다.

539

beware
[bɪˈweər]

v. 조심하다, 주의하다

beware of p. ~을 조심하다
rewarding a. 보람 있는
unaware of p. ~을 알지 못하는
warranty n. 보증, 품질 보증서

어원	-be 상태 + -warn, -ward, -war : watch (E) → '주의해서 지켜보니 조심해라'
유의어	be cautious, be alert, take care
반의어	trust, believe, rely
영영	To be cautious or careful of something or someone potentially dangerous.
예문	Beware of the slippery floor; it's easy to fall. 미끄러운 바닥을 조심하세요. 쉽게 넘어질 수 있습니다.

540

competent
[ˈkɒm.pɪ.tənt]

a. 유능한, 능숙한

competence n. 능숙함, 능력
competitive a. 경쟁력 있는, 경쟁심 강한
compete v. 경쟁하다
competition n. 경쟁, 대회

어원	-com : together + -pet 가서 찾다 → '함께 찾는 경쟁에서 이기니 유능하고 능숙한' * competitor 모두 승리 VS rival 한 사람만 승리
유의어	capable, skilled, proficient
반의어	Incompetent, incapable, unqualified
영영	Having the necessary knowledge, skill, or ability to do something effectively.
예문	She is a competent manager who can handle complex projects. 그녀는 복잡한 프로젝트를 다룰 수 있는 능력 있는 매니저입니다.

541

lad
[læd]

n. 사내애, 청년

lady n. 여자 분, 아가씨
lag v. 뒤쳐지다 뒤떨어지다
lack n. 부족, 결핍 v. 부족하다
landscape n. 풍경, 풍경화

어원	-lad 사내애, 청년 * lady 여자 분, 아가씨
유의어	boy, youth, youngster
반의어	girl, lass
영영	a young boy or youth, often used informally
예문	The young lad was excited to go on his first fishing trip. 어린 소년은 첫 낚시 여행에 흥분했다.

542

suppress
[səˈpres]

v. 진압하다, 억제하다; 참다

어원	-sup, -sub : under + -press → '아래로 누르며 진압하다'
유의어	repress, quell, inhibit
반의어	express, reveal, display
영영	To prevent or restrain something from happening; to subdue or control a feeling or action.
예문	It's important to suppress your anger and stay calm. 분노를 억누르고 침착해 있어야 합니다.

543

alienation
[ˌeɪ.li.əˈneɪ.ʃən]

n. 소외감

alienate v. 소외하다
alien n. 외국인, 외계인
inalienable a. 양도할 수 없는 빼앗을 수 없는

어원	-al, -alien, -alter, altru : other 다른(L) → '다른 이로 만들어 소외시키다' * alter 특성·성질·모양 등이 변함 VS shift 위치·방향을 이동
유의어	estrangement, isolation, detachment
반의어	Inclusion, integration, acceptance
영영	The feeling of being isolated, estranged, or disconnected from one's surroundings or society.
예문	His philanthropic work left a lasting legacy in the community. 그의 자선활동은 지역사회에 지속적인 유산을 남겼습니다.

544

imperial
[ɪmˈpɪə.ri.əl]

a. 제국의, 황제의

imperial a. 제국의, 황제의
imperious a. 오만한, 고압적인
emperor n. 황제, 제왕
empire n. 제국

어원	-imper : emper 절대적 명령 → '절대적 명령을 하는 황제의 제국' * emperor 황제
유의어	regal, royal, majestic
반의어	Non-imperial, non-monarchic, non-sovereign
영영	Relating to an empire or an emperor; grand or majestic in scale.
예문	The imperial palace is a symbol of the country's history. 제국 궁전은 그 나라의 역사의 상징입니다.

545

affirm

[əˈfɜːm]

v. 확언하다, 단언하다, 주장하다

reaffirm v. 재확인하다
affirmative a. 확언적인, 긍정의
affirmatively adv. 긍정적으로, 확정적으로
infirm a. 허약한

어원	-af : to + -firm 강한, 확실한(G) → '~에게 확실하다고 단언하다'
유의어	confirm, assert, declare
반의어	deny, negate, contradict
영영	To state or assert something as true or valid.
예문	She affirmed her commitment to the project. 그녀는 프로젝트에 대한 약속을 재확인했다.

546

remark

[rɪˈmɑːk]

n. 논평, 말 v. 논평하다, 발언하다, 주목하다

marker n. 표지, 표시
leave a mark on p. ~에 큰 영향을 미치다
make a remark p. 말을 하다
markedly adv. 현저하게, 눈에 띄게

어원	-re : again + -mark 표시하다 → '다시 계속 의견을 표시하는 논평'
유의어	comment, observation, statement
반의어	ignore, disregard
영영	spoken or written comment or observation
예문	Her witty remark made everyone in the room laugh. 그녀의 재치 있는 언급으로 방 안에 있는 모든 사람이 웃었다.

547

frantic

[ˈfræn.tɪk]

a. 미친듯이 서두는, 제정신이 아닌

frantically adv. 미친듯이, 광란적으로
frenzy n. 광란, 발작
frustrate v. 좌절감을 주다; 방해하다
fraction n. 단편, 일부, 소량; 분수

어원	-fran, -fren 강한 흥분 → '강한 흥분으로 미친듯이' syn. hectic
유의어	frenzied, panicked, wild
반의어	Calm, composed, collected
영영	Characterized by wild, hurried, or disordered activity or behavior.
예문	She was frantic when she realized she had lost her passport. 여권을 잃어버렸다는 것을 깨닫자 그녀는 광란 상태였습니다.

548

tempt

[tempt]

v. 유혹하다

be tempted to do p. ~하고 싶은 마음이 생기다
temptation n. 유혹
extemporize v. 즉흥적으로 하다
attemp n. 시도, 노력; 시도하다

어원	-tempet : taunt 시도하다, 시험하다, 유혹하다 (L) * tempo 템포를 빠르게 만들어 유혹
유의어	entice, lure, seduce
반의어	deter, dissuade, discourage
영영	Attract or entice someone to do something, typically something unwise or wrong.
예문	The aroma of freshly baked bread tempted her. 막 구운 빵의 향기가 그녀를 유혹했습니다.

549

hibernate

[háibərnèit]

v. 동면하다

hide v. 감추다, 숨다
hibernation n. 동면
hibernal a. 겨울의, 겨울 같은
hierarchy n. 계급, 위계

어원	-hide 감추다 / -hiber(F) 불어로 '겨울' → '겨울에 모습을 감추고 동면하다'
유의어	sleep, rest, dormant
반의어	awaken, rouse
영영	go into a state of inactivity or dormancy during a season
예문	Some animals hibernate during the winter to conserve energy. 겨울 동안 일부 동물은 에너지를 절약하기 위해 동면한다.

550

irrespective

[ìrispéktiv]

a. 상관하지 않는, 고려하지 않고

respect v. 존경하다
disrespect n. 실례, 무례 v. 존경하지 않다
respectively adv. 각각
restitution n. 반환, 복권

어원	-ir, -in : not + -respective 각각의 → '각각 고려하지 않으니 상관하지 않는'
유의어	regardless, regardless of, without regard to
반의어	considerate, mindful, concerned
영영	regardless of, without regard to.
예문	We will consider all applicants irrespective of their background. 우리는 모든 지원자를 그들의 배경과 관계없이 고려할 것이다.

551

impose A on B

p. A를 B에 부과하다, 선고하다

compose v. 구성하다, 작곡하다
depose v. 물러나게 하다, 퇴위시키다
dispose v. 배열하다; 처분하다
poise n. 침착, 균형

어원	-im : in + -pos, -pon, -pound : put 놓다 (L) → '마음 안에 뭔가를 계속 놓아 부담하도록 강요하다'
유의어	enforce A on B, compel B to accept A, thrust A upon B
반의어	liberate B from A, free B from A, release B from A
영영	force or compel B to accept A
예문	The government decided to impose new taxes on imported goods. 정부는 수입품에 대한 새로운 세금을 부과하기로 결정했습니다.

552

come to do

p. ~하게 되다

to do with p. ~와 관계가 있는
do away with p. 폐지하다, 없애다
do one's part in p. 자신의 몫을 다하다
do over p. ~을 다시 하다, 꾸미다

어원	-come 오다
유의어	begin to do, start to do, undertake
반의어	avoid doing, refrain from doing, eschew doing
영영	begin or start to do
예문	He came to regret his decision after seeing the consequences. 그는 결과를 보고 자신의 결정을 후회하게 되었습니다.

553

on one hand

p. 한편으로는

give a hand p. 도와주다
second-hand p. 간접적으로
hand down p. ~을 물려주다
hand out p. 나눠주다

어원	-hand 손 → '한 손이 더해지니 한편으로는'
유의어	firstly, on the one side, from one perspective
반의어	on the other hand, conversely, contrarily
영영	from one perspective or viewpoint
예문	On one hand, I want to travel, but on the other hand, I need to save money. 한편으로는 여행을 하고 싶지만, 다른 한편으로는 돈을 절약해야 합니다.

554

set an example of

p. ~의 본보기가 되다

exempt v. 면제하다 a. 면제의
exemplify v. 예증하다, 예시하다
sampling n. 표본 추출, 샘플링
set A apart from B p. A와 B를 구별하다

어원	-set 설정 + -example 예시 → '예시를 설정하니 본보기가 되다'
유의어	demonstrate, exhibit, show
반의어	fail to exemplify, set a negative example of, be a cautionary tale of
영영	demonstrate or illustrate by one's actions
예문	As a teacher, she always tries to set a good example of hard work for her students. 선생님으로서, 그녀는 항상 자신의 학생들에게 노력의 좋은 본을 보이려고 노력합니다.

555

excuse oneself for

p. ~에 대해 변명하다, 사과하다

inexcusable a. 용서할 수 없는
make an excuse for p. ~에 대한 변명을 하다
accuse v. 고발하다, 기소하다

어원	-ex : out + -cuse : reason → '이유를 밖으로 돌리고 변명을 대니 용서하다'
유의어	apologize for, justify oneself for, offer an explanation for
반의어	blame oneself for, condemn oneself for, criticize oneself for
영영	apologize or justify one's actions
예문	He excused himself for being late to the meeting. 그는 회의에 늦어서 사과했습니다.

556

in any case

p. 어떠한 경우에도

in the event of p. ~의 경우에는
in bulk p. 대량으로
in charge of p. ~을 담당하는
in accordance with p. ~에 준하여, 일치하여

어원	-cas : fall → '사건이 떨어지는 경우'
유의어	regardless, anyhow, nevertheless
반의어	in every case, in each instance, in every scenario
영영	regardless or in any event
예문	In any case, we need to finish this project by the end of the week. 어떤 경우에도, 우리는 이번 주 안에 이 프로젝트를 끝내야 합니다.

557

hold together

p. 단결시키다

hold oneself together p. 침착함을 유지하다
hold out p. ~을 내밀다
hold on p. 붙잡고 있다, 잠시만
hold one's tongue p. 입을 다물다

어원	-hold 잡다 + -together 함께 → '함께 손잡도록 단결시키다'
유의어	remain intact, stay united, stick together
반의어	fall apart, disintegrate, collapse
영영	remain intact or united
예문	The glue helped hold the broken pieces of the vase together. 접착제가 깨진 꽃병 조각들을 함께 붙여주었습니다.

558

catch hold of

p. ~을 (붙)잡다

catch air p. 뛰어오르다
catch on p. 이해하다, 알아듣다
catch wind of p. ~의 낌새를 채다
catch oneself p. 하던 일을 갑자기 멈추다

어원	-catch 잡다 + -hold 갖다 → '잡아서 갖고 있다'
유의어	grasp, seize, capture
반의어	release, let go of, relinquish
영영	grasp or seize firmly
예문	She caught hold of the railing to steady herself. 그녀는 자기 자신을 꾸짖기 위해 난간을 잡았습니다.

559

get into trouble

p. ~을 어려움에 빠뜨리다

go to trouble p. 애를 쓰다, 힘들다
troublesome a. 골치 아픈
get by p. 그럭저럭 살아나가다
get out p. 생산하다

어원	-get into 들어가다 + -trouble 어려움 → '어려움에 들어가도록 하다'
유의어	get in trouble, get into difficulties, encounter problems
반의어	stay out of trouble, avoid trouble, steer clear of trouble
영영	become involved in difficulties or problems
예문	He got into trouble for arriving late to work multiple times. 그는 여러 번 지각해서 문제가 생겼습니다.

560

at all times

p. 항상

all the time p. 항상
by the time p. ~할 즈음에
all the same time p. 동시에
in the nick of time p. 아슬아슬하게 맞춰

어원	-at 지점 + -all + -time → '매 순간 시간이니 항상'
유의어	always, constantly, continuously
반의어	never, seldom, rarely
영영	always or continuously
예문	It's important to wear a helmet when riding a bike at all times. 어느 때나 자전거를 탈 때 헬멧을 착용하는 것이 중요합니다.

Chapter 15.

561	notate	[nóuteit]	v. 악보로 표시하다; 기록하다, 적어두다
562	thorn	[θɔːrn]	n. 가시; 고통을 주는 것
563	frigid	[ˈfrɪdʒɪd]	a. 몹시 추운, 냉담한
564	corrupt	[kəˈrʌpt]	v. 부패시키다, 타락시키다
565	stockpile	[ˈstɒk.paɪl]	n. 비축, 비축량 v. 비축하다
566	trim	[trɪm]	v. (깎아) 다듬다, 없애다; 삭감하다
567	abandon	[əˈbæn.dən]	v. 단념하다, 포기하다, 버리다
568	obsolete	[ˌɒb.səlˈiːt]	a. 쇠퇴한, 구식의
569	gloomy	[ˈɡluː.mi]	a. 우울한
570	commodity	[kəˈmɒd.ə.ti]	n. 상품, 판매 상품
571	overwhelm	[ˌəʊ.vəˈwelm]	v. 제압하다, 압도하다
572	tuition	[tʃuːˈɪʃ.ən]	n. 교육; 수업료
573	diplomacy	[dɪˈpləʊ.mə.si]	n. 공문서; 외교
574	mediate	[ˈmiː.di.eɪt]	v. 조정하다, 중재하다
575	hazard	[ˈhæz.əd]	n. 위험 v. ~을 위태롭게 하다
576	valid	[ˈvæl.ɪd]	a. 유효한
577	discourse	[dískɔːrs --ˊ]	n. 이야기, 대화; 강연, 담론, 담화
578	reckless	[ˈrek.ləs]	a. 무모한, 신중하지 못한
579	assume	[əˈsjuːm]	v. 가정하다, 추측하다; 떠맡다; ~인 체하다
580	conform	[kənˈfɔːm]	v. (행동, 생각을) 같이하다, 순응하다
581	perish	[ˈper.ɪʃ]	v. 멸망하다, 갑자기 죽다; 썩다; 타락하다
582	urge	[ɜːdʒ]	v. 재촉하다, 추진하다; n. 욕구, 충동
583	subordinate	[səˈbɔː.dɪ.nət]	a. 하위의 ; 부차적인, 부수적인; n. 부하
584	deadly	[ˈded.li]	a. 치명적인, 극도의
585	overthrow	[ˌəʊ.vəˈθrəʊ]	n. 타도, 전복 v. 전복시키다, 뒤엎다
586	depict	[dɪˈpɪkt]	v. 묘사하다, 서술하다
587	devote	[dɪˈvəʊt]	v. (노력·돈·시간 따위를) 들이다, 바치다
588	adolescent	[ˌæd.əˈles.ənt]	a. 사춘기 청소년의, 청년의
589	strife	[straɪf]	n. 분쟁, 불화, 반목
590	administration	[ədˌmɪn.ɪˈstreɪ.ʃən]	n. 관리, 행정(부)
591	carry on		p. 계속 수행하다, 계속 ~하다
592	do away with		p. 폐지하다, 없애다
593	commitment to N		p. ~에 대한 헌신
594	react to N		p. ~에 반응하다
595	cold to N		p. ~에 냉담한
596	take A for granted		p. A를 당연하게 여기다
597	on one's own		p. 독자적으로
598	cope with		p. 다루다, 대처하다
599	in a word		p. 한마디로
600	call after		p. ~을 따라 이름 짓다

561

notate

[nóuteit]

v. 악보로 표시하다; 기록하다, 적어두다

note n. 메모, 기록 v. 주목하다, 알아채다
noteworthy a. 주목할 만한
notice n. 통보; 주목
take notice of p. 알다, 주목하다

어원	-no, -not : mark 표시하다, know 알다(L) → '알도록 표시하며 기록하다'
유의어	write down, record, transcribe
반의어	erase, remove, delete
영영	To write down or represent something, typically music or a score, using notation or symbols.
예문	It's important to note the details in the contract. 계약서의 세부 사항을 주목하는 것이 중요합니다.

562

thorn

[θɔːrn]

n. 가시; 고통을 주는 것

thorny a. 가시가 많은
thorned a. 가시가 있는, 가시가 무성한
stalk n. 줄기 v. 몰래 접근하다
stalker n. 스토커

어원	-thorn : stem 줄기 → '줄기나 가지의 가시'
유의어	prickle, spike, barb
반의어	flower, bloom
영영	a sharp, pointed, or prickle-covered projection on the stem or branch of a plant; a source of annoyance or difficulty
예문	She pricked her finger on a thorn while picking roses in the garden. 그녀는 정원에서 장미를 딸 때 가시에 손가락을 찔렸다.

563

frigid

[ˈfrɪdʒ.ɪd]

a. 몹시 추운, 냉담한

frost n. 서리 a. 서리가 낀
freeze v. 얼어붙다 움직이지 않다
freezing a. 영하의, 꽁꽁 얼게 추운
fright n. 공포, 경악

어원	-freeze 얼음으로 변하다(E) → '얼음으로 얼어 붙을 정도로 몹시 추운'
유의어	cold, freezing, icy
반의어	warm, hot
영영	extremely cold; lacking warmth or emotion
예문	The winter in Siberia can be extremely frigid, with temperatures dropping well below freezing. 시베리아의 겨울은 아주 추워서 영하로 기온이 떨어지기도 한다.

564

corrupt

[kəˈrʌpt]

v. 부패시키다, 타락시키다

disrupt v. 붕괴시키다, 분열시키다
erupt v. 분출하다, 폭발하다
dissect v. 해부하다, 분석하다
corruptly adv. 타락하여, 부패하여

어원	-co : together + -rup, -rump : break → '다 같이 상태가 부서지니 부패'
유의어	unethical, dishonest, depraved
반의어	honest, ethical
영영	engage in dishonest or immoral behavior; cause to become dishonest or impure
예문	The corrupt government officials were involved in embezzlement. 부패한 정부 관리들은 횡령 사건에 연루되어 있었다.

565

stockpile

[ˈstɒk.paɪl]

n. 비축, 비축량 v. 비축하다

stock n. 재고품, 저장품; 주식
take stock p. 찬찬히 살펴보다, 점검하다
stock market p. 주식 시장
stockholder n. 주주

어원	-stock 저장 + -pile 더미 → '더미로 저장해서 비축'
유의어	accumulate, hoard, store
반의어	Deplete, use up, exhaust
영영	A large quantity of goods, materials, or supplies stored for future use or emergencies.
예문	The country decided to stockpile emergency supplies for disasters. 그 나라는 재난을 위한 비상 시설을 비축하기로 결정했습니다.

566

trim

[trɪm]

v. (깎아) 다듬다, 없애다; 삭감하다

retailer n. 소매업자
tailor n. 재봉사 v. 맞추다, 조정하다
trimly adv. 정돈하여
trimmed up p. 잘라서 다듬다

어원	-trim : tail → '필요 없는 부분은 잘라 다듬다'
유의어	cut, clip, prune
반의어	expand, enlarge, lengthen
영영	to make something neat and orderly by cutting or removing excess.
예문	She decided to trim her hair to get rid of split ends. 그녀는 열린 머리끝을 없애기 위해 머리를 다듬기로 결정했다.

567

abandon

[əˈbæn.dən]

v. 단념하다, 포기하다, 버리다

abandoned a. 버려진, 방탕한, 타락한
abandonment n. 포기, 자포자기
ban v. 명령으로 금지하다
banish v. 명령으로 추방하다

어원	-ab : away + -ban, -band 명령, 법 → '명령에서 멀어진 것이니 단념하고 포기' * bandit 명령을 듣지 않는 산적 VS contraband 명령에 반대로 하니 밀수(품)
유의어	forsake, desert, leave behind
반의어	retain, keep, hold onto
영영	Leave or desert something or someone completely.
예문	They had to abandon their plans due to bad weather. 나쁜 날씨 때문에 그들은 계획을 포기해야 했습니다.

568

obsolete

[ˌɒb.səlˈiːt]

a. 쇠퇴한, 구식의

obsolescence n. 쇠퇴, 퇴화
obsoleteness n. 못쓰게 됨, 폐기됨
obsoletely adv. 폐기되어
insolent a. 무례한, 거만한

어원	-ob : away + -sol : solo(l) → '떨어져 혼자가 되니 쇠퇴한'
유의어	outdated, outmoded, antiquated
반의어	current, modern
영영	no longer in use or outdated
예문	Some old technology has become obsolete in recent years. 일부 오래된 기술은 최근 몇 년 동안 사용되지 않게 되었다.

569

gloomy

[ˈɡluː.mi]

a. 우울한

gloom n. 우울, 침울; 어둠
groom n. 신랑
gloomy about p. ~에 대해 암울한
gloomily adv. 어둡게, 침울하게

어원	-gloom 우울 * (먹)구름이 어두워 우울한
유의어	dark, dismal, overcast
반의어	cheerful, sunny, bright
영영	Dark or dim; having a dismal or depressing atmosphere.
예문	The rainy, gloomy weather dampened their spirits. 비오고 어두운 날씨로 그들의 기분이 침체되었습니다.

570

commodity

[kəˈmɒd.ə.ti]

n. 상품, 판매 상품

mould v. 틀에 넣어 만들다
mole n. 두더지; 스파이
accommodate v. 맞추다; 숙박시키다
moderate v. 절제하다, 조절하다

어원	-come : with + -mod : measure + -ity(명접) → 규격에 맞춘 상품
유의어	good, product, item
반의어	luxury, rarity, uniqueness
영영	A raw material or primary agricultural product that can be bought and sold.
예문	Oil is a valuable commodity in the global market. 석유는 국제 시장에서 가치 있는 상품이다.

571

overwhelm

[ˌəʊ.vəˈwelm]

v. 제압하다, 압도하다

be overwhelmed with p. ~에 휩싸이다
overwhelming a. 압도적인
oversee v. 감독하다
overweening a. 과시하는, 우쭐대는

어원	-over : superior + -whelm 압도하다 → '위에서 제압하니 압도하다' * 위에서 whale 고래가 짓누르는 느낌
유의어	overpower, overcome, inundate
반의어	underwhelm, fail to impress, disappoint
영영	Overpower or overcome someone or something completely; inundate with a large quantity.
예문	The beauty of the landscape overwhelmed him. 그 풍경의 아름다움이 그를 압도했습니다.

572

tuition

[tʃuːˈɪʃən]

n. 교육; 수업료

intuition n. 직관, 직관력, 통찰력
intuitively adv. 직관에 의하여
tutor n. 개인 지도 교사, 가정교사
counterintuitive a. 직관에 어긋나는

어원	-tuit, -tut : teach / look → '가르치는 교육으로 수업료 받아야지'
유의어	education cost, fees, instruction
반의어	Non-tuition, non-instruction, lack of teaching
영영	The cost or fee for instruction or education at a school, college, or university.
예문	The university increased tuition fees for the upcoming academic year. 대학은 다가오는 학년도를 위해 등록금을 인상했습니다.

573

diplomacy

[dɪˈpləʊ.mə.si]

n. 공문서; 외교

diploma n. 증서, 수료증, 졸업장, 학위
diplomatic a. 외교관의, 외교의
dilemma n. 딜레마, 궁지, 진퇴양난
dioxide n. 이산화물

어원	-di : two + plo 접다 + -ma 단수형 접미사 → '두 번 접은 종이(공문서)를 다루는 외교'
유의어	foreign affairs, international relations, statecraft
반의어	Hostility, conflict, antagonism
영영	The art and practice of conducting negotiations and maintaining relationships between nations and governments.
예문	Diplomacy plays a key role in international relations and negotiations. 외교는 국제 관계와 협상에서 중요한 역할을 합니다.

574

mediate

[ˈmiː.di.eɪt]

v. 조정하다, 중재하다

meditation n. 명상
meditate v. 명상하다
medieval a. 중세의
median a. 중간의

어원	-medi : middle → '가운데서 중재하며 조정하다'
유의어	intervene, arbitrate, negotiate
반의어	escalate, worsen, aggravate
영영	To intervene in a dispute or conflict to help facilitate a resolution.
예문	The mediator helped resolve the conflict between the two parties. 조정자가 두 당사자 간의 분쟁을 해결하는 데 도움을 주었다.

575

hazard

[ˈhæz.əd]

n. 위험 v. ~을 위태롭게 하다

hazardous a. 유해한, 위험한
haze n. 연무, 실안개
in a haza p. (눈이) 흐릿하여
hay n. 건초

어원	-hazard위험 * -haz : haze 안개 때문에 위험한
유의어	risk, danger, peril
반의어	safety, security, certainty
영영	A potential source of danger or risk; a perilous situation.
예문	Crossing the busy road without looking both ways is a hazard. 양쪽을 보지 않고 바쁜 도로를 건너는 것은 위험합니다.

576

valid

[ˈvæl.ɪd]

a. 유효한

validity n. 타당성
valiant a. 용맹한, 단호한
validate v. 유효하게 만들다
validation n. 유효성, 유효성 검증

어원	-val, -vail 가치(L) / strong 강한 → '근거의 가치가 있으니 유효하고 타당한' * price 가격의 가치 VS value 추상적인 가치
유의어	legitimate, acceptable, lawful
반의어	Invalid, void, null
영영	Legally or logically acceptable; sound or justified.
예문	Your passport must be valid for at least six more months to enter the country. 귀하는 이 나라에 입국하려면 여권이 적어도 여섯 개월 이상 유효해야 합니다.

577

discourse

[dískɔːrs --ˊ]

n. 이야기, 대화; 강연, 담론, 담화

accordance n. 일치,, 조화
cordial a. 화기애애한, 다정한
discord n. 의견 차이, 불화
coarse a. 조잡한, 거친

어원	-dis : apart + -cour, -cur : run → '사방에서 달려드는 발 없는 말로 담론'
유의어	discussion, conversation, dialogue
반의어	silence, quietude, muteness
영영	Written or spoken communication or conversation, often of a formal nature.
예문	Their discourse on the topic lasted for hours. 그들의 주제에 대한 담화는 몇 시간 동안 계속되었다.

578

reckless

[ˈrek.ləs]

a. 무모한, 신중하지 못한

reck v. 개의하다, 마음을 쓰다
reckon v. ~라고 생각하다, 여겨지다
reckon in p. ~을 계산에 넣다
recklessly adv. 무모하게

어원	-reck : care + -less 無 → '신경 쓰지 않으니 무모한'
유의어	careless, irresponsible, thoughtless
반의어	cautious, prudent, careful
영영	acting without care or consideration; irresponsible.
예문	His reckless driving led to a serious accident. 그의 무모한 운전으로 심각한 사고가 발생했다.

579

assume

[əˈsjuːm]

v. 가정하다, 추측하다; 떠맡다; ~인 체하다

assumption n. 가정, 전제; 추정, 산정
assumedly adv. 아마
presume v. 가정하다, 추측하다
resume v. 다시 시작하다; n 이력서

어원	-as : to + -sum : take 취하다, 골라 가지다 → '한 방향으로 생각을 취하니 가정'
유의어	suppose, presume, take for granted
반의어	doubt, question, challenge
영영	To take on a particular role, responsibility, or belief without proof or confirmation.
예문	He didn't want to assume anything without concrete evidence. 그는 확실한 증거 없이는 어떤 가정도 하고 싶지 않았다.

580

conform

[kənˈfɔːm]

v. (행동, 생각을) 같이하다, 순응하다

conformity n. 순응
deform v. 흉하게 만들다
reform v. 개혁하다, 개선하다
formiulate v. 정립하다, 공식화하다

어원	-con : together + -form 형태 → '같은 형태니 순응하고 같이 하는 것이다'
유의어	comply, adhere, follow
반의어	Rebel, dissent, oppose
영영	To comply with established rules, standards, or norms; to act in accordance with expectations.
예문	Some individuals choose to conform to societal norms. 어떤 개인들은 사회적 규범에 순응하기로 선택합니다.

581

perish

[ˈper.ɪʃ]

v. 멸망하다, 갑자기 죽다; 썩다; 타락하다

perishable a. 상하기 쉬운, 썩는
perished a. 싸늘해진, 마모된
perishability n. 부패하기 쉬움
perishing a. 망하는, 파괴하는

어원	-peri : away * -ish : finish → '완전히 떠나버리다는 건 죽거나 멸망', '죽으면 몸이 썩는'
유의어	die, expire, pass away
반의어	thrive, flourish, endure
영영	to die or be destroyed, especially due to natural causes.
예문	Without food and water, they feared they would perish in the desert. 음식과 물이 없이, 그들은 사막에서 목숨을 잃을 것을 두려워했다.

582

urge

[ɜːdʒ]

v. 재촉하다, 추진하다; n. 욕구, 충동

urgent a. 긴급한, 절박한, 재촉하는
urgently adv. 긴급하게, 절박하게
urgency n. 긴급함, 절박함, 위급함
ruburd n. 먼 교외

어원	-work, -erg, -urg, -ag 일, 일하다 → '일을 하라고 다그치며 재촉하다'
유의어	desire, impulse, prompt
반의어	discourage, dissuade
영영	strongly encourage or persuade
예문	She had a strong urge to visit her hometown after years away. 그녀는 몇 년 만에 고향을 방문하고 싶은 강한 욕망을 느꼈다.

583

subordinate

[səˈbɔː.dɪ.nət]

a. 하위의 ; 부차적인, 부수적인; n. 부하

subordinative a. 종속적인, 하위의
coordination n. 조정력, 공동 작용
incordinate a. 과도한
extraordinary a. 특별한, 비상한

어원	-sub : under + -ordin : arrange → '아래 순서에 속하니 하급의'
유의어	junior, underling, assistant
반의어	Superior, superior, higher-up
영영	A person who is lower in rank or position within an organization or hierarchy.
예문	Managers need to delegate tasks to their subordinate employees. 관리자는 부하 직원에게 업무를 위임해야 합니다.

584

deadly

[ˈded.li]

a. 치명적인, 극도의

dreary a. 음울한, 따분한
dread v. 몹시 두려워하다
drastic a. 격렬한, 과감한
drape v. (장막을) 드리우다

어원	-dead : death → '죽을 정도로 치명적인'
유의어	lethal, fatal, mortal
반의어	harmless, nonlethal
영영	capable of causing death; extremely harmful or lethal
예문	The snake's bite can be deadly if not treated promptly. 뱀의 물림은 즉시 치료되지 않으면 치명적일 수 있다.

585

overthrow

[ˌoʊ.vəˈθrəʊ]

n. 타도, 전복 v. 전복시키다, 뒤엎다

throw away p. 버리다
throw in p. 덤으로 주다
a stone's throw p. 매우 가까운 거리
thus adv. 이렇게 하여, 이와 같이, 따라서

어원	-over + -throw → '위를 엎으니 전복'
유의어	oust, topple, depose
반의어	Uphold, preserve, maintain
영영	To forcefully remove a government or ruling authority from power.
예문	The rebels planned to overthrow the oppressive government. 반군은 압제적인 정부를 전복하려고 계획했습니다.

586

depict

[dɪˈpɪkt]

v. 묘사하다, 서술하다

picture v. 그리다, 상상하다
depict A as B p. A를 B로 표현하다
depicture v. 상상하다, 묘사하다
diploy v. 전개하다, 배치하다

어원	-de : down + -pict : paint → '그려 내려가며 묘사하다'
유의어	portray, represent, illustrate
반의어	distort, misrepresent
영영	represent or portray something in a picture or description
예문	The painting beautifully depicts the sunset over the ocean. 그 그림은 바다 위의 일몰을 아름답게 묘사하고 있다.

587

devote

[dɪˈvoʊt]

v. (노력·돈·시간 따위를) 들이다, 바치다

devoted to p. ~을 전담하는, ~에 헌신하는
devoted a. 헌신적인, 바쳐진
vow v. 서약하다
avow v. 공언하다, 인정하다

어원	-de : intense + -vot, -vo, -vow 의지 (G) → '의지로 맹세하고 모든 것을 들여 바치다'
유의어	dedicate, commit, consecrate
반의어	neglect, ignore
영영	to give one's time, effort, or attention to a particular purpose or activity; to dedicate or commit oneself to something
예문	She was a devoted fan of the famous singer and attended all his concerts. 그녀는 유명 가수의 헌신적인 팬이었고 그의 모든 콘서트에 참석했다.

588

adolescent

[ˌæd.əˈles.ənt]

a. 사춘기 청소년의, 청년의

adolescence n. 사춘기, 청춘기
adolesce v. 청년기에 이르다
adolescently adv. 청소년기에

어원	-ad : to + -oles, -ales : grow → '어른으로 자라고 있는 청소년'
유의어	teenager, youth, young adult
반의어	Adult, mature, grown-up
영영	A young person who is in the stage of development between childhood and adulthood; a teenager.
예문	Adolescents often experience significant physical and emotional changes. 청소년들은 종종 중요한 신체적 및 정서적 변화를 경험합니다.

589

strife

[straɪf]

n. 분쟁, 불화, 반목

struggle v. 고군분투하다 n. 투쟁, 싸움
strenuous a. 몹시 힘든, 격렬한
stride v. 성큼성큼 걷다, 활보하다
strive v. 투쟁하다, 노력하다

어원	-str : strength 싸우다 → '싸움으로 생긴 분쟁'
유의어	conflict, discord, disagreement
반의어	Harmony, peace, tranquility
영영	Conflict, discord, or disagreement, often resulting in hostility or tension.
예문	Political strife in the country led to social unrest. 그 나라의 정치적 갈등이 사회 불안을 야기했습니다.

590

administration

[ədˌmɪn.ɪˈstreɪ.ʃən]

n. 관리, 행정(부)

administer v. 관리하다, 통치하다, 운영하다
administrative a. 행정상의, 관리상의
admire v. 존경하다, 찬양하다, 감탄하다
make an adjustment p. 조정하다

어원	-ad : to + -minister : serve → '~에 충실히 봉사하는 관리 행정'
유의어	management, governance, leadership
반의어	Rebellion, insurgency, revolt
영영	The process of managing and organizing the affairs of an organization or government.
예문	The administration of the company is responsible for managing daily operations. 회사의 행정 부서는 일상 영업을 관리하는 역할을 담당합니다.

591

carry on

p. 계속 수행하다, 계속 ~하다

carry out p. ~을 수행하다
carry weight p. ~을 중요하게 여기다
miscarry v. 유산하다
miscarriage n. 유산; 실패, 실책

어원	-carry 나르다 + -on 계속 → '계속해서 나르니 임무를 수행하다'
유의어	continue, proceed, persist
반의어	cease, stop, halt
영영	continue or proceed with
예문	Despite the challenges, we must carry on and complete the project. 어려움에도 불구하고, 우리는 계속해서 프로젝트를 완료해야 합니다.

592

do away with

p. 폐지하다, 없애다

to do with p. ~와 관계가 있는
do A up p. A단추를 채우다; 포장하다
do one's part in p. 자신의 몫을 다하다
do over p. ~을 다시 하다, 꾸미다

어원	with(함께) 하는 것을 away(멀리) do(하니) 폐지하다, 없애다
유의어	eliminate, abolish, eradicate
반의어	keep, maintain, retain
영영	abolish or eliminate completely
예문	The company decided to do away with its outdated policies. 그 회사는 구식 정책을 폐지하기로 결정했습니다.

593

commitment to N

p. ~에 대한 헌신

commit v. 전념하다, 헌신하다; 약속하다
commit oneself to p. ~하기로 맹세하다
committed a. 헌신하는, 전념하는
committee v. 의뢰하다, 주문하다 n. 위원회

어원	-com : together + -miss, -mitt, -mist, -mess : course, send → '같은 과정을 밟으며 헌신하고 전념하자고 약속'
유의어	dedication to N, loyalty to N, devotion to N
반의어	disloyalty to N, faithlessness to N, betrayal of N
영영	dedication or loyalty to N
예문	Her commitment to her studies led to her success. 그녀의 학업에 대한 헌신이 그녀의 성공으로 이끌었습니다.

594

react to N

p. ~에 반응하다

reaction n. 반작용; 반응, 대응
reactive a. 반응을 보이는
reactivity n. 반응성, 반작용
enact v. (법률을) 제정하다, 규정하다

어원	-re : back + -act → '행동으로 돌려주니 반응하다'
유의어	respond to N, reply to N, counter N
반의어	ignore N, disregard N, overlook N
영영	respond or respond to N
예문	People react differently to stressful situations. 사람들은 스트레스 상황에 다르게 반응합니다.

595

cold to N

p. ~에 냉담한

coldy adv. 춥게, 차게
coldish a. 쌀쌀한, 약간 추운
coldness n. 추움, 냉담함, 차가움
clumsy a. 서투른, 어색한

어원	-cold 추운 + -to 상대 → '상대에게 쌀쌀하니 냉담한'
유의어	indifferent to N, aloof to N, unresponsive to N
반의어	warm to N, affectionate towards N, loving towards N
영영	indifferent or unresponsive to N
예문	She was cold to him after their argument. 그녀는 그들의 다툼 이후 그에게 냉담했습니다.

596

take A for granted

p. A를 당연하게 여기다

grant v. 주다, 수여하다
grant a wish p. 소원을 들어주다
take it for granted p. ~을 당연하게 여기다
be taken for granted p. 당연시되다

어원	-take 여기다 + -granted 승인된 → '승인된 것으로 여기다'
유의어	assume A, presume A, expect A
반의어	appreciate A, value A, cherish A
영영	assume or consider A as a given
예문	He took her kindness for granted, not realizing how much she did for him. 그는 그녀의 친절을 당연시하고, 그녀가 그를 위해 얼마나 많은 일을 했는지 깨닫지 못했습니다.

597

on one's own

p. 독자적으로

own a. 자신의, 직접 ~한 v. 소유하다
ownership n. 소유
owe A to B p. A는 B덕분이다
all on one's own p. 자력으로, 스스로

어원	-one's + -owe 빚지다 → '스스로에게 빚을 지니 독자적으로'
유의어	independently, by oneself, solo
반의어	with others, together, collectively
영영	independently or without assistance
예문	She traveled around Europe on her own. 그녀는 유럽을 혼자 여행했습니다.

598

cope with

p. 다루다, 대처하다

cope v. 대처하다, 대응하다 n. 사제복
cozy a. 편안한
curb v. 억제하다
curl up p. 동그랗게 말리다, 몸을 웅크리다

어원	-cope : cupe 쿠테타(F) → '쿠테타에 대처하다'
유의어	deal with, handle, manage
반의어	succumb to, be overwhelmed by, be defeated by
영영	deal effectively with or manage
예문	It can be challenging to cope with loss, but with time, healing is possible. 손실에 대처하는 것은 어려울 수 있지만, 시간이 지나면 치유가 가능합니다.

599

in a word

p. 한마디로

word got around p. 소문이 돌았다
word of-mouth p. 구두의, 말로 전하는
wording n. 표현(법), 용어
foreword n. 머리말

어원	-a 하나 + -word 말, 단어(E) → '말 한 마디로'
유의어	briefly, in short, to sum up
반의어	in many words, elaborately, at length
영영	briefly or in summary
예문	In a word, the concert was amazing. 한 마디로, 콘서트는 놀라웠습니다.

600

call after

p. ~을 따라 이름 짓다

so-called p. 소위, 이른바
call back p. ~을 취소하다
call for p. ~을 요구하다, 구하다
call off p. 취소하다, 중지하다

어원	-call 큰 외침(E) + -after 뒤따라 → '뒤따라 부르는 이름이 같으니 따라 이름 짓다'
유의어	name after, designate after, label after
반의어	rename, rebrand, retitle
영영	name or designate in honor of
예문	They decided to call their daughter after her grandmother. 그들은 딸의 이름을 할머니의 이름을 따라 지었습니다.

Chapter 16.

601	discriminate	[dɪˈskrɪm.ɪ.neɪt]	v. 차별하다, 구별하다
602	compulsive	[kəmˈpʌl.sɪv]	a. 강박적인, 충동적인
603	sequence	[ˈsiː.kwəns]	n. 순서, 연속; (연속된) 한 장면
604	portray	[pɔːˈtreɪ]	v. 묘사하다
605	shed	[ʃed]	v. 깎다; 흘리다 n. 간이 창고, 차고; 헛간
606	fortify	[fɔ́ːrtəfài]	v. 강화하다, 요새화하다
607	glide	[glaɪd]	v. 미끄러지듯 가다, 활공하다
608	deposit	[dɪˈpɒz.ɪt]	n. 계약금, 예약금, 예금; 퇴적물, 침전물
609	designate	[ˈdez.ɪg.neɪt]	v. 가리키다, 나타내다; 임명하다
610	entail	[ɪnˈteɪl]	v. (결과를) 수반하다, 필요로 하다
611	combustion	[kəmˈbʌs.tʃən]	n. 연소, 산화, 불에 탐
612	dominate	[ˈdɒm.ɪ.neɪt]	v. (살면서) 지배하다
613	melancholy	[ˈmel.əŋ.kɒl.i]	a. 우울한, 슬픈
614	worship	[ˈwɜː.ʃɪp]	v. 예배하다, 숭배하다
615	contemplate	[ˈkɒn.təm.pleɪt]	v. 심사숙고하다, 신중하게 살펴보다
616	enlightenment	[ɪnˈlaɪ.tən.mənt]	n. 깨달음
617	indebt	[indét]	a. 부채가 있는, 빚이 있는: 은혜를 입은
618	edible	[ˈed.ə.bəl]	a. 먹기에 좋은
619	inhale	[ɪnˈheɪl]	v. 흡입하다
620	breed	[briːd]	v. 번식하다; 새끼를 낳다; 사육하다, 재배하다
621	condemn	[kənˈdem]	v. 비난하다; 선고하다
622	mischance	[ˌmɪsˈtʃɑːns]	n. 불운, 불행
623	superb	[suːˈpɜːb]	a. 장엄한, 화려한, 훌륭한
624	accentuate	[əkˈsen.tʃu.eɪt]	v. 강조하다, 두드러지게 하다
625	abrupt	[əˈbrʌpt]	a. 돌연한, 갑작스러운
626	insist	[ɪnˈsɪst]	v. 주장하다; 요구하다
627	peel	[piːl]	v. (껍질을) 벗기다; 옷을 벗다; 이탈하다
628	sting	[stɪŋ]	v. 찌르다; 자극하다 n. 아픔, 날카로움
629	enormous	[ɪˈnɔː.məs]	a. 거대한, 어마어마한, 엄청난
630	blush	[blʌʃ]	v. 얼굴을 붉히다, 빨개지다
631	at one's convenience		p. ~가 편한 때에
632	take pride in		p. ~을 자랑하다
633	end up		p. 결국 ~이 되다
634	have only to do		p. ~하기만 하면 된다.
635	have a handle on		p. 이해하다, 알아듣다
636	honour A with B		p. A에게 B를 수여하다
637	at no cost		p. 공짜로
638	in a degree		p. 조금은, 어느 정도
639	for fear of		p. ~을 두려워하다, ~을 경외하다
640	at times		p. 때때로

601

discriminate

[dɪˈskrɪm.ɪ.neɪt]

v. 차별하다, 구별하다

crime n. 범죄, 범행
criminal a. 범죄의
discrimination n. 차별
criterion n. 기준

어원	-dis : apart + -crimin : sift → '따로 분리하니 차별하다'
유의어	differentiate, segregate, distinguish
반의어	integrate, include
영영	to unfairly treat or judge someone or a group of people based on their differences, such as race, gender, or religion
예문	It is important not to discriminate against people based on their race or gender. 인종이나 성별에 따라 사람을 차별하지 않는 것이 중요하다.

602

compulsive

[kəmˈpʌl.sɪv]

a. 강박적인, 충동적인

compulsively adv. 강박적으로, 충동적으로
compulsory a. 강제적인, 의무적인
ocmpulsorily adv. 강제적으로, 의무적으로
compulsion n. 충동, 강박감, 강제성

어원	-com 강조 + -pul : drive 몰아가다 → '자신을 완전히 몰아가는 상태니 강박적인'
유의어	obsessive, addictive, uncontrollable
반의어	voluntary, optional
영영	characterized by an irresistible urge or impulse to do something, often repeatedly
예문	His compulsive need to check his phone every few minutes became a problem. 그의 몇 분마다 핸드폰을 확인해야 하는 강박적인 필요성이 문제가 되었다.

603

sequence

[ˈsiː.kwəns]

n. 순서, 연속; (연속된) 한 장면

subsequence n. 다음
subsequent a. 다음의
subsequently adv. 그 뒤에, 나중에
sequel n. 속편, 후속

어원	-sub : after + -secu, -sequ, -su, -sue : follow → '뒤에 따라 나오는 다음' * consequence '함께 나온 즉각적인 결과' VS subsequence '뒤따라 나온 간접적인 결과'
유의어	order, series, arrangement
반의어	Disarray, randomness, chaos
영영	A particular order in which related things follow each other.
예문	The sequence of events in the story is crucial to understanding the plot. 이야기의 사건 순서는 줄거리를 이해하는 데 중요합니다.

604

portray

[pɔːˈtreɪ]

v. 묘사하다

portrayal n. 기술, 묘사
tray n. 쟁반
trading n. 거래, 영업
treaty n. 조약, 협정

어원	-por, -pro : forward + -tray : draw → '앞으로 특징을 끌어내어 표현하다'
유의어	depict, represent, illustrate
반의어	Misrepresent, distort, falsify
영영	To depict or represent someone or something in a particular way, often through art, words, or actions.
예문	The artist used vibrant colors to portray the beauty of nature. 예술가는 자연의 아름다움을 묘사하기 위해 생동감 있는 색상을 사용했습니다.

605

shed

[ʃed]

v. 깎다; 흘리다 n. 간이 창고, 차고; 헛간

shabbily adv. 부적절하게, 초라하게
shab n. 추잡한 것, 구두쇠
shed light on p. 해명하다, ~을 비추다
shave v. 깎다, 면도하다

어원	-sha, -shi, -she, -sho : cut → '나무를 깎고 잘라서 만든 헛간'
유의어	discard, cast off, get rid of
반의어	Accumulate, gather, collect
영영	To discard or get rid of something; to cast off or release.
예문	The snake will shed its skin as it grows. 뱀은 자라면서 피부를 벗을 것입니다.

606

fortify

[fɔ́ːrtəfài]

v. 강화하다, 요새화하다

fortress n. 성채, 요새
forte n. 장점, 장기
enforce v. 강요하다
fortune n. 운; 재산; 성쇠

어원	-for, -forc, -fort : strength 강한(L) + -tude(명접) → '강하게 만들기 위해 요새화하다'
유의어	strengthen, reinforce, secure
반의어	weaken, debilitate, enfeeble
영영	Strengthen or reinforce something, often for the purpose of defense or protection.
예문	They needed to fortify the castle's defenses. 그들은 성의 방어력을 강화해야 했습니다.

607

glide
[glaɪd]

v. 미끄러지듯 가다, 활공하다

slide n. 저하, 하락, 미끄러짐 v. 미끄러 | ㅈ다
sled n. 썰매
slight a. 약간의, 조금의
slip away p. 사라지다, 없어지다

어원	-glide : slide → '미끄러지듯 가다'
유의어	slide, coast, soar
반의어	stumble, trip
영영	to move smoothly and gracefully, often with little effort or resistance
예문	The swan glided gracefully across the serene lake. 백조는 고요한 호수 위를 우아하게 미끄러져 다녔다.

608

deposit
[dɪˈpɒz.ɪt]

n. 계약금, 예약금, 예금; 퇴적물, 침전물

dispose of p. ~을 처리하다
disposition n. 성향, 의향; 정리, 처분
depose v. 물러나게 하다
depot n. 저장소; 정거장

어원	-de : down + -pos : put → '밑에 쌓아둔 예금으로 계약금'
유의어	put, place, lay down
반의어	Withdrawal, removal, taking away
영영	To place or entrust something in a particular location, often for safekeeping.
예문	He made a deposit at the bank to save money for the future. 그는 미래를 위해 돈을 저축하기 위해 은행에 예금을 했습니다.

609

designate
[ˈdez.ɪɡ.neɪt]

v. 가리키다, 나타내다; 임명하다

design v. 고안하다
consign v. 맡기다, 넘겨주다; 보내다
ensign n. 국기
designated a. 지정된, 임명된

어원	-de : down + -sign 부호, 기호 → '아래 지도에 특별한 지역을 가리키다'
유의어	appoint, name, assign
반의어	undesignate, unassign, unname
영영	To assign a specific name, title, role, or status to something or someone.
예문	They had to designate a new leader for the project. 그들은 프로젝트의 새로운 리더를 지정해야 했습니다.

610

entail
[ɪnˈteɪl]

v. (결과를) 수반하다, 필요로 하다

curtail v. 짧게 줄이다; 빼앗다
tailor n. 재봉사; v. 맞추다, 조정하다
in detail p. 상세하게
retail n. 소매, 소매상 a. 소매의, 소매상의

어원	-en : make + -tail 꼬리 → '꼬리를 만드니 결과를 수반'
유의어	involve, necessitate, require
반의어	exclude, omit, disregard
영영	to involve or require as a necessary consequence.
예문	Buying a house can entail a long and complex process. 집을 사는 것은 긴 복잡한 과정을 수반할 수 있습니다.

611

combustion
[kəmˈbʌs.tʃən]

n. 연소, 산화, 불에 탐

burn out p. 소진되다
burnished a. 광을 낸 닦은
blush v. 얼굴을 붉히다, 빨개지다
combustive a. 연소성의

어원	-com : completely + -bu, -bust : burn → '완전히 태워버리는 연소'
유의어	burning, ignition, combustion process
반의어	Extinguishment, quenching, dousing
영영	The process of burning or ignition, typically involving oxygen and fuel.
예문	Combustion is the process of burning fuel to produce energy. 연소는 연료를 태우고 에너지를 생산하는 과정입니다.

612

dominate
[ˈdɒm.ɪ.neɪt]

v. (살면서) 지배하다

domesticate v. 길들이다
predominant a. 두드러진, 우세한, 지배적인
domain n. 영토
dominance n. 지배, 권세, 우세, 우월함

어원	-dom 지배하다 (L) → 둥근 천장 → 건축양식 → '범위 내에서 지배하다' * dom '지배' VS man, main '살다'
유의어	control, overpower, rule
반의어	submit, yield
영영	to have power and control over others or a situation; to be the most prominent or influential
예문	The dominant player on the team scored most of the goals. 팀에서 주도적인 선수가 대부분의 골을 넣었다.

613

melancholy

[ˈmel.ən.kɒl.i]

a. 우울한, 슬픈

mourn v. 애도하다, 슬퍼하다
moan n. 신음 v. 신음하다
bemoan v. 슬퍼하다, 애도하다
lame a. 절름발이의

어원	-melan 검다 + -chole 담즙 → '체액 중에서 흑담즙이 과잉해지는 상태'
유의어	sadness, sorrow, depression
반의어	happiness, joy, elation
영영	a feeling of deep sadness or sorrow.
예문	The rainy weather always puts her in a state of melancholy. 비오는 날씨는 언제나 그녀를 우울한 기분으로 만든다.

614

worship

[ˈwɜː.ʃɪp]

v. 예배하다, 숭배하다

worthy a. ~할 자격이 있는; 훌륭한
be worthwhile to do p. ~할 가치가 있다
wound v. 부상을 입히다 n. 부상, 상처
worshipful a. 숭배하는, 존경하는

어원	-wor : worth + -ship : carry → '가치를 신에게 나르니 숭배'
유의어	veneration, adoration, reverence
반의어	Desecrate, profane, blaspheme
영영	The act of showing reverence, devotion, or adoration to a deity or religious entity.
예문	People gather at the church every Sunday to worship. 사람들은 매주 일요일에 교회에서 예배를 드립니다.

615

contemplate

[ˈkɒn.təm.pleɪt]

v. 심사숙고하다, 신중하게 살펴보다

temper n. 화, 성미, 기질, 기분
lone one's temper p. 화를 내다
temple n. 사원, 절
comtemplative a. 사색적인, 신중히 살피는

어원	-con : completely + -temple 사원, 절 → '절이나 사원 따위에 가서 미래를 유심히 살펴보다'
유의어	consider, meditate, reflect
반의어	neglect, disregard
영영	think deeply or carefully about something
예문	He liked to contemplate the mysteries of the universe. 그는 우주의 신비를 숙고하는 것을 좋아했다.

616

enlightenment

[ɪnˈlaɪ.tən.mənt]

n. 깨달음

enlighten v. 계몽하다, 이해시키다
brighten v. 밝게 하다, 즐겁게 하다
delight v. 기쁨을 주다 n. 기쁨
brilliant a. 탁월한, 찬란한

어원	-en : in + -light, -bright, -brill 빛 → '빛 안에서 깨달음'
유의어	illumination, insight, awareness
반의어	Ignorance, unawareness, lack of knowledge
영영	The Age of Enlightenment, a philosophical and intellectual movement in the 18th century that emphasized reason, science, and individual rights.
예문	Their love was believed to be eternal, lasting beyond this lifetime. 그들의 사랑은 영원하다고 믿어져 이 생애를 초월하는 것입니다.

617

indebt

[indét]

a. 부채가 있는, 빚이 있는: 은혜를 입은

indebted a. 신세를 진, 빚을 진
debt n. 빚, 부채
debtor n. 채무자, 차주
debenture n. 채무증서, 사채권

어원	-in : in + -debt 빚 → '안에 빚이 있는'
유의어	owe, burdened with debt, in debt
반의어	Clear, settle, pay off
영영	Owing money or being financially obligated to someone or an institution.
예문	Taking out a loan can leave you indebted to the bank. 대출을 받으면 은행에 빚지게 될 수 있습니다.

618

edible

[ˈed.ə.bəl]

a. 먹기에 좋은

obesity n. 비만
obese a. 비만인
edible oil p. 식용유
edibility n. 식용으로 적합한 것

어원	-ed : eat + -ible → '먹을 수 있으니 식용의'
유의어	eatable, consumable, digestible
반의어	inedible, uneatable, indigestible
영영	Safe and suitable for eating; something that can be consumed as food.
예문	Some mushrooms in the forest are edible, but others are poisonous. 숲에 있는 몇 가지 버섯은 먹을 수 있지만, 다른 것들은 독성이 있다.

619

inhale
[ɪnˈheɪl]

v. 흡입하다

hale a. 진정한
whale n. 고래

어원	-in : in + -hale : breathe → '안으로 흡입하다'
유의어	breathe in, respire, inspire
반의어	exhale, breathe out
영영	to breathe in air, gases, or other substances into the lungs
예문	You should inhale deeply and exhale slowly to relax your body. 몸을 이완시키기 위해 깊게 들이마시고 천천히 내쉬어야 합니다.

620

breed
[briːd]

v. 번식하다; 새끼를 낳다; 사육하다, 재배하다

breathe v. 호흡하다, 냄새를 풍기다
take a deep breath p. 시몽흡하다
breathtaking a. 숨막히는, 아슬아슬한
breeze n. 산들바람, 미풍

어원	-breed : breath → '생기를 불어 넣어 따뜻하게 유지하며 번식하다'
유의어	raise, rear, propagate
반의어	deter, discourage
영영	to produce offspring through reproduction; a specific type or category of something
예문	The new dog breed they adopted is known for its loyalty and intelligence. 그들이 입양한 새로운 개 종은 충성심과 지능으로 알려져 있다.

621

condemn
[kənˈdem]

v. 비난하다; 선고하다

damn v. 비난하다, 저주하다
indemnify v. ~에게 변상하다, 보상하다
do damage p. 피해를 주다
dawn n. 새벽, 동틀녘

어원	-con : intensive + -demn, -damn : loss → '손해 가는 말을 하니 비난'
유의어	criticize, denounce, censure
반의어	praise, approve, endorse
영영	To express strong disapproval or criticism of something; to pronounce a judgment of guilt or punishment.
예문	The public condemned the politician's actions. 대중은 그 정치인의 행동을 비난했습니다.

622

mischance
[ˌmɪsˈtʃɑːns]

n. 불운, 불행

misguided a. 잘못된, 오도된
miss out on p. ~을 놓치다
misdemeanor n. 경범죄, 비행
demean v. 행동하다, 처신하다

어원	-mis : wrong (E) + chance 행운, 기회 → '놓친 기회니 불운'
유의어	misfortune, accident, bad luck
반의어	Fortune, luck, success
영영	An unfortunate or unlucky event or accident.
예문	It was a simple mischance that led to the accident. 사고로 이어진 것은 단순한 불운이었습니다.

623

superb
[suːˈpɜːb]

a. 장엄한, 화려한, 훌륭한

superior a. 우월한, 우수한, 상급의
summarize v. 요약하다
summation n. 덧셈
superbness n. 당당함; 뛰어남

어원	-superb, -super, -sup, -sur : over → '가장 위에 있으니 화려하고 훌륭한'
유의어	excellent, outstanding, splendid
반의어	awful, poor
영영	excellent; of the highest quality
예문	The view from the mountaintop was absolutely superb. 산 정상에서 보는 풍경은 정말 훌륭했다.

624

accentuate
[əkˈsen.tʃu.eɪt]

v. 강조하다, 두드러지게 하다

accent n. 강세
chant n. 노래, 멜로디, 성가
enchant v. 매혹하다, 황홀하게 하다
cherish v. 소중히 아끼다, 간직하다

어원	-ac : to + -chant, -cent, -cant 노래 → '한 방향으로 노래하니 강조'
유의어	emphasize, highlight, stress
반의어	de-emphasize, downplay, minimize
영영	to emphasize or highlight; to make more noticeable.
예문	The dress is designed to accentuate your curves. 이 드레스는 여러분의 곡선을 강조하기 위해 디자인되었습니다.

625

abrupt

[əˈbrʌpt]

a. 돌연한, 갑작스러운

irruption n. 침입, 돌입, 난입
irruptive a. 침입하는, 관입성의
interrupt v. 방해하다, 중단하다
bankrupt a. 파산한, 부도난

어원	-ab : away + rup : break(L) → '깨뜨리고 터져 나오는'
유의어	sudden, unexpected, sharp
반의어	gradual, steady, smooth
영영	sudden and unexpected; characterized by a sharp change.
예문	His abrupt departure surprised everyone. 그의 급작스러운 떠남은 모두를 놀라게 했다.

626

insist

[ɪnˈsɪst]

v. 주장하다; 요구하다

consist v. ~로 구성되다

어원	-in : on + -sist : stand → '계속해서 의견을 세우는 주장'
유의어	demand, assert, affirm
반의어	acquiesce, yield, concede
영영	To demand or assert something firmly and without wavering.
예문	She will insist on completing the project on time, no matter what. 그녀는 무엇이든지 시간 내에 프로젝트를 완료하도록 주장할 것이다.

627

peel

[piːl]

v. (껍질을) 벗기다; 옷을 벗다; 이탈하다

peer n. 동료, 또래 진구
pee v. 오줌 누다 n. 소변
peek v. 몰래 들여다보다, 엿보다
peet n. 금고

어원	-peel : spade > remove the outer layer → '삽질에서 껍질을 벗기다로' * pee 피같은 껍질을 벗기다
유의어	skin, strip, pare
반의어	cover, coat
영영	remove the outer layer of something, such as fruit or skin
예문	She carefully peeled the skin off the apple. 그녀는 주의 깊게 사과의 피부를 껴 냈다.

628

sting

[stɪŋ]

v. 찌르다; 자극하다 n. 아픔, 날카로움

instinct n. 본능
instigate v. 부추기다, 선동하다
stink v. 고약한 냄새가 나다, 악취가 풍기다
stigma n. 치욕, 오명

어원	-sting, -stinct, -stim : prcik 찌르다, quench 끄다 → '상처를 찌르는 날카로움에 아픔'
유의어	bite, prick, puncture
반의어	soothe, relieve, calm
영영	Cause a sharp, painful sensation, often as a result of a bite, injury, or harsh criticism.
예문	The bee's sting left a painful mark on his arm. 벌의 쏘임으로 그의 팔에 아픈 자국이 남았습니다.

629

enormous

[ɪˈnɔːməs]

a. 거대한, 어마어마한, 엄청난

abnormal a. 이상한, 비정상적인
enormously adv. 어마어마하게, 엄청나게
enormousness n. 거대함, 광대함
norm group p. 기준 집단, 준거 집단

어원	-e : out + -norm 기준, 표준 → '기준에서 벗어나 측정을 할 수 없을 정도로 엄청난'
유의어	massive, huge, colossal
반의어	tiny, small
영영	very large in size, quantity, or extent; immense or colossal
예문	The elephant is an enormous animal that can weigh several tons. 코끼리는 몇 톤에 달하는 거대한 동물이다.

630

blush

[blʌʃ]

v. 얼굴을 붉히다, 빨개지다

flush v. 물을 내리다
burn out p. 소진되다
burnished a. 광을 낸 닦은
combustive a. 연소성의

어원	* -blush : blaze 빨간 빛 → '얼굴에 빨간 빛이 나니 얼굴을 붉히다'
유의어	flush, redden, color
반의어	pale, whiten
영영	to become red in the face due to embarrassment, shyness, or a strong emotional reaction; a reddening of the face
예문	Her cheeks would always blush whenever she received a compliment. 그녀는 칭찬을 받을 때마다 얼굴이 항상 붉어지곤 했다.

631

at one's convenience

p. ~가 편한 때에

conventionally adv. 관습적으로, 관례적으로
convenience n. 편리, 편의
convenience store p. 편의점
adventure n. 모험

어원	-at 시점 + -con : together + -ven : come → '도움이 함께 와서 편한 시점에'
유의어	at one's leisure, when it suits one, whenever one wishes
반의어	at a disadvantage, inconveniently, disadvantageously
영영	at a time or place that is suitable or convenient
예문	You can come for a meeting at your convenience. 편하신 시간에 회의에 참석하실 수 있습니다.

632

take pride in

p. ~을 자랑하다

pride of place p. 가장 눈에 잘 띄는 자리
proudly adv. 자랑스럽게
appraise v. 값을 매기다, 평가하다
precious a. 값비싼, 귀중한

어원	-pric, -priz, -prec, -pra 가치(L) → '가치가 높으니 자랑스러운'
유의어	be proud of, pride oneself on, feel proud about
반의어	be ashamed of, be embarrassed by, be humiliated by
영영	feel proud of or derive satisfaction from
예문	She takes pride in her children's accomplishments. 그녀는 자신의 자녀들의 성취에 자부심을 느낍니다.

633

end up

p. 결국 ~이 되다

end up in p. 결국 ~로 끝나다
end up ing p. 결국 ~하게 되다
end up with p. 결국 ~을 가지게 되다
end up alone p. 결국 혼자 있게 되다

어원	-end 끝 + -up 끝까지 → '끝까지 가보니 결국'
유의어	eventually, ultimately, wind up
반의어	start, begin, initiate
영영	eventually or finally arrive at
예문	If you keep procrastinating, you'll end up failing the exam. 미루다 보면, 시험에서 실패하게 될 거야.

634

have only to do

p. ~하기만 하면 된다.

have something to do with p. ~와 관계가 있다
have a point p. 일리가 있다
have a taste for p. ~에 취미가 있다

어원	-have 갖다 + -only 오직 → '오직 하나만 갖으면 된다'
유의어	need only do, merely need to do, simply have to do
반의어	be unable to do, be prohibited from doing, be prevented from doing
영영	need only to do or simply do
예문	You have only to ask, and I'll help you with your project. 당신이 부탁하기만 하면, 나는 당신의 프로젝트를 도와줄 거야.

635

have a handle on

p. 이해하다, 알아듣다

handy a. 편리한, 손재주 있는
firsthand adv. 직접, 바로 a. 직접의
hand down p. ~을 물려주다
hand out p. 나눠주다

어원	-hand 손 → '손에 익었으니 이해하다'
유의어	understand, grasp, comprehend
반의어	be confused about, be uncertain about, be unclear about
영영	have control or understanding of
예문	He has a handle on the situation and knows how to resolve it. 그는 상황을 잘 다루고 그것을 해결하는 방법을 알고 있습니다.

636

honour A with B

p. A에게 B를 수여하다

dishonor n. 불명예, 치욕
honored a. 명예로운
honorably adv. 명예롭게
a point of honour p. 명예에 관한 문제

어원	-honor 명예 + -with 함께 → 'A에게 명예와 함께 B를 수여하다'
유의어	bestow B upon A, confer B on A, present A with B
반의어	dishonor A, disgrace A, shame A
영영	bestow or confer B upon A as a mark of respect
예문	They honored her with a special award for her humanitarian work. 그들은 인도적인 일에 대한 그녀의 공로를 인정하여 특별 상을 수여했습니다.

637

at no cost

p. 공짜로

constly a. 대가가 큰, 비용이 많이 드는
cost-effectiveness p. 비용 효율성
at one's option p. ~의 마음대로
at peace p. 평화롭게

어원	-at 지점 + -no + -cost 비용 → '비용이 없으니 공짜로'
유의어	for free, free of charge, without charge
반의어	at a cost, with a price, for a fee
영영	free of charge or without payment
예문	The software can be downloaded at no cost. 이 소프트웨어는 무료로 다운로드할 수 있습니다.

638

in a degree

p. 조금은, 어느 정도

some degree of p. 어느 정도의
in a hurry p. 서두르는
ina series p. 잇달아, 연이어
in a word p. 한 마디로

어원	-de : down + -gree : step → '아래까지 단계별로 세는 정도'
유의어	to some extent, somewhat, in part
반의어	absolutely, completely, wholly
영영	to some extent or degree
예문	He succeeded in a degree, but he could have done better. 그는 어느 정도 성공했지만, 더 잘할 수도 있었습니다.

639

for fear of

p. ~을 두려워하다, ~을 경외하다

frighten v. 겁먹게 만들다, 깜짝 놀라게 하다
fright n. 공포, 경악
frigid a. 몹시 추운, 냉담한
fever n. 열, 흥분

어원	-fear 두려움 → '두려움에 경외심까지'
유의어	because of, on account of, out of concern for
반의어	without fear of, unafraid of, fearless of
영영	because of apprehension or concern about
예문	She didn't speak up for fear of offending anyone. 누군가를 화나게 할까봐 그녀는 말을 꺼렸습니다.

640

at times

p. 때때로

timely a. 적시의, 시기 적절한
in a timely manner p. 시기적절한 방법으로
at best p. 잘해봐야
at latest p. 늦어도 ~까지는

어원	-time 시간 → '시간에 맞춰 때때로'
유의어	sometimes, occasionally, from time to time
반의어	consistently, constantly, continually
영영	occasionally or sometimes
예문	She can be difficult to work with at times, but she means well. 때때로 일하긴 어렵긴 하지만, 그녀는 착한 마음을 가지고 있습니다.

Chapter 17.

641	compress	[kəmˈpres]	v. 압축하다, 꽉 누르다
642	foe	[fou]	n. 적, 원수
643	throne	[θrəʊn]	n. 왕좌, 왕위
644	flush	[flʌʃ]	v. (얼굴이) 붉어지다; 물이 쏟아지다
645	shrink	[ʃrɪŋk]	v. 줄어들다
646	lure	[luər]	v. 꾀다, 유혹하다
647	predominant	[prɪˈdɒm.ɪ.nənt]	a. 두드러진, 우세한, 지배적인
648	cultivate	[ˈkʌl.tɪ.veɪt]	v. 기르다, 함양하다, 재배하다; 계발하다
649	intervene	[ˌɪn.təˈviːn]	v. 중재하다, 개입하다
650	tense	[tens]	a. 팽팽한, 긴장한, 절박한; n. 시제
651	warrant	[ˈwɒr.ənt]	n. 영장 v. 보장하다
652	awkward	[ˈɔː.kwəd]	a. 어색한, 곤란한
653	census	[ˈsen.səs]	n. 인구 조사
654	exploit	[ɪkˈsplɔɪt]	v. 이용하다; 개발하다; n. 공, 업적
655	strain	[streɪn]	v. 긴장시키다 n. 힘을 주어 팽팽함
656	possess	[pəˈzes]	v. 소유하다, 지배하다
657	anticipate	[ænˈtɪs.ɪ.peɪt]	v. 예상하다, 기대하다
658	confess	[kənˈfes]	v. 인정하다, 시인하다; 고백하다
659	famine	[fǽmin]	n. 기아, 기근; 결핍
660	ritual	[ˈrɪtʃ.u.əl]	a. 의식 절차; 의식상의, 의례적인
661	fundamental	[ˌfʌn.dəˈmen.təl]	a. 근본적인, 기본적인; 중요한, 필수의
662	substitute	[ˈsʌb.stɪ.tʃuːt]	v. 대체하다, 바꾸다; 대신하다
663	dedicate	[ˈded.ɪ.keɪt]	v. 헌신하다, 전념하다, 바치다
664	captive	[ˈkæp.tɪv]	n. 포로 a. 사로잡힌, 억류된
665	bruise	[bruːz]	n. 멍, 타박상
666	smother	[ˈsmʌð.ər]	v. 질식하게 만들다, 덮어서 불을 끄다
667	starve	[staːrv]	v. 굶주리다, 굶어 죽다, 굶기다, 굶겨 죽이다
668	swallow	[ˈswɒl.əʊ]	n. 제비; v. 삼키다
669	fad	[fæd]	n. (일시적인) 유행
670	thrift	[θrɪft]	n. 절약, 검약
671	attract A to B		p. A를 B로 끌어들이다
672	in the coming year		p. 다음 해에
673	owe A to B		p. A는 B 덕분이다
674	be familiar with		p. ~에 익숙하다, ~을 잘 알다
675	equipped with		p. ~을 갖춘
676	none the worse		p. 더 나쁠 거 없는, 똑같은
677	chop up		p. ~을 잘게 자르다
678	in the air		p. 헛된, 근거 없는
679	take in		p. ~에 참여하다; ~로 받아들이다
680	get around		p. 돌아다니다

641

compress

[kəmˈpres]

v. 압축하다, 꽉 누르다

oppress v. 억압하다
depress v. 낙담시키다; 불경기로 만들다
suppress v. 진압하다, 억제하다; 참다
appress v. 억압하다, 우울하게 하다

어원	-com : completely + -press 누르다 → '완전히 꽉 누르니 압축'
유의어	condense, squeeze, compact
반의어	expand, inflate
영영	press or squeeze something together
예문	Apply a compress to the swollen area to reduce inflammation. 부어 오른 부위에 압축을 적용하여 염증을 줄이세요.

642

foe

[fou]

n. 적, 원수

fortress n. 성채, 요새
forte n. 장점, 장기
enforce v. 강요하다
fortune n. 운; 재산; 성쇠

어원	-foe : enemy with force → '힘을 가진 적'
유의어	enemy, adversary, opponent
반의어	friend, ally, supporter
영영	An enemy or adversary; someone who opposes or is hostile to another.
예문	The hero had to face a formidable foe in the final battle. 주인공은 마지막 전투에서 무시무시한 적에 맞서야 했습니다.

643

throne

[θrəʊn]

n. 왕좌, 왕위

thrive v. 번창하다, 잘 자라다
threat v. 위협하다
thrust v. 세게 밀다; 찌르다
come through p. 극복하다, 이겨내다

어원	-throne : tron 신 또는 성좌의 자리 * thor 토르 → '천둥의 신'
유의어	seat of power, royal chair, sovereignty
반의어	Common seat, ordinary chair, everyday bench
영영	A ceremonial chair or seat of authority for a monarch or ruler.
예문	The king sat on his throne and addressed the court. 왕은 왕위에 앉아 법정을 담담하게 다스렸습니다.

644

flush

[flʌʃ]

v. (얼굴이) 붉어지다; 물이 쏟아지다

blush v. 얼굴을 붉히다, 빨개지다
fluid n. 유동(체), 체액 a. 유동적인
flood n. 홍수, 침수, 범람
fluent a. 유창한

어원	-flu, -flo : flow 흐르다(L) * -sh : push → '눈물이 쏟아지며 울컥하여 얼굴이 붉어짐' * fluid '흐르는 것' VS liquid '액체의 형태'
유의어	redden, blush, glow
반의어	drain, deplete, empty
영영	To flow or rush with force, or to become red in the face due to strong emotion.
예문	After exercising, her cheeks were flushed from the increased blood flow. 운동 후에는 피가 더 흐르면서 그녀의 뺨은 붉게 달아올랐다.

645

shrink

[ʃrɪŋk]

v. 줄어들다

shrimp n. 새우
wrist v. 비틀다; 왜곡하다
wrestle v. 맞붙어 싸우다, 레슬링하다
wrath n. 분노, 노여움

어원	-wrinkle 주름 → '주름처럼 줄어들다'
유의어	contract, reduce in size, diminish
반의어	Expand, grow, increase
영영	To become smaller in size or quantity.
예문	The wool sweater shrank in the wash. 양털 스웨터가 세탁 중에 줄어들었습니다.

646

lure

[luər]

v. 꾀다, 유혹하다

ludic a. 놀기 좋아하는, 놀이의
elusive a. 정의하기 힘든, 찾기 힘든
allure v. 유혹하다, 매혹하다
collude v. 공모하다, 결탁하다

어원	-lure 미끼 → '미끼로 유혹하다'
유의어	entice, attract, tempt
반의어	repel, deter
영영	to attract or entice someone or something to move or go in a particular direction; to tempt or allure
예문	The bright colors of the flowers lured the butterflies to the garden. 꽃의 밝은 색깔이 나비들을 정원으로 유혹했다.

647

predominant

[prɪˈdɒm.ɪ.nənt]

a. 두드러진, 우세한, 지배적인

dormitory n. 기숙사, 공동 침시
predominantly adv. 대개
predominate v. 뛰어나다, 우세하다
dormant a. 휴면기의, 잠복 중인

어원	pre : before + -dom 지배하다 < 둥근 천장 < 건축양식 → '앞서 지배하니 우세하여 두드러진' * dom '지배' VS man, main '살다'
유의어	dominant, prevailing, leading
반의어	subordinate, minor, secondary
영영	Being the most common or influential in a particular situation.
예문	In this region, agriculture is the predominant industry. 이 지역에서 농업이 주요 산업이다.

648

cultivate

[ˈkʌl.tɪ.veɪt]

v. 기르다, 함양하다, 재배하다; 계발하다

cultivation n. 경작, 재배
culture n. 문화; 배양균
acculturation n. 문화적 적응, 사회화
incubation n. 부화, 잠복기

어원	-cult, -colon 재배하다, 경작하다 (L) * culture 문화(경작을 시작하며 발달한 문화)
유의어	grow, nurture, develop
반의어	neglect, abandon, ignore
영영	To prepare and nurture land or plants for growth; metaphorically, to develop or improve something.
예문	Farmers cultivate the land to grow crops. 농부들은 작물을 키우기 위해 땅을 경작한다.

649

intervene

[ˌɪn.təˈviːn]

v. 중재하다, 개입하다

invervention n. 개입, 중재
invent v. 발명하다
in any event p. 아무튼, 어떤 경우에도
prevent v. 막다, 예방하다

어원	-inter : between + -ven : come → '사이에 들어오니 중재하다'
유의어	mediate, interfere, meddle
반의어	Abstain, refrain, stay out
영영	To come between or get involved in a situation in order to influence or modify the outcome.
예문	The teacher had to intervene to stop the students from arguing. 선생님은 학생들의 말다툼을 막기 위해 개입해야 했습니다.

650

tense

[tens]

a. 팽팽한, 긴장한, 절박한; n. 시제

tension n. 팽팽함, 긴장, 홍분
tensely adv. 긴장하여, 딱딱하게
tensile a. 장력의, 신장성 있는
tensive a. 긴장력이 있는

어원	-tend, tens, tent : stretch (L) 밖으로 끌어가다; ~로 향하다 → '끌어 당겨진, 팽팽한', '상태를 나타내는 시제'
유의어	stressed, anxious, nervous
반의어	relaxed, calm
영영	stretched or rigid
예문	The atmosphere in the room became tense as the argument escalated. 논쟁이 격화되면서 방 안의 분위기가 긴장되었다.

651

warrant

[ˈwɒr.ənt]

n. 영장 v. 보장하다

warranty n. 보증, 품질 보증서
guarantee n. 보증; 출연료 v. 보증하다
reward n. 보상; 현상금
beware of p. ~을 조심하다

어원	-war : watch → '경찰 활동이 피해를 줄 수 있어서 법으로 보장' * warranty 문제 생긴 제품 보장 VS guarantee 결함 없다고 보장
유의어	authorize, justify, permit
반의어	Forbid, prohibit, disallow
정장	An official authorization, often in the form of a legal document, permitting a specific action or procedure.
예문	The search warrant allowed the police to enter the premises. 수색 영장은 경찰에게 장소에 들어갈 권한을 부여했습니다.

652

awkward

[ˈɔːkwəd]

a. 어색한, 곤란한

awkwardly adv. 서투르게, 다루기 힘들게
awkwardness n. 어색함, 서투름
ward n. 병동; 구
ward off p. 보호하여 떼어내다, 물리치다

어원	-awk : wrong + -ward 방향 → '잘못된 방향으로 서 있으니 어색한'
유의어	clumsy, ungraceful, ungainly
반의어	graceful, coordinated, adept
정장	lacking skill or dexterity; uncomfortable or clumsy.
예문	He felt awkward at the party because he didn't know anyone. 그는 누구도 모르는 파티에서 어색함을 느꼈다.

653

census

[ˈsen.səs]

n. 인구 조사

censor n. 검열관 v. 검열하다
censrship n. 검열
censure n. 비난 v. 비난하다
cense v. ~에 향을 피우다

어원	-censor 검열하다 * -us 우리 → '우리 사람을 검열하니 인구 조사'
유의어	enumeration, population count, survey
반의어	Non-census, non-enumeration, non-count
영영	An official count or survey of a population, typically recording various demographic and statistical information.
예문	The government conducts a census every ten years to gather population data. 정부는 인구 데이터를 수집하기 위해 10년마다 인구 조사를 실시합니다.

654

exploit

[ɪkˈsplɔɪt]

v. 이용하다; 개발하다; n. 공, 업적

exploiter n. 이용자, 개발자
exploitive a. 자원 개발의, 착취적인
exploitable a. 개발할 수 있는, 이용할 수 있는
exploitation n. 개척, 개발, 착취

어원	-ex : out + -pl, -pli, -plo : use → '밖으로 공적을 드러내니 위해 이용하고 개발'
유의어	use, manipulate, take advantage of
반의어	Neglect, disregard, ignore
영영	To take advantage of someone or something for personal gain; to make use of.
예문	Some companies exploit their workers by paying low wages. 어떤 회사들은 낮은 임금을 지불하면서 노동자들을 착취합니다.

655

strain

[streɪn]

v. 긴장시키다 n. 힘을 주어 팽팽함

stress n. 압박감; 강세 v. 강조하다
constrain v. 강제하다, 억제하다
restrain v. ~을 억누르다, 억제하다
distrain v. 압류하다

어원	-strict, -strai, -strain 팽팽히 누르다 → '팽팽히 눌러 긴장시키다' * strain '힘을 주어 압박' VS constrain '다른 사람에게 억지로 강요'
유의어	stress, tension, pressure
반의어	ease, relax
영영	to exert physical or mental effort to the maximum; a force or pressure applied to an object
예문	Lifting heavy objects without proper technique can strain your back muscles. 올바른 기술 없이 무거운 물건을 들면 등 근육을 부담시킬 수 있다.

656

possess

[pəˈzes]

v. 소유하다, 지배하다

be possessed of p. ~을 소유하다
like all possessed p. 무엇에 홀린듯이
possessed by p. ~에 사로잡힌
posse n. 무장보안대, 경찰대

어원	-pos : power + -sess : sit 앉다 → '힘 있는 사람이 앉아 권력을 소유하다'
유의어	own, have, hold
반의어	lack, be without
영영	to own or have something; to have control or authority over something
예문	She possesses a unique talent for playing musical instruments. 그녀는 악기 연주에 독특한 재능을 가지고 있다.

657

anticipate

[ænˈtɪs.ɪ.peɪt]

v. 예상하다, 기대하다

anticipation n. 예상, 기대
anticipated a. 기대되는, 대망의
antique a. 과거의, 오래된 n. 골동품
incipient a. 초기의, 시조의

어원	-anti, -ante : before + -cip : take → '앞서 차지하는 걸 보니 예상한 모양이다'
유의어	expect, predict, foresee
반의어	overlook, disregard, ignore
영영	to expect or foresee something happening in the future.
예문	They anticipate a busy holiday season at the store. 그들은 가게에서 바쁜 휴가 시즌을 예상하고 있다.

658

confess

[kənˈfes]

v. 인정하다, 시인하다; 고백하다

preface n. 머리말, 서문
prephesy v. 예언하다
prephecy n. 예언
infancy n. 유아기

어원	-con : together + -fess : say → '모두에게 말하며 인정하니 고백'
유의어	admit, acknowledge, own up
반의어	deny, disavow, repudiate
영영	Admit or acknowledge something, especially a wrongdoing or a secret.
예문	She finally decided to confess her feelings to him. 그녀는 마침내 그에게 자신의 감정을 고백하기로 결정했습니다.

659

famine

[ˈfæmɪn]

n. 기아, 기근; 결핍

famish v. 굶주리게 하다
fame n. 명성, 명예
familiar a. 익숙한, 친숙한

어원	-fam, -fames : hunger → '배고픔 때문에 생긴 결핍으로 기아와 기근이'
유의어	starvation, scarcity of food, hunger crisis
반의어	Abundance, plenty, surplus
영영	A severe shortage of food, often resulting in widespread hunger and starvation.
예문	The famine in the region resulted in widespread hunger and suffering. 그 지역의 기근으로 인해 광범위한 굶주림과 고통이 일어났습니다.

660

ritual

[ˈrɪtʃ.u.əl]

a. 의식 절차; 의식상의, 의례적인

ritualize v. 의례적으로 하다
ritually adv. 의식에 따라, 의례적으로
ritualism n. 의식주의
rite n. 의례, 의식, 관례

어원	-rite : ritus 성스러운 관습(L) → '성스러운 관습의 의례' * right와 발음이 비슷하니 '올바르게 치뤄야 하는 의식'
유의어	ceremony, tradition, custom
반의어	Non-ritual, absence of ceremony, lack of tradition
영영	A ceremonial or religious act with established procedures and symbolism.
예문	The temple is considered a sacred place of worship. 이 사원은 신성한 숭배의 장소로 여겨집니다.

661

fundamental

[ˌfʌn.dəˈmen.təl]

a. 근본적인, 기본적인; 중요한, 필수의

fundamentally adv. 근본적으로
found v. 설립하다; ~에 기초를 두다
be founded on p. ~에 기초하다
funding n. 자금, 재정 지원

어원	-fund, -found 바닥, 기초(L) → '기초가 되는 것이니 근본적인' * base '위치가 낮다' VS found '바닥'
유의어	essential, basic, primary
반의어	secondary, nonessential, peripheral
영영	essential, basic, or foundational.
예문	Understanding basic math concepts is fundamental to solving complex equations. 기본 수학 개념을 이해하는 것은 복잡한 방정식을 푸는 데 기본적이다.

662

substitute

[ˈsʌb.stɪ.tʃuːt]

v. 대체하다, 바꾸다; 대신하다

substitue for p. ~의 대체물
substitute A with B p. A를 B로 대체하다
substitute B for A p. A를 V로 대체하다
subsist v. 살아가다; 존재하다

어원	-sub : 대신하여 + -stitu : stand → '대신하여 서게 하다'
유의어	replacement, alternative, stand-in
반의어	Original, genuine, authentic
영영	To replace or use in place of something else.
예문	If you don't have milk, you can substitute it with almond milk. 우유가 없다면 아몬드 우유로 대체할 수 있습니다.

663

dedicate

[ˈded.ɪ.keɪt]

v. 헌신하다, 전념하다, 바치다

dedicated a. 헌신적인
dedication n. 헌신
predict v. 예측하다, 예견하다
dig v. 파다

어원	-de : down + -dic : say → '낮은 위치에서 말하며 헌신하다'
유의어	commit, devote, consecrate
반의어	abandon, forsake
영영	to set aside or commit something for a specific purpose or use; to devote time, effort, or resources to a cause or task
예문	She decided to dedicate her life to helping underprivileged children. 그녀는 박해받는 아이들을 돕는 데 자신의 인생을 헌신하기로 결정했다.

664

captive

[ˈkæp.tɪv]

n. 포로 a. 사로잡힌, 억류된

capture v. 붙잡다, 생포하다
captor n. 획득자, 포획자
captivity n. 속박, 감금, 포로
captivate v. ~을 매혹하다, 마음을 사로잡다

어원	-cap, -chief, -chiev, -cupy, -cip, -cept, -ceive, -ceit : take, hold 잡다, 취하다 (L) → '잡혔으니 포로'
유의어	prisoner, detainee, hostage
반의어	Free, liberated, emancipated
영영	A person or animal that is imprisoned or held against their will.
예문	The explorers were taken captive by the hostile tribe. 탐험가들은 적대적인 부족에게 포로로 잡혔습니다.

665

bruise

[bruːz]

n. 멍, 타박상

break into p. 침입하다, 난입하다
breakthrough n. 획기적 발전; 돌파구
breakage n. 파손, 손상
bruising n. 타박상

어원	-break 깨지다(E) → '몸에서 깨진 곳에 멍'
유의어	contusion, injury, black and blue mark
반의어	heal, recover, mend
영영	a blue or purple mark on the skin caused by injury.
예문	She had a bruise on her arm from accidentally bumping into the table. 그녀는 실수로 탁자에 부딪히면서 팔에 멍이 들었다.

666

smother

[ˈsmʌð.ər]

v. 질식하게 만들다, 덮어서 불을 끄다

smothering a. 숨이 막히는
stcuk a. 꼼짝 못 하는
get stuck with p. 어쩔 수 없이 ~해야 한다
get unstuck p. 빠져나가다

어원	-smo : smoke → '연기로 완전히 뒤덮어 질식하게 하다'
유의어	suffocate, stifle, suppress
반의어	uncover, reveal
영영	to suffocate or stifle someone or something by covering or restricting air or movement
예문	She couldn't breathe as he tried to smother her with a pillow. 그가 베개로 그녀를 질식시키려고 시도하자 그녀는 숨을 쉴 수 없었다.

667

starve

[staːrv]

v. 굶주리다, 굶어 죽다, 굶기다, 굶겨 죽이다

starvation n. 기아, 궁핍, 아사
starve to death p. 굶어 죽다
starved a. 굶주린
stifle v. 굳게 하다

어원	-starve : stiff 뻣뻣해지다 → '굶어 죽으니 뻣뻣해지다' * 굶주리면서 도움을 청하기 위해 stare 응시하다
유의어	hunger, famish, deprive of food
반의어	Overeat, indulge, overindulge
영영	To suffer or die from lack of food; to go without eating for an extended period.
예문	Millions of people in the world starve due to food shortages. 세계적으로 수백만 명의 사람들이 식량 부족으로 굶주립니다.

668

swallow

[ˈswɒl.əʊ]

n. 제비; v. 삼키다

swallow one's pride p. 자존심을 굽히다
swallet n. 지하 수류
swallow hard p. 침을 꿀꺽 삼키다

어원	* -sw : swell 부풀다 → '배가 부푼 걸 보니 뭔가 삼켰다', '먹이를 삼켰다가 새끼에게 주는 제비'
유의어	gulp, ingest, consume
반의어	spit out, expel
영영	take something into the stomach through the mouth
예문	He swallowed his pride and apologized for his behavior. 그는 자존심을 내려놓고 행동에 대한 사과를 했다.

669

fad

[fæd]

n. (일시적인) 유행

fade v. 바래다, 서서히 사라지다
fade away p. 점차 사라지다
faint a. 희미한, 어렴풋한
affair n. 활동, 업무; 사건, 스캔들

어원	-fad : for a day → '하루 동안의 유행'
유의어	trend, craze, fashion
반의어	Permanence, long-lasting trend, sustained fashion
영영	A short-lived and popular trend or fashion that quickly gains and loses popularity.
예문	Wearing bell-bottom pants was a fad in the 1970s. 1970년대에 벨 바지를 입는 것은 유행이었습니다.

670

thrift

[θrɪft]

n. 절약, 검약

twist v. 꼬(이)다, 비틀다 n. 꼬임, 엉킴
threat n. 위협, 협박
thrust v. 세게 밀다; 찌르다
thrill v. 흥분시키다; 흥분, 전율

어원	-thr, -thri 셋, 3 (E) → '3번 나누어 사용하니 절약'
유의어	frugality, economy, thriftiness
반의어	Waste, extravagance, prodigality
영영	The quality of being economical or frugal in managing resources, especially money.
예문	His thrift and frugality allowed him to save a significant amount of money. 그의 검소함과 절약 습관 덕분에 많은 돈을 모았습니다.

671

attract A to B

p. A를 B로 끌어들이다

attract v. 매혹하다
attraction n. 끌림, 명소
subtraction n. 빼기, 공제
subtractive a. 빼는, 차감하는

어원	-at : to + -tract : draw → '원하는 방향으로 당기는 매혹적인 힘'
유의어	draw A to B, entice A towards B, lure A to B
반의어	repel A from B, deter A from B, discourage A from B
영영	draw or pull A toward B
예문	The new marketing campaign aims to attract more customers to the product. 새로운 마케팅 캠페인은 제품에 더 많은 고객을 유치하기 위해 진행됩니다.

672

in the coming year

p. 다음 해에

in some way p. 어떤 점에서는, 혹시
insofar as p. ~하는 한은, ~정도까지는
in the air p. 헛된 근거 없는
in the face of p. ~에도 불구하고, 직면해서

어원	-coming 오는 + -year 연 → '돌아오는 연이니 다음 해에'
유의어	in the next year, in the forthcoming year, in the upcoming year
반의어	in the past year, in the previous year, in the preceding year
영영	in the year that follows the current one
예문	We have ambitious plans for expansion in the coming year. 우리는 다가오는 해에 확장에 대한 야심찬 계획을 가지고 있습니다.

673

owe A to B

p. A는 B 덕분이다

own a. 자신의, 직접 ~한 v. 소유하다
ownership n. 소유
on one's feet p. 독자적으로
all on one's own p. 자력으로, 스스로

어원	-owe 소유하다 * owner에게 빚을 진
유의어	attribute A to B, credit B with A, ascribe A to B
반의어	be indebted to B, be obligated to B, be beholden to B
영영	be indebted or obligated to B for A
예문	He owes his success to years of hard work and dedication. 그의 성공은 오랜 노력과 헌신에 기인합니다.

674

be familiar with

p. ~에 익숙하다, ~을 잘 알다

unfamiliar a. 생소한, 익숙하지 않은
familiarize v. 익숙해지게 하다, 숙지시키다
familiarize A with B p. A를 B에 익숙해지게 하다

어원	-family 가족 → '가족만큼 친숙하니 익숙한'
유의어	know, be acquainted with, recognize
반의어	be unfamiliar with, be ignorant of, be unaware of
영영	have knowledge or experience of
예문	She is familiar with the company's policies and procedures. 그녀는 회사의 정책과 절차에 익숙합니다.

675

equipped with

p. ~을 갖춘

equals v. ~와 같다 n. 등호
equivalent to p. 동등한, 대등한
adequate a. 적절한
equipment n. 장비

어원	-equ : same + -ip : ship → '늘 같은 상태로 배가 나갈 수 있도록 준비를 갖추다'
유의어	provided with, furnished with, supplied with
반의어	lacking, devoid of, unprepared for
영영	furnished or provided with necessary items or tools
예문	The car is equipped with the latest safety features. 그 차는 최신 안전 기능을 갖추고 있습니다.

676

none the worse

p. 더 나쁠 거 없는, 똑같은

make matters worse p. 상황을 더 악화시키다
nothing other than p. 단지 ~뿐인
nothing more than p. ~에 불과한

어원	-none 부정 + -worse : -bad의 비교급 → '더 나쁠 게 없는'
유의어	unaffected, unharmed, undamaged
반의어	better, improved, enhanced
영영	not adversely affected or harmed
예문	Despite the accident, he was none the worse for wear. 사고에도 불구하고, 그는 아무런 손상도 입지 않았습니다.

677

chop up

p. ~을 잘게 자르다

cut A with B p. A를 B로 자르다
cut from the same cloth p. 같은 부류인
cut off p. 잘라버리다; 서둘러 떠나다
cut down on p. ~를 줄이다

어원	-chop : cut into pieces + -up → '잘라서 조각내다'
유의어	cut up, slice, dice
반의어	assemble, construct, build
영영	cut or divide into smaller pieces
예문	The chef chopped up the vegetables for the stir-fry. 요리사가 볶음 요리를 위해 야채를 다져 놓았습니다.

678

in the air

p. 헛된, 근거 없는

in some way p. 어떤 점에서는, 혹시
insofar as p. ~하는 한은, ~정도까지는
in the face of p. ~에도 불구하고, 직면해서
in the course of p. ~되고 있는 중인

어원	-in + -air 공기, 대기, 항공의 → '아무 것도 없는 공기 중인 것처럼 헛된'
유의어	uncertain, unresolved, pending
반의어	certain, definite, resolved
영영	uncertain or unresolved
예문	There's a lot of uncertainty in the air regarding the future of the company. 회사의 미래에 대한 불확실성이 공중에 떠있습니다.

679

take in

p. ~에 참여하다; ~로 받아들이다

take over p. 넘겨 받다; 장악하다
take initiative p. 주도권을 잡다
take sides p. 편을 들다
take on p. ~을 취하다, ~을 태우다

어원	-take 취하다 + -in 안 → '안에 자리를 취하니 참여하다'
유의어	absorb, comprehend, understand
반의어	ignore, overlook, neglect
영영	comprehend or understand
예문	It took him a while to take in the magnitude of the situation. 상황의 심각성을 이해하는 데 시간이 걸렸습니다.

680

get around

p. 돌아다니다

get away from p. ~에서 벗어나다
get down to p. 시작하다, 착수하다
get nowhere p. 아무 쓸모(소용) 없다
get over p. 극복하다

어원	-get 상태 + -around 주변 → '주변을 돌아다니다'
유의어	circumvent, avoid, bypass
반의어	remain stationary, stay in one place, be immobile
영영	circumvent or avoid something
예문	Despite the traffic, we managed to get around the city quickly. 교통이 복잡하지만, 우리는 도시를 빠르게 이동할 수 있었습니다.

Chapter 18.

681	implement	[ˈɪm.plɪ.ment]	n. 도구; v. 실행하다, 시행하다
682	intuition	[ìntjuːˈɪʃən]	n. 직관, 직관력, 통찰력
683	encyclopedia	[ɪnˌsaɪ.kləˈpiː.di.ə]	n. 백과사전
684	alchemy	[ˈæl.kə.mi]	n. 연금술, 신비한 힘, 마력
685	popularity	[ˌpɒp.jəˈlær.ə.ti]	n. 많은 사람들이 알고 있는 사람, 명성
686	stance	[stɑːns]	n. 입장, 태도, 자세
687	correspond	[ˌkɒr.ɪˈspɒnd]	v. ~와 일치하다
688	crack	[kræk]	v. 깨다, 갈라지다; (사건·암호 등을) 풀다
689	temperate	[ˈtem.pər.ət]	a. 온화한, 온난한; 온건한, 도를 넘지 않는
690	inflow	[ˈɪn.fləʊ]	n. 유입, 유입량
691	realty	[ˈrɪəl.ti]	n. 부동산
692	forbid	[fəˈbɪd]	v. 금지하다, 방해하다
693	neglect	[nɪˈglekt]	v. 소홀히 하다, 경시하다; n. 태만, 경시
694	autonomy	[ɔːˈtɒn.ə.mi]	n. 자율성
695	sneak	[sniːk]	v. 살금살금 가다, 몰래 하다
696	inspect	[ɪnˈspekt]	v. 조사하다, 검사하다
697	immense	[ɪˈmens]	a. 거대한, 엄청난, 막대한
698	struggle	[ˈstrʌg.əl]	v. 고군분투하다 n. 투쟁, 싸움, 노력
699	eternal	[ɪˈtɜː.nəl]	a. 끝의, 밖의, 영구적인
700	peer	[pɪər]	n. 동료, 또래 친구
701	homicide	[ˈhɒm.ɪ.saɪd]	n. 살인
702	obesity	[əʊˈbiː.sə.ti]	n. 비만
703	restore	[rɪˈstɔːr]	v. 회복시키다, 복구하다
704	reinforce	[ˌriː.ɪnˈfɔːs]	v. 강화하다
705	timely	[ˈtaɪm.li]	a. 적시의, 시기 적절한
706	dismiss	[dɪˈsmɪs]	v. 해고하다, 무시하다; 일축하다, 해산시키다
707	reluctant	[rɪˈlʌk.tənt]	a. 싫어하는, 꺼리는
708	condense	[kənˈdens]	v. 압축하다; 액화되다, 고체화되다
709	defect	[ˈdiː.fekt]	n. 결점, 결함, 결핍
710	swift	[swɪft]	a. 신속한, 빠른
711	dispose of		p. ~을 처리하다, ~을 없애다
712	approve of		p. ~을 인정하다, ~을 괜찮다고 생각하다
713	vulnerable to N		p. ~에 취약한
714	avail oneself of		p. ~을 이용하다
715	correlated with		p. ~과 서로 관련된
716	fall into place		p. 제자리를 찾다, 아귀가 맞다
717	insofar as		p. ~하는 한은, ~하는 정도까지는
718	hit the books		p. 열심히 공부하다, 열공하다
719	set in one's way		p. 자기 방식이 몸에 밴
720	have something to do with		p. ~와 관계가 있다

681

implement

[ˈɪm.plɪ.ment]

n. 도구; v. 실행하다, 시행하다

complement n. 보충
compliment n. 칭찬, 찬사
implementation n. 이행, 실행
deplete v. 고갈시키다, 소모시키다

어원	-im + -pli : fill → '계획대로 안에 도구를 채워 실행'
유의어	execute, carry out, apply
반의어	abandon, neglect
영영	put a plan, decision, or system into effect
예문	The company plans to implement new safety measures in the workplace. 회사는 직장에서 새로운 안전 조치를 시행하기로 계획하고 있다.

682

intuition

[ɪntjuːɪʃən]

n. 직관, 직관력, 통찰력

tuition n. 교육; 수업료
intuitively adv. 직관에 의하여
tutor n. 개인 지도 교사, 가정교사
counterintuitive a. 직관에 어긋나는

어원	-in : in + -tui : look 보다, 보호하다 → '안을 들여다 보는 직관'
유의어	instinct, gut feeling, hunch
반의어	Logic, reason, rationality
영영	The ability to understand or know something instinctively, without the need for conscious reasoning.
예문	Trust your intuition when making important decisions. 중요한 결정을 내릴 때 자신의 직감을 믿으세요.

683

encyclopedia

[ɪnˌsaɪ.kləˈpiː.di.ə]

n. 백과사전

pedagogue n. 교사
pedagogical a. 교육의, 교육법의
pediatrics n. 소아과
encyclopedic a. 백과사전적인, 아주 해박한

어원	-en : in + -cycle : cycle + -ped : child → '아이들을 위한 전반적인 내용 안에서 교육'
유의어	reference book, compendium, reference work
반의어	Ignorance, unawareness, lack of knowledge
영영	A comprehensive reference work or collection of articles covering a wide range of subjects or topics.
예문	The encyclopedia provides comprehensive information on a wide range of topics. 백과사전은 다양한 주제에 대한 포괄적인 정보를 제공합니다.

684

alchemy

[ˈæl.kə.mi]

n. 연금술, 신비한 힘, 마력

chemistry n. 화학
chemist n. 화하자
biochemistry n. 생화학
alchemic a. 연금술의

어원	-all + -chemi 화학 → '모든 것을 화학으로 바꿀 수 있는 연금술'
유의어	magic, sorcery, transformation
반의어	Chemistry, science, natural philosophy
영영	A medieval and early modern philosophical and proto-scientific tradition that aimed to transform base metals into noble metals and discover the elixir of life.
예문	Alchemy was an ancient practice that aimed to turn base metals into gold. 연금술은 저금속을 금으로 변환하려는 고대의 연습이었습니다.

685

popularity

[ˌpɒp.jəˈlær.ə.ti]

n. 많은 사람들이 알고 있는 사람, 명성

popular a. 인기 있는
populate v. 거주시키다, 거주하다
population n. 인구, 모집단
populous a. 인구가 많은

어원	-popul, -publ 많은 사람들(L) → '많은 사람들에게 인기 있으니 명성'
유의어	fame, recognition, acclaim
반의어	unpopularity, obscurity, insignificance
영영	State of being well-liked or widely admired.
예문	The movie gained popularity worldwide. 그 영화는 전 세계적으로 인기를 얻었습니다.

686

stance

[stɑːns]

n. 입장, 태도, 자세

standard n. 표준, 기준, 수준, 규격
substandard a. 수준 이하의
standee n. 입석
standpoint n. 입장, 견지, 관점

어원	-sta,-sist, -ste, -st, -stitu, -stin, -sti : stand → '서 있는 자세'
유의어	position, standpoint, perspective
반의어	Change, shift, alteration
영영	A position or attitude taken on an issue or topic; a posture or physical position.
예문	The politician's stance on environmental issues is well-known. 정치인의 환경 문제에 대한 입장은 잘 알려져 있습니다.

687

correspond

[ˌkɔr.ɪˈspɒnd]

v. ~와 일치하다

correspond with p. ~와 일치하다
correspondent n. 기자, 특파원
in response to p. ~에 반응하여
spontaneous a. 자발적인, 자연스러운

어원	-cor : together + -respond : 응답하다 → '서로 모두 응답하니 일치하다'
유의어	communicate, exchange, relate
반의어	Differ, disagree, conflict
영영	To communicate with someone through written or electronic means.
예문	We correspond regularly through email. 우리는 정기적으로 이메일을 통해 서신을 주고 받습니다.

688

crack

[kræk]

v. 깨다, 갈라지다; (사건·암호 등을) 풀다

crash n. 사고 v. 충돌하다, 추락하다
crash on p. ~과 충돌하다
crush v. 으스러뜨리다, 밀어넣다, 수셔넣다
crust n. (빵) 껍질, 딱딱한 표면

어원	-crack 깨지는 소리
유의어	fissure, split, fracture
반의어	Seal, close, mend
영영	A narrow opening or fissure, often in a surface or structure.
예문	There was a crack in the glass window. 유리 창에 금이 갔습니다.

689

temperate

[ˈtem.pər.ət]

a. 온화한, 온난한; 온건한, 도를 넘지 않는

temper n. 화, 성미, 기질, 기분
lone one's temper p. 화를 내다
temple n. 사원, 절
contemplate v. 심사숙고하다

어원	-temper : 조절하다, mix 섞다 (L) → '여러 가지 성질이 잘 조화돼서 온화한'
유의어	moderate, mild, restrained
반의어	extreme, excessive, immoderate
영영	moderate or mild in terms of climate or behavior.
예문	The coastal region has a temperate climate with mild winters and cool summers. 해안 지역은 겨울에는 온화하고 여름에는 서늘한 기후를 갖고 있다.

690

inflow

[ˈɪn.floʊ]

n. 유입, 유입량

flow v. 흐르다
float v. 뜨다
afloat a. 떠 있는
fluid n. 유동(체), 체액 a. 유동적인, 부드러운

어원	-in + -flu, -flo : flow 흐르다(L) → '안으로 흐르는 유입량'
유의어	influx, input, arrival
반의어	outflow, efflux
영영	the act of flowing or coming in, especially of a liquid or substance, into a place or container
예문	The inflow of tourists to the city increased significantly after the new airport opened. 새 공항이 개장한 후 도시로의 관광객 유입이 크게 증가했다.

691

realty

[ˈrɪəl.ti]

n. 부동산

real estate p. 부동산
rebate n. 할인, 환불 v. 환불하다
realm n. 왕국, 영역, 범위
combative a. 전쟁을 좋아하는

어원	-real 진짜 → '현실 가치가 있는 부동산'
유의어	real estate, property, land
반의어	illusion, fantasy
영영	real estate; property, including land and buildings
예문	She invested in realty properties as a way to build her wealth. 그녀는 부를 쌓기 위한 수단으로 부동산 투자를 했다.

692

forbid

[fəˈbɪd]

v. 금지하다, 방해하다

bid n. 입찰; v. 값을 매기다; 명령하다
bidder n. 가격 제시자
abide v. 참다, 머무르다
forbidden a. 금지된, 금단의

어원	-for : before 먼저 + -bid : ask → '먼저 요구한 사람이 있어 금지'
유의어	prohibit, ban, prohibit
반의어	Permit, allow, authorize
영영	To prohibit or command someone not to do something; to ban or disallow.
예문	The sign forbids smoking in this area. 이 지역에서 흡연을 금지하는 표지판이 있습니다.

693

neglect

[nɪˈglekt]

v. 소홀히 하다, 경시하다; n. 태만, 경시

denial n. 부인, 부정
negatively adv. 부정적으로
neutrality n. 중립성, 중립
neglected a. 방치된, 도외시된

어원	-neg, -ny, -ne : deny 부인하다 + -lect : gather → '다 모으지 못한 걸 보니 소홀히 했구나'
유의어	ignore, disregard, abandon
반의어	care for, attend to
영영	to fail to care for or pay attention to something or someone, often resulting in harm or deterioration
예문	The neglect of the building led to its deterioration over time. 건물의 방치로 시간이 지남에 따라 그 퇴화로 이어졌다.

694

autonomy

[ɔːˈtɒn.ə.mi]

n. 자율성

autonomate v. 자동화하다
autonomous a. 자율적인
anomy n. 무질서
authentic a. 진정한, 진짜의

어원	-auto 스스로 + -nom 규칙 → '스스로 규칙에 맞추니 자율적인'
유의어	independence, self-rule, sovereignty
반의어	dependence, subordination, reliance
영영	The ability or right to make one's own decisions and govern oneself.
예문	The country gained autonomy and became independent. 그 나라는 자치권을 얻고 독립국이 되었다.

695

sneak

[sniːk]

v. 살금살금 가다, 몰래 하다

snake n. 뱀 v. 꿈틀꿈틀 움직이다
sneaky a. 교활한 비열한
sneakers n. 운동화
snicker n. 낄낄 거리는 웃음 v. 낄낄 거리다

어원	* -sneak : snake → '뱀처럼 살금살금 가다', ' 스니커즈 운동화를 신고 살금살금 가다'
유의어	creep, slink, skulk
반의어	reveal, disclose, expose
영영	To move quietly and stealthily to avoid being detected.
예문	He tried to sneak into the movie theater without buying a ticket. 그는 티켓을 사지 않고 영화관에 몰래 들어가려고 시도했다.

696

inspect

[ɪnˈspekt]

v. 조사하다, 검사하다

on closer inspection p. 더 자세히 살펴보면
inspection 검사, 점검
suspect v. 의심하다, 추측하다
aspect n. 측면, 국면

어원	-in + -spect : look → '마음 속까지 들여다 보며 조사하다'
유의어	examine, scrutinize, check
반의어	ignore, neglect, overlook
영영	to examine or scrutinize something closely.
예문	The quality control team will inspect the products for any defects. 품질 관리 팀은 제품을 결함 여부를 검사할 것이다.

697

immense

[ɪˈmens]

a. 거대한, 엄청난, 막대한

measure v. 측정하다, 평가하다
take measures p. 조치를 취하다
diameter n. 직경, 지름
dimension n. 규모, 차원, 요인

어원	-im : not + -men, -mens, -mea : meausre → '측정하지 못할 정도니 엄청한'
유의어	vast, enormous, colossal
반의어	small, tiny
영영	extremely large in size or degree; vast or enormous
예문	The Grand Canyon's beauty is truly immense and breathtaking. 그랜드 캐년의 아름다움은 정말로 거대하고 아슬아슬하다.

698

struggle

[ˈstrʌg.əl]

v. 고군분투하다 n. 투쟁, 싸움, 노력

strife n. 분쟁, 불화, 반목
strenuous a. 몹시 힘든, 격렬한
stride v. 성큼성큼 걷다, 활보하다
strive v. 투쟁하다, 노력하다

어원	-str : strength 싸우다 + -rug, -rag : rough → '어려움과 싸우며 고군분투하는' * stride '많은 노력에 초점' VS struggle '어려움에 초점'
유의어	strive, endeavor, exert
반의어	ease, breeze, cakewalk
영영	Make a great effort to overcome a difficulty, challenge, or obstacle.
예문	She had to struggle to overcome her fear of public speaking. 그녀는 공개 연설에 대한 두려움을 극복하기 위해 노력해야 했습니다.

699

eternal
[ɪˈtɜːnəl]

a. 끝의, 밖의, 영구적인

terminal n. 터미널
terminated a. 해고된
terminology n. (전문)용어
external a. 끝의, 밖의, 영구적인

어원	-e : out + -termin, -term, -tern 끝, 경계 → '경계를 벗어나니 영구석인' * 고대 로마 신화에서 테르미누스 Terminus 신은 '토지의 경계와 끝'을 뜻
유의어	everlasting, timeless, perpetual
반의어	Temporary, fleeting, impermanent
영영	Without beginning or end; existing outside of time; everlasting.
예문	He's a natural extrovert and enjoys socializing with others. 그는 타고난 외향적 성격이며 다른 사람들과 교류를 즐깁니다.

700

peer
[pɪər]

n. 동료, 또래 친구

peel v. 껍질을 벗기다; 옷을 벗다
pee v. 오줌 누다 n. 소변
peek v. 몰래 들여다보다, 엿보다
compare v. 비교하다

어원	-peer, -par : equal 동등한 (L) → '동등한 조건의 또래나 동료'
유의어	equal, counterpart, colleague
반의어	Superior, higher, more advanced
영영	A person who is of equal standing or rank, often in terms of age or social status.
예문	Her peers respected her for her dedication and leadership. 그녀의 동료들은 그녀의 헌신과 리더십을 존경했습니다.

701

homicide
[ˈhɒm.ɪ.saɪd]

n. 살인

precisely adv. 정확히, 바로
concise a. 거두절미한, 간결한
genocide n. 인종말살, 대량학살
pesticide n. 농약, 살충제

어원	-hom : human + -cid, -cis 잘라 죽이다 → '사람을 죽이니 살인'
유의어	murder, killing, manslaughter
반의어	Survival, non-killing, non-murder
영영	The act of killing another person, either intentionally or unlawfully.
예문	The police are investigating the homicide that occurred last night. 경찰은 어젯밤에 발생한 살인사건을 조사 중입니다.

702

obesity
[oʊˈbiː.sə.ti]

n. 비만

obese a. 비만인
obey v. 복종하다
edible oil p. 식용유
edibility n. 식용으로 적합한 것

어원	-ob : over + -es, -ed : eat → '과하게 먹으니 비만'
유의어	overweight, corpulence, heaviness
반의어	thinness, slenderness, leanness
영영	a medical condition characterized by excessive body fat.
예문	The rise in childhood obesity is a significant health concern. 아동 비만 증가는 중요한 건강 문제이다.

703

restore
[rɪˈstɔːr]

v. 회복시키다, 복구하다

in store for p. ~에게 닥쳐오는
stuff n. 물건, 소지품 v. 채우다, 쑤셔 넣다
storage n. 저장, 보존
soak v. 담그다, 흠뻑 적시다

어원	-re : again + -store 저장 → 다시 힘을 저장하여 복구하니 회복
유의어	repair, renew, revive
반의어	Ruin, damage, destroy
영영	To return something to its original condition or state.
예문	They worked hard to restore the historic building to its former glory. 그들은 역사적인 건물을 옛 영광으로 복원하기 위해 노력했습니다.

704

reinforce
[ˌriːɪnˈfɔːs]

v. 강화하다

reinforcement n. 보강, 강화
workforce n. 노동 인구, 직원 수
forthcoming a. 곧 오려고 하는, 다가오는
forthright a. 솔직 담백한

어원	-re : again + -in, -en : make + -for, -forc, -fort : strength 강한(L) → '다시 하게 만드니 강화'
유의어	strengthen, fortify, bolster
반의어	weaken, undermine
영영	to strengthen or support something, often by adding additional material or support
예문	The additional troops were sent to reinforce the defense of the city. 추가적인 군대가 도시의 방어를 강화하기 위해 파견되었다.

705

timely

[ˈtaɪm.li]

a. 적시의, 시기 적절한

untimeliness n. 시기 상조
tide n. 조수
overtime n. 초과 근무
tiny a. 아주 작은

어원	-time 시간 → '시간에 맞추니 적시의'
유의어	punctual, on time, prompt
반의어	Untimely, late, delayed
영영	Happening at an appropriate or well-chosen moment; punctual.
예문	His timely intervention prevented a disaster. 그의 적시의 개입이 재난을 방지했습니다.

706

dismiss

[dɪˈsmɪs]

v. 해고하다, 무시하다; 일축하다, 해산시키다

dismissal n. 면직, 해고
dismissive a. 거부하는
demise n. 서거, 별세; 양도
emit v. 내뿜다, 방출하다

어원	-dis : away + -mit, -miss, -mess : send(L) → '멀리 보내니 해고'
유의어	let go, release, fire
반의어	Retain, keep, employ
영영	To officially or formally remove someone from a position or role.
예문	The judge decided to dismiss the case due to lack of evidence. 증거 부족으로 판사는 사건을 기각하기로 결정했습니다.

707

reluctant

[rɪˈlʌk.tənt]

a. 싫어하는, 꺼리는

be reluctant to do p. ~하기를 꺼리다
reluctantly adv. 마지못해, 꺼려하며
reluctance n. 내키지 않음, 본의 아님
relinquish v. 포기하다, 양도하다, 단념하다

어원	-re : back + -lug : struggle → '뒤로 떨쳐버리려고 노력하니 꺼리는'
유의어	unwilling, hesitant, resistant
반의어	eager, willing, enthusiastic
영영	Unwilling or hesitant to do something; showing resistance or a lack of enthusiasm.
예문	She was reluctant to speak in front of the large audience. 그녀는 거대한 관객들 앞에서 말하기를 망설였습니다.

708

condense

[kənˈdens]

v. 압축하다; 액화되다, 고체화되다

densely adv. 빽빽이, 밀집하여
density n. 밀도
densify v. 밀도를 높이다
condensed a. 요약한, 응축한, 압축한

어원	-con : together + -dens : -densus(L) 두꺼운, 복잡한(thick); 흐린(cloudy) → '같이 모아 밀집시키니 응축하다'
유의어	compress, reduce, concentrate
반의어	Expand, dilate, inflate
영영	To change from a gas or vapor into a liquid state, often by cooling.
예문	Water vapor in the air can condense into clouds. 공기 중의 수증기는 구름으로 응축될 수 있습니다.

709

defect

[ˈdiː.fekt]

n. 결점, 결함, 결핍

perfect a. 완전한, 완벽한
infect v. 감염시키다
affect v. 영향을 주다, 작용하다
affective a. 감정적인, 정서적인

어원	-de : away + -fac, -fec, -fic, -fy, -fair : make → '질이 떨어지게 만드니 결함'
유의어	flaw, imperfection, fault
반의어	asset, advantage
영영	a flaw or imperfection in something; to abandon one's allegiance or loyalty
예문	The product was recalled due to a manufacturing defect. 제품은 제조 결함 때문에 회수되었다.

710

swift

[swɪft]

a. 신속한, 빠른

swing v. 흔들다, 빙 돌다 n. 그네
switch n. 스위치; 회초리 v. 전환하다
switch over p. 전환하다, 바꾸다
sway n. 흔들림 v. 흔들리다

어원	-swi : swing → '속도가 빠르니 흔들리는'
유의어	fast, quick, rapid
반의어	Slow, sluggish, leisurely
영영	Moving or happening quickly; fast in action or speed.
예문	The cheetah is known for its swift running speed. 치타는 빠른 달리기 속도로 유명합니다.

711

dispose of

p. ~을 처리하다, ~을 없애다

disposal n. 처분, 처리
disposition n. 성향, 의향; 정리, 처분
depose v. 물러나게 하다
deposit n. 계약금; 퇴적물

어원	-de : down + -pos : put → '밑으로 내려놓고 배열 후 처리하다'
유의어	discard, get rid of, eliminate
반의어	acquire, obtain, keep
영영	to get rid of or deal with something
예문	Please dispose of the old furniture properly. 오래된 가구를 적절히 처리해 주세요.

712

approve of

p. ~을 인정하다, ~을 괜찮다고 생각하다

approve v. 승인하다
disapprove of p. ~을 못마땅하게 여기다
proberb n. 속담, 격언
reproval n. 책망, 비난

어원	-a : to + -prov, -prob : 증명하다, 증언하다 (L) → ~에 가서 증명을 거친 후 승인하니 찬성'
유의어	endorse, support, agree with
반의어	disapprove of, reject, oppose
영영	to agree with or support something
예문	The committee will approve of the budget proposal next week. 위원회는 다음 주에 예산 제안을 승인할 것입니다.

713

vulnerable to N

p. ~에 취약한

vulnerable a. 취약한, 연약한
vulnerability n. 취약함, 취약성
invulnerable a. 상처 입지 않는
violence n. 폭행, 폭력, 격렬함

어원	-vulner : wound + -able → '상처가 있어 취약한'
유의어	susceptible to N, at risk of N, prone to N
반의어	immune to N, resistant to N, protected from N
영영	susceptible to harm or damage from N
예문	Young children are vulnerable to infections. 어린 아이들은 감염에 취약합니다.

714

avail oneself of

p. ~을 이용하다

avail v. 쓸모가 있다, 유용하다
available a. 이용할 수 있는, 구할 수 있는
valued a. 소중한
valor n. 용기, 용맹

어원	- av : to + -vail 가치 → '~에게 가치가 있을 때 쓸모가 있어 이용하다'
유의어	utilize, make use of, take advantage of
반의어	avoid, shun, neglect
영영	to make use of or take advantage of something
예문	Students are encouraged to avail themselves of the resources in the library. 학생들은 도서관의 자원을 활용하도록 권장됩니다.

715

correlated with

p. ~과 서로 관련된

correlation n. 연관성, 상호 관련
correlative a. 상호 관계가 있는
relatively adv. 비교적으로, 상대적으로
translate A into B p. A를 B로 고쳐 말하다

어원	-cor : together + -relate 관계 → '모두 관계로 상호 관련하다'
유의어	associated with, linked to, connected with
반의어	unrelated to, independent of, unconnected to
영영	having a mutual relationship or connection with something else
예문	Research has shown that smoking is strongly correlated with lung cancer. 연구 결과 흡연과 폐암 간에 강한 상관 관계가 있음을 보여주었습니다.

716

fall into place

p. 제자리를 찾다, 아귀가 맞다

fall v. 떨어지다 n. 가을
fall down p. 넘어지다
fall apart p. 무너지다
fall for it p. 속아 넘어가다

어원	-fals, -fal, -fail, -faul : deceive 떨어지다 + -place 장소 → '맞는 장소에 떨어진 것이니 아귀가 맞다'
유의어	come together, fit together, make sense
반의어	fall apart, disintegrate, collapse
영영	to become organized or arranged in a satisfactory way
예문	After months of hard work, everything finally fell into place and the project was a success. 수개월간의 노력 끝에, 모든 것이 마침내 잘 맞아 떨어지고 프로젝트는 성공적으로 마무리되었습니다.

717

insofar as

p. ~하는 한은, ~하는 정도까지는

so long as p. ~하기만 하면
as it were p. 소위, 말하자면
in the air p. 헛된 근거 없는
in the course of p. ~되고 있는 중인

어원	-in + -far ~까지 → '범위 내에서 ~까지는'
유의어	to the extent that, as far as, inasmuch as
반의어	to the extent that, to the degree that, only if
영영	to the extent or degree that
예문	You can attend the meeting insofar as it relates to your department's responsibilities. 당신의 부서의 책임과 관련이 있는 한 회의에 참석할 수 있습니다.

718

hit the books

p. 열심히 공부하다, 열공하다

become a hit p. 히트를 치다
hit a plateau p. 정체기에 들다
hit a ceiling p. 노발대발하다
hit it off p. 죽이 맞다

어원	book(책)에 hit(집중)하니 열공하다
유의어	study, cram, revise
반의어	skip studying, ignore the books, neglect learning
영영	to study intensively or rigorously
예문	I need to hit the books and study for my upcoming exams. 나는 교과서를 열심히 공부해서 다가오는 시험을 준비해야 합니다.

719

set in one's way

p. 자기 방식이 몸에 밴

set A apart from B p. A와 B를 구별하다
set A aside p. A를 제쳐두다
set out p. 출발하다
set up p. 조성하다, 만들다

어원	-set 설정하다 + -in + -one's way → '~의 방식 안에서 설정된'
유의어	inflexible, rigid, stubborn
반의어	flexible, adaptable, open-minded
영영	to have established habits, opinions, or routines that are difficult to change
예문	My grandfather is set in his ways and doesn't like to try new things. 제 할아버지는 고집이 세고 새로운 것을 시도하기를 좋아하지 않습니다.

720

have something to do with

p. ~와 관계가 있다

have over p. ~으로 초대하다
have a point p. 일리가 있다
have a taste for p. ~에 취미가 있다
have but to do p. ~하기만 하면 된다

어원	-have 갖다 + -something 무엇 → '무언가 갖고 있으니 관계가 있다'
유의어	be related to, be associated with, be connected to
반의어	unrelated to, disconnected from, irrelevant to
영영	to be related or connected to something
예문	Your attitude has something to do with your success in life. 당신의 태도가 인생에서의 성공과 연관이 있습니다.

Chapter 19.

721	contribution	[ˌkɒn.trɪˈbjuː.ʃən]	n. 기부, 기여, 공헌; 원인제공
722	thrust	[θrʌst]	v. 세게 밀다; 찌르다
723	injure	[ˈɪn.dʒər]	v. 상처 입히다, 다치게 하다
724	endeavor	[enˈdev.ə]	v. 노력 v. 노력하다, 애쓰다
725	incorporate	[ɪnˈkɔː.pər.eɪt]	v. ~을 법인으로 만들다; 합병하다; 포함하다
726	bribe	[braɪb]	n. 뇌물 v. 뇌물을 주다; 매수하다
727	constitution	[ˌkɒn.stɪˈtʃuː.ʃən]	n. 구성, 구조; 헌법
728	confidential	[ˌkɒn.fɪˈden.ʃəl]	a. 은밀한, 내밀한, 기밀의
729	profess	[prəˈfes]	v. 주장하다, 공언하다; ~인 체하다
730	withdraw	[wɪðˈdrɔː]	n. 철회
731	ascribe	[əˈskraɪb]	v. 가까이 쓰다; ~탓으로 돌리다
732	costly	[ˈkɒst.li]	a. 대가가 큰, 비용이 많이 드는
733	invaluable	[invæljuəbl]	a. 매우 귀중한
734	inherent	[ɪnˈher.ənt]	a. 선천적인, 고유의, 내재하는
735	scheme	[skiːm]	n. 계획, 책략; v. 책략을 꾸미다
736	misuse	[mìsjúːs]	v. 잘못 사용하다, 학대하다, 실패하다, 유산하다
737	recognize	[ˈrek.əg.naɪz]	v. 알아보다, 식별하다; 인정하다
738	column	[ˈkɒl.əm]	n. 기둥; 기념비; (신문) 칼럼
739	criterion	[kraɪˈtɪə.ri.ən]	n. 기준
740	abstract	[ˈæb.strækt]	a. 추상적인, 관념적인 n. 개요
741	proficient	[prəˈfɪʃ.ənt]	a. 숙달된, 능숙한
742	flatter	[ˈflæt.ər]	v. 아첨하다, 추켜세우다
743	expel	[ɪkˈspel]	v. 추방하다, 쫓아내다
744	moan	[məʊn]	n. 신음 v. 신음하다
745	impartial	[ɪmˈpɑː.ʃəl]	a. 공평한, 편견 없는
746	obsess	[əbˈses]	v. (마음을) 사로잡다, ~에 집착하게 하다
747	displease	[dɪˈspliːz]	v. 불만스럽게 하다, 불쾌하게 만들다
748	gasp	[gæsp]	v. 헐떡거리다, 숨이 막히다
749	conserve	[kənˈsɜːv]	v. 보존하다, 보호하다
750	tragic	[ˈtrædʒ.ɪk]	a. 비극적인
751	have difficulty in -ing		p. ~하는데 어려움을 겪다
752	adjust A around B		p. A를 B 중심으로[B에 맞춰] 조절하다
753	at an early age		p. 일찍이, 어린 나이에
754	against the laws		p. 불법인, 법에 저촉되는
755	fit in with		p. ~에 잘 들어맞다, 적합하다
756	given that		p. ~이라는 것을 고려하면
757	hand in		p. 제출하다
758	be founded on		p. ~에 기초하다
759	be scared of		p. ~을 두려워하다, ~을 경외하다
760	in contact with		p. ~와 연락하여; ~와 접촉하여

721

contribution

[ˌkɒn.trɪˈbjuː.ʃən]

n. 기부, 기여, 공헌; 원인제공

tribute n. 헌사, 공물
contribute to N p. ~에 기여하다, 원인이 되다
contribute A to B p. A를 B에게 기부하다
make a contribution p. 이바지하다

어원	-con : together + -tribu : assign → '모두에게 할당될 수 있도록 기부하다', '모든 일에 할당되는 원인'
유의어	donation, offering, gift
반의어	Withdrawal, subtraction, deduction
영영	Something that is given, offered, or provided, often in the context of assistance or support.
예문	His contribution to the research project was significant. 그의 연구 프로젝트에 대한 기여는 상당했습니다.

722

thrust

[θrʌst]

v. 세게 밀다; 찌르다

thrive v. 번창하다, 잘 자라다
threat v. 위협하다
throne n. 왕좌, 왕위
come through p. 극복하다, 이겨내다

어원	-threat, -trud, -thrust 밀다 (E) → '세게 미는 것이 곧 찌르기'
유의어	push, force, shove
반의어	Pull, draw, haul
영영	To push or force something with sudden or strong pressure.
예문	The rocket's powerful engines provided the thrust needed for liftoff. 로켓의 강력한 엔진은 발사에 필요한 추진력을 제공했습니다.

723

injure

[ˈɪn.dʒər]

v. 상처 입히다, 다치게 하다

injury n. 상해, 부상
injured a. 부상당한
prejudice n. 선입견, 편견
jury n. 배심원단

어원	-in : not + -ju : right → '옳지 않은 일로 상처를 입히다'
유의어	harm, wound, damage
반의어	heal, mend, repair
영영	to harm or cause physical damage to someone or something.
예문	He managed to injure his ankle while playing soccer. 그는 축구를 하면서 발목을 다치게 되었다.

724

endeavor

[enˈdev.ər]

v. 노력 v. 노력하다, 애쓰다

endear v. 애정을 느끼게 하다
endemic a. 풍토성의
endorse v. 지지하다, 통과시키다
indorse v. 지지하다, 통과시키다

어원	-en : in + -deavor 의무 → '마음 속에 자리잡은 의무 때문에 노력' * 인대가 부어도 일어서려 노력하다, 애쓰다
유의어	effort, attempt, strive
반의어	Abandon, give up, quit
영영	A sincere and purposeful effort to achieve a specific goal or objective.
예문	She made a great endeavor to achieve her dreams. 그녀는 꿈을 이루기 위해 큰 노력을 기울였습니다.

725

incorporate

[ɪnˈkɔː.pər.eɪt]

v. ~을 법인으로 만들다; 합병하다; 포함하다

corporate a. 기업의, 회사의, 공동의
corporation n. 기업, 회사, 법인, 조합
corporately adv. 단체적으로
incorporation n. 포함, 합병

어원	-in : into + -corp : body → '안으로 포함시켜 형체를 갖으니 합병'
유의어	include, integrate, merge
반의어	Exclude, eliminate, omit
영영	To include or integrate something as a part of a larger whole.
예문	The company decided to incorporate sustainable practices into its business model. 그 회사는 지속 가능한 실천 방법을 비즈니스 모델에 통합하기로 결정했습니다.

726

bribe

[braɪb]

n. 뇌물 v. 뇌물을 주다; 매수하다

bride n. 신부
bridegroom n. 신랑
brevity n. 짧음, 간결
breeding n. 사육, 번식

어원	-bribe(F) 거지에게 주던 한 조각의 빵 * bride(신부)를 뇌물로 매수
유의어	corrupt, payoff, inducement
반의어	Legal payment, authorized compensation, legitimate reward
영영	To offer money, goods, or favors to someone in exchange for influence, cooperation, or a desired action.
예문	Offering a bribe to a public official is illegal. 공무원에게 뇌물을 제공하는 것은 불법입니다.

727

constitution

[ˌkɒn.stɪˈtʃuː.ʃən]

n. 구성, 구조; 헌법

constitutive a. 구성적인, 구조의
be consitutive of p. ~을 구성하다
constitutively adv. 구성 요소로서
constitute v. 구성하다; 설립하다; 제정하다

어원	-con : together + -stitu : stand → '법 위에 함께 서게 만드는 구조가 헌법'
유의어	framework, structure, charter
반의어	Destruction, disintegration, breakdown
영영	A fundamental or basic law that establishes the framework and principles of a government or organization.
예문	The constitution of the country outlines the fundamental laws and principles. 그 나라의 헌법은 기본 법률과 원칙을 개요로 제시합니다.

728

confidential

[ˌkɒn.fɪˈden.ʃəl]

a. 은밀한, 내밀한, 기밀의

confident a. 확신하는, 자신감 있는
confidentiality n. 기밀, 비밀
confiding a. 남을 쉽게 믿는
defy v. 반항하다, 도전하다; 무시하다

어원	-con : together + -fi, -fid, -fy 믿다(L) -ent 사람 → '모두 완전히 믿을만한 사람에게만이니 은밀한'
유의어	private, secret, classified
반의어	public, open
영영	meant to be kept secret or private; entrusted with sensitive or classified information
예문	The documents are highly confidential and should not be shared. 그 문서들은 매우 비밀이며 공유해서는 안 된다.

729

profess

[prəˈfes]

v. 주장하다, 공언하다; ~인 체하다

professed a. 공언한, 명백한
profession n. 직업
profile n. 윤곽, 프로필
profane a. 불경스런

어원	-pro : forth + -fess : say → '공공연히 말하다'
유의어	declare, claim, assert
반의어	Deny, renounce, disclaim
영영	To declare openly or publicly, often in a formal or solemn manner.
예문	She didn't profess to be an expert, but she knew a lot about the subject. 그녀는 전문가임을 주장하지 않았지만 그 주제에 대해 많이 알고 있었습니다.

730

withdraw

[wɪðˈdrɔː]

n. 철회

withdrawal n. (예금의) 인출
withhold v. 주지 않다; 억제하다
wither v. 시들다, 말라 죽다
withstand v. 반항하다, 저항하다

어원	-with 밖으로, 반대쪽으로 + draw 끌다 → '반대로 끌다'(E)
유의어	retract, pull back, remove
반의어	deposit, contribute, add
영영	To remove or take back something; to retreat or remove oneself from a situation or place.
예문	The troops had to withdraw from the battle due to heavy losses. 대량의 손실로 인해 부대가 전투에서 철수해야 했습니다.

731

ascribe

[əˈskraɪb]

v. 가까이 쓰다; ~탓으로 돌리다

script n. 대본, 원고
describe v. 묘사하다, 기술하다
insribe v. 글을 쓰다; 깊이 새기다
ascribe A to B p. A를 B탓이라고 돌리다

어원	-a : to + -scrib : write → '~에 따른 결과를 이름으로 쓰다'
유의어	attribute, assign, credit
반의어	dissociate, separate
영영	attribute or assign something to a particular cause
예문	They often ascribe their success to luck rather than hard work. 그들은 종종 성공을 행운에 돌리고 노력이 아닌 것으로 생각한다.

732

costly

[ˈkɒst.li]

a. 대가가 큰, 비용이 많이 드는

cost n. 가격, 원가, 대가
cost-effectiveness p. 비용 효율성
contrast n. 대조, 대비
in contrast p. 대조적으로

어원	-cost 비용 → '비용이 많이 드니 대가가 큰'
유의어	expensive, high-priced, extravagant
반의어	Inexpensive, cheap, affordable
영영	Involving high expenses or expenditures; expensive.
예문	The repairs to the historic building were very costly. 역사적인 건물의 수리는 매우 비용이 많이 들었습니다.

733

invaluable

[invǽljuəbl]

a. 매우 귀중한

value n. 가치 a. 가치가 있는
overvalue v. 지나치게 가치를 주다
valued a. 소중한
valor n. 용기, 용맹

어원	-in : in + -valuable 가치가 있는
유의어	priceless, precious, irreplaceable
반의어	Worthless, valueless, insignificant
영영	Extremely valuable or priceless; beyond estimation in terms of worth.
예문	Her grandmother's advice was invaluable to her throughout her life. 그녀의 할머니의 조언은 그녀의 평생 동안 귀중했습니다.

734

inherent

[ɪnˈher.ənt]

a. 선천적인, 고유의, 내재하는

inherently adv. 타고나서, 본질적으로
inherence n. 고유, 천부, 타고남
inherency n. 고유의 성질, 본래의 속성
adherent a. 들러붙는 n. 지지자

어원	-in : in + -her : stick → '태어날 때부터 몸에 붙어있는'
유의어	innate, intrinsic, natural
반의어	acquired, learned
영영	existing as a natural or essential part
예문	Some skills are inherent, while others can be learned. 일부 기술은 내재적이지만, 다른 것들은 배울 수 있다.

735

scheme

[ski:m]

n. 계획, 책략; v. 책략을 꾸미다

scheme of things p. 사물의 체계
schema n. 스키마, 도식(개인의 인지 구조)
sketch out p. ~을 대략 그리다
situate v. 두다, 위치시키다

어원	-scheme : sketch outline → '개요를 세우고 계획하니 책략'
유의어	plan, strategy, plot
반의어	honesty, sincerity
영영	a plan or program of action designed to accomplish a specific goal; a systematic arrangement or design
예문	They devised a clever scheme to outsmart their competitors in the market. 그들은 시장에서 경쟁자들을 속이기 위한 교묘한 계획을 세웠다.

736

misuse

[mìsjúːs]

v. 잘못 사용하다, 학대하다, 실패하다, 유산하다

misunderstand v. 오해하다
misprint v. 잘못 인쇄하다
mistaken a.. 잘못 알고 있는
mock a. 거짓된, 가짜의, 모의의

어원	-mis : wrong + -use, -uti, -utile, -utili : use → '잘못 사용하는 것이니 실패와 유산과 학대'
유의어	abuse, mistreat, mishandle
반의어	proper use, correct usage, appropriate application
영영	Incorrect or improper use of something.
예문	It's important not to misuse your authority. 권한을 남용하지 않는 것이 중요합니다.

737

recognize

[ˈrek.əg.naɪz]

v. 알아보다, 식별하다; 인정하다

recognise v. 인정하다, 인식하다
recongnizable a. 알아볼 수 있는
unrecognizable a. 인지할 수 없는
cognitive a. 인식의, 인지의

어원	-re : again + -cogn, -gno, -kno, -no, -quaint : know → '다시 알아보고 인정하다'
유의어	identify, acknowledge, perceive
반의어	ignore, overlook
영영	to identify or acknowledge someone or something as familiar or known; to perceive and understand
예문	She couldn't recognize her old friend after so many years. 그녀는 많은 해가 지난 후 예전 친구를 알아보지 못했다.

738

column

[ˈkɒl.əm]

n. 기둥; 기념비; (신문) 칼럼

coma n. 혼수상태, 코마
when it comes to p. ~에 관한한
collocation n. 배치, 배열
columnar a. 원주의, 원형의

어원	-column : columna 꼭대기, 정상 → '꼭대기까지 솟은 기둥', '신문의 기둥 역할을 하는 칼럼'
유의어	pillar, post, support
반의어	Row, line, series
영영	A vertical structural support, or a regular feature in a newspaper or magazine presenting information or opinions.
예문	The newspaper column provides insights into current events. 신문 기사는 현재의 사건에 대한 통찰을 제공합니다.

739

criterion

[kraɪˈtɪə.ri.ən]

n. 기준

criteria n. 기준(criterion의 복수)
crispy a. 바삭바삭한
crucial a. 중요한, 결정적인
discrimination n. 차별

어원	-cri : separate → '구별되는 행동을 나누는 기준'
유의어	standard, guideline, parameter
반의어	Irrelevant factor, non-factor, irrelevant aspect
영영	A standard or rule used for judgment or evaluation.
예문	The main criterion for admission to the program is academic excellence. 이 프로그램 입학의 주요 기준은 학업 우수성입니다.

740

abstract

[ˈæb.strækt]

a. 추상적인, 관념적인 n. 개요

attract v. 끌어들이다
tractor n. 트랙터
retract v. 철회하다, 거부하다
in the abstract p. 추상적으로, 관념적으로

어원	-abs : away + -trac, -tract, -trai, -tray, -treat : draw(L) → '멀리 끌어가는 생각이니 추상적인', '추상적으로 핵심만 모아 놓은 개요'
유의어	conceptual, theoretical, non-concrete
반의어	Concrete, specific, tangible
영영	Existing in thought or as an idea, rather than a physical reality; theoretical or conceptual.
예문	The artist's abstract painting left viewers with various interpretations. 화가의 추상적인 그림은 관람자들에게 다양한 해석을 남겼습니다.

741

proficient

[prəˈfɪʃ.ənt]

a. 숙달된, 능숙한

proficiency n. 숙달, 능숙
proficiently adv. 능숙하게
sufficient a. 충분한
profit n. 이익, 수익

어원	-pro : forth + -fac, -fec, -fic, -fy, -fair : make → '앞서 만드니 능숙한'
유의어	skilled, competent, capable
반의어	inexperienced, unskilled, inept
영영	Skilled or competent in a particular activity or field; having expertise or mastery.
예문	She is proficient in playing the piano. 그녀는 피아노 연주에 능숙합니다.

742

flatter

[ˈflæt.ər]

v. 아첨하다, 추켜세우다

어원	-flat, -flare : blow → '바람만 불어넣는 말이니 아첨'
유의어	compliment, praise, sweet-talk
반의어	insult, criticize
영영	praise someone insincerely or excessively to gain favor
예문	She tried to flatter her boss in the hope of getting a promotion. 그녀는 승진을 얻기 위해 상사를 아첨하려고 노력했다.

743

expel

[ɪkˈspel]

v. 추방하다, 쫓아내다

repel v. 물리치다, 쫓아버리다
propel v. 추진하다, 밀어내다
compel v. 강요하다, 억지로 ~시키다
impel v. 재촉하다

어원	-ex : out + -pel, -peal, pul : drive 몰다 → '바깥으로 모니 추방하고 쫓아버리다'
유의어	eject, remove, oust
반의어	Admit, accept, welcome
영영	To force someone to leave or eject them from a place, organization, or group.
예문	The school decided to expel the student for repeated misconduct. 학교는 반복된 불행한 행동으로 학생을 퇴학시키기로 결정했습니다.

744

moan

[məʊn]

n. 신음 v. 신음하다

mournful a. 신음 소리를 내는, 슬퍼하는
bemoan v. 슬퍼하다, 애도하다
lament v. 슬퍼하다 애도하다, 한탄하다
lame a. 절름발이의

어원	-moan : mourn 슬픔 → '슬픔에 나오는 신음'
유의어	groan, lament, wail
반의어	rejoice, celebrate, delight
영영	Make a low, mournful sound expressing pain, discomfort, or unhappiness.
예문	The injured man let out a moan of pain. 다친 남자는 고통의 토로를 내뱉었습니다.

745

impartial

[ɪmˈpɑːʃəl]

a. 공평한, 편견 없는

impart v. 나누어 주다
counterpart n. 상대, 대응; 복사물
couple A with B p. A를 B와 결부시키다
have no part in p. ~에 관계가 없다

어원	-im : in + -part 나누다 → '내 안에 있던 것을 공평하게 나누는'
유의어	unbiased, neutral, fair
반의어	Biased, prejudiced, unfair
영영	Treating all parties or people fairly and without bias; neutral and objective.
예문	The judge must remain impartial and unbiased during the trial. 판사는 재판 중에 공정하고 편견 없이 유지해야 합니다.

746

obsess

[əbˈses]

v. (마음을) 사로잡다, ~에 집착하게 하다

obsessive a. 사로잡힌, 강박적인
obsessively adv. 집요하게, 강박적으로
be obsessed with p. ~에 집착하다, 사로잡히다
residue n. 나머지, 쓰레기

어원	-ob : to + -sid, -sess, -set : sit 앉다 → '나를 향하여 앉게 하니 마음을 사로잡다'
유의어	fixate, preoccupy, haunt
반의어	detach, disconnect
영영	to have an excessive and persistent preoccupation or fixation on something or someone
예문	He would obsess over his mistakes and couldn't move on. 그는 자신의 실수에 집착하고 다음으로 나아갈 수 없었다.

747

displease

[dɪˈspliːz]

v. 불만스럽게 하다, 불쾌하게 만들다

displeased a. 불만스러운, 불쾌한
unpleasant a. 불쾌한
pleasant a. 즐거운, 기분이 좋은
plead v. 간청하다; 탄원하다, 변호하다

어원	-dis : bad + -pla, -plac, -plas, -pleas, -plead 기쁘게 하다 → '기쁘게 하지 않으니 불만스럽다'
유의어	upset, disappoint, offend
반의어	satisfy, please
영영	to cause someone to feel unhappy or dissatisfied; to not meet someone's expectations or desires
예문	His actions did not please his boss, and he was reprimanded for his behavior. 그의 행동은 상사를 기쁘게 하지 않았고, 그의 행동으로 인해 비난을 받았다.

748

gasp

[gæsp]

v. 헐떡거리다, 숨이 막히다

gap n. 격차
garbage n. 쓰레기
gasping adv. 숨이 턱 막히며
gasp for p. ~을 갈망하다

어원	-gasp : open the mouth widely → '입을 크게 벌리며 헐떡거리다' * gas 가스 때문에 숨이 막혀 헐떡거리다
유의어	pant, wheeze, breathe heavily
반의어	breathe, exhale
영영	catch one's breath suddenly, usually due to surprise or shock
예문	She let out a gasp of surprise when she saw the birthday cake. 그녀는 생일 케이크를 보고 놀라서 숨을 크게 들이마셨다.

749

conserve

[kənˈsɜːv]

v. 보존하다, 보호하다

conservation n. 보호, 보존
conservative a. 보수적인, 신중한
subserve v. 돕다, 공헌하다
deserve v. ~할 만한 가치가 있다

어원	-con : intensive + -serv : keep → '함께 지키니 보존'
유의어	preserve, protect, save
반의어	waste, squander
영영	to protect and preserve something, especially natural resources, from harm or depletion
예문	It's important to conserve energy by turning off lights when not in use. 사용하지 않을 때는 조명을 끄는 등 에너지를 절약하는 것이 중요하다.

750

tragic

[ˈtrædʒ.ɪk]

a. 비극적인

tragedy n. 비극
tragical a. 비극적인, 비참한
tragically adv. 비참하게, 비참하게도

어원	-trag : goat 염소 → '신에게 염소를 제물로 바치니 비극'
유의어	heartbreaking, sorrowful, lamentable
반의어	fortunate, joyful
영영	involving a serious and unfortunate event or situation
예문	The tragic accident left the whole community in mourning. 비극적인 사고로 인해 전체 지역 사회가 애도에 잠겼다.

751

have difficulty in -ing

p. ~하는데 어려움을 겪다

hand in p. 제출하다
take the blame for p. ~에 대한 책임을 지다
pass A in -ing p. ~하느라 돈[시간]을 쓰다
be busy in -ing p. ~하느라 바쁘다

어원	-have 갖다 + -difficulty 어려움
유의어	struggle with, find it hard to, have trouble with
반의어	excel in, succeed in, thrive in
영영	to struggle or experience challenges in doing something
예문	She has difficulty in speaking in front of large audiences. 그녀는 대규모 청중들 앞에서 말하는 데 어려움을 겪습니다.

752

adjust A around B

p. A를 B 중심으로[B에 맞춰] 조절하다

adjust to N p. ~에 적용하다, 조정하다
adjusted a. 조정된, 조절된
maladjusted a. 적응이 안 되는
adjustment n. 조절 적응

어원	-ad : to + -just : right → '올바른 방향으로 맞추니 적용하다' syn. adapt to
유의어	adapt A to B, modify A for B, accommodate B with A
반의어	change B for A, alter B to fit A, modify B to accommodate A
영영	to make changes to A to accommodate or fit with B
예문	We need to adjust our schedule around the new project deadline. 우리는 새로운 프로젝트 마감일을 중심으로 일정을 조정해야 합니다.

753

at an early age

p. 일찍이, 어린 나이에

at an angle p. 비스듬히
at all times p. 항상
at a loss p. 어쩔 줄을 모르는
at a distance p. 멀리서

어원	-early 일찍, 어린 + -age 나이 → '일찍부터 어린 나이에'
유의어	in childhood, when young, from a young age
반의어	in later life, in adulthood, in maturity
영영	during childhood or at a young age
예문	She started learning to play the piano at an early age. 그녀는 어린 나이에 피아노를 배우기 시작했습니다.

754

against the laws

p. 불법인, 법에 저촉되는

against the one's will p. ~의 의지에 반하여
against the wall p. 벽에 기대다
act up p. 버릇없이 굴다; 상태가 나쁘다
against the odds p. 역경을 무릅쓰고

어원	-a : anti + -ga : gone * 그리스 신화에서 영원한 생명을 얻은 영웅 고네(Gone) → '영원한 생명에 반하여'
유의어	illegal, unlawful, prohibited
반의어	legal, lawful, permitted
영영	not in accordance with established rules or regulations
예문	Stealing is against the laws of society. 도둑질은 사회의 법에 반하는 행위입니다.

755

fit in with

p. ~에 잘 들어맞다, 적합하다

fit in p. ~에 맞추다, 어울리다
fit into p. 적합하다, 어울리다
fit together with p. ~와 잘 맞다
fitter n. 설비 기술자

어원	-fit 맞추다 (* 주로 형용사와 어울려 a good fit, bad fit, perfect fit)
유의어	blend in with, conform to, harmonize with
반의어	clash with, oppose, contradict
영영	to be compatible or harmonious with something
예문	I hope my ideas fit in with the team's overall vision. 나의 아이디어가 팀의 전체적인 비전과 조화를 이루기 바랍니다.

756

given that

p. ~이라는 것을 고려하면

give in to p. ~에 굴복하다
give A the benefit of any doubt p. A를 속는 셈 치고 믿어보다
give or take p. 대략

어원	-given 주어진 + -that → 'that이하 상황이 주어진 것을 고려하면'
유의어	considering that, since, in view of the fact that
반의어	despite the fact that, regardless of the fact that, in spite of the fact that
영영	considering the fact that
예문	Given that it's raining outside, we should bring umbrellas. 밖이 비온다는 것을 감안하여 우산을 가져가야 합니다.

757

hand in

p. 제출하다

hand in hand p. 손을 마주잡고, 제휴하여
take the blame for p. ~에 대한 책임을 지다
pass A in -ing p. ~하느라 돈[시간]을 쓰다
be busy in -ing p. ~하느라 바쁘다

어원	-hand 손 + -in 안 → '정해진 기간 안에 손으로 제출하다'
유의어	submit, turn in, deliver
반의어	keep, withhold, retain
영영	to submit or give something to someone in authority
예문	Please hand in your assignments by Friday. 금요일까지 과제를 제출해 주세요.

758

be founded on

p. ~에 기초하다

found v. 설립하다; ~에 기초를 두다
foundation n. 토대, 기초
founding a. 기초적인
confound v. 당황케 하다, 혼동하다

어원	-fund, -found 바닥, 기초(L) → 기초가 바닥에 있다 * base '위치가 낮다' VS found '바닥'
유의어	based on, built on, grounded on
반의어	unfounded, baseless, groundless
영영	to be based or established on something
예문	The company is founded on the principles of honesty and integrity. 그 회사는 정직과 성실의 원칙 위에 설립되었습니다.

759

be scared of

p. ~을 두려워하다, ~을 경외하다

scare a. 희귀한, 드문 v. 위협하다
scarecrow n. 허수아비
frighten v. 겁먹게 만들다, 깜짝 놀라게 하다
fright n. 공포, 경악

어원	-scare : rare 드문 → '드문 현상이니 위협적이이라 겁먹은' (* 중세 영어로 '겁, 두려움' 뜻)
유의어	afraid of, frightened of, fearful of
반의어	unafraid of, fearless of, courageous in the face of
영영	to be afraid of something
예문	Many people are scared of spiders. 많은 사람들이 거미를 무서워합니다.

760

in contact with

p. ~와 연락하여; ~와 접촉하여

contagious a. 전염성의
in conclusion p. 결론적으로, 끝으로
in commotion p. 동요하고 있다
in contrast to p. ~와는 대조적으로

어원	-con : together + -tac : touch → '함께 닿으니 연락'
유의어	in touch with, connected with, communicating with
반의어	isolated from, separate from, disconnected from
영영	having communication or connection with someone or something
예문	He is in contact with his family every day. 그는 매일 가족과 연락을 합니다.

Chapter 20.

761	fertile	[ˈfɜː.taɪl]	a. 기름진, 비옥한
762	doom	[duːm]	n. 운명, 파멸, 죽음
763	occupy	[ˈɒk.jə.paɪ]	v. 차지하다, 점령하다
764	indicate	[ˈɪn.dɪ.keɪt]	v. 말로 가리키다, 나타내다, 암시하다
765	inhabit	[ɪnˈhæb.ɪt]	v. 살다, 서식하다
766	ruthless	[ˈruː.θləs]	a. 무자비한, 냉정한
767	desperate	[ˈdes.pər.ət]	a. 절망적인, 자포자기의, 무모한; 필사적인
768	assure	[əˈʃúər]	v. 확신시키다, 보장하다
769	legitimate	[ləˈdʒɪt.ə.mət]	a. 합법의, 적법의
770	publicity	[pʌbˈlɪs.ə.ti]	n. 홍보, 공표, 평판, 널리 알려짐
771	embrace	[ɪmˈbreɪs]	v. 껴안다, 받아들이다
772	mature	[məˈtʃʊər]	a. 성숙한, 신중한
773	determine	[dɪˈtɜː.mɪn]	v. 결정하다, 측정하다, 판정하다
774	advent	[ˈæd.vent]	n. 등장, 출현
775	segment	[ˈseg.mənt]	n. 부분, 조각 v. 분할하다
776	obtain	[əbˈteɪn]	v. 얻다, 획득하다
777	nominate	[ˈnɒm.ɪ.neɪt]	v. 임명하다, 공천하다
778	vicious	[víʃəs]	a. 잔인한, 사악한
779	appropriate	[əˈprəʊ.pri.ət]	a. 적당한, 타당한
780	conceal	[kənˈsiːl]	v. 숨기다
781	fascinate	[ˈfæs.ən.eɪt]	v. 매료하다, 매혹시키다
782	insulate	[ˈɪn.sjə.leɪt]	v. 단열 처리를 하다, 방음 처리를 하다
783	reap	[riːp]	v. 수확하다
784	manifest	[ˈmæn.ɪ.fest]	n. 화물 목록; a. 명백한; v. 분명히 나타내다
785	crawl	[krɔːl]	v. 기어가다
786	imply	[ɪmˈplaɪ]	v. 내포하다, 넌지시 나타내다, 암시하다
787	deed	[diːd]	n. 행동, 행위, 사실, 실행; 권리증서
788	mutual	[ˈmjuː.tʃu.əl]	a. 상호간의, 서로의, 공통의
789	illuminate	[ɪˈluː.mɪ.neɪt]	v. 빛을 비추다, 밝히다
790	hereby	[ˌhɪəˈbaɪ]	adv. 이에 의하여, 이로써
791	cut from the same cloth		p. 같은 부류인
792	in the mood for		p. ~하고 싶은, ~에 마음이 내켜서
793	go with		p. (계획, 제의 등을) 받아들이다 / 어울리다
794	catch oneself		p. 하던 말(일)을 갑자기 멈추다
795	blow away		p. 날려버리다; ~을 감동시키다
796	free from		p. ~에서 벗어난
797	couple A with B		p. A와 B를 결부시키다
798	a great deal of		p. 많은, 다량의
799	in partnership with		p. ~와 제휴하여, 협력하여
800	call off		p. 취소하다, 중지하다

761

fertile

[ˈfɜːrtaɪl]

a. 기름진, 비옥한

fertilize v. 비옥하게 만들다, 기름지게 하다
fertilization n. 토지 비옥화; 시비, 수정
fertilizer n. 비료
fertility n. 비옥함, 기름짐; 번식력, 출산력

어원	-fer : bear 낳다 + -ti : terra 땅 → '땅에서 생명이 나오니 비옥한'
유의어	productive, fruitful, rich
반의어	barren, infertile, unproductive
영영	Capable of producing abundant offspring or crops; rich in resources or possibilities.
예문	The fertile soil in the valley was ideal for farming. 계곡의 풍부한 토양은 농업에 이상적이었다.

762

doom

[duːm]

n. 운명, 파멸, 죽음

indeed adv. 실제로
misdeed n. 악행, 비행
deem v. ~으로 생각하다, 간주하다
be doomed p. 불행한 운명(결말)을 맞다

어원	-deed, -deem, -doom : doed 행해진(E) → '행해진 그대로 판단하여 운명이라 생각'
유의어	fate, destiny, catastrophe
반의어	salvation, success, prosperity
영영	a grim or catastrophic fate or outcome.
예문	The impending storm seemed to spell doom for their outdoor picnic. 임박한 폭풍은 야외 소풍에 좋지 않은 전조로 보였다.

763

occupy

[ˈɒk.jə.paɪ]

v. 차지하다, 점령하다

occupation n. 직업, 직종
occupancy 점유; 사용권; 이용률; 거주권
occupied a. 사용 중인, 바쁜, 점령된
preoccupy v. 선점하다

어원	-oc, -ob 가까이 + -cup : hold + -y 동접 → '가까이 가서 잡는 것이니 점유하고 사용'
유의어	inhabit, reside, dwell
반의어	Vacate, abandon, leave
영영	To take or hold possession or control of a place, often by force or through settlement.
예문	Protesters decided to occupy the city square until their demands were met. 시위대는 그들의 요구가 충족될 때까지 도시 광장을 점거하기로 결정했습니다.

764

indicate

[ˈɪn.dɪ.keɪt]

v. 말로 가리키다, 나타내다, 암시하다

indicator n. 지표, 지수; 징후, 조짐
indication n. 지시 징표, 징후
be indicative of p. ~을 나타내다, ~을 보여주다
dictator n. 독재자

어원	-in 안 + -dic : say + -ate → '안에 의미를 넣어 나타내다'
유의어	show, suggest, point out
반의어	Conceal, hide, obscure
영영	To point out, show, or suggest something; to make known or demonstrate.
예문	The arrow will indicate the direction to the nearest exit. 화살표는 가장 가까운 출구 방향을 가리킬 것입니다.

765

inhabit

[ɪnˈhæb.ɪt]

v. 살다, 서식하다

habitat n. 서식지, 거주지
inhabitant n. 서식인, 거주자
rehabilitate v. 원상태로 돌리다, 복귀시키다
rehab n. 재활

어원	-in + -hab, -hib, -ab 살다, 유지하다 / have 갖다 → '안에 사는 것이 습관이 되니 거주하다' (L)
유의어	reside, occupy, dwell
반의어	vacate, abandon, desert
영영	to live in or occupy a place.
예문	Many species of fish inhabit the coral reefs in this area. 이 지역의 산호초에는 다양한 종류의 물고기가 서식하고 있다

766

ruthless

[ˈruː.θ.ləs]

a. 무자비한, 냉정한

ruth n. 슬픔, 비애, 후회
ruthlessness n. 무자비함, 냉정함
regreful a. 유감스러운
reimburse v. ~에게 변상하다, 갚다

어원	-ruth 슬픔 + -less 無 → '슬픈 감정까지 없으니 무자비한'
유의어	merciless, pitiless, cruel
반의어	compassionate, merciful, kind-hearted
영영	Showing no compassion or mercy; harsh and unrelenting.
예문	The ruthless dictator ruled with an iron fist. 무자비한 독재자가 철저하게 통치했습니다.

767

desperate

[ˈdes.pər.ət]

a. 절망적인, 자포자기의, 무모한; 필사적인

desperately adv. 절망적으로, 자포자기식으로
desperation n. 자포자기, 절망
desperate a. 절망적인, 자포자기의
despair n. 절망 v. 절망하다

어원	-de : down + -sper, -spar, -spair 희망 → '희망이 떨어져 절망적이기에 더 필사적인'
유의어	hopeless, despairing, frantic
반의어	Hopeful, optimistic, confident
영영	Feeling a sense of urgency and despair, often due to extreme circumstances.
예문	He was in a desperate situation and needed help urgently. 그는 절박한 상황에 있었고 긴급한 도움이 필요했습니다.

768

assure

[əʃúər]

v. 확신시키다, 보장하다

ensure that p. ~을 보장하다
insure v. 보험에 들다
ensure v. 책임지다, 보장하다
reassure v. 안심시키다

어원	-a : to + -sure 확실한 → '~에게 확신시키다'
유의어	reassure, guarantee, promise
반의어	doubt, question
영영	make someone feel certain or confident
예문	He wanted to assure his family that everything would be alright. 그는 가족에게 모든 것이 괜찮을 것이라고 확신시키고 싶었다.

769

legitimate

[ləˈdʒɪt.ə.mət]

a. 합법의, 적법의

legit a. 합법의, 진짜의, 적당한
legitimacy n. 합법성, 적법, 정당성
illicit a. 불법의
legislation n. 입법, 법률 제정

어원	-leg, -leag, -loy : law 법률, 위임하다 → '법을 따르니 합법의'
유의어	legal, lawful, valid
반의어	Illegitimate, unauthorized, illegal
영영	In accordance with the law or accepted rules; valid and legal.
예문	The company has a legitimate reason for its decision. 그 회사는 그 결정에 대한 정당한 이유가 있습니다.

770

publicity

[pʌbˈlɪs.ə.ti]

n. 홍보, 공표, 평판, 널리 알려짐

public speaker p. 대중 연설가
republic n. 공화국, 공화제 국가
publicly adv. 공개적으로, 공공연하게
publish v. 출판하다, 발표하다

어원	-popul, -publ 많은 사람들(L) → '많은 사람들을 선동하는 홍보니 평판이 널리 알려짐'
유의어	promotion, advertising, exposure
반의어	Privacy, obscurity, anonymity
영영	The act or process of creating awareness and attention to something through various forms of media or promotion.
예문	The new product received a lot of publicity in the media. 새 제품은 언론에서 많은 홍보를 받았습니다.

771

embrace

[ɪmˈbreɪs]

v. 껴안다, 받아들이다

embracement n. 포옹 수락
bracelet n. 팔찌
embarrass v. 부끄럽게 하다, 다오항하다
brave a. 용감한, 용기 있는

어원	-em : in + -brace 팔 → 팔 안에 들어오도록 껴안다
유의어	hug, cuddle, clasp
반의어	reject, push away
영영	hold someone or something closely; accept or adopt willingly
예문	They shared a warm embrace upon reuniting after years apart. 멀리 떨어져 있던 시간이 지난 후 다시 만나면서 따뜻한 포옹을 나눴다.

772

mature

[məˈtʃʊər]

a. 성숙한, 신중한

premature a. 시기 상조의
prematurely adv. 이르게, 시기 상조로
immature a. 미숙한
immaturity n. 미성숙, 미발달

어원	-mature 성숙한 * amateur 아마추어 -a : not + -mature 성숙한 → '성숙하지 못하니 비전문가'
유의어	grown, developed, fully grown
반의어	immature, juvenile, inexperienced
영영	Fully grown or developed; showing adult qualities or characteristics.
예문	His mature outlook on life impressed his peers. 그의 삶에 대한 성숙한 시각은 동료들을 감동시켰습니다.

773

determine

[dɪˈtɜː.mɪn]

v. 결정하다, 측정하다, 판정하다

determined a. 확고한, 결연한, 결정된
be determined to do p. ~하기로 결심하다
determination n. 확고함, 결연함, 결정
determinant n. 결정 요인

어원	-de : completely + -termin 끝, 경계 → '완전히 고민을 끝내고 내린 결정' * 고대 로마 신화, 테르미누스 Terminus 신은 '토지의 경계와 끝, 고정불변의 것'을 뜻함
유의어	decide, ascertain, conclude
반의어	hesitate, waver
영영	to decide or settle something conclusively; to ascertain or establish something with certainty
예문	Your attitude and effort will determine your success in this endeavor. 당신의 태도와 노력이 이 노력에서의 성공을 결정할 것이다.

774

advent

[ˈæd.vent]

n. 등장, 출현

venture n. 모험, 모험적인 사업
venture into p. ~로 과감히 들어가 보다
adventure n. 모험 v. 모험을 걸어보다
adventious a. 우연한

어원	-ad : to + -ven, vent : come → '~방향으로 다가와 등장하니 출현'
유의어	arrival, coming, appearance
반의어	departure, exit
영영	arrival or coming of a significant event or person
예문	The advent of technology has changed the way we live. 기술의 도래는 우리의 삶 방식을 바꿨다.

775

segment

[ˈseg.mənt]

n. 부분, 조각 v. 분할하다

insect n. 곤충
section n. 부분
separate v. 분리하다
dissect v. 해부하다, 분석하다

어원	-sec, -sect, -seg 자르다 (L) → '잘라진 것이니 부분, 조각' * -cid, -cis '자르다' / '잘라서 죽이다'
유의어	section, part, portion
반의어	Whole, entirety, complete entity
영영	A distinct part or section of something that is separate or distinct from the whole.
예문	The documentary was divided into several segments for easier viewing. 다큐멘터리는 더 쉬운 시청을 위해 여러 부분으로 나누어졌습니다.

776

obtain

[əbˈteɪn]

v. 얻다, 획득하다

obtainable a. 얻을 수 있는
contain v. 포함하다, 담고 있다
retain v. 계속 유지하다; 보유하다
sustain v. 유지하다, 지지하다

어원	-ob : to + -tain : hold → '~을 향한 후 잡으니 얻다'
유의어	acquire, get, secure
반의어	Surrender, relinquish, give up
영영	To acquire, gain, or secure something through effort, action, or request.
예문	He had to obtain a permit before starting construction. 공사를 시작하기 전에 그는 허가를 획득해야 했습니다.

777

nominate

[ˈnɒm.ɪ.neɪt]

v. 임명하다, 공천하다

nomination n. 임명, 지명
denominate v. ~라고 부르다, 명명하다
renown n. 명성, 유명
synonym n. 동의어, 유의어

어원	-nomin, -no : name 이름(L)
유의어	appoint, propose, name
반의어	dismiss, reject, disqualify
영영	to propose or suggest someone for a position or honor.
예문	She was nominated for the prestigious award. 그녀는 훌륭한 상을 받기 위해 노미네이트되었다.

778

vicious

[víʃəs]

a. 잔인한, 사악한

victory n. 승리
victom n. 피해자, 희생자
convict v. 유죄를 선고하다 n. 죄수
convince v. 확신시키다, 납득시키다

어원	-vict 승리 → '승리를 위해 뭐든 하니 잔인한'
유의어	cruel, brutal, malicious
반의어	gentle, kind, benevolent
영영	extremely cruel, aggressive, or violent.
예문	The dog turned vicious after being mistreated. 개는 학대를 당한 후 사나워졌다.

779

appropriate
[əˈprəʊ.pri.ət]

a. 적당한, 타당한

appropriately adv. 적합하게, ~에 어울리게
property n. 재산, 부동산, 자산; 소유물
properly adv. 적절하게, 알맞게
propaganda n. 선전, 선전 활동

어원	-ap : to + -propr : proper 맞춰진 → '같은 방향으로 맞춰져 적당한, 타당한'
유의어	suitable, proper, fitting
반의어	inappropriate, unsuitable, unfitting
영영	suitable or fitting for a particular purpose.
예문	It's important to dress appropriately for a formal event. 공식 행사에 적절한 옷을 입는 것이 중요하다.

780

conceal
[kənˈsiːl]

v. 숨기다

concealment n. 은폐
concealable a. 숨길 수 있는
concealer n. 은닉자
reveal v. 드러내다, 밝히다

어원	-con : together + -cult, -cel, -ceal : hide → '모두 감추다'
유의어	hide, cover, keep secret
반의어	reveal, uncover, expose
영영	to hide or keep something secret.
예문	He tried to conceal his surprise when she revealed the surprise party. 그는 그녀가 의외의 파티를 공개할 때 놀라지 않으려고 노력했다.

781

fascinate
[ˈfæs.ən.eɪt]

v. 매료하다, 매혹시키다

fashion n. 유해으 인기, 풍조
fascination n. 매료, 매혹, 매력
fascinating a. 매혹적인
fashionably adv. 유행을 따라서

어원	-fasc 마법 + -in + -ate 동접 → '마법처럼 한 순간에 빠지게 매료하다'
유의어	captivate, enchant, bewitch
반의어	bore, repel
영영	attract or captivate someone's interest or attention
예문	The exotic wildlife in the jungle always fascinated him. 그 정글의 이국적인 야생 동물은 항상 그를 매혹시켰다.

782

insulate
[ˈɪn.sjə.leɪt]

v. 단열 처리를 하다, 방음 처리를 하다

insulator n. 단열재
insulation n. 단열 처리, 방음 처리
peninsula n. 반도
in isolation p. 고립된 채로

어원	-isle, -insul, -isol : island 섬 → '섬처럼 열과 소리가 못 들어가는'
유의어	isolate, protect, shield
반의어	Conduct, transfer, transmit
영영	To protect or isolate from the transfer of heat, sound, or electricity.
예문	Good insulation helps keep the house warm in the winter. 좋은 단열재는 집을 겨울에 따뜻하게 유지하는 데 도움이 됩니다.

783

reap
[riːp]

v. 수확하다

strip v. 뜯어내다; 옷을 벗기다
strip A of B p. A에서 B를 제거하다
strip away p. ~을 벗겨내다
rip off p. 뜯어내다, 훔치다

어원	-reap : rip → '땅에서 곡식을 뜯어내다'
유의어	harvest, gather, collect
반의어	sow, plant
영영	harvest or gather a crop
예문	After months of hard work, they were finally able to reap the rewards. 몇 달간의 노력 끝에 그들은 마침내 보상을 얻을 수 있었다.

784

manifest
[ˈmæn.ɪ.fest]

n. 화물 목록; a. 명백한; v. 분명히 나타내다

manually adv. 수동으로, 손으로
manifestly adv. 명백하게, 분명하게
manifestation n. 징후, 명시, 나타남
manifesto n. 성명서, 선언문

어원	-man : hand + -fest : fist 주먹 → '손을 주먹으로 치며 목록을 세니 명백한'
유의어	demonstrate, reveal, display
반의어	hide, conceal
영영	display or show clearly
예문	His commitment to the project was manifest in his dedication and hard work. 프로젝트에 대한 그의 헌신과 노력은 명확하게 나타났다.

785

crawl

[krɔːl]

v. 기어가다

creep v. 기어가다
cripple n. 불구자; v. 불구자가 되다
cringe n. 비굴한 태도 v. 굽실대다
reptile n. 파충류

어원	-crawl : claw → '발톱을 사용해 천천히 기어가다'
유의어	creep, slither, inch
반의어	sprint, rush
영영	to move forward slowly by dragging the body along the ground or a surface, typically on hands and knees
예문	The baby started to crawl across the room for the first time. 아기는 처음으로 방 안을 기어다녔다.

786

imply

[ɪmˈplaɪ]

v. 내포하다, 넌지시 나타내다, 암시하다

implied a. 내재된, 함축된
implant v. 심다, 주입시키다
implicit a. 내재적인, 암시적인

어원	-im : in + -pli, -ply, -ploy, -ploit, -plex : weave 짜다 → '안에 의미가 엮여 있어 내포하다, 암시하다'
유의어	suggest, insinuate, indicate
반의어	deny, contradict
영영	to suggest or indicate something without explicitly stating it; to hint or insinuate
예문	Her smile implies that she is happy with the news. 그녀의 미소는 그녀가 그 소식에 만족한다는 것을 시사한다.

787

deed

[diːd]

n. 행동, 행위, 사실, 실행; 권리증서

indeed adv. 실제로
misdeed n. 악행, 비행
deem v. ~으로 생각하다, 간주하다
doom n. 운명, 파멸, 죽음

어원	-deed, -deem, -doom : doed 행해진(E) → '행할 권리를 증서로'
유의어	action, act, accomplishment
반의어	misdeed, wrongdoing, offense
영영	an action or act; a legal document representing ownership.
예문	Her kind deeds made a positive impact on the community. 그녀의 친절한 행동들이 지역사회에 긍정적인 영향을 미쳤다.

788

mutual

[ˈmjuːtʃuˌəl]

a. 상호간의, 서로의, 공통의

mutually adv. 상호간에, 서로 합의되어
mutually exclusive p. 상호 배타적인
commute v. 교환하다, 대체하다; 통근하다
mutation n. 돌연변이; 변화, 변천

어원	-mut : change 바꾸다 → '바꾸기로 상호간 합의'
유의어	shared, common, reciprocal
반의어	individual, separate
영영	shared or experienced by two or more parties
예문	They have a mutual respect for each other's opinions. 그들은 서로의 의견을 상호 존중한다.

789

illuminate

[ɪˈluːmɪˌneɪt]

v. 빛을 비추다, 밝히다

illuminated a. 빛으로 켜지는
illuminating a. 명료하고 이해하기 쉬운
illumination n. 빛, 조명, 깨달음
illusion n. 환상, 착각, 오해

어원	-il, -im, -in, -ir ~하게 하다 (L) + -lus, -lustr, -lumin : shine / play → '빛을 비추니 명백히 하다'
유의어	light up, brighten, elucidate
반의어	Darken, obscure, shadow
영영	To provide light or clarity to something, often by shining a light.
예문	The lanterns illuminated the path through the dark forest. 등불들은 어두운 숲을 통과하는 길을 밝혀 주었습니다.

790

hereby

[ˌhɪəˈbaɪ]

adv. 이에 의하여, 이로써

hereafter adv. 이후로, 사후로, 내세에
thence adv. 거기서부터
henceforth adv. 이후, 이제부터는
then again p. 그러지 않고, 반대로

어원	-here 지금 + -by → '지금 곁에 있는 너로 인하여'
유의어	thus, accordingly, by this means
반의어	thereby, thus, accordingly
영영	by means of this, as a result of this.
예문	I hereby declare this meeting open. 나는 이렇게 세션을 열겠다고 공식 선언합니다.

791

cut from the same cloth

p. 같은 부류인

cut out p. 멈추다; 급히 떠나다
cut A with B p. A를 B로 자르다
chop up p. ~을 잘게 자르다
cut off p. 잘라버리다; 서둘러 떠나다

어원	-cut 자르다 + -cloth → '같은 천에서 잘랐으니 같은 부류인'
유의어	similar, alike, cut from the same mold
반의어	different, dissimilar, unrelated
영영	to be very similar in character or nature
예문	Sarah and I have similar opinions because we're cut from the same cloth. 사라와 나는 같은 유형의 사람이기 때문에 의견이 비슷합니다.

792

in the mood for

p. ~하고 싶은, ~에 마음이 내켜서

in the light of p. ~의 관점에서
in the face of p. ~에 직면하여
in the mood to do p. ~하고 싶은
in the same way p. 이와 마찬가지로

어원	-mood : mode : fit → '현장에 맞춰진 기분'
유의어	inclined to, disposed to, feeling like
반의어	uninterested in, disinclined to, unwilling to
영영	to feel like doing something or to have the desire for something
예문	I'm in the mood for Italian food tonight. 오늘 밤에 이탈리아 음식이 먹고 싶어요.

793

go with

p. (계획, 제의 등을) 받아들이다 / 어울리다

go up p. (가격, 기온 등이) 오르다
go through p. 통과되다, 성사되다, 해결되다
go over p. 점검하다, 검토하다
go out of one's way p. 굳이 뭔가를 하다

어원	- go with 함께 가니 잘 어울리는
유의어	accompany, match, complement
반의어	clash with, conflict with, contradict
영영	to accompany or complement something
예문	The blue curtains go with the new sofa. 파란색 커튼은 새로운 소파와 잘 어울립니다.

794

catch oneself

p. 하던 말(일)을 갑자기 멈추다

catch air p. 뛰어오르다
catch on p. 이해하다, 알아듣다
catch wind of p. ~의 낌새를 채다
catch hold of p. ~을 붙잡다

어원	oneself(자신)을 catch(잡고) 깨닫거나 후회할 수 있는 일을 멈추다
유의어	realize, become aware, snap out of it
반의어	remain unaware, continue unaware, overlook
영영	to become aware of something that one was not initially conscious of
예문	She caught herself before revealing the surprise. 그녀는 놀람을 드러내기 전에 자신을 잡았습니다.

795

blow away

p. 날려버리다; ~을 감동시키다

blowout n. (자동차 타이어) 펑크
burst v. 폭발하다; 갑자기 ~하다
outburst v. 폭발하다
balsting n. 폭파, 분쇄

어원	-blizzard, -blast : bhle, bhel : blow, swell → '누군가 날려버릴 정도로 감동시키다'
유의어	impress, amaze, astound
반의어	disappoint, underwhelm, bore
영영	to impress or amaze someone greatly
예문	The performance blew away the audience with its intensity. 공연은 강렬함으로 관객들을 놀라게 했습니다.

796

free from

p. ~에서 벗어난

for free p. 무료로
freely adv. 자유롭게
freeway n. 고속도로
frequency n. 빈번, 빈도; 주파수, 진동수

어원	-free 자유
유의어	devoid of, without, liberated from
반의어	bound by, constrained by, limited by
영영	not constrained or restricted by something
예문	The house is free from pests since we hired an exterminator. 집은 해충이 없으니까 우리가 해충 퇴치업체를 고용한 이후입니다

797

couple A with B

p. A와 B를 결부시키다

impart v. 나누어 주다
counterpart n. 상대, 대응; 복사물
coupled with p. ~과 결합하여
have no part in p. ~에 관계가 없다

어원	-couple : 선, 연결 + -with → '선으로 ~와 결합하여'
유의어	pair A with B, match A to B, combine A and B
반의어	disconnect A from B, separate A from B, decouple A from B
영영	to combine or associate A with B
예문	The chef couples the steak with a red wine reduction sauce. 요리사는 스테이크와 레드 와인 리덕션 소스를 함께 제공합니다.

798

a great deal of

p. 많은, 다량의

strike a deal p. 계약을 맺다
new deal p. 뉴딜 정책
deal in p. 장사하다
the real deal p. 실질적인 것, 진짜

어원	-great 많은 + -deal 거래 → '많은 거래를 할 수 있는 양이니 많은'
유의어	a lot of, plenty of, a large amount of
반의어	a little of, a small amount of, a fraction of
영영	a large amount or quantity of something
예문	He has a great deal of experience in the field of finance. 그는 금융 분야에서 많은 경험을 가지고 있습니다.

799

in partnership with

p. ~와 제휴하여, 협력하여

in some way p. 어떤 점에서는, 혹시
in retrospect p. 돌이켜 생각해 보면
in public p. 공공장소에서(공연히)
in particular p. 개별적으로, 특별하게

어원	-part, -port 부분 → '의무를 부분 나눠가진 동반자 관계' * partner 동등한 권리의 사람 VS participate 동등하게 나누는
유의어	collaborating with, working together with, in association with
반의어	independently of, apart from, solo
영영	collaborating or working together with someone
예문	Our company works in partnership with several local businesses. 우리 회사는 여러 지역 사업체들과 파트너십을 맺고 있습니다.

800

call off

p. 취소하다, 중지하다

call after p. ~을 따라 이름짓다
call back p. ~을 취소하다
call for p. ~을 요구하다, 구하다
so-called p. 소위, 이른바

어원	-call 큰 외침(E) + -off 떨어져 → '불려지지 않아 떨어지니 취소'
유의어	cancel, abandon, revoke
반의어	proceed, continue, carry on
영영	to cancel or abandon something that was previously planned or scheduled
예문	Due to the bad weather, they had to call off the outdoor event. 나쁜 날씨로 인해 그들은 야외 이벤트를 취소해야 했습니다.

Chapter 21.

801	distribute	[dɪˈstrɪb.juːt]	v. 분배하다, 배포하다, 분류 배치하다
802	genuine	[ˈdʒen.ju.ɪn]	a. 진짜의; 진실된
803	cosmopolitan	[ˌkɒz.məˈpɒl.ɪ.tən]	a. 세계적인, 국제적인
804	polish	[ˈpɒl.ɪʃ]	v. 닦다, 윤내다 n. 광택제
805	overtake	[ˌəʊ.vəˈteɪk]	v. 따라잡다, 앞지르다
806	plural	[ˈplʊə.rəl]	n. 복수 a. 여러 개의
807	sacrifice	[ˈsæk.rɪ.faɪs]	n. 희생; 제물 v. 희생하다, 바치다
808	critical	[ˈkrɪt.ɪ.kəl]	a. 위태로운, 위험한, 비판적인; 중요한
809	outdo	[ˌaʊtˈduː]	v. ~을 능가하다
810	pathetic	[pəˈθet.ɪk]	a. 한심한, 형편없는; 애처로운
811	enchant	[ɪnˈtʃɑːnt]	v. 매혹하다, 황홀하게 하다
812	enlist	[ɪnˈlɪst]	v. 도움을 요청하다; 입대하다
813	eccentric	[ɪkˈsen.trɪk]	a. 괴짜인, 별난
814	resolve	[rɪˈzɒlv]	v. 결심하다; 해결하다
815	discharge	[dɪsˈtʃɑːdʒ]	v. 해임하다, 내보내다, 방출하다; 이행하다
816	execute	[ˈek.sɪ.kjuːt]	v. 처형하다; 실행하다
817	requisite	[ˈrek.wɪ.zɪt]	n. 필수품 a. 필요한
818	embarrass	[ɪmˈbær.əs]	v. 울타리로 가로 막다, 난처하다
819	undertake	[ˌʌn.dəˈteɪk]	v. 떠맡다, 책임을 지다; 약속하다; 시작하다
820	fury	[ˈfjʊə.ri]	n. 격노, 격한 분노
821	aesthetic	[esθétik]	a. 심미적, 미학적, 미적인
822	heritage	[ˈher.ɪ.tɪdʒ]	n. 전통문화(유산)
823	discipline	[ˈdɪs.ə.plɪn]	n. 규율, 통제, 학문, 기강, 훈련
824	lessen	[lésn]	v. 줄이다
825	fragile	[frǽdʒəl]	a. 부서지기 쉬운, 깨지기 쉬운; 허약한
826	assemble	[əˈsem.bəl]	v. 더욱 (목적이) 동일하다, 모으다 n. 조립
827	grief	[griːf]	n. 큰 슬픔
828	deplete	[dɪˈpliːt]	v. 고갈시키다, 소모시키다
829	tyrant	[ˈtaɪə.rənt]	n. 폭군, 독재자
830	sustain	[səˈsteɪn]	v. 유지하다; 부상을 입다; 지지하다; 부양하다
831	persist in		p. 고집하다
832	so long as		p. ~하기만 하면
833	strike a deal		p. 계약을 맺다
834	by now		p. 이제는, 이미
835	go along with		p. ~에 동조하다, 찬성하다
836	in the way		p. ~의 방식대로
837	draw on		p. 그림을 그리다; ~에 의존하다
838	do one's part in		p. ~에서 자신의 몫을 다하다
839	set out		p. 출발하다
840	in case of		p. ~의 경우에는

801

distribute

[dɪˈstrɪb.juːt]

v. 분배하다, 배포하다, 분류 배치하다

distribution n. 분배, 배포, 유통
distributive a. 분배적인
distributor n. 배급 업자
redistribution n. 보답; 징벌, 보복

어원	-dis : apart + -trib, -tribut : allot 할당하다 → '값진 것을 따로 떼어주니 분배하다' * allocate 배분하다 VS distribute 분배하다
유의어	allocate, dispense, apportion
반의어	collect, hoard
영영	give out or share something among a group
예문	Volunteers distribute food to the homeless every week. 자원봉사자들은 매주 무주택자들에게 음식을 배포한다.

802

genuine

[ˈdʒen.ju.ɪn]

a. 진짜의; 진실된

ingenuity n. 재주, 재간, 독창성
ingenious a. 재능이 있는, 영리한
gentil a. 온화한, 상냥한
genie n. (아라비아난이트의) 요정, 정령

어원	-gen, -gn : birth 태어나다, 낳다 / produce 생성하다 (G) → '태생 그대로니 진짜의'
유의어	authentic, real, true
반의어	Fake, counterfeit, phony
영영	Authentic, real, or true; not fake or counterfeit.
예문	Her smile was genuine and showed her true happiness. 그녀의 미소는 진실하며 진정한 행복을 나타냈습니다.

803

cosmopolitan

[ˌkɒz.məˈpɒl.ɪ.tən]

a. 세계적인, 국제적인

political a. 정치적인
politics n. (이해) 관계, 정략; 정치
politeness n. 공손; 예의바름
polish v. 닦다, 윤내다 n. 광택제

어원	-cosmo 세계 + -polit, -polic, -polis 많은, 시민, 도시 (G) → '세계의 도시들을 아우르니 세계적인'
유의어	worldly, sophisticated, cultured
반의어	provincial, narrow-minded, parochial
영영	Familiar with and at ease in many different countries and cultures; worldly.
예문	New York City is known for its cosmopolitan atmosphere. 뉴욕 시는 세계적인 분위기로 유명합니다.

804

polish

[ˈpɒl.ɪʃ]

v. 닦다, 윤내다 n. 광택제

polished a. 광이 나는, 세련된
polishing n. 연마, 연마공
refurbish v. 개조하다, 재단장하다
refurbished a. 혁신된, 일신된

어원	-pol 닦다→ '닦으니 광이 나는' (* 대부분 polishes)
유의어	shine, buff, gloss
반의어	tarnish, dull, roughen
영영	to make something smooth, shiny, or refined through a process of cleaning or improvement.
예문	She spent hours polishing her shoes until they shone brilliantly. 그녀는 신발을 빛나게 할 때까지 몇 시간 동안 닦았다.

805

overtake

[ˌəʊ.vəˈteɪk]

v. 따라잡다, 앞지르다

overcome v. 극복하다, 이기다
overflow v. 넘치다, 물에 잠기게 하다
overdose n. 과량, 지나친 투여
oeveestimate v. 과대평가하다

어원	-over + -take 오다(E) → '넘기면서 취하니 따라잡다'
유의어	surpass, exceed, outstrip
반의어	lag behind, fall behind
영영	pass by or go beyond in a race or journey
예문	The faster car was able to overtake the slower one on the race track. 빠른 자동차가 레이스 트랙에서 느린 자동차를 추월할 수 있었다.

806

plural

[ˈplʊə.rəl]

n. 복수 a. 여러 개의

surplus a. 과잉의
nonplus n. 어찌할 바를 모름
plurality n. 득표차, 초과 득표수
pluralize v. ~을 복수형으로 나타내다

어원	-plus 더하기 (L) → '더해서 여러 개의' * plus '더해서 남게 되는 것' VS sum '더해서 목표에 도달한다'
유의어	multiple, several, various
반의어	singular, singular form, singular number
영영	The grammatical form indicating more than one item, person, or thing.
예문	"Cats" is the plural form of the word "cat." "Cats"는 "cat"의 복수형이다.

807

sacrifice

[ˈsæk.rɪ.faɪs]

n. 희생; 제물 v. 희생하다, 바치다

sacrifice n. 희생, 제물
sacrificial a. 제물로 바쳐진
saint a. 성인
sacred a. 신성한; 종교적인

어원	-sacr, -sacri, -saint : holy + -fic : make → '신성한 의식을 위해 제물을 만드느라 희생'
유의어	offering, ritual, surrender
반의어	Preserve, keep, retain
영영	The act of giving up something valuable or cherished, often for a greater cause or purpose.
예문	Many cultures have rituals involving the sacrifice of animals. 많은 문화에서는 동물 희생을 포함한 의식을 가지고 있습니다.

808

critical

[ˈkrɪt.ɪ.kəl]

a. 위태로운, 위험한, 비판적인; 중요한

critically adv. 비판적으로
critic n. 비평가
hypocrisy n. 우유부단; 위선
crisis n. 위기

어원	-cri : separate → '무리와 떨어진 위기에 비판적인', '비판으로 다뤄야 할 정도로 중요한'
유의어	crucial, essential, vital
반의어	Non-critical, unimportant, insignificant
영영	Expressing disapproval or criticism; involving careful analysis and evaluation.
예문	The critical examination of the evidence revealed new insights. 증거의 비판적인 검토는 새로운 통찰력을 드러냈습니다.

809

outdo

[ˌaʊtˈduː]

v. ~을 능가하다

outgrow v. ~보다 커지다
outnumber v. ~보다 수가 많다
outshine v. ~보다 더 빛나다
outrun v. ~보다 빨리 달리다

어원	-out : more than + -do → '지금 하는 것 이상이니 능가'
유의어	surpass, outperform, excel
반의어	Underperform, fall short, do worse
영영	To surpass or outperform someone or something in a particular area.
예문	The team worked hard to outdo their competition in the tournament. 팀은 대회에서 경쟁 상대를 능가하기 위해 노력했습니다.

810

pathetic

[pəˈθet.ɪk]

a. 한심한, 형편없는; 애처로운

sympathy n. 동정, 공감
antipathy n. 반감, 혐오
apathy n. 냉담, 무관심
pathetically adv. 가여울 정도로

어원	-path, -pati, -pass : suffer 고통을 겪다 → '고통 받는 처지니 불쌍한'
유의어	pitiful, miserable, wretched
반의어	impressive, admirable
영영	deserving of sympathy or compassion due to being pitiful or sad; causing feelings of pity
예문	It was a pathetic sight to see the abandoned and hungry stray kittens. 버려진 굶주린 길고양이들을 보는 것은 불쌍한 광경이었다.

811

enchant

[ɪnˈtʃɑːnt]

v. 매혹하다, 황홀하게 하다

enchanting a. 황홀한, 매혹적인
enchantment n. 매직, 황홀, 마법
chant n. 노래, 멜로디, 성가
accentuate v. 강조하다, 두드러지게 하다

어원	-en : make + -chant, -cent, -cant 노래 → '노래로 유혹하니 매혹적인'
유의어	captivate, bewitch, charm
반의어	repel, disgust
영영	to delight or captivate someone with charm, beauty, or magic; to cast a spell on
예문	The beautiful melody seemed to enchant everyone who heard it. 아름다운 멜로디는 듣는 사람들을 마법에 걸린 듯 만들었다.

812

enlist

[ɪnˈlɪst]

v. 도움을 요청하다; 입대하다

enlistment n. 입영, 모병
enlisted a. 사병의
enlistee n. 지원병
enlist in p. ~에 입대하다

어원	-en : in + -list 명부 → '군 명부에 이름을 올려 국가를 위해 도움을 요청하다'
유의어	join, sign up, recruit
반의어	discharge, release, expel
영영	To recruit or enroll someone, typically into a cause, organization, or military service.
예문	He decided to enlist in the army to serve his country. 그는 나라를 위해 병역에 자원 입대하기로 결정했다.

813

eccentric

[ɪkˈsen.trɪk]

a. 괴짜인, 별난

centralize v. 집중시키다
concentrate v. 집중하다
concentrate A on B p. A를 B에 집중시키다
concentraion n. 집중; 농축; 농도

어원	-ec : out + centr 가운데 → '중심에서 벗어난'
유의어	unconventional, odd, quirky
반의어	Normal, conventional, mainstream
영영	Unconventional, peculiar, or deviating from common behavior or norms.
예문	Her eccentric fashion sense always drew attention. 그녀의 별난 패션 감각은 항상 주목을 끌었습니다.

814

resolve

[rɪˈzɒlv]

v. 결심하다; 해결하다

resolution n. 결심, 결의; 해결, 해답
resolved a. 결심한, 결심이 굳은
unresolved a. 해결되지 않은
dissolute a. 방탕한, 타락한

어원	-re : again + -solv : loosen → '엉킨 것을 다시 풀어 해결하다'
유의어	determine, decide, settle
반의어	hesitate, waver
영영	make a firm decision; settle or find a solution
예문	They made a resolution to exercise regularly and eat healthier. 그들은 규칙적으로 운동하고 더 건강하게 식사하기로 결심했다.

815

discharge

[dɪsˈtʃɑːdʒ]

v. 해임하다, 내보내다, 방출하다; 이행하다

in charge of p. ~에 대한 책임이 있다
recharge v. 재충전하다
charisma n. 카리스마
charity n. 사랑, 자비, 박애; 자선(단체)

어원	-dis 반대 + -char : carriage → '짐을 내려주고 해임하다'
유의어	release, dismiss, fire
반의어	Load, fill, charge
영영	The act of releasing or sending someone or something away, or the flow or emission of a substance.
예문	The hospital will discharge the patient once they have fully recovered. 환자가 완전히 회복하면 병원에서 퇴원됩니다.

816

execute

[ˈek.sɪ.kjuːt]

v. 처형하다; 실행하다

execution n. 실행, 수행, 처형
executive a. 운영의, 집행의 n. 운영진, 중역
seriously adv. 진지하게

어원	-ex : out + -ecu, -secu : follow → '법적 효력을 밖으로 실행되도록 따르니 처형'
유의어	carry out, perform, implement
반의어	Pardon, forgive, absolve
영영	To carry out or perform a task, action, or order; also, to put someone to death as a punishment.
예문	The CEO decided to execute the company's new strategy. 최고 경영자는 회사의 새로운 전략을 실행하기로 결정했습니다.

817

requisite

[ˈrek.wɪ.zɪt]

n. 필수품 a. 필요한

require v. 필요로 하다, 요구하다
acquire v. 습득하다, 획득하다
conquer v. 정복하다, 이기다
quest n. 탐구, 탐색

어원	-re : again + -quir, -quer, -quest, -quisit : seek 구하다 → '계속해서 구해야 하는 필수품'(L)
유의어	necessary, required, essential
반의어	optional, unnecessary, dispensable
영영	Necessary or required for a particular purpose; essential or indispensable.
예문	Safety equipment is a requisite for any construction site. 안전 장비는 모든 공사 현장에 필수품입니다.

818

embarrass

[ɪmˈbær.əs]

v. 울타리로 가로 막다, 난처하다

barrier n. 장벽, 장애물
barricade n. 통행 차단물, 장애물
barn n. 외양간, 헛간
embargo n. 제재 v. 출입항을 금지하다

어원	-em 수정 접두사 + -bar, -bat 말뚝, 막대 때리며 싸우다(E) → '말뚝으로 울타리를 만들어 막으니 난처하다'
유의어	disconcert, abash, make uncomfortable
반의어	Comfort, ease, relieve
영영	To cause someone to feel self-conscious, awkward, or ashamed.
예문	She felt embarrassed when she tripped and fell in front of a crowd. 그녀는 군중 앞에서 비틀거리고 넘어지면서 부끄러움을 느꼈습니다.

819	어원	-under : below + -take 떠맡다 → '밑에서 떠맡은 책임', '책임을 맡고 일에 착수하다'
undertake	유의어	embark on, tackle, take on
[ˌʌn.dəˈteɪk]	반의어	abandon, give up, relinquish
v. 떠맡다, 책임을 지다; 약속하다; 시작하다	영영	to commit to or start a task or project.
undertaking n. 사업; 인수; 약속 undertaker n. 기업가; 장의사 intake n. 흡입구, 흡입량 retake v. 되찾다, 탈환하다	예문	The company will undertake a major expansion project next year. 회사는 내년에 대규모 확장 프로젝트를 수행할 것이다.

820	어원	-fur 털 → '털을 세우고 달려드는 맹수의 격한 분노'
fury	유의어	anger, rage, wrath
[ˈfjʊə.ri]	반의어	calmness, tranquility
n. 격노, 격한 분노	영영	intense, violent anger or rage
furious a. 격노하는, 몹시 화를 내는 furiously adv. 격노하면서, 몹시 화를 내면서 fuzzy a. 보풀로 덮인; 흐릿한 furl v. (돛·깃발) 걷다; (우산을) 접다	예문	His fury was evident when he found out his car had been stolen. 그의 분노는 자동차가 훔쳐진 사실을 알게 되었을 때 명백했다.

821	어원	-a : to + -esthet, -aesthet : feel 느낌, 감각 → '~쪽으로 아름다움을 느끼니 심미적'
aesthetic	유의어	artistic, beautiful, pleasing
[esθétik]	반의어	Ugly, unattractive, displeasing
a. 심미적, 미학적, 미적인	영영	Concerned with beauty or the appreciation of beauty; artistic or visually pleasing.
aesthetics n. 미학, 감성론 aesthetical a. 심미적인, 미적인 aesthetically adv. 미학적으로, 심미적으로 aestheticism n. 유미주의, 탐미주의	예문	The design of the building was praised for its modern aesthetic. 건물의 디자인은 현대적인 미적 감각으로 칭찬받았습니다.

822	어원	-hered, -heir, -herit : 상속 + -age(명접) (L) → '상속인이 받는 유산'
heritage	유의어	legacy, inheritance, tradition
[ˈher.ɪ.tɪdʒ]	반의어	Loss, abandonment, abandonment
n. 전통문화(유산)	영영	The cultural, historical, or natural legacy passed down from one generation to the next.
hereditary a. 유전적인, 세습되는 inherit v. 물려받다, 상속하다 heir n. 상속인, 후계자 herald n. 전조, 전령 v. 예고하다, 알리다	예문	His feelings of alienation from his peers made him withdraw from social activities. 동료들로부터의 소외감 때문에 그는 사회 활동에서 물러났습니다.

823	어원	-dis : apart 떨어져서 + -cip : take → '떨어진 각 분야의 학문을 취하는'
discipline	유의어	control, self-control, training
[ˈdɪs.ə.plɪn]	반의어	Disorder, chaos, anarchy
n. 규율, 통제, 학문, 기강, 훈련	영영	The practice of maintaining order and control through rules, regulations, or training; also, a branch of knowledge or field of study.
disciple n. 제자, 문하생, 신봉자 disciplined a. 훈련된 self-discipline p. 자제, 자기 수양 principle n. 교장	예문	The military requires a high level of discipline from its soldiers. 군대는 병사들에게 높은 수준의 규율을 요구합니다.

824	어원	-less 덜 → '덜 남도록 줄이다'
lessen	유의어	reduce, diminish, decrease
[lésn]	반의어	intensify, increase, amplify
v. 줄이다	영영	To make something smaller, reduce in amount or intensity.
unless conj. ~하지 않으면 lesson n. 교훈, 수업, 가르침 let down p. 기대를 저버리다 let go p. (걱정·근심 등을) 떨쳐버리다	예문	Taking breaks during work can help lessen stress. 일하는 동안 휴식을 취하는 것은 스트레스를 줄이는 데 도움이 될 수 있다.

825

fragile

[frædʒəl]

a. 부서지기 쉬운, 깨지기 쉬운; 허약한

friction n. 마찰, 불화
fragment n. 파편, 조각
fracture n. 골절, 균열
fraction n. 단편, 일부, 소량; 분수

어원	-frag : break + -ile ~하기 쉬운<형접> → '부서지기 쉬우니 허약한'
유의어	delicate, breakable, frail
반의어	sturdy, robust
영영	easily broken or damaged
예문	Handle the fragile glassware with care to avoid breakage. 유리 용품을 부러뜨리지 않으려면 주의해서 다뤄야 합니다.

826

assemble

[əˈsem.bəl]

v. 더욱 (목적이) 동일하다, 모으다 n. 조립

assembly n. 의회, 집회; 조례; 조립
ensemble n. 합창, 합주; 앙상블
dissemble v. 숨기다, 가장하다
resent v. ~에 분개하다, 원망하다

어원	-a : to + -sem 비슷한 → '한 방향으로 비슷한 것들을 모아 조립하다'
유의어	gather, collect, convene
반의어	Disassemble, take apart, break down
영영	To gather or collect together into one place or group; to put together parts to form a whole.
예문	The team will assemble at the meeting room in 10 minutes. 팀은 10분 후에 회의실에서 모일 것입니다.

827

grief

[griːf]

n. 큰 슬픔

grieve v. 비통해 하다, 슬프게 하다
grievance n. 불만
aggrieve v. 고통을 주다, 괴롭히다
grudge n. 원한, 유감

어원	-grav, -griev : heavy 무거움; 고통 → '마음이 무거우니 슬프다'
유의어	sorrow, sadness, mourning
반의어	joy, happiness, elation
영영	Intense sadness or sorrow, especially due to a loss or tragedy.
예문	She experienced profound grief after losing her loved one. 그녀는 사랑하는 사람을 잃은 후 깊은 슬픔을 경험했다.

828

deplete

[dɪˈpliːt]

v. 고갈시키다, 소모시키다

complete v. 완성하다 a. 완성한
replete a. 가득한, 충만한
implement n. 도구 v. 실행하다, 시행하다
complex a. 복잡한 n. 건물 단지

어원	-de : down + -ple, -pli : fill → '완전히 채웠던걸 떨어뜨리니 고갈'
유의어	exhaust, drain, consume
반의어	replenish, fill
영영	to reduce or diminish the quantity or resources of something, often to an insufficient level
예문	Overfishing has led to the depletion of marine resources in the area. 과잉 어업으로 인해 그 지역의 해양 자원 고갈이 발생했다.

829

tyrant

[ˈtaɪə.rənt]

n. 폭군, 독재자

tyrannosaur n. 티라노사우르스
tyrannical a. 폭압적인
tyranny n. 폭정, 폭압
typhoon n. 태풍

어원	-tyrant : tyranno 폭군 * tyrannosaur 티라노사우르스(-tyrant 폭군 + -saur : lizard)
유의어	dictator, autocrat, oppressor
반의어	Benevolent ruler, just leader, fair monarch
영영	A ruler or leader who exercises oppressive and cruel authority; a despot.
예문	The people rebelled against the tyrant ruler who oppressed them. 사람들은 자신들을 억압한 폭군 지배자에게 반란을 일으켰습니다.

830

sustain

[səˈsteɪn]

v. 유지하다; 부상을 입다; 지지하다; 부양하다

obtain v. 얻다, 획득하다
contain v. 포함하다, 담고 있다
retain v. 계속 유지하다; 보유하다
sustenance n. 지속, 유지

어원	-sus : sub + -tain : hold → '무너지지 않고 아래를 잡아 유지하다'
유의어	maintain, support, uphold
반의어	weaken, debilitate
영영	to support, uphold, or maintain something, often over an extended period of time
예문	The organization works to sustain clean drinking water in remote areas. 그 단체는 외진 지역에서 깨끗한 음용수를 유지하기 위해 노력하고 있다.

831

persist in

p. 고집하다

persist v. 고집하다, 주장하다
persistence n. 고집, 완고
persistent a. 고집하는
persistently adv. 끈덕지게, 고집스럽게

어원	-per : through + -sist : stand → '끝까지 서있으며 고집하고 주장하다'
유의어	continue, persevere in, keep on
반의어	abandon, give up, cease
영영	to continue firmly or obstinately in an opinion or a course of action
예문	Despite the challenges, she persisted in her efforts to learn a new language. 어려움에도 불구하고, 그녀는 새로운 언어를 배우기 위한 노력을 계속했습니다.

832

so long as

p. ~하기만 하면

insofar as p. ~하는 한은
as it were p. 소위, 말하자면
in the air p. 헛된 근거 없는
in the course of p. ~되고 있는 중인

어원	-so 그렇게 + -long → '그렇게 오래 ~하기만 하면'
유의어	as long as, provided that, if
반의어	unless, provided that not, if not
영영	provided that, as long as
예문	You can borrow my car so long as you return it by tomorrow. 당신이 내일까지 차를 반납한다면 내 차를 빌릴 수 있어요.

833

strike a deal

p. 계약을 맺다

a great deal of p. 많은, 다량의
new deal p. 뉴딜 정책
deal in p. 장사하다
the real deal p. 실질적인 것, 진짜

어원	-strike 치다 + -deal 거래 → '조건을 치면서 계약을 맺다'
유의어	make a deal, negotiate an agreement, reach a settlement
반의어	disagree, fail to reach an agreement, break off negotiations
영영	to reach an agreement or come to terms with someone
예문	After negotiations, they finally struck a deal on the terms of the contract. 협상 끝에 그들은 마침내 계약 조건에 대해 합의에 이르렀습니다.

834

by now

p. 이제는, 이미

now and then p. 이따금
not that p. 이제서야
noadays adv. 요즘에는
by the look of it p. 보기에, 아무래도

어원	-now 지금
유의어	by this time, at this point, already
반의어	until now, up until this point, hitherto
영영	at the present time, by this point
예문	By now, you should have received the package in the mail. 지금쯤이면 우체통으로 소포를 받았어야 합니다.

835

go along with

p. ~에 동조하다, 찬성하다

go over p. 점검하다, 검토하다
go for p. ~을 좋아하다, ~를 찾다
go hand in hand p. ~와 관련이 있다
go off p. (알람·경보 등이) 울리다

어원	-go 가다 -with → '함께 가니 동조하다'
유의어	agree with, comply with, conform to
반의어	oppose, disagree with, resist
영영	to agree or comply with something
예문	I'll go along with your plan if you can convince me it's the right choice. 당신이 그것이 올바른 선택이라고 날 설득할 수 있다면, 나는 당신의 계획을 받아들일 거야.

836

in the way

p. ~의 방식대로

make one's way p. 나아가다
stand in the way p. 방해가 되다
be in the way p. 방해가 되다
in no way p. 결코 ~하지 않다

어원	-in 안 + -way 방식 → '~의 방식 안에서'
유의어	obstructing, blocking, hindering
반의어	out of the way, clear, unobstructed
영영	obstructing or hindering progress or movement
예문	Your backpack is in the way; please move it so I can pass. 네 배낭이 가로막고 있어요; 제가 지나갈 수 있게 좀 옮겨주세요.

837

draw on

p. 그림을 그리다; ~에 의존하다

draw A out p. A를 끌어내다
draw A from B p. A를 B로부터 끌어내다
drawer n. 서랍; 수표 발행인
draw attention to p. ~에 관심을 끌다

어원	-draw 당기다 + -on → '붙어 당기는 것이 의존하다'
유의어	utilize, use, employ
반의어	abstain from, refrain from, avoid
영영	to use something as a resource or inspiration
예문	The artist drew on her own experiences to create a powerful piece of artwork. 예술가는 강력한 작품을 만들기 위해 자신의 경험을 활용했습니다.

838

do one's part in

p. ~에서 자신의 몫을 다하다

for the most part p. 대체로
have no part in p. ~에 관계가 없다
partial a. 부분적인; 불공평한; 편애하는
particle n. 소량, 미량; 소립자

어원	-do 하다 + -part 나의 파트, 몫 → '파트에서 몫을 다하다'
유의어	contribute, play one's role in, fulfill one's responsibility in
반의어	neglect one's duty, shirk responsibility, fail to contribute
영영	to fulfill one's share of responsibility or obligation
예문	Everyone needs to do their part in conserving energy to protect the environment. 모든 사람들은 환경 보호를 위해 에너지 절약에 기여해야 합니다.

839

set out

p. 출발하다

set A apart from B p. A와 B를 구별하다
set A aside p. A를 제쳐두다
set in one's way p. 자기 방식이 몸에 밴
set up p. 조성하다, 만들다

어원	-set 설정하다 + -out → '기본 설정을 벗어나 출발'
유의어	embark on, start, begin
반의어	abandon, give up, cease
영영	to begin a journey or a task with a particular aim or purpose
예문	We set out early in the morning to beat the traffic. 우리는 아침 일찍 출발해서 교통을 피하기 위해 떠났습니다.

840

in case of

p. ~의 경우에는

in charge of p. ~을 담당하는
in commotion p. 동요하고 있는
in contact with p. ~와 연락하여
in contrast to p. ~와는 대조적으로

어원	-cas : fall → '사건이 떨어지는 경우'
유의어	in the event of, if, should
반의어	regardless of, despite, in spite of
영영	in the event of, if there should be
예문	In case of emergency, please dial 911 for assistance. 긴급 상황이 발생한 경우, 도움을 요청하려면 911로 전화하세요

Chapter 22.

841	utter	[ˈʌt.ər]	a. 극단적인 v. 밖으로 소리를 내다
842	testify	[ˈtes.tɪ.faɪ]	v. 증언하다, 진술하다
843	primary	[ˈpraɪ.mər.i]	a. 제1의, 주요한, 최초의, 주된
844	defeat	[dɪˈfiːt]	v. 패배시키다, 좌절시키다
845	proclaim	[prəˈkleɪm]	v. 선언하다, 공표하다
846	commemorate	[kəˈmem.ə.reɪt]	v. 기념하다, 기념식을 거행하다
847	exterminate	[ikstə́ːrmənèit]	v. 근절하다, 박멸하다
848	liken	[ˈlaɪ.kən]	v. ~에 비유하다, 견주다
849	verdict	[ˈvɜː.dɪkt]	n. 판결, 평결
850	defiance	[dɪˈfaɪ.əns]	n. 믿음을 무너뜨리는 것, 반항
851	submerge	[səbˈmɜːdʒ]	v. 물 속에 잠기다, 가라앉히다
852	bury	[ˈber.i]	v. 파묻다, 매장하다
853	insure	[ɪnˈʃɔːr]	v. 보험에 들다
854	altitude	[ˈæl.tɪ.tʃuːd]	n. 높이, 고도, 해발
855	admiral	[ˈæd.mər.əl]	n. 해군대장, 제독
856	oppress	[əˈpres]	v. 억압하다
857	mortgage	[ˈmɔː.gɪdʒ]	n. 저당물, 담보, 보증
858	engage	[ɪnˈgeɪdʒ]	v. 약속하다, 참가하다; 사용하다; 고용하다
859	raid	[reɪd]	n. 습격, 급습; v. 급습하다
860	disinterested	[dɪˈsɪn.trə.stɪd]	a. 사욕이 없는, 공평한, 흥미가 없는
861	detach	[dɪˈtætʃ]	v. 말뚝을 뽑다, 분리하다, 파견하다
862	folklore	[ˈfəʊk.lɔːr]	n. 민속, 전통문화
863	hostility	[hɒsˈtɪl.ə.ti]	n. 적개심
864	undermine	[ˌʌn.dəˈmaɪn]	v. 밑을 파다; 훼손시키다, 손상시키다, 약화시키다
865	query	[kwíəri]	v. 질문하다; n. 질문, 의문
866	distort	[dɪˈstɔːt]	v. 왜곡하다; 바꾸다, 비틀다
867	mimic	[ˈmɪm.ɪk]	v. 흉내내다
868	regress	[rɪˈgres]	v. 되돌아가다, 퇴행하다, 퇴보하다
869	mash	[mæʃ]	n. 사료, 으깬 음식 v. 으깨다
870	gracious	[ˈgreɪ.ʃəs]	a. 우아한, 품위 있는
871	inherit from		p. ~에서 물려받다
872	opposite to N		p. ~과 반대의
873	cease to do		p. ~이 아니게 되다
874	be obligated to do		p. 의무적으로 ~해야 하다
875	as it were		p. 소위, 말하자면
876	at the heart of		p. ~의 중심에
877	on one's feet		p. 독자적으로
878	in one's interest		p. 가장 이익이 되는
879	at peace		p. 평화롭게; 안심하고; 의좋게; 죽어서
880	away from		p. ~로부터 떨어져

841

utter

[ˈʌt.ər]

a. 극단적인 v. 밖으로 소리를 내다

do one's utmost p. 전력을 다하다
outskirt n. 주변, 교외
utterly adv. 완전히, 철저히
utterance n. 말, 발화

어원	-utter : out의 비교급 → '밖으로 말을 꺼내니 완전한 사실'
유의어	say, speak, articulate
반의어	withhold, retain, keep
영영	Speak, pronounce, or express something clearly and distinctly.
예문	She didn't utter a single word during the entire meeting. 그녀는 전체 회의 동안 한 마디도 하지 않았습니다.

842

testify

[ˈtes.tɪ.faɪ]

v. 증언하다, 진술하다

testimony n. 증언
protester n. 항의자, 시위자
attest v. 증명하다
detest v. 몹시 싫어하다, 혐오하다

어원	-test 증명하다, 증언하다(L) + -fy 동접 → '증명하기 위한 진술' * prove 코앞에 증거 VS test 객관적인 근거'
유의어	witness, declare, attest
반의어	deny, refute, contradict
영영	To give evidence or speak under oath in a court of law.
예문	The witness will testify in court about what they saw. 목격자는 본인이 본 것에 대해 법정에서 증언할 것이다.

843

primary

[ˈpraɪ.mər.i]

a. 제1의, 주요한, 최초의, 주된

prime a. 가장 중요한, 최상의 n. 전성기
primacy n. 제일
primarily adv. 주로, 본래
primitive a. 원시의, 원시적인

어원	-prim, -prin, -pri : first 최고의, 첫 번째 (L) * prime 최상의; 전성기
유의어	main, principal, chief
반의어	Secondary, auxiliary, subordinate
영영	Of first importance or priority; the most basic or fundamental.
예문	Learning to read is a primary skill for young children. 읽는 법을 배우는 것은 어린 아이들에게 필수적인 기술입니다.

844

defeat

[dɪˈfiːt]

v. 패배시키다, 좌절시키다

feat n. 위업, 업적
feature n. 생김새, 특징, 특색
fever n. 열, 흥분
defease v. 무효화하다, 파기하다

어원	-de : away + -fac, -fec, -fic, -fy, -fair : make 만들다 → '이뤄내지 못하게 만들다'
유의어	loss, failure, overthrow
반의어	Victory, triumph, success
영영	To overcome or prevail over an opponent or obstacle; to win a victory.
예문	Despite their best efforts, they suffered a defeat in the battle. 최선을 다해도 그들은 전투에서 패배를 입었습니다.

845

proclaim

[prəˈkleɪm]

v. 선언하다, 공표하다

claim v. 주장하다
claimable a. 요구할 수 있는
exclaim v. 외치다
clamorous a. 시끄러운

어원	-pro : forward + -claim, -cil : cry out 외치다 / call 부르다 → '앞서서 말하니 선언하고 공표하다'
유의어	declare, announce, state
반의어	suppress, silence
영영	to announce or declare something officially and publicly
예문	The king proclaimed a national holiday to celebrate the victory. 왕은 승리를 축하하기 위해 국경일을 선포했다.

846

commemorate

[kəˈmem.ə.reɪt]

v. 기념하다, 기념식을 거행하다

Memorial day p. 현충일
memoir n. 회고록
immemorial a. 기억에 없는, 옛날의
commemoration n. 기념, 기념 행사

어원	-com : together + -memor 기억(L) → '함께 기억하는 기념일'
유의어	celebrate, honor, remember
반의어	forget, neglect, ignore
영영	To honor or remember an event, person, or occasion with a ceremony or tribute.
예문	The ceremony was held to commemorate the anniversary of the historic event. 이식은 역사적 사건의 기념일을 기리기 위해 열렸다.

847

exterminate
[ikstə́ːrmənèit]

v. 근절하다, 박멸하다

terminal n. 터미널
terminated a. 해고된
terminology n. (전문)용어
eternal a. 끝의, 밖의, 영구적인

어원	-ex : out + -termin, -term, -tern 끝, 경계 (G) → '끝내고 완전히 아웃시키니 근절' * 고대 로마 신화, 테르미누스 Terminus 신은 '토지의 경계와 끝'을 의미
유의어	eliminate, annihilate, eradicate
반의어	nurture, protect, preserve
영영	to completely destroy or eliminate something, especially pests or threats.
예문	The pest control company was hired to exterminate the mice in the house. 해충 퇴치 업체가 집에 있는 쥐를 박멸하기 위해 고용되었다.

848

liken
[ˈlaɪ.kən]

v. ~에 비유하다, 견주다

likely to do p. ~할 것 같다, 가능성이 있다
as likely as not p. 아마, 십중팔구
likelihood n. 있음직함, 가망성
likewise adv. ~와 마찬가지로

어원	-like 유사한 → '닮은점이 있어 비유하며 견주다'
유의어	compare, equate, analogize
반의어	Differentiate, distinguish, contrast
영영	To compare or draw a similarity between two things or concepts.
예문	Some people liken the experience to a rollercoaster ride. 어떤 사람들은 그 경험을 롤러코스터 타는 것에 비유합니다.

849

verdict
[ˈvɜː.dɪkt]

n. 판결, 평결

verify v. 대조확인하다, 입증하다, 증명하다
verification n. 입증, 검증, 확인
indicate v. 나타내다; 암시하다
contradict v. 반발하다

어원	-ver : true + -dict : say → '진실을 말하다'
유의어	judgment, decision, ruling
반의어	acquittal, exoneration, vindication
영영	A formal decision or judgment in a legal case; an opinion or conclusion.
예문	The jury reached a unanimous verdict of guilty. 배심원단은 모두 유죄의 판결을 내렸습니다.

850

defiance
[dɪˈfaɪ.əns]

n. 믿음을 무너뜨리는 것, 반항

defy v. 반항하다, 도전하다; 무시하다
defiant a. 도전적인
perfity n. 배반, 불성실
confident a. 확신하는, 자신감 있는

어원	-de : dis 반대 + -fy : trust → '믿음에 반대하니 반항과 저항'
유의어	resistance, disobedience, rebellion
반의어	submission, obedience, compliance
영영	Open resistance or refusal to obey or conform to something.
예문	His defiance of the rules led to disciplinary action. 그의 규칙에 대한 도전으로 인해 징계 조치가 취해졌습니다.

851

submerge
[səbˈmɜːdʒ]

v. 물 속에 잠기다, 가라앉히다

submerged a. 침수의; 가난한
submergence n. 침수, 침몰
submersed a. 침수의
subdivide v. 세분하다

어원	-sub : under + -merge, -ners : sink 잠기다 / plunge 던져 넣다 → '아래로 잠기게 하다'
유의어	immerse, plunge, submerse
반의어	Emerge, surface, appear
영영	To completely immerse or cover something underwater.
예문	The submarine can submerge to great depths in the ocean. 잠수함은 바다의 깊은 곳으로 잠수할 수 있습니다.

852

bury
[ˈber.i]

v. 파묻다, 매장하다

burial n. 매장, 매장식
burrow n. 굴; 숨는 곳; 피난처
blush v. 얼굴을 붉히다, 빨개지다
combustion n. 연소, 산화, 불에 탐

어원	-bury 묻다 < build → '올리기 전에 흙을 파서 묻다'
유의어	inter, entomb, lay to rest
반의어	unearth, disinter, exhume
영영	Place a dead body in the ground; conceal or hide something.
예문	They had to bury their beloved pet in the backyard. 그들은 사랑하는 애완 동물을 뒷마당에 묻어야 했습니다.

853

insure
[ɪnˈʃɔːr]

v. 보험에 들다

insurance n. 보험
insured a. 보험에 든
insurer n. 보험업자, 보험회사
ensure v. 책임지다, 보장할, 보증하다

어원	-in : 안에 + -sure 확신 → '마음 안에 확신이 서게 하는 보험' * insure 만약의 대비책 VS assure 확실한 안심 VS ensure 확실한 준비
유의어	ensure, safeguard, protect
반의어	risk, endanger, jeopardize
영영	Provide or obtain insurance coverage; protect against financial loss or risk.
예문	It's important to insure your valuable possessions. 소중한 물건을 보험 가입하는 것이 중요합니다.

854

altitude
[ˈæl.tɪ.tʃuːd]

n. 높이, 고도, 해발

altimeter n. 고도계
altar n. 제단
altitudinal a. 고도의, 표고의

어원	-alt 높은 + -tude 명접 → '높이를 나타내는 고도'
유의어	height, elevation, altitude above sea level
반의어	depth, profundity, shallowness
영영	The height above sea level or ground level; elevation.
예문	The plane reached a cruising altitude of 35,000 feet. 비행기는 35,000 피트의 고도로 비행했습니다.

855

admiral
[ˈæd.mər.əl]

n. 해군대장, 제독

miracle n. 기적
admiration n. 존경, 감탄, 찬양
admiring a. 감탄하는, 찬양하는
marvel n. 놀라운 일 v. 놀라다

어원	-ad : to + -mir, -mar, -mor : wonder → '~에 경탄할만한 대상을 해군대장으로'
유의어	naval officer, commander, fleet admiral
반의어	Ordinary seaman, sailor, crew member
영영	A high-ranking naval officer responsible for commanding a fleet.
예문	The admiral led the naval fleet into battle. 해군 함대를 지휘하는 대장은 해군 대장입니다

856

oppress
[əˈpres]

v. 억압하다

repress v. 억누르다, 억압하다
depress v. 낙담시키다; 불경기로 만들다
suppress v. 진압하다, 억제하다; 참다
appress v. 억압하다, 우울하게 하다

어원	-op : against + -press 누르다 → '반대로 누르니 억압'
유의어	suppress, subjugate, persecute
반의어	liberate, free
영영	to treat with unjust or cruel exercise of authority or power; to burden or weigh down heavily
예문	The authoritarian government tried to oppress dissenting voices. 권위주의적인 정부는 이의를 제기하는 목소리를 억압하려고 했다.

857

mortgage
[ˈmɔːr.ɡɪdʒ]

n. 저당물, 담보, 보증

mortal a. 죽어야 할 운명의, 치명적인
mortality n. 사망자수, 사망률
mortician n. 장의사
mortify v. 굴욕감을 주다, 당황하게 만들다

어원	-mort : death + -gage : pledge 서약 → '돈을 갚지 못하면 죽음을 담보로 갚겠다니 보증'
유의어	loan, debt, mortgage loan
반의어	Ownership, full payment, no debt
영영	A loan secured by real estate, where the borrower uses their property as collateral.
예문	They took out a mortgage to buy their dream home. 그들은 꿈의 집을 사기 위해 주택 모기지를 냈습니다.

858

engage
[ɪnˈɡeɪdʒ]

v. 약속하다, 참가하다; 사용하다; 고용하다

engage in p. 관여하다, 참여하다
engage witih p. ~을 다루다, 관여하다
engagement n. 참여, 관여, 개입
engaging a. 매력 있는

어원	-en : in + -gage : pledge 서약 → '서약에 들어간 것이니 고용과 동시에 관여를 약속', '서약으로 약혼을 약속'
유의어	involve, participate, commit
반의어	disengage, withdraw, detach
영영	To become involved or participate in an activity or conversation.
예문	The teacher tried to engage the students in a lively discussion. 선생님은 학생들을 활기찬 토론에 참여하도록 시도했다.

859

raid

[reɪd]

n. 습격, 급습; v. 급습하다

raider n. 침략자
afraid a. 두려운, 걱정인
give a ride p. 태워주다
rail n. 철도, 레일

어원	-raid : ride → '말을 타고 급습하다'
유의어	assault, attack, incursion
반의어	defend, protect, guard
영영	A sudden attack or assault, typically by a military force or law enforcement.
예문	The police conducted a raid on the illegal drug operation. 경찰은 불법 마약 작전에 습격을 가졌습니다.

860

disinterested

[dɪˈsɪn.trə.stɪd]

a. 사욕이 없는, 공평한, 흥미가 없는

uninterested a. 무관심한, 냉담한
uninteresting a. 재미 없는
be interested in p. ~에 관심이 잇는
in the interest of p. ~을 위하여

어원	-dis : away + -interest 관심 → '관심과 거리가 머니 무관심한'
유의어	impartial, unbiased, neutral
반의어	biased, partial, prejudiced
영영	Impartial or unbiased; not influenced by personal interest or bias.
예문	The judge must be disinterested in the outcome of the case. 판사는 사건의 결과에 무관심해야 합니다.

861

detach

[dɪˈtætʃ]

v. 말뚝을 뽑다, 분리하다, 파견하다

attach A to B p. A를 B에 붙이다
attachment n. 부착
detachment n. 분리, 탈착
be detached from p. ~에서 분리되다

어원	-de : away + -tach, -tak 말뚝, 막대; 들러붙게 하다 → '말뚝에서 멀리 분리하다'
유의어	separate, disconnect, disengage
반의어	attach, connect, affix
영영	to separate or disconnect one thing from another.
예문	You can detach the keyboard from the tablet. 키보드를 태블릿에서 분리할 수 있습니다.

862

folklore

[ˈfəʊk.lɔːr]

n. 민속, 전통문화

lore n. 전통적인 지식이나 이야기
folktale n. 민간 설화, 전설
folky a. 소탈한, 흔한
folkish a. 민속적인

어원	-folk 사람들, 서민 + -lore 설화 → '서민들 이야기니 민속'
유의어	traditional stories, legends, oral history
반의어	Modern culture, contemporary traditions, current customs
영영	The traditional beliefs, stories, customs, and practices of a particular culture or community, often passed down orally.
예문	Believers often think about what happens in the hereafter after they pass away. 믿는 사람들은 자신이 죽은 뒤에 어떤 일이 벌어질지에 대해 생각합니다.

863

hostility

[hɒsˈtɪl.ə.ti]

n. 적개심

host n. 주인
hospital n. 병원
hostile a. 적대적인, 비우호적인
hostage n. 담보물, 인질

어원	-host, -hospit : host, guest, stranger 낯선 사람 (E) → '낯선 사람에게 생기는 적개심'
유의어	enmity, animosity, aggression
반의어	friendliness, amicability
영영	a state of strong opposition, animosity, or antagonism towards someone or something
예문	The ongoing hostility between the two countries has caused tension in the region. 두 나라 간의 지속적인 적대감으로 인해 그 지역에서 긴장이 일어났다.

864

undermine

[ˌʌn.dəˈmaɪn]

v. 밑을 파다; 훼손시키다, 손상시키다, 약화시키다

underlie v. ~의 밑에 있다; 우선하다
mineral a. 광물의; 무기물
undergo v. 겪다, 경험하다
undertake v. 떠맡다, 책임을 지다

어원	-under : below + -mine 파다 → '밑을 파서 손상시키니 약화시키다'
유의어	weaken, sabotage, subvert
반의어	Strengthen, support, fortify
영영	To weaken or erode the foundation, support, or authority of something, often secretly or subtly.
예문	Negative comments can undermine a person's self-esteem. 부정적인 의견은 개인의 자존감을 훼손할 수 있습니다.

865

query

[kwíəri]

v. 질문하다; n. 질문, 의문

questionnaire n. 설문지
unquestioned a. 의심의 여지가 없는
in question p. 문제의, 논의가 되고 있는
queer a. 기묘한, 괴상한

어원	-quir, -quer, -quest, -quisit : seek 구하다, ask 묻다 (L) → '원하는 것을 구하기 위한 탐구와 질문'
유의어	question, inquiry, interrogation
반의어	Answer, respond, reply
영영	A question or inquiry seeking information or clarification.
예문	He sent a query to the customer support team regarding his order. 그는 주문에 관한 문의를 고객 지원 팀에 보냈습니다.

866

distort

[dɪˈstɔːt]

v. 왜곡하다; 바꾸다, 비틀다

extort v. 강탈하다, 강요하다
contort v. 뒤틀다, 일그러뜨리다
retort v. 보복하다, 반박하다
torch n. 햇불; 휴대용 전등

어원	-dis : away + -tort 비틀다 → '본래의 모습과 떨어지도록 비트니 왜곡'
유의어	twist, warp, deform
반의어	Clarify, elucidate, explain
영영	To twist or alter the shape, meaning, or appearance of something in a misleading or harmful way.
예문	The funhouse mirrors distorted their reflections into strange shapes. 편의점 거울은 그들의 반영을 이상한 모양으로 왜곡시켰습니다.

867

mimic

[ˈmɪm.ɪk]

v. 흉내내다

imitation n. 모바으 모조품
mimicry n. 흉내
macula n. 흠, 오점
immaculate a. 깨끗한, 순결한

어원	* mimic 모습이나 행동을 흉내 VS imitate 모양을 복제하듯 만듦
유의어	imitate, copy, emulate
반의어	Original, genuine, authentic
영영	To imitate or copy the actions, speech, or behavior of someone or something.
예문	He could mimic the voices of various celebrities perfectly. 그는 다양한 유명인의 목소리를 완벽하게 흉내 낼 수 있었습니다.

868

regress

[rɪˈgres]

v. 되돌아가다, 퇴행하다, 퇴보하다

digression n. 여담; 탈선
digressive a. 지엽적인, 주제를 벗어나는
regress v. 되돌아가다, 퇴행하다, 퇴보하다
transgress v. 넘다, 벗어나다; 위반하다

어원	-re : again + -gress : go → '뒤로 가니 퇴보하다'
유의어	relapse, deteriorate, revert
반의어	progress, advance
영영	return to a former or less developed state
예문	Some children may regress in their behavior when faced with stress. 스트레스를 겪을 때 일부 어린이는 행동에서 후퇴할 수 있다.

869

mash

[mæʃ]

n. 사료, 으깬 음식 v. 으깨다

smash v. 박살내다, 부딪치다
mash on p. ~을 누르다
mass n. 질량
massive a. 거대한

어원	-mash : crush into mass → '으깨서 덩어리로 만든 사료'
유의어	crush, squash, pulp
반의어	uncrush, separate, disconnect
영영	to crush or press something into a soft and pulpy mass.
예문	Mash the potatoes until they are smooth and creamy. 감자를 부드럽고 크림 같아질 때까지 으깨세요.

870

gracious

[ˈɡreɪʃəs]

a. 우아한, 품위 있는

grace n. 우아함; 친절함
graceful a. 우아한, 품위를 지키는
gracefully adv. 우아하게, 품위 있게
disgrace n. 불명예, 망신

어원	-grat, -gree, -grac : pleasing 기쁘게 하는 → '보는 사람에게 기쁨을 주는 우아함'
유의어	courteous, polite, kind
반의어	discourteous, impolite, rude
영영	courteous, polite, and showing kindness to others.
예문	The host was gracious and welcoming to all the guests. 주인은 모든 손님들에게 친절하고 환영받는 분이었다.

871

inherit from

p. ~에서 물려받다

hereditary a. 유전적인, 세습되는
inheritance n. 상속, 유산
heir n. 상속인, 후계자
herald n. 전조, 전령 v. 예고하다, 알리다

어원	-in, -en : make + -her, -heir, -hered 상속 → '상속받도록 만들다' * hair 머리카락 검사로 친자 확인
유의어	receive from, be left with, acquire through inheritance
반의어	disinherit, deprive of inheritance, exclude from inheritance
영영	to receive or be entitled to receive property or a characteristic from someone by legal succession
예문	She inherited her grandmother's antique jewelry collection. 그녀는 할머니의 고대 보석 수집품을 상속 받았습니다.

872

opposite to N

p. ~과 반대의

oppose v. 반대하다
as opposed to p. ~과는 대조적으로
opponent n. 상대, 적
depot n. 저장소; 정거장

어원	-ob, -oc, -of, -op 밖으로, 반대쪽으로 (L) + -pos : put 놓다 → '반대쪽에 놓다'
유의어	contrary to N, conflicting with N, different from N
반의어	similar to N, alike to N, comparable to N
영영	contrary or contrary to the nature or characteristics of N
예문	His opinion is opposite to mine on this matter. 그의 의견은 이 문제에 대해 내 의견과 반대입니다.

873

cease to do

p. ~이 아니게 되다

cease v. 그만두다, 멈추다, 끝나다
ceaseless a. 끊임없는
incessant a. 끊임없는
precedence n. 우선(함)

어원	-ceas : go away → '일을 하던 중에 가버리니 중단'
유의어	stop doing, discontinue, halt
반의어	continue to do, persist in doing, keep doing
영영	to stop doing something
예문	The factory will cease to operate after this month. 그 공장은 이번 달 이후 운영을 중단할 것입니다.

874

be obligated to do

p. 의무적으로 ~해야 하다

obligate v. 의무를 지우다
oblige v. 의무를 지우다
obligatory a. 의무적인
obligation n. 의무

어원	-ob : to + -lig, -ly, -li : bind 묶다 → '~에 묶인 의무니 ~해야 한다'
유의어	be required to do, be compelled to do, be duty-bound to do
반의어	free from obligation, optional, voluntary
영영	to be required or compelled to do something
예문	As a citizen, you are obligated to pay taxes. 시민으로서, 세금을 내는 것이 당신의 의무입니다.

875

as it were

p. 소위, 말하자면

insofar as p. ~하는 한은
so long as p. ~하기만 하면
in the air p. 헛된 근거 없는
in the course of p. ~되고 있는 중인

어원	it were(과거에서 말했던 것을) ~대로(as) 말하자면
유의어	so to speak, in a manner of speaking, as if
반의어	exactly as, precisely like, in fact
영영	used to indicate that a word or phrase is being used in a figurative or metaphorical sense
예문	He was, as it were, the king of the neighborhood. 그는, 말하자면, 그 동네의 왕이었습니다.

876

at the heart of

p. ~의 중심에

heartbeat n. 심장 박동
heartbreaking a. 가슴 아프게 하는
warmhearted a. 마음이 따뜻한
heartless a. 무정한

어원	-at 지점 + -heart 마음(E) → '마음이 머무른 중심에'
유의어	central to, core of, essence of
반의어	peripheral to, away from, on the outskirts of
영영	central to, fundamental to
예문	Education lies at the heart of social progress. 교육은 사회적 진보의 핵심에 있습니다.

877

on one's feet

p. 독자적으로

set foot p. 발을 들여놓다
footfall n. 발소리
footpath n. 보도
footprint n. 발자국

어원	-on 접촉 + -one's 개인의 + -foot, -feet, -fet 발 → '개인의 발자취니 독자적으로'
유의어	standing, upright, on foot
반의어	off one's feet, sitting, lying down
영영	standing up, in a standing position
예문	After resting for a while, she was back on her feet and ready to continue. 잠시 쉰 뒤, 그녀는 다시 일어나서 계속할 준비가 되었습니다.

878

in one's interest

p. 가장 이익이 되는

in the interests of p. ~을 위해
in the best interest of p. ~을 위해 최선인
disinterest n. 이해 관계가 없음, 무관심
uninterested a. 무관심한, 냉담한

어원	-in 안 + -interests 이익 → '안에 품을 이익이 가장 기대되는'
유의어	advantageous to, beneficial to, in one's favor
반의어	against one's interest, to one's detriment, disadvantageously
영영	beneficial or advantageous to someone
예문	It's in your best interest to save money for the future. 미래를 위해 돈을 저축하는 것이 당신의 이익에 맞습니다.

879

at peace

p. 평화롭게; 안심하고; 의좋게; 죽어서

make peace with p. ~와 평화롭게 지내다
at no time p. 결코 ~하지 않다
at one's option p. ~의 마음대로
at one another p. 서로

어원	-peas, -pais 결합 → '결합을 이끄는 친목과 화합으로 평화'
유의어	calm, tranquil, serene
반의어	in turmoil, unsettled, disturbed
영영	in a state of tranquility or calmness
예문	After years of conflict, the country is finally at peace. 수년간의 갈등 끝에, 그 나라는 마침내 평화로워졌습니다.

880

away from

p. ~로부터 떨어져

awe n. 경외심 v. 경외심을 느끼다
awe-inspiring a. 경외심을 자아내는
awful a. 끔찍한 지독한
awesome a. 아주 멋진, 굉장한

어원	-a + -way + -from ~로부터 → '~로부터 떨어져서'
유의어	apart from, distant from, removed from
반의어	towards, closer to, near to
영영	distant or separated from
예문	He moved away from the city to live a quieter life in the countryside. 그는 조용한 삶을 살기 위해 도시에서 멀어졌습니다.

Chapter 23.

881	hostage	[ˈhɒs.tɪdʒ]	n. 담보물, 인질
882	optical	[ɑ́ptikəl]	a. 눈의, 시각의; 빛을 이용하는
883	interface	[iˈntərfeiˌs]	n. 경계면 v. 조정하다; 접촉하다, 접속하다
884	associate	[əˈsəʊ.si.eɪt]	v. 관련시키다; 교제하다 n. 동료, 친구
885	allot	[əˈlɒt]	v. 할당하다, 배당하다
886	sacred	[ˈseɪ.krɪd]	a. 신성한; 종교적인
887	fulfill	[fʊlˈfɪl]	v. 다하다, 이행하다, 충족하다
888	ban	[bæn]	v. 명령으로 금지하다
889	apparent	[əˈpær.ənt]	a. 또렷한, 명백한, 외견상의, 겉보기에는
890	prosper	[ˈprɒs.pər]	v. 번영하다, 성공하다
891	barometer	[bəˈrɒm.ɪ.tər]	n. 기압계
892	resist	[rɪˈzɪst]	v. 반대하다; 견디다, 참다, 저항하다
893	affair	[əˈfeər]	n. 활동; 업무; 사건, 스캔들; 불륜, 정사
894	undo	[ʌnˈduː]	v. 풀다, 열다; 망치다; 원상태로 돌리다
895	pregnant	[ˈpreg.nənt]	a. 임신한; 내포한, 의미 심장한; 풍요한, 충만한
896	drain	[dreɪn]	v. 배수하다, 물을 빼나다
897	obscure	[əbˈskjʊər]	a. 어두운, 분명치 않은
898	verify	[ˈver.ɪ.faɪ]	v. 대조확인하다, 입증하다, 증명하다, 검증하다
899	steer	[stɪər]	v. 키를 잡다, 조종하다; 이끌다, 나아가게 하다
900	chronic	[ˈkrɒn.ɪk]	a. 만성의, 시간의
901	revalidate	[ˌriːˈvæl.ɪ.deɪt]	v. 갱신하다, 재허가하다, 재확인하다
902	vessel	[ˈves.əl]	n. 선박; 혈관; 용기
903	commence	[kəˈmens]	v. 시작하다, 시작되다, 개시하다; 학위를 받다
904	seizure	[síːʒər]	n. 몰수, 장악; 발작, 경련
905	irritate	[ˈɪr.ɪ.teɪt]	v. 짜증나게 하다; (피부 등을) 자극하다
906	sumptuous	[ˈsʌmp.tʃu.əs]	a. 호화로운, 값비싼
907	compatible	[kəmˈpæt.ə.bəl]	a. 양립할 수 있는, 조화되는; 호환되는
908	malnutrition	[ˌmæl.njuːˈtrɪʃ.ən]	n. 영양 부족, 영양 실조
909	encounter	[ɪnˈkaʊn.tər]	v. 우연히 만나다
910	admit	[ədˈmɪt]	v. 시인하다, 인정하다; 입학을 허가하다
911	refer to N		p. ~에 돌리다; 회부하다; 언급하다
912	in consultation with		p. ~와 협의하여
913	deprive A of B		p. A에게서 B를 빼앗다
914	as to		p. ~에 대한
915	get A out of the way		p. (더는 문제가 되지 않도록) A를 치우다
916	back out		p. 물러나다, (하기로 했던 일에서) 빠지다
917	clean out		p. 깨끗이 치우다
918	cut off		p. 잘라버리다; 서둘러 떠나다
919	give a hand		p. 도와주다
920	come up with		p. ~을 떠올리다, ~을 생각해 내다

881	어원	-host, -hospit : host, guest, stranger 낯선 사람 (E) → '손님을 모시다' * 고대 로마는 전쟁이 끝나고 패전국의 왕자 등을 인질로 데려와 손님으로 모심
hostage	유의어	captive, prisoner, detainee
	반의어	Free person, unconfined individual, independent
[ˈhɒs.tɪdʒ]	영영	A person who is held captive or taken as a prisoner, often to force others to fulfill certain demands.
n. 담보물, 인질		
host n. 주인 hospital n. 병원 hospitality v. 환대, 후한 대접 hostile a. 적대적인, 비우호적인	예문	The hostage situation was resolved peacefully. 인질 사태가 평화적으로 해결되었습니다.
882	어원	-opt, opin : see → '시력은 눈이 빛을 받아들이는 것'
optical	유의어	visual, related to sight, ocular
	반의어	non-optical, nonvisual, non-sighted
[ɑptikəl]	영영	Related to sight, vision, or the use of light.
a. 눈의, 시각의; 빛을 이용하는		
optic a. 눈의, 눈과 관련된 optics n. 광학 optician n. 안경상, 안경 판매상 opt for p. ~을 선택하다	예문	The telescope is an optical instrument used for stargazing. 망원경은 별자리 관찰에 사용되는 광학 기기입니다.
883	어원	-inter : between + -fac 겉면, 앞면(L) → '서로가 겉면을 마주하고 접촉하다'
interface	유의어	connection, interaction, linkage
	반의어	disconnect, separate
[iˈntərfeiˌs]	영영	a point where two systems or components meet and interact
n. 경계면 v. 조정하다; 접촉하다, 접속하다		
surface n. 위의 면, 표면 superficial a. 표면상의 forefront n. 맨 앞, 가장 중요한 위치 facile a. 손쉬운, 수월한	예문	The new software has a user-friendly interface. 새로운 소프트웨어는 사용자 친화적인 인터페이스를 가지고 있습니다.
884	어원	-as : to + -soc 결합 → '~에 일을 결부짓는 것이 연관시키다'
associate	유의어	colleague, partner, coworker
	반의어	Disassociate, disconnect, disjoin
[əˈsəʊ.si.eɪt]	영영	To connect or link one thing with another; a person with whom one is connected or associated.
v. 관련시키다; 교제하다 n. 동료, 친구		
associate A with B p. A를 B와 연관시키다 associated a. 관련된, 지지하는 association n. 연상, 연관성 dissociated v. 분리시키다	예문	She is an associate professor at the university. 그녀는 대학에서 부교수입니다.
885	어원	-at : to + -lot 무더기 → '한 방향으로 한 무더기씩 할당하다'
allot	유의어	allocate, assign, distribute
	반의어	Withhold, keep, retain
[əˈlɒt]	영영	To allocate or distribute something, often resources or tasks, among various individuals or groups.
v. 할당하다, 배당하다		
lot n. 지역, 부지; 무더기; 제비 뽑기; 많음 a lot of p. 많은 lotion n. 로션 allotted a. 할당된	예문	Each team member was allotted a specific task to complete. 각 팀 멤버는 완료할 특정 작업을 할당 받았습니다.
886	어원	-sacr, -sacri, -saint : holy 신성한
sacred	유의어	holy, divine, consecrated
	반의어	Profane, secular, unholy
[ˈseɪ.krɪd]	영영	Regarded as holy, divine, or spiritually significant; deserving reverence or respect.
a. 신성한; 종교적인		
saint n. 성인 sacrifice n. 희생, 제물 sacrificial a. 제물로 바쳐진 sacrificially adv. 희생적으로	예문	The temple is considered a sacred place of worship. 이 절은 숭배의 신성한 장소로 여겨집니다.

887

fulfill

[fʊlˈfɪl]

v. 다하다, 이행하다, 충족하다

self-fulfilling p. 자기 충족적인
refill v. 다시 채우다
fulfillment n. 완수, 이행
fuel v. 증가시키다, 기름을 넣다; 연료

어원	-full + -fill 채우다 → '주어진 임무량을 가득 채워 이행하다'
유의어	accomplish, achieve, complete
반의어	disappoint, fail
영영	carry out or achieve a task or promise
예문	His dream was to fulfill his lifelong ambition of becoming an astronaut. 그의 꿈은 우주 비행사가 되는 평생의 포부를 이루는 것이었다.

888

ban

[bæn]

v. 명령으로 금지하다

banish v. 명령으로 추방하다
abandon v. 단념하다, 포기하다
abase v. 떨어뜨리다, 비하하다
debase v. (품위·가치 따위를) 떨어뜨리다

어원	-ban, -band 명령, 법(E) → '명령으로 금지하다'
유의어	prohibit, forbid, bar
반의어	allow, permit
영영	to officially prohibit or forbid something; a formal restriction or prohibition
예문	Smoking is banned in all public buildings in this city. 이 도시의 모든 공공건물에서 흡연이 금지되어 있다.

889

apparent

[əˈpær.ənt]

a. 또렷한, 명백한, 외견상의, 겉보기에는

appar a. 명백한, 분명한
apparently adv. 겉보기에
apparel n. 의류, 의복
transparence n. 투명, 명백

어원	-ap : to + -par : appear → '~방향으로 뚜렷이 보이니 명백한'
유의어	evident, obvious, clear
반의어	hidden, concealed, obscure
영영	readily seen or understood; obvious.
예문	The problem became apparent when the machine stopped working. 기계가 작동을 멈추면서 문제가 명백해졌다.

890

prosper

[ˈprɒs.pər]

v. 번영하다, 성공하다

prosperity n. 번영
proper a. 적절한, 적당한
proscribe v. 금지하다, 배척하다
prosecute v. 기소하다, 추진하다

어원	-pro : forward + -sper, -spair : hope 희망 → '희망에 따라가니 성공하니 번영'
유의어	thrive, succeed, flourish
반의어	Decline, fail, falter
영영	To succeed or thrive, often in terms of wealth, growth, or well-being.
예문	The small business began to prosper after implementing new strategies. 새로운 전략을 시행한 후 소규모 사업이 번창하기 시작했습니다.

891

barometer

[bəˈrɒm.ɪ.tər]

n. 기압계

barbell n. 바벨, 역기
dimension n. 규모; 차원; 요인
diameter n. 직경, 지름
geometry n. 기하학

어원	-bar, -baro 압, 중량 + -meter : measure → '압력을 측정하는 것'
유의어	pressure gauge, weather indicator, atmospheric instrument
반의어	Irrelevant, unimportant, insignificant
영영	An instrument used to measure atmospheric pressure.
예문	The barometer is used to measure changes in atmospheric pressure. 기압 변화를 측정하는 데 바로미터가 사용됩니다.

892

resist

[rɪˈzɪst]

v. 반대하다; 견디다, 참다, 저항하다

resistance n. 저항, 반항, 반대
resistant a. 저항하는, 반항하는
resister n. 저항자
irresistible a. 저항할 수 없는, 너무 매력적인

어원	-re : against + -sist : stand → '반대에 서다'
유의어	oppose, withstand, defy
반의어	yield, surrender
영영	withstand or oppose the force or temptation
예문	It was difficult to resist the temptation of the delicious chocolate cake. 맛있는 초콜릿 케이크의 유혹을 저항하기 어려웠다.

893

affair

[əˈfeər]

n. 활동; 업무; 사건, 스캔들; 불륜, 정사

fair a. 타당한, 공정한 n. 품평회, 박람회
Job fair p. 취업 박람회
unfair a. 불공평한, 부당한
faint a. 희미한

어원	-a : not + -fair 공정한 → '공정하게 업무를 처리하지 못해서 난 스캔들'
유의어	matter, issue, event
반의어	Divorce, separation, split
영영	An event or situation, often of a personal or intimate nature; also, an ongoing activity or matter.
예문	The scandal became a major political affair. 이 스캔들은 주요 정치적 사안이 되었습니다.

894

undo

[ʌnˈduː]

v. 풀다, 열다; 망치다; 원상태로 돌리다

undoing n. 풀기, 열기; 취소; 실패
undone a. 열려 있는; 파멸한
uneven a. 평평하지 않은, 불규칙한; 홀수의
unfold v. 펴다, 펼치다; 나타내다; 전개하다

어원	-un : reverse + do → '하다의 반대니 원상태로 돌리다'
유의어	reverse, cancel, overturn
반의어	do, perform
영영	to reverse or cancel the effects of something that has been done; to unfasten or untie
예문	He desperately tried to undo the damage caused by his mistake. 그는 자신의 실수로 인한 피해를 되돌리려 애를 썼다.

895

pregnant

[ˈpreɡ.nənt]

a. 임신한; 내포한, 의미 심장한; 풍요한, 충만한

pregnancy n. 임신
impregnate v. 임신시키다; 주입하다
progeny n. 자손
prioritize v. 우선적으로 처리하다

어원	-pre : before + -gn, -gen : birth → '탄생 이전의 상태니 임신한', '임신한 몸이니 풍만한'
유의어	expectant, with child, in the family way
반의어	barren, infertile, childless
영영	expecting a child; carrying a developing fetus.
예문	She just found out she's pregnant and is excited about becoming a mother. 그녀는 방금 임신한 사실을 알게 되었으며 어머니가 되는 것에 기대감을 갖고 있다.

896

drain

[dreɪn]

v. 배수하다, 물을 빼내다

dry a. 마른, 건조한
drought n. 가뭄
draw A out p. A를 끌어내다
drawer n. 서랍; 수표 발행인

어원	-dr : drought 가뭄 → '물을 빼내 마르게 하다'
유의어	empty, empty out, deplete
반의어	Fill, clog, block
영영	A pipe or channel for carrying away liquid waste or excess water.
예문	The sink had a clogged drain that needed to be cleared. 싱크대에는 청소가 필요한 막힌 배수구가 있었습니다.

897

obscure

[əbˈskjʊər]

a. 어두운, 분명치 않은

optic a. 눈의, 눈과 관련된
optics n. 광학
optician n. 안경상, 안경 판매상
opposite to p. ~와 반대의

어원	-ob, -oc, -of, -op 밖으로, 반대쪽으로 (L) + -scure 덮다 → '밖을 덮어 놓으니 어두운'
유의어	unclear, vague, ambiguous
반의어	clear, evident, obvious
영영	Unclear, vague, or hidden from view.
예문	The meaning of the poem was quite obscure and open to interpretation. 그 시의 의미는 상당히 모호하고 해석의 여지가 있었습니다.

898

verify

[ˈver.ɪ.faɪ]

v. 대조확인하다, 입증하다, 증명하다, 검증하다

verification n. 입증, 검증, 확인
veterinarian n. 수의사
indicate v. 나타내다; 암시하다
contradict v. 반발하다

어원	-ver 사실, 진실 (L) → '진실을 찾아가는 과정에서 증거를 들어 대조확인하다'
유의어	confirm, validate, authenticate
반의어	refute, disprove, debunk
영영	To confirm the accuracy or truth of something.
예문	Please provide documents to verify your identity. 신원을 확인하기 위한 문서를 제공해 주세요.

899

steer

[stɪər]

v. 키를 잡다, 조종하다; 이끌다, 나아가게 하다

steering wheel p. 핸들
steep a. 가파른
steering n. 조타, 조종
steerage n. 3등 선실; 키 조종

어원	-ste, -sta : stand → '올바르게 서도록 조종하여 이끌다'
유의어	guide, direct, navigate
반의어	drift, meander
영영	to guide or control the direction of a vehicle or course of action
예문	He had to steer the boat carefully to avoid the rocks in the river. 그는 강에서 바위를 피하기 위해 보트를 주의 깊게 조종해야 했다.

900

chronic

[ˈkrɒn.ɪk]

a. 만성의, 시간의

chronically adv. 만성적으로
chronicity n. 만성, 만성적임
chronicle v. 기록에 남기다 n. 연대기
anachronism n. 시대 착오

어원	-chron 시간(G) → '질질 시간을 끄니 만성의'
유의어	persistent, long-term, constant
반의어	acute, sudden
영영	persisting for a long time or recurring frequently; typically used to describe a medical condition or problem
예문	He had been suffering from chronic back pain for years. 그는 몇 년 동안 만성 등통을 앓고 있었다.

901

revalidate

[ˌriːˈvæl.ɪ.deɪt]

v. 갱신하다, 재허가하다, 재확인하다

validate v. 유효하게 만들다
validity n. 타당성
invalidate v. 틀렸음을 입증하다, 무효로 하다
invalid a. 병약한, 근거 없는

어원	-re : again + -val, -vail 가치(L) / strong 강한 → '다시 가치를 확인하니 갱신하다' * price 일반적 가치 VS value 추상적 가치
유의어	reassess, reconfirm, reexamine
반의어	invalidate, disapprove, reject, revoke
영영	to confirm or validate something once more, often after a certain period of time has passed
예문	She had to revalidate her driver's license after it expired. 운전 면허가 만료되었기 때문에 그녀는 다시 운전 면허를 갱신해야 했다.

902

vessel

[ˈves.əl]

n. 선박; 혈관; 용기

vesselled a. 배에 실은; 용기에 담긴
vesselful n. 배 가득; 용기 가득
vacation n. 방학
vein n. 정맥

어원	-van, -vat, -vas, -ves, -vain, -void, -vac, was : empty 속이 빈 → '속이 비어 있어 배가 뜬다고 생각; 속이 빈 혈관이나 용기'
유의어	ship, boat, container
반의어	Emptiness, void, vacuum
영영	A ship or large boat; a container or object designed to hold liquids or other substances.
예문	The ship was a sturdy vessel capable of crossing the ocean. 그 배는 대양을 건널 수 있는 튼튼한 선박이었습니다.

903

commence

[kəˈmens]

v. 시작하다, 시작되다, 개시하다; 학위를 받다

commerce n. 상업, 교섭
come up with p. ~을 떠올리다
come up p. 발생하다, 생기다
come to do p. ~하게 되다

어원	-com : together + -men : initiate 시작하다 → '다 왔으니 시작'
유의어	begin, start, initiate
반의어	conclude, finish
영영	to begin or start something, often with a formal or ceremonial action; to initiate or embark on
예문	The graduation ceremony will commence at 10 AM tomorrow. 졸업식은 내일 오전 10시에 시작될 것이다.

904

seizure

[síːʒər]

n. 몰수, 장악; 발작, 경련

seize v. 붙잡다, 장악하다
seek to do p. ~하려고 애쓰다, 노력하다
segregate v. 분리하다, 인종차별하다
snatch v. 낚아채다, 잡아채다; n. 잡아챔

어원	-seize 붙잡다 → '전부 붙잡아 장악 후 몰수'
유의어	fit, convulsion, attack
반의어	release, letting go, relinquishment
영영	A sudden and uncontrolled episode of an illness or a seizure of property or assets.
예문	He suffered a seizure and was rushed to the hospital. 그는 발작을 겪고 병원으로 급속히 이송되었습니다.

905

irritate

[ˈɪr.ɪ.teɪt]

v. 짜증나게 하다; (피부 등을) 자극하다

irritable a. 짜증을 잘 내는, 화가 난
get irritated with p. ~에 짜증이 나다
itch n. 가려움 v. 가렵다
irrigate v. 물을 대다, 관개하다

어원	-irrit 싸움 + -ate 동섭 → '짜증나게 하다' * itch 가려움
유의어	annoy, provoke, agitate
반의어	calm, soothe
영영	provoke or annoy someone
예문	The constant noise from the construction site began to irritate the residents. 공사 현장에서 들리는 지속적인 소음이 주민들을 화나게 했다.

906

sumptuous

[ˈsʌmp.tʃu.əs]

a. 호화로운, 값비싼

consume v. 소비하다
consumptive a. 소비의, 소모성의
overconsume v. 과다 섭취하다
consummate v. 완성하다 a. 완벽한

어원	-sume : take → '돈으로 값비싼 물건들을 취하니 호화로운'
유의어	luxurious, lavish, opulent
반의어	plain, simple, modest
영영	luxurious, extravagant, or splendid.
예문	The banquet was a sumptuous affair with gourmet dishes. 연회는 고급 음식이 있는 화려한 행사였다.

907

compatible

[kəmˈpæt.ə.bəl]

a. 양립할 수 있는, 조화되는; 호환되는

compared to p. ~과 비교하여
in comparison with p. ~과 비교할 때
incompatibility n. 불일치, 호환되지 않음
compatibly adv. 잘 어울려서, 양립하여

어원	-com : together + -pat : feel → '함께 느끼니 잘 지내고 양립할 수 있는'
유의어	harmonious, suitable, congruent
반의어	Incompatible, conflicting, contradictory
영영	Capable of existing or working together without conflict; harmonious.
예문	The software must be compatible with different operating systems. 이 소프트웨어는 다양한 운영 체제와 호환되어야 합니다.

908

malnutrition

[ˌmæl.njuːˈtrɪʃən]

n. 영양 부족, 영양 실조

malodor n. 악취
malign a. 유해한, 악성인
malice n. 악의, 원한
malaria n. 학질, 말라리아

어원	-mal : bad(L) +-neutrition 영양
유의어	undernourishment, poor nutrition, starvation
반의어	nourishment, nutrition, health
영영	a condition resulting from a lack of proper nutrition.
예문	Malnutrition can lead to serious health problems. 영양 실조는 심각한 건강 문제로 이어질 수 있습니다.

909

encounter

[ɪnˈkaʊn.tər]

v. 우연히 만나다

counteract v. 대항하다, 거스르다, 대응하다
counterbalance v. 반대로 행동하다
discount v. 할인하다, 무시하다 n. 할인
counterfeit a. 가짜의, 위조의 v. 위조하다

어원	-en : make + -counter 반대 → '반대편에서 만남이 만들어지다'
유의어	meet, confront, face
반의어	avoid, evade
영영	to come across or meet someone or something, especially unexpectedly or by chance
예문	During their expedition, they encountered a rare species of bird. 원정 중에 그들은 희귀한 새 종을 만났다.

910

admit

[ədˈmɪt]

v. 시인하다, 인정하다; 입학을 허가하다

admit to N p. ~한 것을 인정하다
admittance n. 입장, 입회
admission n. 입장료, 입장권; 승인, 허가
admission to N p. ~에게 하는 인정

어원	-ad : to + -mit, -miss, -mess : send(L) → '(비난·사람 등을)(안으로) 들여보낸 것을 인정하다'
유의어	confess, acknowledge, concede
반의어	deny, reject
영영	confess or acknowledge something as true
예문	He had to admit his mistake and apologize to his friend. 그는 자신의 실수를 인정하고 친구에게 사과해야 했다.

911

refer to N

p. ~에 돌리다; 회부하다; 언급하다

refer v. ~에 돌리다; 조회하다; 언급하다
refer to A as B p. A를 B로 칭하다
be referred to as p. ~라고 불리다
with reference to p. ~에 관하여

어원	-re : again + -fer : carry → '특정 사안을 참조하는 추천서', '다시 의미를 전하려고 언급'
유의어	allude to, mention, cite
반의어	disregard N, ignore N, overlook N
영영	to mention or allude to something
예문	The textbook refers to several important historical events. 그 교과서는 여러 중요한 역사적 사건을 언급합니다.

912

in consultation with

p. ~와 협의하여

consult v. 상담하다, 상의하다
counsel n. 권고, 조언, 변호인 v. 권고하다
counselor n. 상담사, 카운슬러
consultant n. 고문 컨설턴트, 상담가

어원	-con : together + -sult, -sal : leap 뛰어오르다 → '함께 문제 해결을 위해 뛰어 오르는 것이 권고하는 것이 자문'
유의어	in discussion with, in collaboration with, in coordination with
반의어	independently of, unilaterally, without consulting
영영	with the advice or input of someone
예문	The decision was made in consultation with all department heads. 모든 부서장들과 협의를 통해 결정이 내려졌습니다.

913

deprive A of B

p. A에게서 B를 빼앗다

deprive v. 물러나게 하다, 퇴위시키다
deprivation n. 박탈, 부족, 궁핍
deprived a. 궁핍한, 불우한
deprecate v. 반대하다, 비난하다

어원	-de : away + -priv : separate → '잘라서 떼어내니 물러나게 하는 것이다'
유의어	strip A of B, rob A of B, deny A access to B
반의어	provide A with B, grant A access to B, endow A with B
영영	to take away or deny someone something that they need or desire
예문	The drought deprived the region of its water supply. 가뭄으로 인해 그 지역은 물 공급을 박탈당했습니다.

914

as to

p. ~에 대한

so long as p. ~하기만 하면
as it were p. 소위, 말하자면
in the air p. 헛된 근거 없는
in the course of p. ~되고 있는 중인

어원	-as ~로서 + -to 목표 → '목표를 향한 자세니 ~에 대한'
유의어	regarding, concerning, with respect to
반의어	unrelated to, disconnected from, unconnected to
영영	concerning or regarding something
예문	We haven't made a decision as to where we'll go on vacation. 휴가 때 어디로 갈지에 대한 결정을 내리지 않았습니다.

915

get A out of the way

p. (더는 문제가 되지 않도록) A를 치우다

get off the ground p. 순조롭게 출발하다
get something out p. ~을 생산하다
get to the point p. 핵심에 이르다
get the hang of p. ~에 익숙해지다

어원	-get 얻다 + -out 꺼내다 + -way 길 → '길에서 문제가 되지 않도록 꺼내니 치우다'
유의어	remove A, clear A, eliminate A
반의어	bring A forward, facilitate A, encourage A
영영	to remove or eliminate something that is obstructing or hindering
예문	Let's get these boxes out of the way so we can move the furniture. 가구를 옮길 수 있도록 이 상자들을 비켜 놓읍시다.

916

back out

p. 물러나다, (하기로 했던 일에서) 빠지다

back and forth p. 왔다 갔다 하는
backyard n. 뒷마당, 뒤뜰
backdrop n. 배경
bacteria n. 박테리아, 세균

어원	-back 뒤, 거꾸로, 다시(E) + -out → '아웃이 되어서 물러나다'
유의어	withdraw, retreat, pull out
반의어	commit, proceed, continue
영영	to withdraw from an agreement or commitment
예문	He promised to help, but then he backed out at the last minute. 그는 도와줄 것을 약속했지만 마지막 순간에 취소했습니다.

917

clean out

p. 깨끗이 치우다

clean agent p. 세정제
cleanliness n. 청결
clear a. 분명한, 확실한 v. 치우다
clearly adv. 명백하게

어원	-clean 깨끗한 + -out 강조 * pure 성분이 섞여있지 않은 VS clear 어지러져 있지 않은
유의어	empty, clear, purge
반의어	fill, stock, replenish
영영	to remove or empty completely
예문	We need to clean out the garage before we can park the car inside. 차를 안에 주차하기 전에 차고를 청소해야 합니다.

918

cut off

p. 잘라버리다; 서둘러 떠나다

cut A with B p. A를 B로 자르다
cut from the same cloth p. 같은 부류인
cut out p. 멈추다; 급히 떠나다
chop up p. ~을 잘게 자르다

어원	-cut 자르다 + -off 떨어져 → '잘리고 무리에서 떨어져 급히 떠나다'
유의어	disconnect, sever, detach
반의어	connect, link, join
영영	to remove or separate by cutting
예문	The storm cut off power to the entire neighborhood. 폭풍이 전체 동네에 전기를 차단했습니다.

919

give a hand

p. 도와주다

on one hand p. 한편으로는
second-hand p. 간접적으로
hand down p. ~을 물려주다
hand out p. 나눠주다

어원	-give 주다 + -hand 손 → '손길을 주니 도와주다'
유의어	help, assist, lend a hand
반의어	hinder, obstruct, impede
영영	to offer assistance or help
예문	Can you give me a hand with these groceries? 이 식료품들을 들 때 도와 줄 수 있니?

920

come up with

p. ~을 떠올리다, ~을 생각해 내다

come down with p. 병에 걸리다, 들리다
come up p. 발생하다, 생기다
come to do p. ~하게 되다
come to one's senses p. 정신이 들다

어원	-come 오다 + with 함께 → '~와 함께 머리 속에 떠 오른 생각'
유의어	devise, concoct, think of
반의어	fail to produce, lack creativity, be unoriginal
영영	to produce or devise something, especially a plan or idea
예문	She always comes up with creative solutions to problems. 그녀는 항상 문제에 대한 창의적인 해결책을 생각해 냅니다.

Chapter 24.

921	enact	[ɪˈnækt]	v. (법률을) 제정하다, 규정하다
922	catholic	[kǽθəlik]	a. 천주교의, 보편적인 n. 천주교도
923	fabulous	[ˈfæb.jə.ləs]	a. 멋진, 굉장한
924	weird	[wɪəd]	a. 기이한, 기묘한
925	exclusive	[ɪkˈsklu.sɪv]	a. 독점적인, 전용의, 배타적인
926	legislate	[ˈledʒ.ɪ.sleɪt]	v. 법률을 제정하다
927	moral	[ˈmɒr.əl]	a. 도덕적인
928	prestige	[presˈtiːʒ]	n. 명성, 위신
929	tolerate	[ˈtɒl.ər.eɪt]	v. 용인하다, 너그럽게 보아주다
930	hospitality	[ˌhɒs.pɪˈtæl.ə.ti]	v. 환대, 후한 대접
931	monetary	[ˈmʌn.ɪ.tri]	a. 금전의, 금융의
932	violence	[ˈvaɪə.ləns]	n. 폭행, 폭력; 격렬함
933	propel	[prəˈpel]	v. 나아가게 하다, 추진하다
934	refuse	[rɪˈfjuːz]	v. 거절하다, 사절하다
935	meditate	[ˈmed.ɪ.teɪt]	v. 명상하다
936	fiery	[ˈfaɪə.ri]	a. 불의, 불같은, 화염의
937	disturb	[dɪˈstɜːb]	v. 방해하다, 어지럽히다
938	aptitude	[ˈæp.tɪ.tʃuːd]	n. 소질, 적성
939	suit	[suːt]	v. 적합하다 n. 정장; 소송
940	cruel	[ˈkruː.əl]	a. 잔혹한, 잔인한
941	spur	[spɜːr]	n. 박차, 자극 v. 원동력이 되다
942	exclaim	[ɪkˈskleɪm]	v. 외치다, 큰 소리로 말하다
943	dispatch	[dɪˈspætʃ]	v. 보내다, 파견하다, 급파하다; 죽이다, 해치우다
944	merchant	[ˈmɜː.tʃənt]	n. 상인, 무역상
945	cling	[klɪŋ]	v. 꼭 붙잡다, 매달리다; 달라붙다;애착을 갖다
946	fraction	[ˈfræk.ʃən]	n. 단편, 일부, 소량; 분수
947	perplex	[pəˈpleks]	v. 당황하게 하다
948	eliminate	[iˈlɪm.ɪ.neɪt]	v. 제거하다, 없애다
949	prominent	[ˈprɒm.ɪ.nənt]	a. 돌출한; 눈에 띄는, 탁월한
950	backfire	[ˌbækˈfaɪər]	v. 역효과가 나타나다
951	as we speak		p. 바로 지금, 이 순간에도
952	be prone to do		p. ~하기 쉬운
953	intent on		a. ~에 열중하고 있는
954	be subject to N		p. (특히 나쁜 영향을 받아) ~될 수 있는
955	bring about		p. 일으키다, 야기하다, 초래하다; 낳다
956	have a breakdown		p. 고장이 나다
957	come in handy		p. 쓸모가 있다, 도움이 되다
958	consistent with		p. ~와 일치하는
959	in decline		p. 쇠퇴하여, 기울어
960	go for		p. ~를 좋아하다, ~를 찾다

921	어원	-en : make + -ac, -act, -ag, -ig : do 행하다, act 작용하다(L) → '행동을 하게 만드는 법 제정'
	유의어	pass, adopt, establish
enact	반의어	Repeal, abolish, revoke
[ɪˈnækt]	영영	To make into law through a formal legislative process; to put something into practice.
v. (법률을) 제정하다, 규정하다		
enactment n. 법률 제정, 입법 agent n. 대리인, 중개상 exact to the life p. 실물 그대로의 react to N p. ~에 반응하다	예문	The Age of Enlightenment was a period of intellectual growth and reason. 개화 시대는 지적 성장과 이성의 시기였습니다.

922	어원	-cathedral : chair 대성당 → '대성당에서 의식을 행하는 천주교의' * castle 성과 닮은 성당
	유의어	universal, all-encompassing, comprehensive
catholic	반의어	Non-Catholic, non-denominational, non-religious
[kǽθəlik]	영영	Relating to the Roman Catholic Church or its beliefs and practices; also, universal or all-encompassing in scope.
a. 천주교의, 보편적인 n. 천주교도		
castle n. 성 cathedral n. 대성당 catholicism n. 천주교 catholicity n. 보편성, 포용성	예문	The university offers a diverse curriculum, reflecting a catholic approach to education. 대학은 다양한 교과과정을 제공하여 교육에 대한 포괄적인 접근을 반영합니다.

923	어원	-fa, -fe, -fess, -phe : talk 말하다 → '말을 불려서 하는 과장하니 멋진'
	유의어	fantastic, incredible, marvelous
fabulous	반의어	Unimpressive, ordinary, unexceptional
[ˈfæb.jə.ləs]	영영	Extremely good, wonderful, or remarkable; often used to describe something as excellent.
a. 멋진, 굉장한		
fabular a. 우화의, 우화적인 fabric n. 직물, 천; 구조 fabricate v. 제작하다; 꾸며내다, 날조하다 at one's face value p. 액면 그대로	예문	The view from the mountaintop was absolutely fabulous. 산 정상에서의 경치는 정말 멋졌습니다.

924	어원	* -weak 약한 → '약해 보일 정도로 기이한'
	유의어	strange, unusual, bizarre
weird	반의어	normal, ordinary, conventional
[wɪəd]	영영	Strange, unusual, or unconventional in a way that is unsettling.
a. 기이한, 기묘한		
weak a. 약한 weed n. 잡초 weird out p. 멍하다 weirdly adv. 불가사의하게	예문	The strange noise coming from the old house sounded quite weird. 오래된 집에서 들리는 이상한 소리가 상당히 기묘하게 들렸다.

925	어원	-ex : out + -clu, -clp, -clud, -clos : close → '바깥을 닫아버린 것이니 독점적인'
	유의어	selective, restricted, limited to few
exclusive	반의어	Inclusive, open, accessible
[ɪkˈskluː.sɪv]	영영	Limited to a particular person, group, or category; not open to others.
a. 독점적인, 전용의, 배타적인		
exclude v. 제외하다, 배제하다 exclusively adv. 독점적으로, 배타적으로 exclusion n. 제외, 배제, 차단 excluding prep. ~을 제외하고	예문	The exclusive club only admitted members by invitation. 이 독점적인 클럽은 초대장으로만 회원을 받았습니다.

926	어원	-leg, -legis : law + -lat : carry → '법을 나르다'
	유의어	make laws, enact legislation, pass laws
legislate	반의어	repeal, abolish, annul
[ˈledʒ.ɪ.sleɪt]	영영	Make or enact laws through a formal legislative process.
v. 법률을 제정하다		
legislation n. 입법, 법률제정 legit a. 합법의, 진짜의, 적당한 illicit a. 불법의 privilege n. 특권, 특전	예문	The government plans to legislate new regulations for the industry. 정부는 그 산업을 위한 새로운 규정을 제정하기로 계획하고 있습니다.

927	어원	-mo, -mod, -mold 척도(L) → '척도에 맞춰 살아가니 도덕적인'
moral	유의어	ethical, virtuous, righteous
	반의어	Immoral, unethical, corrupt
[ˈmɒr.əl] a. 도덕적인	영영	Relating to principles of right and wrong behavior; ethical.
morale n. 사기, 의욕 immoral a. 부도덕한 amoral a. 도덕을 모르는 morality n. 도덕성	예문	The moral of the story is to always be kind to others. 이 이야기의 교훈은 항상 다른 사람에게 친절해야 한다는 것입니다.

928	어원	-prestige : illusion → '환상처럼 힘 있는 명성' * -pre : before + -stig : bind → '앞에 높게 묶여있는 현수막의 명성'
prestige	유의어	status, reputation, standing
	반의어	Disrepute, disesteem, lack of respect
[presˈtiːʒ] n. 명성, 위신	영영	The reputation, status, or esteem associated with someone or something, often due to achievements or influence.
prestigious a. 명망 있는, 일류의 prestigeful a. 명성이 있는 of prestige p. 신망이 있는 precious a. 소중한, 귀중한	예문	The award added to the prestige of the accomplished actor. 그 상은 성취한 배우의 명성을 높였습니다.

929	어원	-toler 참다 + -ate 동접 → '프랑스의 관용 정신(톨레랑스)' * tolerance '태도와 상태의 인내' VS toleration '행동의 인내'
tolerate	유의어	endure, bear, withstand
	반의어	reject, resist
[ˈtɒl.ər.eɪt] v. 용인하다, 너그럽게 보아주다	영영	endure or accept something, even if unpleasant
toilet n. 변기(통), 화장실 tolerance n. 관용, 용인, 허용 toleration n. 묵인, 용인 tolerant a. 내성이 있는, 관대한	예문	It's important to tolerate different opinions and viewpoints. 다른 의견과 시각을 용인하는 것이 중요하다.

930	어원	-host, -hospit : guest, host, stranger 낯선 사람 (E) → 'guest를 환대하니 후한 대접'
hospitality	유의어	welcome, friendliness, generosity
	반의어	hostility, unfriendliness, rudeness
[ˌhɒs.pɪˈtæl.ə.ti] v. 환대, 후한 대접	영영	The friendly and generous reception and treatment of guests or strangers.
hospital n. 병원 hotel n. 호텔 hospitable a. 환대하는, 친절한 hospice n. 말기 환자용 병원	예문	The warm hospitality of the host made the guests feel welcome. 호스트의 따뜻한 환대로 손님들은 환영받는 느낌을 받았다.

931	어원	-moneta : money
monetary	유의어	financial, fiscal, economic
	반의어	Non-monetary, non-financial, non-cash
[ˈmʌn.ɪ.tri] a. 금전의, 금융의	영영	Relating to money or currency, often involving financial matters.
monetize v. 화폐로 주조하다 monetization n. 화폐 주조, 통화 제정	예문	The central bank is responsible for controlling the country's monetary policy. 중앙 은행은 국가의 통화 정책을 통제하는 책임이 있습니다.

932	어원	-viol 침해, 폭력 → '격렬하게 폭행하며 침해하니 폭력적인' * walking violation → '농구에서 드리블 반칙 용어'
violence	유의어	brutality, aggression, force
	반의어	Non-violence, peace, non-aggression
[ˈvaɪə.ləns] n. 폭행, 폭력; 격렬함	영영	The use of physical force to cause harm, injury, or damage; often associated with aggression or brutality.
violent a. 폭력적인, 격렬한 violently adv. 격렬하게, 맹렬히 inviolable a. 신성한, 범할 수 없는 violet n. 제비꽃, 보라색	예문	The violence in the city escalated, leading to concerns for public safety. 도시 내의 폭력이 확산되어 공공 안전에 대한 우려가 높아졌습니다.

933

propel

[prəˈpel]

v. 나아가게 하다, 추진하다

propeller n. 프로펠러, 추진기
propellant n. 추진력
propulsive a. 추진하는
promote n. 승진 v. 승진시키다, 증진하다

어원	-pro : forth + -pel, -peal, pul : drive 몰다 → '앞으로 몰다'
유의어	drive, push, thrust
반의어	Halt, stop, hinder
영영	To drive or push something forward or in a particular direction.
예문	The jet engine can propel the aircraft at high speeds. 제트 엔진은 비행기를 높은 속도로 추진할 수 있습니다.

934

refuse

[rɪˈfjuːz]

v. 거절하다, 사절하다

confuse A with B p. A와 B를 혼동하다
diffuse v. 확산시키다, 분산되다
transfuse n. 수혈
perfume n. 향수

어원	-re : back + -fus : pour → '거꾸로 퍼부으니 거절'
유의어	reject, decline, deny
반의어	accept, agree, consent
영영	Reject or decline something; say no to an offer or request.
예문	She had to refuse the invitation due to a prior commitment. 그녀는 이전 약속 때문에 초대를 거절해야 했습니다.

935

meditate

[ˈmed.ɪ.teɪt]

v. 명상하다

meditation n. 명상
mediate v. 조정하다, 중재하다
medieval a. 중세의
median a. 중간의

어원	-me, -med, -men, -medi : middle 중간 (L) / think 생각하다 → '깊은 생각의 중간에 들어가니 명상'
유의어	contemplate, reflect, ponder
반의어	agitate, disturb
영영	engage in deep contemplation or reflection
예문	He likes to meditate to relax his mind. 그는 마음을 진정시키기 위해 명상을 좋아한다.

936

fiery

[ˈfaɪə.ri]

a. 불의, 불같은, 화염의

misfire v. 불발이 되다
infirm a. 허약한
fierce a. 사나운, 맹렬한
affirm v. 확언하다, 단언하다

어원	-fier : fire 불 → '불이 나서 화염의'
유의어	passionate, intense, blazing
반의어	calm, peaceful, placid
영영	Burning with a flame or intense heat; passionate or fervent.
예문	Her fiery passion for the cause inspired others to join the movement. 그녀의 불타는 열정은 다른 이들을 운동에 참여하도록 자극했습니다.

937

disturb

[dɪˈstɜːb]

v. 방해하다, 어지럽히다

disturbance n. 방해, 폐해
disturbing a. 충격적인, 불안감을 주는
disturbed a. 정신적 장애가 있는
distribute v. 분배하다, 배포하다

어원	-dis : utterly + -turb : confused / -tur : shake → '완전히 혼란해지게 방해하다'
유의어	upset, agitate, perturb
반의어	calm, soothe, placate
영영	Upset, interrupt, or bother.
예문	Please do not disturb me while I'm working. 일하고 있는 동안 저를 방해하지 마세요.

938

aptitude

[ˈæp.tɪ.tʃuːd]

n. 소질, 적성

attitude n. 태도, 자세, 의견, 심정
apt a. ~하는 경향이 있는, ~하기 쉬운
arbitrary a. 제멋대로인 변덕스러운
arbitrate v. 중재하다, 조정하다

어원	-apt, -att : fit 적합하게 하다 → '적합한 일을 찾았으니 소질과 적성에 맞는' * apt 개인적 차원의 적성이나 적응 VS att 다른 사람들에게 적용
유의어	talent, capability, skill
반의어	Inaptitude, incompetence, lack of skill
영영	Natural ability or talent for a particular activity, skill, or field.
예문	Her aptitude for mathematics was evident from a young age. 그녀의 수학에 대한 적성은 어린 나이부터 명백했습니다.

939

suit

[suːt]

v. 적합하다 n. 정장; 소송

suitor n. 소송인, 구혼자
suite n. 스위트룸; 세트, 묶음
suitable a. 적합한, 적절한
unsuitable a. 부적절한, 적임이 아닌

어원	-su : follow + -it : fit → '따라 맞춰입는 옷'
유의어	fit, match, befit
반의어	mismatch, clash
영영	a set of clothes consisting of a jacket and pants or a skirt
예문	She wore a stylish suit to the business meeting. 그녀는 비즈니스 미팅에 스타일리시한 정장을 입었다.

940

cruel

[ˈkruːəl]

a. 잔혹한, 잔인한

rude a. 무례한
rubbish n. 쓰레기, 헛소리
crude n. 원유 a. 대충의, 미가공의
rug n. 깔개, 융단

어원	* -crus : rude(무례)를 지나서 잔인한
유의어	brutal, ruthless, inhumane
반의어	kind, compassionate
영영	causing pain, suffering, or distress to others without mercy or compassion; harsh or inhumane
예문	Animal cruelty is a serious issue that needs to be addressed. 동물 학대는 해결해야 할 심각한 문제이다.

941

spur

[spəːr]

n. 박차, 자극 v. 원동력이 되다

spring n. 봄; 영수철, 스프링
offspring n. 자손, 짐승의 새끼
sprint n. 단거리 달리기 경주
sprout n. 새싹 v. 새싹이 나다

어원	-spur : spring → '박차고 튀어 나오게 하는 원동력'
유의어	stimulate, motivate, encourage
반의어	discourage, deter, dissuade
영영	Stimulate or encourage someone to take action or achieve something.
예문	The coach's words of encouragement spurred the team to victory. 코치의 격려의 말이 팀을 승리로 이끌었습니다.

942

exclaim

[ɪkˈskleɪm]

v. 외치다, 큰 소리로 말하다

claim v. 주장하다
reclaim v. 되찾다, 개선하다
decalim v. 연설하다, 낭독하다; 비난하다
proclaim v. 선언하다

어원	-ex : out + -claim, -cil : cry out 외치다 / call 부르다 → '바깥으로 말하니 큰 소리로 외치다'
유의어	cry out, shout, declare
반의어	whisper, mumble, mutter
영영	to cry out or speak suddenly and loudly, typically expressing surprise or strong emotion.
예문	She exclaimed with joy when she received the good news. 그녀는 좋은 소식을 듣고 기쁨에 소리쳤다.

943

dispatch

[dɪˈspætʃ]

v. 보내다, 파견하다, 급파하다; 죽이다, 해치우다

pedal n. 발의 발판
pedestal n. 주춧돌; 기초
expedition n. 원정, 탐험
pedestrian n. 보행자

어원	-dis : intensive + -patch, -ped : foot → '급하게 발을 내딛다'
유의어	send, transmit, convey
반의어	receive, accept, take in
영영	Send off, transmit, or deal with a task or assignment promptly and efficiently.
예문	The company decided to dispatch a team to investigate the issue. 회사는 문제를 조사하기 위해 팀을 파견하기로 결정했습니다.

944

merchant

[ˈmɜːrtʃənt]

n. 상인, 무역상

market n. 시장
emrchandise v. 장사하다, 매매하다
merchandising n. 판매, 판촉
commerce n. 상업, 무역

어원	-merc : trade 장사하다, reward 보상하다 + -ant 사람 → '장사하는 사람'
유의어	trader, seller, retailer
반의어	Customer, buyer, shopper
영영	A person or business involved in buying and selling goods or commodities, often on a commercial scale.
예문	The local merchant sold fresh fruits and vegetables at the market. 지역 상인은 시장에서 신선한 과일과 채소를 팔았습니다.

945		
	어원	-cling : stick 달라붙다 → '달라 붙으니 애착을 갖다'
cling	유의어	adhere, stick, hold on
	반의어	release, let go
[klɪŋ]	영영	to hold on tightly or adhere strongly to something; to be emotionally attached or dependent
v. 꼭 붙잡다, 매달리다; 달라붙다;애착을 갖다		
clinging n. 집착하는 것 cliff n. 절벽, 낭떠러지 clip v. 자르다, 깎다; 짧은 영상 clerk n. 사무원, 직원	예문	The wet clothes clung to her body after she fell into the river. 강에서 떨어진 후 젖은 옷이 그녀의 몸에 붙었다.

946		
	어원	-fra , -frag, -frac, -fring : break 부수다 → '작게 부순 부분, 숫자를 부수니 분수'
fraction	유의어	portion, part, segment
	반의어	Whole, entirety, complete entity
[ˈfræk.ʃən]	영영	A numerical quantity that represents a part of a whole, often expressed as a ratio of two numbers.
n. 단편, 일부, 소량; 분수		
friction n. 마찰, 불화 fragment n. 파편, 조각 fracture n. 골절, 균열 in a fraction of a second p. 순식간에	예문	A fraction of the population participated in the protest. 인구의 일부만 시위에 참여했습니다.

947		
	어원	-per 완전히 + -pli, -ply, -ploy, -ploit, -plex : weave, twine, fold(E) → '완전히 문제를 꼬아 당황하게 하다'
perplex	유의어	confuse, puzzle, bewilder
	반의어	clarify, elucidate, simplify
[pəˈpleks]	영영	Confuse or puzzle someone; make someone uncertain or doubtful.
v. 당황하게 하다		
complex a. 복잡한 complicate v. 복잡하게 하다 perplexed a. 어찌할 바를 모르는 in perplexity p. 당혹하여	예문	The complex problem continued to perplex the scientists. 복잡한 문제는 여전히 과학자들을 당황하게 했습니다.

948		
	어원	-e : out + -limi, -limit, -limin : border 경계 → '경계 밖으로 치워 제거하다'
eliminate	유의어	remove, get rid of, eradicate
	반의어	add, include, retain
[iˈlɪm.ɪ.neɪt]	영영	to completely remove or get rid of something.
v. 제거하다, 없애다		
unlimited a. 한계가 없는 elimination n. 배제, 제거 preliminary a. 예비의, 서두의 delimit v. 범위를 정하다	예문	The goal is to eliminate waste and promote recycling. 목표는 폐기물을 제거하고 재활용을 촉진하는 것이다.

949		
	어원	-pro : forth + -min, -mini, -minim 작은 (L) / 돌출하다 → '앞으로 돌출하니 두드러지는'
prominent	유의어	distinguished, notable
	반의어	inconspicuous, obscure
[ˈprɒm.ɪ.nənt]	영영	standing out or noticeable; widely recognized or well-known
a. 돌출한; 눈에 띄는, 탁월한		
eminence n. 저명함, 탁월함 imminent a. 긴박한 menace n. 위협, 협박 prominently a. 두드러지게, 현저하게	예문	The prominent scientist was awarded the Nobel Prize for his groundbreaking research. 그 유명한 과학자는 그의 혁신적인 연구로 노벨상을 받았다.

950		
	어원	-back + -fire 발사 → '뒤로 발사하니 역효과가 나타나다'
backfire	유의어	boomerang, rebound, misfire
	반의어	Succeed, go well, work out
[ˌbækˈfaɪər]	영영	To have an unintended negative consequence, often as a result of an action or plan.
v. 역효과가 나타나다		
misfire v. 불발이 되다 fiery a. 불의, 불같은, 화염의 fierce a. 사나운, 맹렬한 affirm v. 확언하다, 단언하다	예문	His plan to impress his boss backfired and led to misunderstandings. 상사를 감동시키려는 그의 계획은 역효과를 일으키고 오해를 불러왔습니다.

951

as we speak

p. 바로 지금, 이 순간에도

speak badly of p. 험담하다, 헐뜯다
as it were p. 소위, 말하자면
in the air p. 헛된 근거 없는
in the course of p. ~되고 있는 중인

어원	-as : when + we speak 우리가 말하다 → '우리가 말하는 지금 이 순간에도'
유의어	currently, right now, at this very moment
반의어	previously, before, formerly
영영	at the current moment, right now
예문	The negotiations are ongoing as we speak. 우리가 말하는 현재에 협상이 진행 중입니다.

952

be prone to do

p. ~하기 쉬운

prone a. 경향이 있는; ~하기 쉬운
lie prone p. 엎드려 눕다
plonk v. 뛰어다니다
progressive a. 진보적인

어원	-pro : forward → '앞서 나서는 경향이 있으니 ~하기 쉬운'
유의어	be inclined to do, tend to do, have a tendency to do
반의어	be unlikely to do, rarely do, seldom do
영영	to have a tendency or inclination to do something
예문	He is prone to exaggeration when telling stories. 그는 이야기할 때 과장하는 경향이 있습니다.

953

intent on

a. ~에 열중하고 있는

intend to do p. ~할 작정이다
intently adv. 골똘히, 열중하여
intention n. 의사, 의도
unintended a. 의도하지 않은

어원	-in 안 + -tend, -test 뻗다, 펼치다 + -on 접촉 → '의지가 안에서 뻗어 나와 펼치는 것이니 ~에 전념'
유의어	determined to, focused on, committed to
반의어	indifferent to, apathetic towards, unconcerned about
영영	determined or resolved to do something
예문	She is intent on finishing her novel by the end of the month. 그녀는 이번 달 말까지 자신의 소설을 완성하기로 결심했습니다.

954

be subject to N

p. (특히 나쁜 영향을 받아) ~될 수 있는

subject n. 주제, 학과, 주어; 피실험자
subjective a. 주관적인
subjectivity n. 주체성, 주관성
be subjected to N p. ~을 받다; ~을 겪다

어원	-sub : under + -ject : throw → '아래에 던져져 ~을 당하는'
유의어	be vulnerable to N, be susceptible to N, be liable to N
반의어	be immune to N, be unaffected by N, be exempt from N
영영	to be susceptible or liable to experience something
예문	Outdoor events are subject to cancellation in case of bad weather. 야외 행사는 날씨가 안 좋은 경우에는 취소될 수 있습니다.

955

bring about

p. 일으키다, 야기하다, 초래하다; 낳다

bring A to bear p. A에 집중하다
bring oneself to p. ~할 마음이 생기다
bring to the table p. ~을 제공하다
bring up p. 기르다, 교육하다

어원	-bear, -bir, -bri 나르다, 가져오다, 데려오다 + -about 이것저것 → '이것저것 사건들을 가져와 일으키고 야기하다'
유의어	cause, induce, generate
반의어	prevent, hinder, impede
영영	to cause or make something happen
예문	The new law brought about significant changes in the industry. 새로운 법률이 산업에 중요한 변화를 가져왔습니다.

956

have a breakdown

p. 고장이 나다

break into p. 침입하다, 난입하다
breakthrough n. 획기적 발전; 돌파구
breakage n. 파손, 손상
bruising n. 타박상

어원	-have 갖다 + -breakdown 고장 → '고장난 물건을 소유'
유의어	suffer a breakdown, experience a breakdown, undergo a breakdown
반의어	function smoothly, operate efficiently, run without problems
영영	to experience a sudden failure or collapse
예문	After working non-stop for weeks, she had a breakdown and needed time off. 몇 주 동안 쉬지 않고 일한 후, 그녀는 정신적 붕괴를 겪었고 휴가를 필요로 했습니다.

957

come in handy

p. 쓸모가 있다, 도움이 되다

handy a. 편리한, 손재주 있는
firsthand adv. 직접, 바로 a. 직접의
hand down p. ~을 물려주다
hand out p. 나눠주다

어원	-come 오다 + -handy 손재주 있는 → '손재주가 있으면 도움이 된다'
유의어	be useful, be convenient, be practical
반의어	be useless, be impractical, be inconvenient
영영	to be useful or convenient
예문	Having a flashlight came in handy during the power outage. 전기가 나간 상황에서 손전등이 유용하게 쓰였습니다.

958

consistent with

p. ~와 일치하는

consist of p. ~으로 구성되다
consistency n. 일관성
consistently adv. 일관되게, 지속적으로
consist in p. ~에 근거하다

어원	-con : together + -sist : stand → '같은 모습으로 일치하게 서 있으니 일관성'
유의어	in line with, compatible with, congruent with
반의어	conflicting with, contradictory to, incompatible with
영영	in agreement or harmony with something
예문	His actions are not consistent with his words. 그의 행동은 그의 말과 일관되지 않습니다.

959

in decline

p. 쇠퇴하여, 기울어

declare v. 단언하다, 공언하다
incline v. ~할 마음이 내키게 하다
clinical a. 임상의
recline v. 기대다

어원	-de : down + -clin, -clim 기울이다 → '마음이 아래로 기울니 거절하다'
유의어	deteriorating, decreasing, waning
반의어	improving, rising, advancing
영영	experiencing a gradual decrease or deterioration
예문	The old factory is in decline due to lack of investment. 투자 부족으로 인해 오래된 공장은 쇠퇴하고 있습니다.

960

go for

p. ~를 좋아하다, ~를 찾다

go for naught p. 헛되이 하다
go over p. 점검하다, 검토하다
go hand in hand p. ~와 관련이 있다
go off p. (알람·경보 등이) 울리다

어원	-go 가다 + -for ~를 찾아서
유의어	opt for, choose, select
반의어	avoid, shun, reject
영영	to choose or select something
예문	I'll go for the chicken salad, please. 제가 치킨 샐러드로 주문할게요.

Chapter 25.

961	ascend	[əˈsend]	n. 오르다; 승진하다
962	perspiration	[ˌpɜː.spərˈeɪ.ʃən]	n. 땀, 발한; 엄청난 노력
963	divert	[daɪˈvɜːt]	v. (방향을) 전환하다
964	factual	[ˈfæk.tʃu.əl]	a. 사실에 입각한, 사실적인
965	odor	[ˈoʊ·dər]	n. 냄새, 악취
966	grant	[grɑːnt]	v. 주다, 수여하다
967	successive	[səkˈses.ɪv]	a. 연속적인, 연이은
968	acknowledge	[əkˈnɒl.ɪdʒ]	v. 인정하다; 사례하다, 감사하다
969	numerous	[ˈnjuː.mə.rəs]	a. 많은
970	prone	[proʊn]	a. 경향이 있는, ~하기 쉬운; 어드려 있는
971	armament	[ˈɑː.mə.mənt]	n. 장비, 병기
972	manufacture	[ˌmæn.jəˈfæk.tʃər]	v. 제조하다, 생산하다, 만들다 n. 제조, 생산
973	tumble	[ˈtʌm.bəl]	v. 휙 뒤집다 n. 곤두박질, 재주 넘기
974	vague	[veig]	a. 애매한, 막연한
975	accumulate	[əˈkjuː.mjə.leɪt]	v. 모으다, 축적하다, 누적시키다, 점차 늘어나다
976	impulse	[ímpʌls]	n. 충동, 자극
977	endure	[ɪnˈdʒʊər]	v. 지속하다, 견디다
978	fixate	[fɪkˈseɪt]	v. 정착(고정)시키다, 집착하다
979	tin	[tɪn]	n. 주석(원소기호 Sn), 통조림; (원통형) 통
980	omit	[əʊˈmɪt]	v. 생략하다, 빠뜨리다
981	monastery	[mɑ́nəstèri]	n. (남자) 수도원
982	calculate	[ˈkæl.kjə.leɪt]	v. 계산하다
983	shorthand	[ʃɔˈrthæˌnd]	n. 속기, 약칭 v. 속기하다
984	ultraviolet	[ˌʌl.trəˈvaɪə.lət]	a. 자외선의
985	barren	[ˈbær.ən]	a. 불모의, 황량한
986	disrupt	[dɪsˈrʌpt]	v. 붕괴시키다, 분열시키다, 방해하다
987	inevitable	[ɪˈnev.ɪ.tə.bəl]	a. 불가피한, 부득이한, 필연적인
988	enroll	[ɪnˈroʊl]	v. 등록하다, 명부에 올리다, 가입하다
989	patron	[ˈpeɪ.trən]	n. 후원자; 고객, 단골
990	greed	[griːd]	n. 탐욕, 식탐
991	a majority of		p. 대다수의
992	bring A to a stop		p. A를 세우다, A를 정지시키다
993	jump to a conclusion		p. 성급하게 결론을 내리다
994	cup of tea		p. 선호하는 일, 기호[취미]에 맞는 일
995	by heart		p. 외워서
996	get a handle on		p. 이해하다, 알아듣다
997	keep up to date		p. 최신 정보를 계속 유지하다
998	go off		p. (알람·경보 등이) 울리다
999	half off		p. 반값 할인
1000	at most		p. 기껏해야

961

ascend

[əˈsend]

n. 오르다; 승진하다

ascent n. 상승, 오르막길
descendant n. 자손, 후손
escalate v. 증가시키다; 확대되다
scale n. 규모; 계급, 등급; 축적, 비율

어원	-a : to + -scend, -scent, -scal : climb 오르다 → '~한 방향으로 오르다 * -gra, -gre 한발자국씩 간다 VS -scen 높이를 정하고 위로 간다
유의어	climb, rise, mount
반의어	descend, fall
영영	move upward or climb
예문	The hikers began their journey to ascend the steep mountain. 등반하기 위해 가파른 산으로 여행을 시작했다.

962

perspiration

[ˌpɜː.spərˈeɪ.ʃən]

n. 땀, 발한; 엄청난 노력

perspire v. 땀을 흘리다
transpire v. 새다, 누설되다
conspire v. 공모하다, 음모를 꾸미다
perspiratory a. 땀나는, 발한 작용의

어원	-per : through + -spir : breathe → '숨구멍으로 땀을 흘리다'
유의어	sweat, sweatiness, moisture
반의어	Dryness, lack of sweating, absence of sweat
영영	The act of sweating; moisture excreted through the sweat glands of the skin.
예문	After the intense workout, his face was covered in perspiration. 격렬한 운동 후에 그의 얼굴은 땀으로 뒤덮여 있었습니다.

963

divert

[daɪˈvɜːt]

v. (방향을) 전환하다

diverse a. 다양한, 가지각색의
divorce v. 이혼하다; 분리하다
invert v. 뒤집다, 거꾸로 하다
convert v. 변환하다

어원	-di, -dis : aside + -vert, -vers, -vorc : turn 돌리다(L) → '떨어뜨려서 방향을 전환하다'
유의어	redirect, reroute, change course
반의어	Direct, guide, steer
영영	To redirect or change the course of something, often to a different destination or purpose.
예문	The diversion of the river altered the landscape of the region. 강의 방향전환은 그 지역의 지형을 변경했습니다.

964

factual

[ˈfæk.tʃu.əl]

a. 사실에 입각한, 사실적인

factor n. 요소, 요인
factor in p. ~을 고려하다, ~을 계산에 넣다
by a factor of p. ~배로
manufacture v. 제조하다, 생산하다 n. 제조

어원	-fac, -fec, -fic, -fy, -fair : do 하다 (L) → '행하여 실제가 된'
유의어	true, accurate, real
반의어	Unfactual, false, fictional
영영	Based on facts or reality; accurate and objective.
예문	The report is based on factual information and data. 이 보고서는 사실적인 정보와 데이터를 기반으로 합니다.

965

odor

[ˈoʊ·dər]

n. 냄새, 악취

odd a. 이상한; 홀수의; 남은, 임시의
odorless a. 악취가 없는
odometer n. 주행기록장치
period n. 길 주변; 기간, 주기

어원	-odd 홀수; 이상한 + -or, -ora, -orat 말하다(L) → '이상하게 말할 때 냄새가' * 오 더러워~
유의어	scent, fragrance, smell
반의어	fragrance, scent, aroma
영영	A distinctive smell or scent, often a characteristic or recognizable smell.
예문	The strong odor of flowers filled the room. 꽃들의 강한 냄새가 방을 가득 채웠습니다.

966

grant

[grɑːnt]

v. 주다, 수여하다

grant a wish p. 소원을 들어주다
take A for granted p. A를 당연하게 여기다
take it for granted p. ~을 당연하게 여기다
be taken for granted p. 당연시되다

어원	-cre, -cred, -creed : believe 믿다(G) → 프랑스어 granter '신뢰를 가지고 승인하여 주다'
유의어	give, award, bestow
반의어	Deny, refuse, reject
영영	To give or bestow something, often as an official or formal act of generosity or approval.
예문	She received a grant to fund her research project. 그녀는 연구 프로젝트를 자금 지원하기 위해 장학금을 받았습니다.

967

successive

[sək'ses.ɪv]

a. 연속적인, 연이은

succeed v. 성공하다; 뒤를 잇다 계승하다
succeed to p. 계승하다, 상속하다
in successtion p. 연속으로
a succession of p. 일련의

어원	-suc : sub + -cess : go → '아래로 대를 이어가는 굴레니 연속'
유의어	consecutive, sequential, following
반의어	non-successive, isolated, sporadic
영영	Following in order or sequence; occurring one after another.
예문	They won three successive championships in a row. 그들은 연이은 세 번의 선수권 대회에서 우승했습니다.

968

acknowledge

[ək'nɒl.ɪdʒ]

v. 인정하다; 사례하다, 감사하다

know better than to do p. ~할 정도로 어리석지
않다
acquaint v. 정보를 주다, 숙지시키다
reacquaint v. 다시 알게 하다

어원	-ad : to + -cogn, -gno, -kno, -no, -quaint : know → '~쪽으로 잘 알고 있다고 인정하며 사례하고 감사'
유의어	admit, recognize, confess
반의어	deny, refuse
영영	admit the truth or existence of something
예문	It's important to acknowledge the efforts of those who contributed to the project. 프로젝트에 기여한 사람들의 노력을 인정하는 것이 중요하다.

969

numerous

['njuː.mə.rəs]

a. 많은

number n. 숫자
denumber v. 제거하다, 수를 뺏다
numberously adv. 수없이 많이, 다수로
enumerate v. 열거하다

어원	-numer : number → '숫자가 수없이 많은'
유의어	many, numerous, countless
반의어	few, scarce, rare
영영	existing in large numbers; many.
예문	There are numerous reasons why people choose to travel. 사람들이 여행을 선택하는 이유는 다양하다.

970

prone

[prəon]

a. 경향이 있는, ~하기 쉬운; 어드려 있는

어원	-pro : forward → '앞서 나서는 경향이 있으니 ~하기 쉬운'
유의어	inclined, disposed, likely
반의어	upright, vertical, standing
영영	Likely or inclined to experience or do something.
예문	Some people are prone to allergies in spring. 봄에 알레르기가 잘 발생하는 사람도 있습니다.

971

armament

['ɑː.mə.mənt]

n. 장비, 병기

arm n. 팔; 무장 v. 무장시키다
armor n. 갑옷
unarmed a. 비무장의
unarm v. 무장 해제하다

어원	-arm 팔, 무기 * army 군대
유의어	weaponry, arms, military equipment
반의어	Disarmament, demilitarization, denuclearization
영영	Military weapons and equipment used for defense or warfare.
예문	The country increased its armament in response to a growing threat. 그 나라는 증가하는 위협에 대응하기 위해 군비를 강화했습니다.

972

manufacture

[ˌmæn.jəˈfæk.tʃər]

v. 제조하다, 생산하다, 만들다 n. 제조, 생산

factory n. 공장
manufactured a. 제조된
manufacturing n. 제조(업)
manufacturer n. 제조 회사, 제조업자

어원	-manu : hand + -fac : make → '손으로 만드니 제조하다'
유의어	produce, make, fabricate
반의어	Unmake, disassemble, break down
영영	The process of making goods or products, often through mechanical or industrial means.
예문	The company manufactures high-quality electronics. 그 회사는 고품질 전자제품을 생산합니다.

973

tumble

[ˈtʌm.bəl]

v. 휙 뒤집다 n. 곤두박질, 재주 넘기

tumbler n. 텀블러 컵; 휙 도는 것
stumble v. 휘청이다 n. 비틀거림, 휘청임
fumble v. 더듬거리다, 더듬어 찾다
bumble v. 갈팡질팡하다

어원	-tumble 휙 돌다 → '휙 돌아 굴러 떨어지니 추락' * swirl '좌우로 소용돌이 치는' VS tumble '위 아래로 휙 도는'
유의어	fall, trip, topple
반의어	stand, rise, ascend
영영	to fall suddenly or clumsily; to roll or toss about.
예문	The child accidentally tumbled down the stairs. 아이가 우연히 계단을 넘어 떨어졌다.

974

vague

[veig]

a. 애매한, 막연한

extravagant a. 낭비하는, 사치스러운
extravagance n. 낭비, 사치
vale n. 계곡
avalanche n. 눈사태, 쇄도

어원	-vag : wander 떠돌아다니다 → '그냥 떠돌아 다니니 막연한'
유의어	unclear, indefinite, ambiguous
반의어	clear, distinct, precise
영영	Unclear or not clearly defined; lacking detail or precision.
예문	The instructions were vague, and I couldn't understand what to do. 지시사항이 모호해서 어떻게 해야 할지 이해하지 못했다.

975

accumulate

[əˈkjuː.mjə.leɪt]

v. 모으다, 축적하다, 누적시키다, 점차 늘어나다

accumulation n. 축적, 누적
accumulative a. 축적이 되는, 누적되는
accumulatively adv. 축적되어, 누적되어
cumulative a. 누적되는, 가중의

어원	-ac, -ad : add + -cumul : heap up → '쌓아 올리며 더하니 축적하다' * cumulate 쌓아 올리다 VS accumulate 단계 적으로 쌓아 올리다
유의어	gather, amass, collect
반의어	Disperse, scatter, spread out
영영	To gather or collect over time, often gradually or in increasing quantities.
예문	Over time, dust and dirt can accumulate on the furniture. 시간이 지남에 따라 먼지와 더러움이 가구에 축적될 수 있습니다.

976

impulse

[ímpʌls]

n. 충동, 자극

pulse n. 맥박, 진동, 파동
impulsive a. 충동적인, 즉흥적인
impulsively adv. 충동적으로
impure a. 순수하지 않은, 불결한

어원	-im : in + -pul : drive → '마음 안이 몰리는'
유의어	urge, instinct, inclination
반의어	Inhibition, restraint, control
영영	A sudden and strong urge or desire to do something; a brief and spontaneous action.
예문	She bought the dress on impulse without thinking it through. 그녀는 생각하지 않고 충동적으로 그 드레스를 샀습니다.

977

endure

[ɪnˈdʒʊər]

v. 지속하다, 견디다

endurance n. 인내력
endurable a. 견딜 수 있는, 참아낼 수 있는
unendurable a. 견딜 수 없는, 참을 수 없는
enduring a. 참을성이 강한

어원	-en, -em : in + -dur 지속하다, 계속하다 → '수술 때 안을 파고드는 고통을 계속해서 견디는'
유의어	withstand, tolerate, bear
반의어	Surrender, yield, give in
영영	To withstand or tolerate something difficult or challenging; to persist or continue in spite of adversity.
예문	Despite the hardships, she had the strength to endure and persevere. 어려움에도 불구하고, 그녀는 참고 인내하는 힘을 가지고 있었습니다.

978

fixate

[fɪkˈseɪt]

v. 정착(고정)시키다, 집착하다

fixated a. 집착하는
fixedness n. 정착, 고착, 고정
fixture n. 고정적인 요소
affix v. (우표 등을) 붙이다

어원	-fix 고정 + -ate 동접
유의어	focus, obsess, concentrate
반의어	release, free, liberate
영영	To become overly focused or obsessed with a particular idea, object, or person.
예문	She tended to fixate on small details and couldn't see the bigger picture. 그녀는 작은 세부 사항에 집착하는 경향이 있어 큰 그림을 볼 수 없었다.

979

tin

[tɪn]

n. 주석(원소기호 Sn), 통조림; (원통형) 통

tidy up p. ~을 깔끔하게 정리하다
timely a. 적시의, 시기 적절한
tide n. 조수(밀물과 썰물)
tiny a. 아주 작은

어원	-tin 주석(원소기호 Sn), 통조림 A tin of beans 콩 통조림 한 개
유의어	metallic element, metal, can
반의어	Valuable metal, precious metal, superior metal
영영	A chemical element with the symbol Sn, often used to coat other metals to prevent corrosion.
예문	Tin cans are commonly used for food packaging. 주로 음식 포장용으로 주석캔이 사용됩니다.

980

omit

[oʊˈmɪt]

v. 생략하다, 빠뜨리다

omission n. 생략, 탈락
emit v. 내뿜다, 방출하다
remit v. 보내다, 환송하다
intromit v. 삽입하다

어원	-o, -ob : away + -mit : send → '보내서 없어지니 생략'
유의어	exclude, skip, leave out
반의어	include, add, incorporate
영영	To leave out or exclude something that should be included.
예문	Don't forget to omit sensitive information from the report. 보고서에서 민감한 정보를 빠뜨리지 않도록 주의하세요.

981

monastery

[mάnəstèri]

n. (남자) 수도원

monk n. 수도승
monetary a. 금전의, 금융의
monotony n. 하나의 소리, 무변화, 지루함

어원	-mon, -mono 하나(G) → '혼자 생활해야 하는 수도원'
유의어	convent, abbey, cloister
반의어	secular, non-religious, worldly
영영	A place where monks or nuns live, work, and worship as part of a religious community.
예문	The monastery on the hill was a place of peace and meditation. 언덕 위의 수도원은 평화와 명상의 장소였습니다.

982

calculate

[ˈkæl.kjə.leɪt]

v. 계산하다

calculable a. 계산할 수 있는, 의지할 수 있는
incalculable a. 헤아릴 수 없는, 무수한
calculation n. 계산 결과, 산출
calculus n. 미적분학

어원	-calculus 작은 돌(L) → '옛날 양치기가 양의 수를 셀 때 작은 돌을 이용했다'
유의어	compute, estimate, figure
반의어	guess, estimate, conjecture
영영	Determine a value or outcome through mathematical or logical methods.
예문	He needed to calculate the total cost of the project. 그는 프로젝트의 총 비용을 계산해야 했습니다.

983

shorthand

[ˈʃɔːrthæ̀nd]

n. 속기, 약칭 v. 속기하다

handy a. 편리한, 손재주 있는
firsthand adv. 직접, 바로 a. 직접의
hand down p. ~을 물려주다
hand out p. 나눠주다

어원	-short + -hand 손 → '짧은 시간에 손으로 쓰는 속기'
유의어	abbreviated writing, stenography, shorthand notation
반의어	full text, longhand, detailed writing
영영	A system of writing or symbols used for rapid writing and transcription, often using abbreviations or symbols.
예문	She uses shorthand to take notes during meetings. 그녀는 회의 중에 속기법을 사용해 메모를 합니다.

984

ultraviolet

[ˌʌl.trəˈvaɪə.lət]

a. 자외선의

infrared n. 적외선 a. 적외선의
violet n. 제비꽃; 보라색
violent a. 폭력적인, 격렬한
vulnerable to N p. ~에 취약한

어원	-ultra : over + -violet : 보라색 → '보라색 빛의 파장보다 짧고 에너지가 큰 자외선'
유의어	UV, invisible radiation, ultraviolet light
반의어	infrared, visible, visible light
영영	A type of electromagnetic radiation with shorter wavelengths than visible light, often abbreviated as UV.
예문	Too much exposure to ultraviolet rays can damage the skin. 자외선에 지나치게 노출되면 피부를 손상시킬 수 있다.

985

barren

[ˈbær.ən]

a. 불모의, 황량한

barrenness n. 불모, 황량함
bare a. 헐벗은 v. 드러내다
barefoot a. 맨발의
barber n. 이발사, 이발소

어원	-bar 벌거벗은, 초기의, 원시의 → '산이 벗겨졌으니 헐벗은'
유의어	desolate, lifeless, sterile
반의어	fertile, productive
영영	incapable of producing offspring, crops, or results; unproductive and desolate
예문	The desert was barren, with no signs of life. 사막은 생명의 흔적이 없는 황량한 곳이었다.

986

disrupt

[dɪsˈrʌpt]

v. 붕괴시키다, 분열시키다, 방해하다

disruption n. 방해, 혼란; (환경) 파괴
erupt v. 분출하다, 폭발하다
dissect v. 해부하다, 분석하다
corrupt v. 부패시키다

어원	-dis : apart + -rup, -rump : break → '부수고 나누며 방해하니 혼란시키다'
유의어	disturb, interrupt, disarrange
반의어	facilitate, aid
영영	to interrupt or disturb the normal course of something; to cause disorder or chaos
예문	The sudden power outage disrupted the meeting. 갑작스러운 정전으로 회의가 중단되었다.

987

inevitable

[ɪˈnev.ɪ.tə.bəl]

a. 불가피한, 부득이한, 필연적인

evite v. 피하다, 기피하다
inevitably adv. 불가피하게
alleviate v. 경감시키다, 완화시키다
longevity n. 장수

어원	-in : not + -evit 피하다 → '피할 수 있는 것이 아닌'
유의어	unavoidable, certain, inescapable
반의어	Avoidable, preventable, escapable
영영	Certain to happen; unavoidable.
예문	Change is inevitable; it's a part of life. 변화는 불가피하며, 그것은 삶의 일부입니다.

988

enroll

[ɪnˈroʊl]

v. 등록하다, 명부에 올리다, 가입하다

enrollment n. 등록, 입학, 정원, 신청, 진학
enrollment rate p. 등록률
play a role in p. ~하는 데 역할을 하다
rotary a. 도는 n. 회전하는 기계

어원	-en : in + -rol : roll → '두루마리로 된 문서에 기입하는'
유의어	register, sign up, join
반의어	Unenroll, withdraw, drop out
영영	To officially register or sign up for a course, program, or membership.
예문	Parents can enroll their children in the after-school program. 부모님은 자녀를 방과 후 프로그램에 등록할 수 있습니다.

989

patron

[ˈpeɪ.trən]

n. 후원자; 고객, 단골

patriot n. 애국자
petty a. 사소한, 하찮은, 옹졸한
patter n. 재잘거림
patronage n. 후원

어원	-patr, -patter : father 아버지 → '아버지처럼 돌봐주시는 후원자'
유의어	supporter, sponsor, benefactor
반의어	Critic, opponent, adversary
영영	A person who supports or provides financial or other assistance to a person, organization, or cause.
예문	The art gallery had many patrons who supported the artists. 그 예술 갤러리에는 아티스트를 지원하는 많은 후원자가 있었습니다.

990

greed

[griːd]

n. 탐욕, 식탐

greedy a. 탐욕스러운, 욕심 많은
grudge n. 원한, 유감
grusome a. 고통스러운
grumble v. 투덜거리다

어원	-greed : hungry → '배고픔에 생기는 식탐' * -gre : great 큰 욕심이 식탐
유의어	avarice, covetousness, rapacity
반의어	generosity, altruism, selflessness
영영	Excessive and insatiable desire for wealth, possessions, or power.
예문	His greed for wealth led to unethical business practices. 그의 부의 탐욕이 비윤리적인 비즈니스 행태로 이어졌다.

991

a majority of

p. 대다수의

majestic a. 장엄한, 웅장한, 당당한
majority n. 대다수, 다수파
majesty n. 위엄, 폐하
major in p. ~을 전공으로 하다

어원	-major, -master, -mayor, -magni, -majes, -maxim : great (L) → '거대한 수니 대다수'
유의어	most, the greater part of, the larger portion of
반의어	a minority of, less than half of, a small portion of
영영	more than half of a total
예문	A majority of voters supported the new policy. 대다수의 투표자가 새로운 정책을 지지했습니다.

992

bring A to a stop

p. A를 세우다, A를 정지시키다

bring A to bear p. A에 집중하다
bring on p. ~을 야기하다, 초래하다
bring to the table p. ~을 제공하다
bring up p. 기르다, 교육하다

어원	-bear, -bir, -bri 나르다, 가져오다, 데려오다 + -stop 정지 → '데려오다 정지'
유의어	halt A, stop A, cease A
반의어	start A, initiate A, begin A
영영	to cause A to halt or cease
예문	The police officer brought the speeding car to a stop. 경찰관은 과속 중인 차를 정지시켰습니다.

993

jump to a conclusion

p. 성급하게 결론을 내리다

in conclusion p. 결론적으로, 끝으로
conclusive a. 결정적인
in contrast to p. ~와는 대조적으로
include out p. ~을 제외하다, 빼다

어원	-con : intensive + -clud, -clude, -clos : close, shut → '논의를 완전히 끝내고 결론을 내리다'
유의어	leap to a conclusion, rush to a conclusion, hastily conclude
반의어	hesitate, deliberate, take time to decide
영영	to reach a conclusion prematurely or without sufficient evidence
예문	It's not wise to jump to conclusions without all the facts. 모든 사실을 갖추지 않고 결론을 미리 내리는 것은 현명하지 않습니다.

994

cup of tea

p. 선호하는 일, 기호[취미]에 맞는 일

cuppa n. 한 잔의 차, 홍차
cupid n. 큐피드
tease v. 놀리다
tear n. 눈물 v. 찢다, 파괴하다

어원	-tea 차 → 차를 무척 선호하는 영국인들은 전쟁 보급품에서도 차가 꼭 있었다고 한다.
유의어	preference, liking, taste
반의어	dislike, aversion, distaste
영영	someone's preferred taste or interest
예문	Rock music isn't really my cup of tea. 록 음악은 내 취향이 아니에요.

995

by heart

p. 외워서

heartbeat n. 심장 박동
heartbreaking a. 가슴 아프게 하는
warmhearted a. 마음이 따뜻한
at the heart of p. ~의 중심에

어원	-by 수단 + -heart 마음(E) → '마음을 수단으로 기억에 넣어서 외움'
유의어	from memory, memorized, by memory
반의어	unfamiliarly, unknown, unlearned
영영	to memorize something thoroughly
예문	She knows all the lyrics to the song by heart. 그녀는 그 노래 가사를 외우고 있습니다.

996

get a handle on

p. 이해하다, 알아듣다

handy a. 편리한, 손재주 있는
firsthand adv. 직접, 바로 a. 직접의
hand down p. ~을 물려주다
hand out p. 나눠주다

어원	-get 얻다 + -hand 손 → '손에 익었으니 이해하다'
유의어	grasp, understand, comprehend
반의어	lose understanding of, be confused about, misunderstand
영영	to gain understanding or control of something
예문	It took me a while to get a handle on the new software. 새 소프트웨어를 이해하는 데 시간이 걸렸습니다.

997

keep up to date

p. 최신 정보를 계속 유지하다

out of date p. 시대에 뒤떨어진, 구식의
date back to p. ~까지 거슬러 올라가다
daybreak n. 새벽, 동틀녘
heyday n. 전성기, 한창 때

어원	-keep 유지하다 + -date 날짜 → '계속해서 날짜마다 정보를 쫓다'
유의어	stay updated, remain current, stay informed
반의어	fall behind, lag behind, be outdated
영영	to stay informed about the latest developments or information
예문	It's important to keep up to date with the latest news and developments. 최신 뉴스와 발전 사항을 계속해서 따라가는 것이 중요합니다.

998

go off

p. (알람·경보 등이) 울리다

go for naught p. 헛되이 하다
go over p. 점검하다, 검토하다
go hand in hand p. ~와 관련이 있다
go out of one's way p. 굳이 뭔가를 하다

어원	-go 가다 + -off 떨어져 → '자리에서 떨어지게 알람이 울리다'
유의어	explode, detonate, burst
반의어	ignite, explode, detonate
영영	to become rotten or spoiled, to explode or detonate
예문	The alarm clock went off at 6:00 AM. 알람 시계가 아침 6시에 울렸습니다.

999

half off

p. 반값 할인

halfway a. 중간의, 불완전한
half-round p. 반원, 반원형 몰딩
halfhearted a. 열의가 없는
half-holiday p. 반공휴일

어원	-half 중간, 절반 → '원래 가격에서 절반만 떼서 할인'
유의어	discounted by fifty percent, at fifty percent off, half-price
반의어	full price, regular price, unaltered price
영영	discounted by fifty percent
예문	All items in the store are half off today. 오늘 상점의 모든 상품이 반값 세일 중입니다.

1000

at most

p. 기껏해야

at best p. 잘해봐야
at the cost of p. ~의 비용을 지불하고
at the last minute p. 막판에, 마지막 순간에
at latest p. 늦어도 ~까지는

어원	-at 지점 + -most 최고 → '최고 위치에 있어 봤자'
유의어	at the maximum, no more than, up to
반의어	at least, a minimum of, not less than
영영	no more than, maximum or highest possible
예문	The repair will take two hours at most. 수리는 최대 2시간이 걸릴 것입니다.

무지개보카 고등 초급

발 행 | 2024년 3월 4일
저 자 | 김동원
펴낸이 | 한건희
펴낸곳 | 주식회사 부크크
출판사등록 | 2014.07.15(제2014-16호)
주 소 | 서울특별시 금천구 가산디지털1로 110 SK트윈타워 A동 305호
전 화 | 1670-8316
이메일 | info@bookk.co.kr

ISBN | 979-11-410-7472-2

www.bookk.co.kr
ⓒ 김동원 2024
